Gender on the Market

University of Pennsylvania Press
New Cultural Studies

Joan DeJean, Carroll Smith-Rosenberg,
Peter Stallybrass, and Gary Tomlinson,
Editors

University of Pennsylvania Press
Series in Contemporary Ethnography

Dan Rose and Paul Stoller, General Editors

University of Pennsylvania Press
Publications of the American Folklore Society
New Series

Patrick Mullen, General Editor

Gender on the Market

Moroccan Women and
The Revoicing of Tradition

Deborah A. Kapchan

PENN

University of Pennsylvania Press
Philadelphia

Published by
University of Pennsylvania Press
Philadelphia, Pennsylvania 19104-4011

Library of Congress Cataloging-in-Publication Data

Kapchan, Deborah A. (Deborah Anne)
    Gender on the market : Moroccan women and the revoicing of tradition / Deborah A.
Kapchan.
        p.   cm. — (New cultural studies) (Series in contemporary ethnography) (Publications
of the American Folklore Society. New series)
    Includes bibliographical references and index.
    ISBN 0-8122-3155-4 (cloth : alk. paper). — ISBN 0-8122-1426-9 (pbk. : alk. paper)
    1. Women merchants — Morocco.   2. Markets — Morocco.   3. Women — Morocco —
Economic conditions.   4. Women — Morocco — Social conditions.   I. Title.
II. Series.   III. Series : Series in contemporary ethnography.   IV. Series : Publications of
the American Folklore Society.   New series (Unnumbered)
HF3882.K37   1996
381'.18'082 — dc20   95-51427
                                                                              CIP

To my parents

And to Hannah Joy,

Berber, Russian, Swede, Hungarian, Scot
Christian, Muslim, Jew

Contents

List of Figures

Transcription and Transliteration

Moroccan Arabic is not only quite different from other dialects in the Middle East and North Africa, it also varies from region to region. My ear is tuned to the dialects of Beni Mellal and Marrakech and my transliterations reflect this. In my rendering of the language, I have consulted both Harrell (1962) and Heath (1987). Whereas Heath follows strict morphological rules in his use of hyphenation, however, I use hyphens in the following cases:

1. to indicate definite articles before nouns: l-bir, the well
2. to indicate prepositions when they are not followed by a vowel: f-l-bir, in the well
3. to indicate possessives: saṭl-ək f-l-bir. Your bucket is in the well.
4. to indicate objects: shəfna-hum. We saw them.
5. to indicate verbal prefixes marking duration and gender: kay-mshi, he goes; kat-mshi, she goes; or ghadi y-mshi, he will go; ghadiya t-mshi, she will go.

For consonants, I have followed the system used by the *International Journal of Middle Eastern Studies*. For vowels, however, I have diverged from this system. Moroccan Arabic does not employ long vowels as in Classical Arabic [CA]. Rather, there are what Heath refers to as "full vowels" (a, i, u). Unlike those in Classical Arabic, they "have no one-to-one relationship to shorter counterparts, and ... are not especially prolonged phonetically. They do, however, commonly reflect CA long vowels ... in inherited vocabulary" (Heath 1987 : 23). In general, full vowels represent the phonemic rendering of the Moroccan vowel system. In addition to these, there are short vowels, which are always word-medial in Moroccan Arabic [MA] and change according to their environment. For the sake of simplicity, I have used the schwa (ə) to represent these sounds. ay is a dipthong, similar to the English pronunciation of "they." I refer the reader to Heath's book *Ablaut and Ambiguity* (1987) for a more thorough delineation of Moroccan dialectal variations than is given here.

The consonants not found in English are rendered as follows:

gh is a voiced uvular fricative, pronounced like a French "r"
kh is a voiceless uvular fricative, similar to the last consonant in Bach
' is a voiced pharyngeal fricative, corresponding to the letter 'ayn in Classical Arabic
' is a glottal stop, the Arabic letter hamza.

The emphatic consonants in Arabic are shown with a dot under the letter that most resembles it in English: thus, ḍ, ṣ, ṭ, ḥ

Unless otherwise noted, plurals are marked with an "s."

Names of cities and towns as well as proper names are written as they have been officially or conventionally translated in Morocco. This means that some words are preceded by the article "el" (as in El Ksiba) instead of "al" or simply "l" and that emphatic markings are absent. When quoting a previous transcription from Moroccan Arabic in English or French it has been my policy not to change anything.

Words that appear frequently in the text are found in the glossary in the appendix. Speakers of other dialects of Arabic will note that the possessive preposition "of" in Moroccan Arabic is sometimes rendered dyal (or dyol [pl.]) as in bǝnt dyal-i, my daughter.

In presenting the discourse in this manuscript, I have tried to remain faithful to the music of Moroccan Arabic. In most cases conventional punctuation and typeface — commas, periods, dashes, italics — are sufficient to alert the reader to regular rhythms, repetition, parallelism, and rhymes. Where necessary, closed-up ellipses (...) indicate larger natural pauses or breaths. Code switching, when it occurs, is noted by enclosing the Berber [B], Classical Arabic [CA], or French [F] within curved brackets { }. Unless noted, all texts were originally spoken in Moroccan Arabic [MA].

The texts in the appendices give a detailed poetic transcription of oral discourses found in Chapters Three and Four. In addition to the above-mentioned conventions, here line breaks indicate pauses or rests; loud or stressed words are written in CAPITAL letters; and vowels that are drawn out are indicated by a colon after the vowel (ha:rd = haaaaard). All other information relevant to the keying of the performances is enclosed in square brackets [ ].

Acknowledgments: Possession by Three Spirits

It was June, 1982, and we stood facing Toubkal, the highest mountain in North Africa. I had arrived in Morocco two weeks earlier, having spent the previous four years as a student living in Manhattan's East Village. Looking up at another village, its brown earthen shelters carved directly out of the landscape, I felt the euphoria that often accompanies radical change.

I had come to Morocco to teach English, but had time to travel with two other Americans before beginning work. Our trek began at the foot of the High Atlas Mountains, about 65 kilometers south of Marrakech, in a place called Imlil. We had come by bus from El-Jadida, legs stiff from hours of being cramped in small metal-framed seats, and heads dizzy with the bus fumes that rose up from the holes in the floor. For the last ten kilometers we rode in a rickety taxi up narrow and broken roads.

It was already mid-afternoon, too late to begin our climb. One of my traveling companions talked for a few minutes to a local villager, who invited us to be his guests for the night. It was past dusk when we arrived at one of the mountain homes we had viewed from below.

We were escorted into a small rectangular room with thick mud walls and a small window that looked out on the valley. Our host lit candles, brought tea, then brought a ṭajin of goat meat and vegetables. We heard him talking to his wife in the kitchen, but she appeared only briefly. After our meal he gave us some wool blankets and left us to sleep on the foam rubber banquettes lining the main room. In the morning we had coffee, bread, and butter on the terrace, which was the roof of the house below. The milkfat rose to the top of my glass and the butter smelled strong and unfamiliar, making me feel a little queasy.

After breakfast we started our hike up the mountain path. The light green wheat had grown tall in the mountain fields and the sky was cloudless and calm. The brilliant sun warmed the cool air and reflected on the mountain streams that the Berber communities had so carefully channeled and terraced into irrigation canals. Our plans were to reach the refuge, a stone house where climbers can spend the night before the steep ascent to the summit. After that, inexperienced mountain climbers needed a guide.

Well into our climb we noticed a sprightly woman, perhaps in her mid-thirties, approaching us from below. She was not following the dirt road that curved around the mountainside, but energetically cut her own path, scaling rocks and shrubs. We had already come across young girls out shepherding and groups of women collecting wood, but this woman was alone. She was not dressed like a Berber in a belted tunic with a ḥayk pulled up over her head and shoulders, but wore a jəllaba, a zippered overgown made of synthetic fabric and worn primarily in the cities. As she got closer she called out to us, and we saw that she was climbing bare-footed.

She told us that she was on her way to a marabout, a saint's tomb further up the mountain. This marabout, she said, had blessing (baraka) and those who made the pilgrimage also received blessing. Perhaps because we were strangers she felt free to talk to us. She said she was possessed by three spirits (jnun) — a Muslim, a Christian, and a Jew. These spirits did not cohabit her body peacefully but were making life difficult for her and her family. She was going to the marabout to persuade the Jewish and the Christian spirits to leave her body, to pacify them, or to convert them to Islam.

We watched her as she continued up the mountain with the ease and speed of a bobcat. Soon she had left us far behind. By the time we arrived at the marabout, a white-domed structure attached to a stone compound of sleeping quarters, she was nowhere to be seen.

More than a decade later, the image of this woman has come to represent for me the embodied plurality of my subsequent experiences in Morocco. She was a hybrid of sorts. And although I am now an analyst of culture, an ethnographer, I too have experienced multiple roles in Morocco — teacher, researcher, wife, daughter-in-law, sister-in-law, mother. My understanding of Moroccan culture arises from within these identities and from all the people who I have encountered and spent time with during the four years of my stay.

In Beni Mellal, Abdelmajid and Fatiha Boustati, Ali Bouanani as well as the entire Drobi family (Abdelmajid, Fatoma, Hafida, Mohamed, Norreddine and Saadia, Um Drobi) have provided me with an anchor and made me feel at home. Amina Belkentaoui and Si Mohamed Chahid have been loyal friends; we have seen each other through the births of our children and the unfolding of our careers. Latifa Farid and Abderrafia Sofiane have cared for me when I was sick, fed me when I was hungry (and even when I wasn't!), argued Moroccan politics with me, and generally taken me into their lives and hearts. They occupy a very special place in my own.

Hssaine Aggour, who now lives in the United States, has been an intermittent housemate, a persistent Arabic teacher, and an incomparable storyteller. He is, above all, a brother. His continuing contribution to my understanding of Moroccan culture cannot be overemphasized.

My research assistants, Si Mohamed Zidouh and Abdelmajid Hafidi, worked for long hours, often in the hot sun, with an incredible amount of humor and determination. I am thankful to both of them for debating with me, explaining to me, and involving me in their own lives and dramas. Generous thanks also go to Saadia Aarbaoui, Rahma Atlassi, Abderahman Berkali, Abdullah Berkali, Saadia Daodi, Khaddouj Ennouhi, Amina Karmi, Halima Karmi, Fatima Sadra'wi, Zohra Tamezoujt, and Fatima Zereka. Our neighbors Hajja Zohra Khalid and her mother Hajja Selha Amin, have enriched my life by opening their doors to me in times of birth and in times of death.

I have other people to thank for their hospitality, generosity, discussions, and friendship in Morocco. In Rabat, Professors Mohamed Dahbi, Abdelhai Diouri, Abdelkebir Khatibi, Fatima Mernissi, and Abdelmjid Zeggaf have all offered me their time and ideas. In Casablanca, Soumaya Naamane-Guessous has done the same. I have also benefited from conversations with Drs. Abdellatif Chadli and Zahra Ikhwan.

My affiliation with the University of Pennsylvania began before I formally initiated graduate study, when Dan Wagner hired me in 1984 to be a research assistant with the university's Literacy Project in Morocco. What I learned in that pivotal year about women, literacy, and social class in Morocco provided much of the basis for this book. My thanks to him as well as to Rachida Abdouh, Aisha Bint Mohamed, Mary Eno, Zhor Harfi, Hafida Khamar, Naima Lachgar, Beverly Seckinger, Jennifer Spratt, and Fatima Tamezoujt, who all shared this experience with me to differing degrees. In the Department of Folklore and Folklife, Margaret A. Mills and Robert Blair St. George gave generously of their time and thoughts in the writing of this manuscript. Most abundant thanks go to Roger D. Abrahams, whose analysis and intellectual enthusiasm have shaped my thinking in numerous and important ways.

For reading and commenting on one or more chapters I extend my thanks to Arjun Appadurai, Steve Caton, M. E. Combs-Schillings, Elizabeth Warnock Fernea, Webb Keane, Fedwa Malti-Douglas, Dan Rose, Peter Stallybrass, Joel Sherzer, Pauline Turner Strong, Katharine Young, and Yael Zerubavel. Dale Eickelman provided invaluable commentary and critique of the entire manuscript, as did Hasan El-Shamy, Robert Fernea, Patrick Mullen, Susan Slyomovics, and Paul Stoller. Aziz Abbassi read the text with a careful eye, adding insight to my interpretations. I am indebted to him, to El-Houcine Haddad and to Mary Shapiro for their help with the transliterations.

I have had the privilege of working with exceptional colleagues and graduate students both at the Folklore Institute at Indiana University and in the Department of Anthropology at the University of Texas at Austin. Their enthusiasm and inspiration have been invaluable to me. Special thanks are also due to Roger Allen, David Azzolina, Richard Bauman, Dan Ben-Amos, Ann Richman Beresin, Wafa Berrada, Nadia Bouamar, Hamid Bouhamid, Najib Bounahai, Charles Briggs, Polly Byers, Steven Feld, Jan Garnert, Henry Glassie, Kenny Goldstein, Lahcen Haddad, Fatima Hajjarabi, Paul Hanson, Mary Lawrence Hicks, Amy Horowitz, Joy Jacobson, Deanna Kemler, Barbara Kirshenblatt-Gimblett, Jimmy Lavita, John Mac-Dowell, Geneviève Massourre, Susan Ossman, John Roberts, Amy Shuman, Emily Socolov, Beverley Stoeltje, Catharine Nislick Schumer, Greg Urban, Kate Wilson, and Youssef Zerkani. Buck VanWinkle provided computer assistance at a crucial moment. Kathleen D. Connors read the final draft carefully before it went to the Press. Her editorial skills and personal generosity find no equal. Dr. Camille Aumasson was the first to instill in me a love for North Africa. In a mysterious way, his life is between the lines of this book. Pour ceci je le remercie ainsi que sa famille, Dr. Christine Chaubier, Dr. Robert Chaubier, Isabelle et Jean-Philippe Chaubier.

Some of this research was funded by a Fulbright Fellowship administered by the Institute of International Education and the Moroccan American Commission for Educational and Cultural Exchange. Edward Thomas, the Commission's former director in Rabat, has been instrumental in facilitating my research in many kind ways. The University of Pennsylvania Press, and in particular Alison Anderson and Patricia Smith, have helped this book come into being.

My final thanks go to my family, on both sides of the ocean. My parents-in-law in Morocco have welcomed me into their fold. The stillness of their company when we sit in the garden late on a summer evening, the weight of that silence, has made me reconsider the meaning of Fate. My sisters and brothers-in-law and all of their children have taught me more than I would have learned as a social scientist "in the field." For this, I am deeply grateful.

On this side of the ocean my family has also been integral in the writing of this book. In particular, my mother Nancy has generously provided innumerable hours of loving childcare for my daughter Hannah Joy. And to Yahya Tamezoujt, who has refused to be an informant but has continued to be my partner, my thanks.

With the exception of the public oratory transcribed in Chapters Three and Four (for which permission was obtained after the initial recording), all the discourse in this manuscript was recorded with the full knowledge and consent of my acquaintances in the marketplace, my friends, my family, and their neighbors. More important to me than the texts, however, is the talk (*l-hadra*) that has informed my understanding of them. Where are the boundaries of the private here? The private and the public become open categories. Their hybridization, and their shifting boundaries, present themselves as questions in this book as they have in my life.

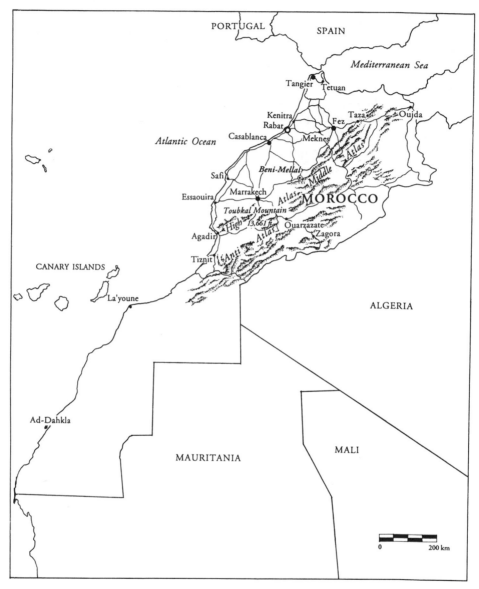

Figure 1. Map of Morocco. Beni-Mellal is the agricultural province of Morocco. Located at the foot of the Middle Atlas Mountains, it is on the road between Fez and Marrakech.

Introduction: The Dialogic Enterprise of Women in Changing Social Contexts

> The market: its pure product is relentless displacement — of traditions, beliefs, values, and natural objects, and it is through language that this awesome reconfiguration of humanity takes shape; it endlessly reconfigures the planetary landscape and reunifies the human species within a highly differentiated frame of frames that lies concealed from us and, alternately, openly defies us to understand it.
>
> — Rose (1991 : 112)

A woman sits on a mat laid on a rocky dirt hill in a marketplace at the foot of the Middle Atlas Mountains in Morocco. Before her are five piles of minerals and herbs, including dried sea urchins, some roots, and a blue fluorescent rock that is chipped for use. It is market day and she has come to do business. About a dozen people surround her, a few of them men. She caresses a small hedgehog and offers her audience samples of home-made remedy: black pellets, a mixture of ground animal parts, herbs, olive oil, and honey. By the reaction of those who have thrown the concoction from their palms into their mouths, it is not disagreeable to the taste. Her sales pitch is loud; she is competing with other herbalists in the vicinity, including men with microphones:

"Here you are, sir. Take this hedgehog and slaughter it," she said, holding the animal in the air. "Here, here is real medicine of truth, taken from a book. And whatever is in books doesn't contain lies. Here you are. Just bring a hedgehog and slaughter it. I beg of you, whoever is dizzy or sick with hemorrhoids, the ill person who has a sick uterus, whoever has a cold or who feels his shoulders tense or has a stiff back. Bring a hedgehog like this one. Take the hedgehog and slaughter it. And when you slaughter it, from its belly take out its intestines, take off its legs, and leave the hedgehog with its needles, with its bones, with its head, with its meat, and with its blood, because that is what the book said to do. Take this hedgehog and fry it in a clay pot until it burns. When the hedgehog is cooked, take it and put it in the heart of a mortar and pound it until it becomes a powder. That powder, put it here by itself. Then add these five herbs. Use them for five days in a row as the book says.

"If you want to buy these herbs prepared, have faith (*niya*)[1] and leave the yoke here on my shoulders. There's nothing more difficult than responsibility. Here, woman, even my family eats them in the morning and in the afternoon. I have brought up five children on them, by God I swear."

How is this woman perceived? She is a self-described mother of five, unveiled in the marketplace of Beni Mellal — a provincial capital with a regional population of over 350,000.[2] She speaks of the cure of the viscera. She ingests her product on the spot to demonstrate its safety and efficacy and offers her audience samples. She swears by God, invokes the authority of the written word, and encourages her audience to put their belief in the herbs and to leave the rest, the responsibility, to her. Her presence in the suq is anomalous: she is a mother and breadwinner. Aggressive and crafty in the skills of the marketplace, she speaks to men as well as to women forthrightly and with authority, using public genres of speech.

Her oratory is characteristic of the marketplace, a composite of oaths, formulae, axiomatic sayings, and, in this case, feminine testimony. Her musical intonation is comprised of long litanies of similarly stressed syllables. The hybrid quality of marketplace genres (the intertextual and intergeneric borrowings between religious quotation, bargaining, hawking, swearing, storytelling, and divining) set them apart from the more intimate, monosexual, and ritualized speech events of the private domain. Despite the quality of monologue in her speech, the social role of the female hawker introduces dialogue and the process of "dialogization" (Bakhtin 1981) into a public space occupied by both men and women — in the marketplace the authority of every voice is put into question by the presence and competition of all others.

Women's Performance Genres

This study begins by examining women's emergence into a discursive domain formerly dominated by men — the marketplace (*suq*). Women's presence as petty traders in Morocco is not new (Hajjarabi 1987, 1988; Troin 1975), yet the last decade has seen a dramatic increase in their visibility and a major reorganization of the sexual division of labor. Since my first visit to Beni Mellal in 1982, women marketers have expanded their trade from foodstuffs and items manufactured at home to contraband (cloth, cassette recorders, perfume) that they bring from the northern border towns with Spain. Even more significant is women's presence as orators in the performance section of the marketplace, the *ḥalqa*. Although still few in number, women's voices in the halqa mark an important shift in the meaning and function of oral genres in the public realm.

In order to illuminate how marketplace culture and relations of commodity are both experienced and interpreted in the process of their political emergence, I focus on social performances that are either born in the market or arise in marketplace conditions, paying particular attention to feminine discourse. The intersection of marketplace relations with performance is a crossroads where the past meets the future, a place where tradition is re-created and "the modern" (*al-ʿasri*) is socially and personally incorporated. By turning an eye, an ear—indeed our whole sensorium—to these performances, it is possible to apprehend what commodification means to those whose lives are being radicalized by its processes, as well as the sometimes violent, sometimes blissful nature of that change as it is experienced by its agents and mediators.

There is one theoretical trajectory that informs all of the following essays on Moroccan marketplace culture and feminine performance: it is the tripartite notion (1) that the marketplace—in both its local, itinerant form and its international guise—is a forum for transition; (2) that transition relies on an intensification of social license; and (3) that in granting permission for the opening of social boundaries and categories, license, in turn, provides the conditions for the hybridization of social and expressive forms.[3] The performances analyzed here create new roles and values within a modernizing and complex society by carving out unique discursive domains, giving new life to old usages, mixing categories, appropriating symbols, and revoicing expressive forms. These dynamics are apprehended in verbal and non-verbal genres such as marketplace oratory, ritual behavior, body-marking, gossip, and storytelling, as well as in live and mediated entertainment. The breakdown and new fusion of private and public categories means that characteristics usually associated with the public sphere—the "impersonal heterogeneous, mediated, officialized, commodified, and centralized"—are evidenced in face-to-face encounters among small groups, while the more "intimate forms of domestic, sociable and work encounters" are emerging in public forms of display (Bauman 1989:178).

Analysis of both the empirical and symbolic hybridization of feminine expressive forms provides key insights into the social transformation now occurring in Morocco. Linguistically, hybridization is witnessed in the mixing of formally noncompatible genres and registers; in the moral economy, it manifests itself in the collision of the values of honor and reciprocity with those of the (inter)national marketplace and commodity culture; in the gender realm, it is exemplified in the redefinition of gendered space and new formulations of social authority. This study posits marriage and market exchange as part of a unified field, one which is undergoing radical and pervasive change. One consequence of this change is seen in the reorganization of socio-symbolic space: as the private realm is bombarded with public messages from the marketplace, the public realm is being infiltrated with a rhetoric of privacy, a sort of "feminine speaking."

Performance Genres and Embodiment

In Beni Mellal, women's performance genres have everything to do with how they experience their bodies and gender in the larger society. The changes in women's use of speech genres correspond to changes in their discursive practices and physical dispositions, what Bourdieu (1977, following Mauss 1950) refers to as *habitus* — the gestural and emotional-aesthetic ethos structuring identities of difference. Women's words, their bodies, and their sociopolitical relation to symbolic and physical space are intertwined (cf. Pandolfo 1989). Just as "speech and action supplement each other and do each other's work in a web of unbroken pattern,"[4] so do performance genres and habitus make up an inseparable, if mutable, pair.[5]

Speech genres like the one cited above have a distinctive role in mediating and creating imagined communities at the state and local level, whether these communities are organized around bonds of nationalism, ethnicity, class status, or gender.[6] As repositories of history and tradition, speech genres are often sites of contest, arenas for the discursive reconstruction of identity, intertextual fields where competing tropes battle for metonymic dominance or accede to hybrid complexity (cf. Malti-Douglas 1991). Insofar as "a society chooses and codifies the acts that correspond most closely to its ideology,"[7] examination of public and mediated genres of speech provide direct access to cultural values and their transformation.[8] Performed genres are particularly significant in creating new and hybrid identities, as actors use them to maintain, reinforce, or revise the social imagination according to their interests.

Discourses about genres are discourses about boundaries — interpretive, stylistic, and pragmatic.[9] As Jameson notes, genres are institutions, social contracts imbued with ideology. Our use of genre is thus a political, if not always a conscious, choice. This is because all generic expression bears an indexical relation to "prior discourse" (Bakhtin 1981:342). Genres contain the sediment of the past (Jameson 1981:140–41); they are built upon the words of others. Whether a speaker establishes connection with that past, thereby upholding "tradition" and its inherent authority, or whether she changes the relation of words, space, and performer to construct difference, has important consequences for social change (Briggs and Bauman 1992). In the latter case, such generic reorientations, or "revoicings," leave their impress on the larger social imaginary (Kapchan 1993b). The extent to which expressive hybridizations effect social transformation depends on the density of their performativity — that is, on the degree to which they are appropriated into a public culture as icons of difference and change.[10] This is particularly true of speech genres, which, despite their ephemerality, maintain a deep rootedness to their context of enunciation.

Gender and Genre in the Middle East and North Africa

The study of verbal genres in the Middle East and North Africa (MENA) has produced a rich literature, exploring the construction of both personal and community identities and the relation of expressive life to issues of political economy, gender construction, and cultural ethics (see Fernea and Malarkey 1975 for an early overview of anthropological studies of the area; cf. Abu-Lughod 1989; Antoun 1976). These studies have demonstrated the role of speech genres in mediating conflict (Caton 1990; Meeker 1979), encoding affect (Abu-Lughod 1990b; Grima 1992), voicing dissent (Abu-Lughod 1986; Joseph 1980; Mills 1991), and creating community and tradition (Tapper and Tapper 1987; Webber 1991[11]). All these genres are associated with one gender or the other[12] and help to constitute the definition of gender for the larger community. Many are contextualized in homogeneous social settings, assuming either a single world view and morality or two complimentary and gender-based value systems.[13]

This study parts with the traditional mapping of gender and genre in the Middle East and North Africa by locating verbal art in a context of heterogeneity, where discourses of religion, morality, and kinship vie with those of self-interest, capitalism, and commodification. The examination of feminine speech genres in the marketplace takes us into the realm of expressive hybridity involving a plurality of coded messages, ideologies, and power relations.[14]

Study of the expressive dimensions of women's lives in Beni Mellal quickly becomes an exploration of what Moroccan sociologist Mernissi has referred to as "pitilessly rapid change" (1987:viii). The examination of women's linguistic and bodily practices illuminates how they are inscribing new values into a fast-changing cultural landscape, while being scripted *into* the commodification and stratification of social life. From the carnivalized ambience of the local marketplace to the vagaries of the international market as it weaves into women's ritual and narrative lives, I track the changes taking place in the worlds — real and imagined, narrated and embodied — of Moroccan women. Focusing on the multivocalic dimensions of expressive culture, I examine hybrid genres of verbal and nonverbal art as prime sites of sociocultural transformation (cf. Hanks 1987).[15] The salience of performativity[16] in these different genres (or genres of difference) — the degree to which they are public, reflexive, and agentive — becomes an index to changing power relations in the social context. By examining the relations of intertextuality in feminine performances in Beni Mellal, Morocco, it is possible to perceive the changes women are effecting in both the poetic and the public spheres.[17] I argue that their relation to these performative genres is highly ambiguous, deliberately polysemic, and ultimately hybrid in nature.

Performing Hybridity

It is unnecessary to insist on a bounded definition of a hybrid genre, which is, in any case, an oxymoron insofar as hybrid genres are actually anti-genres, defying categorical definition.[18] Although the most obvious hybrid genres are those which combine different ethnic identities,[19] hybridity is effected whenever two or more historically separate realms come together in any degree that challenges their socially constructed autonomy.[20] More productive than definitions, however, is shifting the focus to the *instrumentality* of hybrid genres — what do these inherently ambiguous and self-reflexive forms accomplish? And how are they generated?[21]

On the linguistic level, hybridization is akin to the concept of creolization, the mixing of two languages to form a third language which generates its own grammar and reproduces itself.[22] Although a creole language as such does not exist in Morocco,[23] the process of cultural creolization does (cf. Hannerz 1987); the nation of Morocco is composed of a plurality of ethnicities, histories, and languages that together form conceptions of what it is to be Moroccan. Given its diverse population as well as the historical permeability of its borders, it is not hard to understand why Moroccan sociologist and essayist Abdelkebir Khatibi encourages transgression against any force that would reduce Morocco's diversity to a single sphere of identity:

> This is our very chance, the demand for a transgression to be declared and sustained continuously against any kind of self-sufficiency. Furthermore, a thought which is not inspired by its own poverty is always elaborated to dominate and humiliate; a thought which is not minority, marginal, fragmentary and incomplete, is always a thought of ethnocide. This . . . is not a call for a philosophy of the poor and its exaltation, but a call for a plural thought which does not reduce others (societies and individuals) to the sphere of its self-sufficiency. To disengage from such a reduction is, for every thought, an incalculable chance. (Khatibi 1983 : 17–18)

Moroccan identity is difficult to fix, changing according to one's geopolitical and linguistic vantage point. Although Arabic is the national language, there is a large Berber population, speaking three different regional dialects: Tamezight, Tachilhit, and Tariffit. The recent Moroccan link with the western Sahara makes the Saharan presence and dialect an important one to reckon with as well. Extracultural influences are also varied; there are two Spanish enclaves in the north — Melilla and Ceuta — and emigration to both Spain and France continues to have a significant impact on the Moroccan culture and economy. Urbanization scrambles these points of identity, but doesn't erase them; rather, urban areas provide a striking example of the coexistence of peoples and languages as they exchange both goods and social identities.

Although the terms "creolization" and "hybridization" both refer to a process of linguistic and symbolic contact, I have chosen the latter to describe what is occurring in the expressive economies of Moroccan women. "Hybridization," an extra-linguistic term, offers the possibility of examining the mixing of linguistic forms on the pragmatic, symbolic, generic, and semantic levels while avoiding the limitations of the purely grammatical use of the term. The word "hybrid" is particularly apt, expressing not an agglutinative process, or one that cuts and pastes, but an actual *mixing and blending* of forms. Viewed pragmatically, the process of hybridization produces new forms in the expressive economy which inherit certain "traditions" from their progenitors yet are unique unto themselves.

The linguistic economy of the Moroccan marketplace is characterized by hybrid language, wherein at least two different ethics (or symbols, genres) meet, partially merge, and produce a new and complex sign. This form of hybrid language is endemic to marketplace culture; it defies borders, shows up uninvited in traditional contexts, and wreaks havoc on our comfortable conceptions of category and definition. The market is a place where many voices, ethics, and nations are represented, providing a unique arena for the examination of expressive and sociopolitical transition.

More people had gathered around the herbalist, despite the intensity of the late morning sun. Some squatted down, some lingered around the periphery of bodies that formed a semicircle around the seated woman.

"This is taken from a book," she said loudly, directing her comments to a woman who was tasting the sample of herbs she had just given her to eat. "Here you are. This woman asked me to fix her 100 riyals worth of herbs. This 100 wasn't wasted in the wilderness. Will it come back to her or not? It will come back double and triple.

"God make you find it in paradise," Fatima said, handing over the herbs wrapped in newspaper. "Say Amen," she directed the crowd.

"Amen," they repeated.

"Give me your hand, my sister. God heal you. Everyone say, Amen."

"Amen."

"Now, you. This, what is this? This is what God has given. Do you see these herbs? If there's not a hedgehog and these five herbs and honey and oil, or if it has more or less [of one thing than it should], may God break my head! I give my word by God. And those who have faith in God and want to take some from me, give me 100 riyals. If you want them separately here they are. If you want them prepared, here they are. Trust me." A woman motioned to Fatima for some herbs, holding up a ten dirham note.

"Okay, my sister, you want 100 francs, right?[24] Here you are. You see these herbs? Here I am. I gathered them, I washed them and I pounded them and sifted them and prepared them.

"They cure the pains of hemorrhoids, the pains of gastritis, colds of the bladder. Here you are." She counted the herbal pills she was placing in a newspaper. "Here's one God,[25] here's two, here's three, here's four, here's five, here's six, here's seven, here's eight, here's nine, here's ten. Ten for 1000 francs and five for 100 riyals.

"Who hasn't tasted them? Who wants to taste them? Here, woman, put them in your mouth," she said, handing out a sample. "Okay, woman, do you want 100 [riyals] or 1000 francs? How much do you want?"

"Give me 100."

"Ah! You only want 100 riyals. Okay. In the name of God (*Bismillah*).[26] Here, taste some. Here, my sister, here are five. Use them five days in a row. Here's one God, here's two, here's three, here's four, here's five. Do you want them unground? Here they are."

"Will these five herbs be enough to cure stomach pains?"

"What shall I add? That's enough, just five. Here you are, sir. This 100, let's say it was wasted on this woman. Will it return or not? It will return. If I wasted her 100 riyals, may God waste my health. And now I don't owe you anything."

"Will you be here next market?" asked the same woman.

"Insha'llah, if God lets us live we'll be here," Fatima answered. "And here you are. Use them. Do you know what they cure? Potions, the pain of hemorrhoids, the pains of gastritis. Whoever wants them ground, here they are. And whoever wants them unground, here they are. Here's 'stone breaker,' here's kabar, here's 'the tree that isn't moved by the wind,' here's the hedgehog, here's 'the silk of the arid land's spices,' which is grown in Chaouia.

"Here, my sister, use these herbs for five days. When you finish with life's business and your prayers and you go to sleep, open one and put it in the palm of your hand and throw it in your mouth and follow it with hot tea. If I've wasted your 100, if we don't meet again in this life, we'll meet again in the next. Tomorrow in front of God you'll take a piece of my skin [as payment for sins in paradise].

"If there's not a hedgehog and the herbs and oil and honey. And don't be afraid; they won't hurt you in this summer [heat]. To the contrary, they're good for hemorrhage if it's in your head. They're good for blood pressure if it goes up. They're good for dizziness. They're good for fainting. They're good for the mouth that wakes up spicy like asphalt.

"Whoever has an old cold or whoever [just] wants to try these herbs, give me 100 riyals like this woman. Here they are. 100 riyals won't empty or fill your pocket. It won't make you poor or rich. If you trust the drugs of the Ḥajj, of Mecca, or of Moulay Abdelqader, may God make you meet up with their vendors. Here you are, sir, here's one God, here's two. And whoever wants to taste them, I'll give them some. Whoever wants them without tasting [first], here they are.

"Here's the hedgehog, here are the herbs. Take them to your house and prepare them. Here, sir. By God, I am the slave of God to serve his other slaves. Here's one God, here's one who has no partner [two], here's three, here's four, here's five. These five, their price is 100 riyals. You won't get richer, and you won't get poorer. It won't empty your pocket. It won't fill your pocket. All of them from the dirt, neither from money nor gold.

"Do you see these herbs here? It's on my shoulders if they don't cure the pains of hemorrhoids, the pains of the stomach or the woman who has a sick uterus or whoever of you can't keep the purity of ablutions because of a sick bladder, or whoever has a sore back because of physical or mental work, or whoever has sore knees because of cold and whoever has arteries that are burning and hurting. Here you are, these are the herbs that work even on asthma. The responsibility is on my shoulders.

"Whoever wants to cure his health and get well, bring this hedgehog here. This hedgehog has a lot of curing possibilities for Muslims. Except that Satan prevents you, the son of a bitch, from buying; may God curse him. The hedgehog and kabar and honey, they are medicine. The hedgehog and the kabar here, doctors make penicillin from them. They fight rheumatism, the 'nest of the flower.'[27] This, this kabar, do you see this kabar here? It has a lot of curing power. This kabar, where does it grow? It grows in the west, it grows in Sidi Kacem, in the Ḥayella and in the west. Do you see this herb here? This is good for the old and the new cold. But if you want to cure your health, bring the hedgehog.

"Listen, whoever wants to cure himself by himself, I won't be jealous of you. The jealous one will go to hell, even if he prays day and night. Whoever wants to cure his health and get rid of old and new colds and cure himself of hemorrhoids, to vomit up potions, and [get rid of] colds that leave the body through foul-smelling perspiration or pain in the intestine or a cold in the intestines, here you are, sir. If God gave you the intelligence of day, and if God makes it possible for you to find a hedgehog, take it and slaughter it. It only has a pleasant smell.

"Take his hedgehog and slaughter it. Here, here is real medicine of truth, taken from a book. And whatever is in books doesn't contain lies. Here you are. Just bring a hedgehog and slaughter it. When the hedgehog is cooked, take it and put it in the heart of a mortar and pound it until it becomes a powder. That powder, put it by itself, but bring its own vegetables, the vegetables of the hedgehog: first is the flower of the prickly pear. That cures the cold of the bladder. Second, bring the 'stone-breaker.' And listen, if God gave you the intelligence of day, these are the vegetables of the hedgehog.

"You see, when you fry and grind and sift and bring the flowers of the prickly pear, that cleans the bladder. Bring this herb: it's for the kidneys if they're sick, it's called 'stone-breaker.' Bring this herb. These are the vegetables of the hedgehog, sir. This is the third: bring kabar for those who have rheumatism or an old cold or a new one or hemorrhoids. This is the third. Bring *this* herb here, it's called 'the tree that isn't taken by the wind.' It grows in the Sahara. It's good for blood pressure if it goes up and down and [the removal of] potions; and it's good for diabetes this herb. Bring a small piece. Grind it and sift it. Do you see, when you prepare these four: flower of the prickly pear, and stone-breaker, and kabar, and the tree that isn't taken by the wind; bring these herbs. Here, you all see these herbs. These are good. They clean the intestines if they are hard. These are good. Do you see these five? Well, pound them and sift them. And the hedgehog, slaughter and cook and sift it. And knead them with wild honey and olive oil and make them like this. Here they are.

"And whoever wants to prepare them by themselves, here they are. Whoever wants them already ground, I'll gather them up here. Bring them to your house and pound them and sift them. Don't call me a liar or a son of a bitch (*wald l-ḥaram*).

"And whoever of you doesn't know how or doesn't have honey or oil or the means to grind them, I'll give them to you prepared. I gathered them and washed them and pounded them and sifted them and cooked the hedgehog and sifted all of it. If they have additions or subtractions, God subtract from my health, from here." Fatima smacked her side.

"Whoever wants some from me give me a hundred. By the truth of God, if I've wasted your 100 riyals, tomorrow next to God — here, you are all more than twelve witnesses[28] — if I've wasted your 100 riyals, tomorrow next to God, you'll take a piece of my meat, from here. And whoever wants to taste a little, taste a little. Here they are, mixed with honey and with oil. If you eat some it's better than salted butter or almonds or walnuts. It's the sweetest thing to eat. It's good for hemorrhage if it's in your head. It's good for the person who has bitterness in his heart.

"I gathered them and washed them and ground them and from the book it's copied. Here are the herbs, here they are."

The importance of the written word in this discourse is clear. "Here, here is real medicine of truth," says Fatima, "taken from a book. And whatever is in books doesn't contain lies." If, as Hart asserts (1976), women's magic and herbalism have been based on oral tradition while men's practices have employed written texts, this differentiation no longer holds true. Fatima validates her practices with written materials, authorizing her presence in the public sphere with credentials that are socially esteemed across gender lines. Drawing on a canon of both written and oral sources, the herbalist establishes her identity with her male predecessors. Yet the advent of women herbalists in the marketplace publicizes these realms from the *feminine* perspective. Magic is no longer "the exclusive affair of women concealed from men" (Bourdieu 1966:221), nor is the practice of herbalism confined to the home. Both the business of magic and a subordinate belief system are given public credence and affirmation.

Yet the herbalist's place in the market is still ambiguous. Despite the herbalist's mastery of a rich, complex, and multivocalic form of verbal art, the emergence of women as popular performers in the public space of the market comes at a time when the marketplace itself is being devalued. All over Morocco itinerant marketplaces are being replaced with permanent stalls and boutiques which are instituting the policy of fixed pricing (prix fixe).

Public Privacies and Private Publications:
Hybrid Space and the (Pure) Middle Class

The private and the public realms are distinguished operationally after the onset of social mobility, as people are confronted increasingly with the stranger and the strange. Interaction with the foreigner has always been a condition of the itinerant marketplace in Morocco, which is why women's roles there become important for understanding the changes in society generally: the presence of women in this most public of domains, whether in the country or in the city, challenges the notion of separate spheres, putting class and gender struggles into vivid relief. During times of stability the ritualized role reversals of the marketplace are less threatening, being more easily categorized as low and polluting, distanced from the "higher" strata of the social body. In an unstable socioeconomic climate, the site of the marketplace is perceived as an actual site of contagion and subversion.[29] In Morocco, marketplace discourse and behavior is under close surveillance by politicians and civic leaders. Itinerant marketplaces are being pushed further outside town or are being razed altogether and replaced with centrally located, permanent, and more expensive shops. The phenomenon of prix fixe is gaining momentum, silencing the voices of negotiation.[30]

The transformation of the body that the herbalist promises is an apt metaphor for the changes that women themselves are experiencing in Beni Mellal, where appearances have changed dramatically in the last ten years. The availability of public education for both girls and boys not only has created a large job market for educators, but has contributed to the mass urbanization already underway. Along with a boom in middle-class housing construction comes a surging expansion of the service economy. There is an overabundance of small shops that sell daily-need items and a proliferation of cafés, bakeries, clothing boutiques, and franchised shoe stores. Fast food restaurants, specializing in barbecued chicken, ground beef, and fries, cater to a growing number of single professionals and civil servants. Television, a possession of the elite only twenty-five years ago, is now in virtually every home, advertising luxury products with sexy images and selling a bourgeois ethic to both rural and urban populations.

Other technologies are also changing the face of the provinces. More and more people are driving cars, some purchased in Europe, some bought with high-interest credit through Moroccan banks. The train and bus systems connecting urban and provincial centers in Morocco have been privatized, expanded, and made comfortable, encouraging national travel and accommodating personal and professional mobility. Inner-city buses serve towns that have mushroomed into urban sprawl. Telephone booths have begun to appear on street corners, where one can witness lines of a dozen or more people waiting for hours just to exchange greetings with friends who have been lucky enough to have a telephone installed in their homes (in 1991 requests for home installation exceeded the company's ability to fulfill demand in Beni Mellal). Because telephone service is expensive, the status achieved by merely waiting in line for the telephone objectifies the consumer who displays her- or himself on the street.

Although there is severe unemployment, especially among the educated, the changes in consumption and social expression that have transpired in the last decade are dramatic. In the current climate of class stratification, the open-air marketplace becomes symbolic of a disappearing peasantry and the urbanizing poor.

Women in the marketplace are also in the street — and in great numbers. It is only in response to what Mernissi calls "a world of shifting, volatile sexual identity" that polarization of the private and public spheres takes shape (1987: xxviii). For every call to "tradition" (however recently defined), there are a multiplicity of voices rallying for new and hybrid definitions of social identity. Because the private/public dichotomy is challenged by social practice, its maintenance must be continually supervised. Traced here are the tensions created by the on-going construction of polarities and the hybridization that threatens to demystify them.

Daily routines provide several examples of how the privatization of public life becomes a privatization of the body. Whereas going to the public oven used to be the only way to bake the daily bread, private ovens are now common. Young women no longer want to deliver the leavening bread in the morning and pick it up before lunch; they prefer to own a gas oven, for prestige and convenience. But this also works to keep them off the streets and in the homes, an outcome not unnoticed by their families. Likewise with the public bath (*ḥammam*), as more middle-class housing is being built with hot water facilities. Although women are not completely ready to forgo their hours of steam, sweat, and naked gossip at the public bath, these trips are becoming more a supplement to hygiene than a weekly or bi-weekly necessity. Women able to exercise choice often complain that the public bath is dirty or dark. By removing themselves from this public institution, they constitute themselves as a class apart. Individual alienation thus becomes a marker of middle-class status. Many working women simply do not have the time to spend at the bath, for the ḥammam is a ritualistic process that involves moving from the hot to the warm to the cool room several times in succession, scrubbing, rinsing off *ḥǝnna* and *ghasul* from the hair, sweating, and scrubbing again.

The creation of middle-class housing also restructures private and public space, removing opportunities for social exchange across classes. High-rise buildings elevate the middle class above street level and curtail most forms of outside sociability. Balconies put the public in view yet allow only restricted and distanced contact. Apartment dwellers must either descend to the street (in formal street attire) or accommodate themselves to a new interiority. This is particularly significant as Moroccans are used to being "outside" even when inside their homes. In traditional urban architecture there is an open garden (*ryaḍ*) in the middle of the house, where the family eats and gathers for leisurely tea-drinking. This allows the women of the house to be outside while still secluded from the gaze of and encounter with the stranger. Lower-class housing may imitate the ryaḍ by leaving an opening in the ceiling around which cinderblock rooms are built. Roofs, being flat, are used for laundering, drying clothes, and cooking. Even modest dwellings have accessible gardens or outdoor kitchen areas that are privatized with makeshift bamboo screens. New middle-class housing, however, encloses domestic and leisure space. Voices do not float from garden to garden as they do in old city architecture and there is no neutral area between domiciles in which to linger and talk with neighbors. Practical problems arise under these new conditions. An enclosed domestic space severs the inhabitants from the sun's warmth in winter and deprives them of the cool circulation of breezes in the sweltering summer months. There is also the problem of where to slaughter animals, for even in semi-urban centers like Beni Mellal animals are bought live in the marketplace to be killed and prepared at home. In urban and rural centers alike, the ritual sacrifice of a sheep is mandatory for each head of household once a year on the day of the Great Feast (*'id l-kbir*). Apartment rooftops may serve this purpose, though butchers profit from the arrangement by slaughtering animals for a fee.

The interiorizing of middle-class life closes off the nuclear family from a more interactive and visible community, one that was open to the gaze and moralizing of outsiders.[31] Gossiping has always served as a bridge between the private and the communal, an intimate discourse with repercussions in the public realm. Gossip is not only a genre that functions to establish the honor or dishonor of community members, but a field of contestation and subversion wherein struggles for power and domination are played out. Despite the closing of domestic space—or perhaps because of it—daily "talk" (*l-hadra*) remains a key genre for discerning the re-organization of power relations as they play in and through multiple spheres.

Television has also changed the timber of community life. The hum of television sets (and refrigerators) now overrides the music of the cicadas in the evening. Informal outdoor gatherings among neighbors and kin, once a common sight after dark, are more likely to occur inside the house around the television screen, altering the standards of oral communication. This is especially so as satellite dishes (*parabole*) become increasingly common, bringing images from Algeria, Egypt, France, Italy, Poland, Scandanavia, Turkey, and the United States into the Moroccan domestic sphere. Television opens the home and exposes its occupants to transglobal images that adulterate the "safe" and "traditional." The media has raised a plethora of new social issues, among them the possibility for the transformation of social categories of class and gender (see Ossman 1994).[32]

Despite a certain curtailment of public mobility, middle-class women are still very visible. In Beni Mellal there is a street local youths have nick-naked "look at me street" (*zənqat shufu-ni*). In the warm weather a large part of the population take to the main boulevard after sundown to promenade and display themselves. Young mothers push the newest status commodity, the stroller, walking with either girlfriends or husbands. This latter phenomenon makes public the new nuclear family and the "gender bonding"[33] that is occurring there, at least superficially. It also speaks of the desire for leisure time to be enjoyed with mixed company. Couples visit other couples with a frequency unheard of a generation ago. The nuclear family is in vogue and the young urbanized educated class is its proponent. The opportunity for social display is now available to women without incurring social stigma, marking a significant change.

Some street activity does involve transgression, however. The prominence of cars (owned primarily by men) brings an increase in casual sexual liaisons and prostitution. Cars provide a private place for meetings between young, mostly high-school-aged girls and older men who are affluent enough to own or have access to a vehicle. When a slow-moving car follows a group of girls, people say the driver and his friends are "hunting" (kaysaydu). Marriage may result from such informal meetings, yet this form of interaction is highly frowned upon, though recognized as symptomatic of the "opening" of the streets (and schools) to women. As both reputable and disreputable girls promenade in the evening, it is democratically impossible to close the street to the female half of the population.

Feminine Transgression and Hybrid Ethnography

My focus on the narrative construction of an emergent middle class in Beni Mellal makes this study necessarily positioned. Much of the book is a reading of the voices of the lower classes, the folk (sha'b), while also examining the mentalité of an educated and consuming class that defines itself in contradistinction to the folk. This is not unintentional for, although change often comes from "below," it is also an indisputable fact that women's emergence into the public sphere is economically motivated. The speech event quoted earlier is a performance on which the vendor's livelihood depends. Such inroads into new territories are always initially transgressive; yet the transition of feminine self-conceptions, the reflexivity of their status as commodities (though not always as controlling commodities) and their new patterns of work and consumption are impelling changes in all spheres of society. These roles imply changing genres which encode new relations of power and authority.[34]

As the media redefine current markets and circumscribe territories of newly sanctioned desire, women not only become commodities in their marital relation to men, but are fetishized as consumers, made into signs attributed with a false agency. "These images of agency are increasingly distortions of a world of merchandising so subtle that the consumer is consistently helped to believe that he or she is an actor, where in fact he or she is at best a chooser" (Appadurai 1990 : 16). Taking account of the massive influence of television advertising on cultural values complicates the analysis of feminine discourse. "Hawking" is no longer confined to the suq but permeates the neighborhoods with an electric televised drone. Since a majority of commercials target a feminine audience, their fetishization as consumers via the creation of new needs and desires is visible to such an extent that terms of agency themselves (transgression, constitution, creation) must be scrutinized with care.

What follows is an analysis of feminine expressive forms, focusing on the active, creative, and subversive while assuming that reactive, opposing, and entropic counter-forces are to be reckoned with. The voices in this book are often counter-hegemonic and transgressive, voices of the margins (cf. Tsing 1993). Although emphasis on transgression has been associated with a subtle form of Orientalism — making extoic objects of those who break the law — in this text the "powerless" speak with voices that reveal them to be anything but impotent constructions of a Western gaze. Rather, this study telescopes the borderlands between law and its contestation in the realm of expressive culture, illuminating the creativity and agency that arise at such junctures (cf. Lavie, Narayan, and Rosaldo 1993).

Other books could have been written: one that examined the dialogue between verbal texts and their literary predecessors (see Mills 1991 for an excellent example), or one that explored the economic aspects of women's movement into new and public realms. Instead I have focused on the emergence of women's expressive culture and the way it determines and responds to larger spheres of influence. When one piece of the kaleidoscope changes, so does the entire configuration. Likewise formal transformations in speech and performance genres affect the enactment of social and ideological practices. The dialogues and narratives that follow are only partial in their representation of emerging identities, and I have taken care to demonstrate how they are embedded in larger discourses of gender, religion, capitalism, and class.

Any examination of public genres of expression cannot ignore the contours of its own generic forms. Several genres of ethnographic writing are employed in this text, some objectifying and analytical, others less so. Although the boundaries between fiction, science, and anthropology may have blurred in recent years, it is also true that unclear divisions may cause injurious misrepresentation.[35] To this end, careful transliteration and eth-nopoetic transcription of key texts are included, providing the reader with a basis for alternate interpretations, while subtexts are elaborated on in footnotes.[36] In addition, my own positioning in several sub-communities in Beni Mellal is made as clear as possible.

The focus on speech genres in this manuscript takes much from the work of scholars dedicated to understanding cultural texts through analysis of discourse and its performance,[37] while also demonstrating the difficulty of positing any whole-cloth notion of cultural aesthetics. Combining de-scription, quoted texts, and my own analyses, I draw freely from the ludic, the dramatistic, and the textual idioms that circulate in ethnographic writ-ing (Geertz 1983:33). Such a hybrid focus is offered as an alternative to analyses that are either overly objective or that reify the subject and personal narrative above all other modus operandi. In seeking to trace movement and meaning in the discursive and physical domains of Moroccan women, these chapters move between the voices of particular subjects and the voices of the analyst, between embodied practice and the "prior discourse" that infiltrates and determines the present context. As genre analysis makes clear, processes of objectification are not the privileged domain of the ethnogra-pher, but are implicated in all social performances that seek to augment cultural and economic capital (Bourdieu 1984). By making my interpre-tive frame as explicit as possible, I hope to combine object and subject in a weave of difference, wherein readers, speakers, actors, and writer all recog-nize themselves and their multiple motives.

Notes

1. *Niya* may also be translated as belief, good intention, or naiveté. See Rosen (1984).

2. This statistic is taken from a government tourist publication, *Le Maroc en chiffres*, funded by La Banque Marocaine du Commerce Extérieur and published in 1988 (Casablanca: Impression Idéale).

3. See Chapter 2 for a discussion of hybridization in Bakhtin's sense.

4. Sapir (1933). Reprinted in Sapir (1963).

5. The way a performer's learned habits of body and mind inform and act on the values and stances already coded in genre, as well as those of the audience, pro-vide proof that the *embodiment* of genre is a central focus of study for those inter-ested in the way expressive forms work to change social norms and categories (Bourdieu 1977; Hanks 1987, 1990). The significance of genre to social practice has

been eloquently formulated by Hanks who notes that the "relation between an agent, the agent's body, the location of action, and the conventional categories of language [genre] and gesture is a social construction par excellence" (1990:7; cf. 1987).

6. The subject of genre is receiving renewed attention from literary scholars and anthropologists alike (Abu-Lughod 1986, 1993; Bauman 1992; Behar 1990; Besnier 1989; Briggs 1988; Briggs and Bauman 1992; Caton 1990; Feld 1990; Gal 1990; Hanks 1987; Haring 1992a, 1992b; Kirshenblatt-Gimblett 1989; Malti-Douglas 1991; Perloff 1992; Sherzer 1987; Stewart 1991; Todorov 1990). Feminists have compared generic convention to Lacan's "law of the father" — a pervasive and ultimately hegemonic structure that must be challenged by a return of the repressed (Benstock 1991; Irigaray 1991). Social critics following in Bakhtin's wake view genre as a particular world view, one in which alternate realities and rules may be constructed to challenge and sometimes overturn the classical, the high, the status quo (Bakhtin 1981, 1986; cf. Briggs 1992; Hanks 1987). What seems certain is that while some are proclaiming the death of genre, or at least its transfiguration beyond identifiable bounds, others — particularly subaltern groups — are creating genres (some quite conventional) in a project of "strategic essentialism" (Spivak 1993) that carves out a recognizable identity in the public sphere.

7. Todorov (1990:19).

8. See B. Anderson (1983) on the effects of print capitalism on the development of "imagined communities."

9. Genres may often be defined by their linguistic "style," as Briggs and Bauman note, "Genre styles are constellations of co-occurrent formal elements and structures that define or characterize particular classes of utterances. The constituent elements of genre styles may figure in other speech styles as well, establishing indexical resonances between them" (1992:141). Transformation in genre is indexical of larger social transformation. Thus "a subset of diacritical generic features may be combined with those that characterize another genre to effect an interpretive transformation of genre, a phenomenon that Hymes terms 'metaphrasis'" (Briggs and Bauman 1992:141; cf. Urban 1984).

10. As repositories of history, genres take on particular importance in times of political upheaval or socio-emotional change (Hanks 1987; Haring 1992a); they are the site of historicization in the dialogue between past and present, between ideology and practice.

11. See also Abu-Lughod (1993); Beeman (1986); cf. N. Tapper (1990).

12. It is appropriate to speak of two genders in the Middle Eastern context — the heterosexual dyad of male and female. For despite the largely homosocial context created by sex segregation, open homosexuality is taboo and considered deviant.

13. Though Abu-Lughod (1993) acknowledges the hetereogeneity of all positioned cultural encounters, her work has built on a community that shares a moral ethic (Abu-Lughod 1986). Later work (1990a, 1993) points toward the fracturing of this ethic.

14. Scholars have often examined speech events in light of gender considerations (see Gal 1990; Philips 1980 for reviews), paying attention to verbal expression

that not only reflects differences in the sexual division of labor, but often challenges existent inequalities (Abu-Lughod 1990a; Briggs 1992; Caraveli 1986; Herzfeld 1990). Although social theorists argue for the hegemony of codes and their re-production (Bourdieu and Passeron 1977), there are clearly expressive practices which strain against convention (Wollard 1985), practices that instantiate themselves into a more centered position so that definitions of category and genre are also transformed.

15. As a term of analysis, the word "hybrid" is both engaging and problematic. On one hand, it exists in contrast to an imagined purity, an anti-hybridity, which it defies and threatens to subvert. On the other, it seems to obliterate difference en-tirely by incorporating all identities into, say, the homogeneity of late capitalist cul-ture (cf. Jameson 1983 on pastiche). In fact, both these theoretical positionings are faulted. Hybrid forms are not born of the pure. Although it is interesting to trace genealogical threads, they do not unravel into a more authentic past. To mix meta-phors, there are hybrid turtles all the way down. One of the useful byproducts of a hermeneutics that begins with the hybrid, is that it reveals the very constructed — even contrived — nature of anything considered pure. The delineation of a pure category — whether it be an epic, a race, or a sexual identity — reveals more about the worldviews and ethics of scholars and their times than it does about anything real "out there." In this sense, the metaphor of hybridity does not launch the cultural critic into a search for purer roots, but rather deconstructs the motives for such a search in the first place.

Nor do hybrid forms erase all identities of difference. The "leading edge of change," remarks Lee (1993:174) "lies in the intersections and interstices of pro-cesses beyond the nation-state that have their own global infrastructure. Hybrid spaces created by diasporic migrations are inhabited by bilingual and bicultural resi-dent nomads who move between one public sphere and another." The "hybrid spaces" created by cultural movement and the complex expressive forms arising at such junctures challenge all notions of categorization and objectification. K. Stewart notes that the cultural critic can only track "its constituting forms and modes of social deployment . . . following along in its wake, tracing its interpretive moves and their actual effects" (1991:395). All closed interpretations are refracted by the hybrid artform, which at once sets in place and supercedes the terms of its making. Indeed, the Latin American scholar Nestor García Canclini asserts that intercultural hybrid identities, like that of the mestizo, help relativize and dissolve the "hallowed antino-mies of cultural thought such as tradition/modern, erudite/popular, oppressor/op-pressed" (Lauer 1993). Conceptions of the hybrid in García Canclini's work (1990), entitled *Culturas hibridas: estrategias para entrar y salir de la modernidad*, grow out of both the cultural and biological hybridity of Latin American citizens and their reception and creation of modernity. (My thanks to Ana-Maria Ochoa for bringing this work to my attention.)

Although it may be argued that "since there have always been plunderings, borrowings and intertextuality, the task of the critic seems to be confined to the accumulation of new hybrids" (Franco 1993:141), there is reason to analyze the im-pact of "new hybrids" in the larger political economy. If intertextuality has always made for hybrid forms, it is not the case that hybridity is self-replicating or that its issue and impact is predictable. The very notion of the hybrid entails the veering of a traditional trajectory in an other and often unexpected direction. What's more, intentional hybridization must be viewed as a political force, a strategy of empowerment as well as an instrument of domination. Attention to new hybrid forms is thus not reductionist or confining, but critical to cultural analysis.

Applied to expressive forms, hybridization may be defined as an aesthetic process which allows for the simultaneous coexistence or combination of forms and voices, as well as their mutual blending and transmutation. There are different degrees of hybridity, ranging from mixed genres (such as festival, wherein forms are clearly delineated yet multiple; cf. Smith 1972:68) to the actual blending of forms wherein all notions of generic boundary are put into question. This is not simply bricolage, a "making do" by combining the different elements at hand. Hybrid artforms are more motivated than makeshift. When they enter public discourse, they are historically driven and politically strategic.

The term "hybrid" has a more limited use in folklore studies than it does in Bakhtin's works (Abrahams n.d.; Dorst 1983; Hanks 1987; Haring 1992a). Yet the way the term has been appropriated and defined by folklore scholars reveals that fascination with hybridization has solid scholarly precedent. This is particularly true of studies devoted to large scale cultural enactments and display events (see Abrahams 1977). The festival literature in folklore scholarship marked a new stream of inquiry, that of anti-structure, play, and license as they are exhibited in complex cultural performances and enactments (Abrahams 1969, 1977, 1983; Abrahams and Bauman 1978; Babcock 1978; Bauman 1977; Davis 1986; Dundes and Falassi 1975; Falassi 1987; Smith 1972, 1975; S. Stewart 1978, 1984; Stoeltje 1981, 1987, 1988; Sutton-Smith 1972; Turner 1982; for a recent examination of these issues, see Noyes 1992). The emergence of the festival literature in folklore studies had a hybridizing effect of its own as it introduced a festive "vocabulary" into the discipline of folklore. Literature on "play" was also proliferating at the time. (See Abrahams 1977; Caillois 1961; Huizinga 1967; Sutton-Smith 1979; Turner 1974 for some exemplary works.)

The interest in hybrid genres may be divided into two categories: synchronic studies concerned with categorically and formally ambiguous genres (Abrahams 1985; Bauman 1992; Dorst 1983) and more diachronic studies which focus on how socio-cultural and ideological change is effected in the expressive realm (Hanks 1987; Haring 1992a; S. Stewart 1991; see also Feld in press; Urban 1991). I argue here for the necessity of both these perspectives in order to understand the function and import of hybrid phenomena as they negotiate sociocultural change, connecting issues of hybridization in the formal realm of poetics to those of sociocultural transformation or creolization (see Abrahams 1983, n.d.; Bauman 1989; Hannerz 1987). Such an approach is by no means new (see Briggs 1988, chap. 1 for an overview). What remains to be examined, however, is how aesthetic hybridizations reflect and constitute hybridization at larger levels of social change.

For examples of works that relate hybridization and expressive culture see Abrahams (1993); Bauman (1989); Briggs (1993); Dorst (1990); Kirshenblatt-Gimblett (1992); see also Appadurai (1990, 1991); Hannerz (1987).

16. I take dialogic liberty with the notion of "performativity" in this context. While drawing upon its definition in speech act theory as language which performs,

or does something (see Silverstein 1976), I also allow it to resonate with the concept of performance as a cultural enactment or public display (see Abrahams 1977).

17. Unlike practices in West Africa and South America (see Robertson 1984; Seligmann 1993), women vendors and orators in the heterosexual Moroccan marketplace do not have a long history. In 1976, Hart wrote that "going to market is almost exclusively a male concern; all women, save the poor and the elderly, are rigidly excluded — as indeed they are from the mosque" (1976 : 69). Three years later, Geertz asserted that "overall, the bazaar is an emphatically male realm, and so far as Sefrou is concerned there is not a single woman of any real importance in either the trade or the artisan worlds" (1979 : 240, n. 30). Even Troin, who, in 1975, noted the increasing participation of women in the markets of the Jbala region of northern Morocco, referred to women's gradual "whittling" at "certain sectors of the commercial sector, *usually reserved for men*" (1975 : 64, emphasis mine). Although these analyses do not represent the whole of market practices in Morocco, it is clear that the division of labor in the open-air marketplace has changed considerably in the last decade. The presence or absence of women in the Moroccan marketplace varies according to region. In some places, their presence as vendors has a much longer history than it does in Beni Mellal where this research was carried out (see Troin 1975). It is clear, however, that women's roles in the itinerant marketplace are changing dramatically in all regions. Not only are they sellers of contraband — a recent category of vendor in my research site of Beni Mellal — but they are becoming orators in the ḥalqa — the performance area of the market. This is a role that is historically unprecedented in all of the markets that I have been able to research.

18. Mills warns against applying the "hybrid" qualifier indiscriminately. Of a narrative she recorded in Afghanistan, Mills says, "To say that this story partakes of religious heroic themes and of romantic quest literature is not to say that the tale is generically hybrid but only that the generic categories we might want to impose on Islamic popular literature do not capture the unities which operate across our distinctions" (1991 : 156). Her remarks call attention to the danger of erroneous classification, as ethnographers impose ethnocentric (etic) definitions of genre in inappropriate contexts.

19. For example, North African rai (Gross, McMurray, and Swedenburg 1994).

20. Following Bakhtin, unintentional hybridization is realized whenever conventional relations of indexicality are subverted and replaced with new associations, that is, whenever an agent alters the naturalized relationships between style, content, and context (or embodied use). In this rendering, unintentional hybridization is synonymous with creativity or linguistic evolution. (See Silverstein 1976; see also Urban 1984, 1991).

21. That hybrid genres are not new is demonstrated in the example of the *Thousand and One Nights*. As a work that has been through various incarnations throughout nearly ten centuries, it represents a conglomerate of cultural, geographical, and historical influences. Although the earliest manuscript dates from the ninth century, this is only a fragment. It is not until the fifteenth century that a definite corpus of stories (of anonymous authorship), written in Arabic, emerges in manuscript form. This corpus is an amalgamation of three distinct cultural narrative traditions. It

comprises Persian stories (which contain Indian elements) that were translated into Arabic around the tenth century; stories composed in Baghdad between the tenth and twelfth centuries; and, finally, stories composed in Egypt mostly in the thirteenth and fourteenth centuries (Gerhardt 1963:9; cf. Kilito 1992; Malti-Douglas 1991). Each of these "layers of story-material" is distinguished by its own vocabulary, idiom, and structural form, and is recognizable to students of Arabic literature, if not to the lay reader. This culturally diverse narrative layering in *1001 Nights* makes it difficult for any one people to lay claim to the stories. Gabrieli (1956, as quoted and translated by Gerhardt 1963:3–4) asserts that the *1001 Nights* is characterized by "an Arabic veneer" but that "every connoisseur of the genuinely Arabic will feel in the complex whole of the modern *1001 Nights* something diluted, impoverished, superficial and fictitious, in comparison with the more ancient literary manifestations of the Arabic spirit." Such value judgments arise from an elitism that privileges written literature over oral and "pure" genealogy over literary and cultural mixing. The hybrid nature of the stories combined with their colloquial parlance makes Arab scholars reluctant to include *1001 Nights* in the representative literature of "high" Arabic culture. These same factors make this work highly interesting to the folklorist, if problematic.

The first problem encountered is that this oeuvre cannot be easily situated in time and space. Its unknown authors are from different cultures and different time periods. A close reading of *1001 Nights* shatters the illusion that these stories grew up as an organic body of texts; rather, *1001 Nights* is a grafted and reconstructed body that speaks in multiple languages, code-switching at often irregular intervals. As a multivocal text, it speaks for not one ethnic consciousness but for several, for not one period of history, but for many.

Because of the long history of *1001 Nights* as both written text and oral performance, the two traditions have grown up around each other with such tenacity that they are virtually inseparable (witness the colloquial language of oral performance and the literariness of some of the narrative techniques). There is a double influence here: not only have the oral versions affected the written (and vice-versa) within a particular *synchronic* frame, but later translations have, in a sense, looped back into performance versions which are then again recycled as "oral narrative" into the literary traditions. In other words, the stories told in the Moroccan marketplace today may well come from an Arabic translation of Galland's *Mille et une nuit* (written in French), which the Moroccan narrator then elaborates or reduces to create a second order oral text (Galland included a first order one) which itself may enter the written tradition when collected and documented. Gerhardt (1963:456–57) quotes Stith Thompson as asserting that "the task of separating literary from genuine popular tradition is extraordinarily difficult in these [Moslem] countries, and sometimes quite impossible [1946:17]."

Although there is little recourse to native generic categories, there is some historical evidence for native sentiment concerning *1001 Nights*. Gerhardt (42–3) remarks that educated readers in the Arabic-speaking world have always held the stories in low esteem by virtue of their predominantly fictitious nature. She quotes Wehr: "This judgement dates back to the Abassid period, when the erudite deemed a fictitious story incompatible with higher literature. Purely narrative literature, which had no didactic or cultural purpose and, moreover, did not employ classical Arabic, was considered trifling. Thus, the *1001 Nights*, and fiction in general, was relegated to the obscurity of an anonymous activity and found its public among people of humble condition" (1959 : 287–88).

To judge from the situation in present-day Morocco, these conditions have not greatly changed. Although stories from the *1001 Nights* can be bought in little chapbooks at the marketplace, the stories are also told by professional storytellers in the suq. The audience, as in the Abassid period, is still comprised of "people of humble condition," that is, men who are illiterate and/or fairly marginal to mainstream society — often unemployed or old men with time on their hands, and unsupervised children seeking diversion. The middle and upper strata of Moroccan society are conspicuously absent from public storytelling circles. This is not to say, however, that the storyteller in Moroccan society has always been devalued. To the contrary, storytellers only a generation ago were revered and their deaths would bring out the entire community to pay their respects (Abdelmjid Zeggaf, personal communication; I am indebted to Dr. Zeggaf for his acute analysis of the effects of media on both family structure and oral genres in Morocco).

22. Linguists are familiar with these questions, having explored the effects of cultural contact in analyses of creole languages and cultures. Hymes notes that "One loanword does not a convergence make. Yet it is essential to take different degrees and consequences of convergence into account. Indeed, when we think of creolization and convergence as kin, we often seem to think of more than convergence in the strict sense of approximation of one variety to another. We have in mind mingling, coalescence, even fusion, of two varieties, especially as involves grammar. Creolization as convergence implies not only approximation, nor mixture even, but *creativity*, the adaptation of means of *diverse provenience to new ends*" (Hymes 1971 : 76; emphasis added). In these studies, "hybridization" has been used to describe processes of both blending and resistance, inextricable from notions of individual and social creativity (Whinnom 1971; cf. Hymes 1971 : 76). The contemporary work in hybridity, however, is cross-disciplinary, evident in studies of popular culture, media, immigrant populations, subaltern studies, history, and expressive culture. As empirical reality — whether historical, linguistic, or social — hybridity offers a unique analytical vantage point on the politics of culture. As trope, the notion of hybridization challenges notions of purity and authenticity — not by positing a model wherein one culture assimilates to another more dominant culture (as in studies of linguistic creolization or acculturation), but by acknowledging the intricate and complex weave of any plural community.

23. In Morroco, multiple languages coexist and may be employed in daily conversation (classical Arabic, Moroccan Arabic, the dialects of Berber, French, or Spanish) and code-switching is frequent.

24. In the Beni Mellal suq vendors and buyers use two monetary denominations — riyals (there are twenty riyals in one dirham, about 12 cents) and francs (five francs are worth one riyal, and there are 100 francs in a dirham).

25. One of the precepts of Islam is the profession of faith, the *shahada* or creed, which states that "There is no God but God and Muḥammad is his Prophet." The herbalist invokes the idea of the one God while she is counting the herbs, making

her discourse double-voiced; that is, her words index both religious discourse and sales rhetoric.

26. Actually three words, *bi-smi-llah* is often said on initiating any action — entering a house or beginning a meal, for example. Because the phrase is said with such frequency, I have chosen to transcribe it as one word, as I have the phrase *insha'llah*, "if God wills."

27. "The nest of the flower" is a euphemism for a sexually transmitted disease.

28. According to traditional Islamic law, twelve witnesses are needed to establish a legal fact in the absence of written proof (see Rosen 1984:124–25).

29. See Agnew (1986); Davis (1978); Seligmann (1993) on the historical and contemporary power of market spaces.

30. Bourgeois market negotiations are removed from the site of exchange and take place only among a designated few. In late capitalism, bargaining tends to survive in labor negotiations, development contracts, and other "bids" for political power.

31. See Rosen (1978) for an example of the power of social commentary in the Moroccan context.

32. Abdelmjid Zeggaf, personal communication.

33. Yael Zerubavel suggested this term for what is happening in the Moroccan context today, namely an (albeit relative) move towards the center as opposed to the extremes of the gender poles as traditionally established.

34. Sabra Webber documented this in Tunisia, where women who have traditionally told *khurafat* (fantasy stories) are beginning to utilize the male genre of *hikayat* (true stories): "in appropriating and restructuring what traditionally have been men's stories, women are symbolically asserting their right to a significant place in the male world — outside the house" (1985:316).

35. Geertz (1983) discusses the blurred genres of social science, while Said (1978) and Abu-Lughod (1991, 1993) bring attention to the potential danger of not understanding the impact of objectifying categories.

36. In the body of this manuscript, most discourses are transcribed in paragraph form as opposed to being lined out as poetry. This is for the ease of the reader. The rhythm of the narratives should nonetheless be clear from the repetition and parallelism present in the discourse. In the appendix I have provided a more poetic rendering of marketplace oratory, drawing on the work of Tedlock (1983) and Sherzer (1990).

37. See Abrahams (1983); Bauman (1977, 1986); Bauman and Sherzer (1974); Brenneis (1986, 1987); Briggs (1988); Feld (1990); Hymes (1974); Kirshenblatt-Gimblett (1976); Sherzer (1983, 1987, 1990); Urban (1991).

PART ONE

Women in the Market

Any movement that believes it can subvert a system by its infrastructure is naive. Seduction is more intelligent, and seemingly spontaneously so. Immediately obvious — seduction need not be demonstrated, nor justified — it is there all at once, in the reversal of all the alleged depth of the real, of all psychology, anatomy, truth, or power. It knows (this is its secret) that *there is no anatomy*, nor psychology, that all signs are reversible. Nothing belongs to it, except appearances — all powers elude it, but it "reversibilizes" all their signs. How can one oppose seduction?

— Jean Baudrillard, *Seduction* (10)

Imagine someone who abolishes within himself [sic] all barriers, all classes, all exclusions, not by syncretism but by simple discard of that old specter: *logical contradiction*; who mixes every language, even those said to be incompatible; who silently accepts every charge of illogicity, of incongruity; who remains passive in the face of Socratic irony (leading the interlocutor to the supreme disgrace: *self-contradiction*) and legal terrorism (how much penal evidence is based on a psychology of consistency!). Such a man would be the mockery of our society: court, asylum, polite conversation would cast him out: who endures contradiction without shame? Now this anti-hero exists; . . . the confusion of tongues is no longer a punishment, the subject gains access to bliss by the cohabitation of languages *working side by side*: the text of pleasure is a sanctioned Babel.

— Roland Barthes, *The Pleasure of the Text* (6)

1. In the Place of the Market

Keep away from the crowded markets [and] you will escape all evil
— Moroccan proverb[1]

The woman's market is volatile
He who enters beware!
They'll show you a ton of profit
And walk away with your capital

— Sidi Abderaḥman al-Majdub

A lie is not a lie; it is only a formula, a substitute, a long way around, a polite manner of saying: None of your business.

— Paul Bowles, *The Spider's House* (9)

When I first went to Beni Mellal in 1982 there were plenty of women in the marketplace. Apart from the vendors of wool, eggs, bread, and chickens, however, women were primarily buying rather than selling. The scene is different today. There are now so many women marketers in Beni Mellal that they have had to set up their goods outside the market walls. There is no room for them within. Women have also begun to hawk herbs in the ḥalqa, the performance section of the marketplace. Their role as herbalists and their elaborate oratory in the suq mark a feminine entry into what has historically been a male domain.

Marketplaces are very sensitive registers of the sociopolitical climate (Claire Robertson, personal communication; see also Agnew 1986; Davis 1978; Robertson 1984; Troin 1975). They are increasingly being recognized as key sites for the redefinition of ethnic and gender identities (Seligmann 1993). This is because the marketplace — both in its local itinerant form and in its international guise — is a forum for transition. Goods and values trade hands in the market and identities are negotiated. While the cultural and transnational movement facilitated by the market relies on an intensification of social license, the opening of social boundaries provides the conditions for the hybridization of social and expressive forms. The marketplace puts all rules of appropriate behavior into question.

Margins and Limen: The Locality of the Suq in Beni Mellal

"Why did they move the suq down the hill to the plain?" I asked Hadda, a long-time resident of Beni Mellal and an old family friend. My sister-in-law Zohra and I had come to visit her in her new house. Although she no longer lived in the countryside, Hadda still kept goats and chickens on her roof. I knew that for many years after her husband died she had sold used goods in the marketplace in order to support herself and three daughters. "She would come around to all the neighbors, and ask them for the things they no longer needed," my mother-in-law told me. "Then she'd take them to the marketplace, the poor woman."

When I asked Hadda about women vendors, she refused to speak of her experience; it was clearly a source of embarrassment to her. She had always been scrupulously veiled when selling and intended to keep that identity hidden. Now she was happy to be supported by her working daughters. We were drinking tea in her living room, a large color television flashing images at us from the corner of the room, when Hadda explained how urbanization had forced the marketplace to move:

"The city is moving out. It's getting bigger. There are more and more houses. They have to distance the suq from the sons of Adam. Ah!" she exclaimed, "When the medina [city] encompasses the suq it will be the center! They'll start to drive the animals in the midst of people. It's not good. And they make their dung, they ruin the street. The suq must always be outside. Always. They must be outside, those things."

The suq is now found at the lowest altitude of Beni Mellal. Before the rapid expansion of this provincial capital, the suq used to be the city limit. Today the suq has expanded down onto the plain. The sloping site of its first home is still populated with corrugated tin structures that shelter tinkers, shoemakers, sewing-machine repairmen and barbers. The "old suq," as it is called, is also a garbage dump, a public bathroom, and the place where a couple of storytellers and their audiences gather every afternoon about two hours before sunset (Figure 2). On market days the old suq is also populated with clairvoyants under umbrellas or in tents (Figure 3), *kuwways* (traditional healers whose technique is cauterization) and sellers of herbs, incense and potions, many with microphones and sophisticated sales spiels. This is the part of the marketplace designated as the performance site, the ḥalqa.

Below the ḥalqa is the suq proper, enclosed on three sides with stone walls, with a slaughterhouse on the fourth and farthest end. In recent years the Beni Mellal marketplace has grown outside its walls, due primarily to a

Figure 2. A storyteller holds forth in the "old market," now the place of the ḥalqa. Below are the tents of the new market.

proliferation of women sellers of contraband. They sit on the ground with large pieces of plastic laid out before them, displaying synthetic cloth, bikini underwear from Spain, pajamas, cheap perfume. The wool sellers sit under canvas tents with skeins of home-dyed bright blue and red wool. Outside their tents are piles of rags, sold by the kilo, to make rugs. All along the western wall are women, many quite elderly, with different-sized piles of used clothing for sale.

Inside the suq walls men vendors are the majority, though women do sell bread, chicken, and eggs. The inner western wall is lined with rafia-carpeted café stalls displaying tin teapots, clay *ṭajins*,[2] and fried dough. Further north there are the potters. The eastern and southern walls are lined with used furniture, bed springs, metal parts, junk; there are also a few tinkers repairing metalware. In toward a labyrinth of tents there is butchered meat, livestock, pots and pans, vegetables, mint, cloth, used and new books, gold jewelry. In the cold and wet seasons people walk through a mixture of mud, rotten vegetables, and donkey manure, their breath visible in front of their faces as they bargain for a few meters of woollen *jǝllaba*

Figure 3. A clairvoyant gives counsel in the ḥalqa.

cloth or a *qanṭar*[3] of wheat. Some stop to ask the day's price on a bouquet of absinthe leaves for a potent tea. In the hot and dry seasons the ground is hard and odors are loose. Outside the suq walls garbage is piled and only partially burned. Upon entering there is a procession of smells: bottles of tar, blood of slaughtered livestock, curry and cinnamon and cloves under tents, meat and fat grilling on spits, the oily smell of synthetic fabric rolled and piled in tents. People elbow, squeeze, and push their way through the crowd, stopping to listen to an argument between a vendor and client, or going about their business of buying vegetables or selecting the cloth and gold for a trousseau. Others scream "*bal-ək*" "watch out," as they drive their animals through the crowd.

There are eight market sites in the Beni Mellal region. Beni Mellal is the largest suq, though the ones at Souk Sebt and Kasba Tadla are nearly as big (see Figure 4). Tuesday is suq day in Beni Mellal. On Saturday many of the vendors travel by car, bus, or taxi to Souk Sebt, about forty kilometers

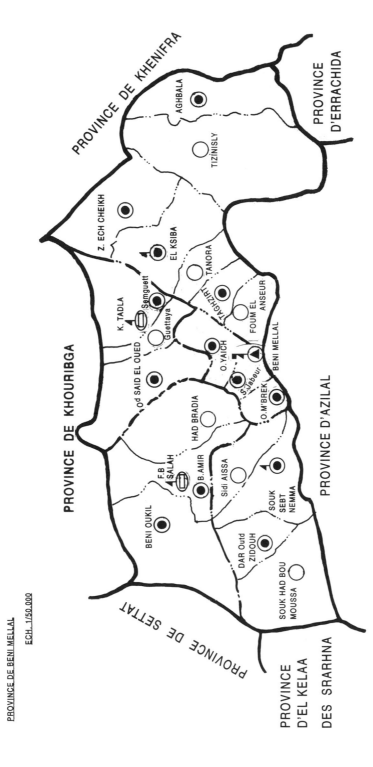

PROVINCE DE BENI MELLAL

ECH. 1/50.000

Figure 4. The Province of Beni Mellal; neighboring towns are on the itinerant marketplace circuit.

to the northwest. Wednesday suq is in Fqih Ben Salah, Friday in Kasba Tadla, Sunday in El Ksiba. Other markets in the area include those of Had El-Bradia, Ouled Yaich, and Zaouia Ch-Cheikh. Vendors travel to any or all of these markets, depending on their proximity or lucrative promise. As long as they pay the marketplace tax collector (*mul ș-șunk*) for their spot in the suq, vendors are free to market their goods. Some sellers do business only in the town or city where they reside.

The Body of the Market

The suq has already moved once in Beni Mellal to accommodate town expansion and remain on its outer limits. But urbanization is taking place so rapidly that there is now a poor residential quarter below the suq. Town officials plan to move the suq once again — this time well beyond the limits of town so there is no risk of habitation encompassing it again. This will make the suq much less accessible to town people who, lacking mules, donkeys, and carts, will have to take a city bus[4] or travel there by motor-scooter. Everyone is aware of this, though no one knows when it will happen. This impending move is symbolic: distancing the traditional institution of the itinerant weekly suq will act to separate the emergent middle and upper classes, who prefer boutiques and can afford to pay the higher prices of the neighborhood greengrocer, from the lower echelon of society who buy used clothing and rely on price negotiation to economize every penny. The recent completion of gardens surrounding a fountain in the center of town, along with the demolition of old stores and the reconstruction of a new boutique center indicates that the suq project will soon be part of city renovation.

For now the suq is below the cemetery. Next to it on the eastern side is a walled quarter of low-income housing. Neighborhoods are usually not walled in Beni Mellal, unless the walls function to hide the embarrassment of poverty.[5] This quarter was a shantytown that the city razed when the suq became its neighbor. It was replaced with a rectilinear grid of one- and two-room cement shelters surrounded by a wall so that suq-goers (at one time, comprising the majority of heads of households, women or men) would not be obliged to confront destitution.

Efforts to cover up the borders of impoverishment notwithstanding, the marketplace is still populated with the poor and socially disenfranchised. The grotesque imagery characteristic of literary markets is not absent (Bakhtin 1986). Even though there are taboos in Moroccan culture surrounding urination and defecation, it is common to see people (considered "country") squatting at the suq walls in order to relieve themselves. The marketplace, and especially the area of the ḥalqa, is dense with young mothers in rags, sleeping or listless children in their laps. Women's limbs and torsos are glimpsed through tent flaps of traditional healers, while blind men and women chant blessings with open palms, and those with physical handicaps ask for alms.[6] There is no stigma attached to begging, no issue of pride involved. Poverty and physical lack entitle one to beg. The poor are considered the charge of the faith; there is an obligation (*wajib*) to take care of them with charitable contributions.

In this context it becomes problematic to gloss the "grotesque," as Bakhtin does, as a quality of marketplace experience which "liberates man [sic] from all the forms of inhuman necessity that direct the prevailing concept of the world" (1968:49). Bakhtin equates the openness of marketplace experience with social renewal, a shared liberation that leans towards counter-hegemonic communitas. Yet the suq is not a carnival. Although it shares many carnivalesque attributes, the market does not give rise to the kind of crowd euphoria found in festival celebrations (Abrahams 1987; Falassi 1987) and mardi gras (Turner 1987); rather it embodies a plurality of experience wherein different bodies rejoice, accuse, or yawn in uneven moments and unpredictable movements. The market is a body that has not been colonized by a privileged symbol—eating, defecating, cursing, cauterization, and social intercourse about sexuality are all found at the suq and each embodies intense sensations that bid equally for pleasure and pain.

It is virtually impossible to mirror the market as a single entity. There is no primary suq experience that defines the market, no sovereignty in a place where a rich butcher sells four skinned calves next to an old man in rags who is meting out vials of liquid asphalt for a few riyals. The market has no physical center.[7] It is not a grid but a series of tangential crossings. Even a labyrinth has a more traceable middle, a place from which paths unwind. But the suq's organization (unlike the city's, which has a *centre-ville*) is an anti-organization. One circulates among the tents with a certain learned radar, like blood coursing through the body. Nothing in the suq is fixed; everything is negotiable. Values in this institution are slippery, mutable, and mutually influential.

Metaphors of regeneration are certainly applicable to the Moroccan suq, even to such destitute figures as the nursing beggar; but the liberating forces of the grotesque and the carnivalesque must be relativized here. Marketplace humor, as well as all affective hyperbole, is a vital aspect of the unsettling of categories in marketplace speech, but laughter does not drown out the real sufferings the marketplace presents. Nor is the "inhuman necessity" Bakhtin refers to ever absent from the Moroccan context.

The Marketplace, the Fair, and Carnival

Market day (*nhar suq*) has traditionally been marked as a day of intensified consumption, commodity exchange, and celebration. The correlation of market day with a holiday, when the normal rhythms of daily life change tempo, is preserved in the French term *jour ferié*, a day set apart for the commemoration of a civil or religious celebration or remembrance. The word *ferié* comes from the Latin *ferioe*, "days of rest," which is a derivation of *feria*, "market," or "fair." These terms come from a period when work stopped at fixed and regular intervals in the calendrical cycle (usually weekly) in order that people could go to the market and attain material, psychological, and spiritual provisions (fairs often took place on religious holy days). But the word *ferié* is not without its secular connotations and paradoxes. A related Latin noun, *foria*, means diarrhea and the word *foire*, or fair, eventually came to be used figuratively as a place where disorder and confusion reign. *Faire la foire* in contemporary French means to abandon oneself to a life of debauchery.

Market day in Morocco does not necessarily coincide with the religious *jour ferié* in the Islamic calendar (*nhar j-jəmʿa*, "meeting day," or Friday), but it does function as a day that is set apart from the rest of the week, a day for limited rest, relative feast, and civil commemoration. The polluting qualities of the marketplace are also evident in the Moroccan context. The suq is the most prominent social metaphor for a site that embodies dirt, confusion, and shameful enactments. It is a place of dirt and words. In fact, what we refer to as "dirty words," or "street talk" in English is referred to in Moroccan dialect as *al-klam dyal suq*, "words of the suq."[8]

The marketplace has a special status in the Moroccan imagination as a symbol of disorder, a locus with no center. When people are loud and unruly in a public setting such as a post office or a bank, the question of "Is this a suq or what?" (*wəsh suq hada u la?*), serves to intimidate the crowd into orderly behavior. Another common expression, "He's into the suq in his head" (*dakhəl suq ras-u*), means that one minds one's own business. Someone who is "into his own suq" is non-imposing, but may also be suspiciously aloof. The suq represents a terrain through which one may promenade almost indefinitely with rapt attention, a place wherein one is easily and perhaps menacingly lost.

The Marketplace and the Value of Gold

In a context that lends itself easily to adjectives such as "grotesque" and "unruly," the presence of the gold market in the suq is a seeming anomaly. The presence of women selling gold signifies a move in women's roles in the marketplace from periphery to center. Gold is a very important commodity in Morocco and has a direct symbolic connection to feminine power and status.[9] Its display in the form of necklaces, pendants, bracelets, and rings signals not only the financial assets but the actual value of its wearer on the marriage market. The gold a woman wears is her own, considered by Moroccan women as an investment and insurance against hard times. It is the first purchase a woman makes with her money, sometimes saved in small increments for years on end.

Women come to the suq to buy gold or to sell it for more liquid capital (*flus* "money"). Trade in gold is always done with weights and measures and women are savvy about the going prices. There is little bargaining in gold exchange. The weight of the object times the value per ounce equals the price.

One of the more traditional adornments sold at the gold market is a coin that was current during the French Protectorate, called *l-luiz* ("louis d'or" in French). Women used to covet these coins, bringing them out only on special occasions. They are still collected and worn as earrings, necklaces, and belts. Although considered a symbol of backward "country" people for several decades, they are now back in fashion. Because these coins are almost a century old, jewelers pretend they are rare and charge more than their value in weight. One jeweler confided to me that luiz are plentiful in France, available at half the price charged in Morocco. The creation of this "lack" of luiz in Morocco and the willingness of women to pay such a high price for these decorative coins alerts us to their symbolic importance. The display of luiz is a show of a particular kind of wealth. A women who is decorated with "money" has a certain degree of autonomy, for the gold is hers, not her husband's. A woman with gold is a more valuable (and dangerous) object than a woman with none, but she is also an essentialized symbol, a reminder to herself and to others of her market worth. Yet the very presence of gold in the suq is an ambiguous one. Its value is set apart from, yet clearly mixed up with, the dirt and confusion of its surroundings.

It is one of the hallmarks of gold in Morocco that it is found in contexts associated not only with high status but with pollution, dirt, and ambiguity. Its presence in the marketplace is one example of this.

The Ḥalqa, the Hybrid Circle

The suq is constructed as socially "low," the locus of popular performance and chicanery. Performance in the suq takes the form of public oratory, sales spiels for potions that remove spells, acrobatic displays, competitive boxing, storytelling, and doom-saying. These spectacles usually take place in the ḥalqa, the section of the suq reserved for performance. The ḥalqa is space of play and leisure, a place for boys to watch their peers being coached in a boxing match, a place for old men to have their heads shaved,[10] a place for the unemployed to pass the time drinking tea and listening to epic tales. It is also a place for women who frequent clairvoyants, herbalists, and fqihs — men learned in the Qur'an, who write charms for them and give them counsel (see Figure 5). The ḥalqa is the public arena for social license, a site where almost anything can be said with impunity.[11] Because of the expressive liberties taken in the ḥalqa, it is a marginal site; a man of honor would be embarrassed to be found there.

In Beni Mellal the ḥalqa is in the old market site that rises on the first slope of the Middle Atlas mountains, dominating the view of the plain and the main area of the suq. The old suq is the designated place for ḥalqa performers, but their enactments are mobile, created whenever a circle of people gather. The audience defines the ḥalqa (literally "link" [of a chain] or "circle"); there can be no ḥalqa without a minimum number of people surrounding a performer. The *ḥlayqi* (masc. sing.) is obliged to draw out and elaborate the introduction to his spiel until a large enough audience has been lured to constitute a circle. The "art of the draw" is essential; one must be skilled in attracting an audience, making the market a site of seduction. Delaying the consumption of market goods — performances or appropriable commodities — is the art of the marketplace. One lingers in moments of transition, in promises of acquisition,[12] and in the words and postures that facilitate social exchange.[13]

Entering the old market, people immediately flock to the ḥalqa with the highest density of bodies. The more difficult it is to see the entertainer, the more the audience is convinced that it is worthwhile to do so. Some performers entice with unusual feats such as contortion or snake charming;

Figure 5. A fqih writing a charm in the ḥalqa.

others use verbal prowess in humor, bawdiness, or religious doom-saying. Some use microphones, many simply scream. Women orators enjoy a special status because their presence in the market is relatively novel. Both men and women gather around these herbalists and spell-specialists, not only because they are attracted by the spiel, but because the spiel-maker[14] commands attention by virtue of being a woman in a public and formerly male role.

The physical and symbolic space of the ḥalqa calls up imagery of performance and unethical behavior, associated with lies, physical dirt, chicanery, and "cheap" entertainment. "Buying and selling is better than robbery," goes a popular saying.[15] The confluence of performance and transgression is not arbitrary. The most common form of popular performance — singing and dancing done by female performers, or *shikhat* — has long been emblematic of sexual libertinism. The in-mixing of the sexes in a celebratory context has the effect of either licit or illicit transgression.

In-mixing is a primary reason that marketplace performance is considered a less-than-reputable activity. Hybridity is the trademark of marketplace interaction. The term "hybrid" in Moroccan Arabic (*mkhallat* "mixed") gathers its meaning in contrast to an imagined homogeneity, symbolized in marriage patterns with patrilineal cousins, for example, who have "one blood" (*dam waḥəd*). Tribal mentality holds this purity of blood relation as an ideal, even if rarely attained in Morocco (H. Geertz 1979). But the suq is an extra-familial territory, representing all of the dangers of the strange and the stranger. As a proverb explains, "brotherhood is neither bought not sold";[16] market relations have no place in the familial system of fraternity. Codes of honor cannot be taken for granted here, nor can the practice of religious principles[17]: "Keep away from the crowded markets [and] you will escape all evil."

Despite the untrustworthy quality of marketplace activity, or perhaps because of it, the values of honor, fraternity, and honesty are often invoked. The use of moral discourses imputes hybridity to marketplace speech by contaminating religious invocation with lies, fraternity with hypocrisy, and categories of honor with inversion. There is no pure language of the marketplace; not only are different registers used, but different dialects of Arabic and Berber are interspersed conversationally. Cultural diglossia makes even the language of currency negotiable.[18] The suq is the site of creolization, a symbolic domain that embodies social contagion, a hybridizing force which the developing middle class both fears and desires (Stallybrass and White 1986).

There are several ways in which this reconfiguration and fusing of different orders is manifest. Because performance takes place in the space of buying and selling, it is subject to immediate commodification. Stories and advice, like goods such as potions and incense, are given a price. The *site of discourse* thus determines the value and interpretation of the speech events that emerge. The marketplace contributes political consequence to performance by making it a commodity where goods are evaluated by the privileged symbol of money. The value of the "items sold" in the ḥalqa is nominal, ranging from a few cents to a dollar. Ḥalqa performers (with the exception of herbalists) are people who pass the hat much like beggars, likewise dependent upon a populace that participates in (or at least aspires to) the dominant modes of production to earn their livelihood. Ḥlayqiya (pl.) are socially devalued because their goods are often intangible or ephemeral and because their activities challenge dominant notions of what constitutes value in society. Performers in the ḥalqa are excluded from a material economy whose primary value is the generation of capital, yet included in it as an example of refuse.

The Merchant as Trickster

The suq is a place of exaggeration where people permit themselves to lose their tempers, scream, and accuse others at the slightest provocation. Self-interest, cunning, and lying are expected. But these are not necessarily "bad" characteristics; they may actually be heroic insofar as they permit the underdog to triumph over his or her enemies (Roberts 1989; see also E. Basso 1987). The adaptive quality of such "tricksters" gives them access to heroic status, especially in conditions like colonialism which demand a less-than-confrontational strategy.

There is a long tradition of idealizing the trickster in North African folktales (see Moulieras 1987; Basset 1987). In Morocco the most famous trickster goes by the name of "Jḥa," sometimes portrayed as a vendor, as in the following account, told to me by Hssaine Aggour, a primary school teacher and consummate verbal artist:

Jḥa was out of work, but he had an idea about how to make some money. He went and gathered some shit. He rolled it into little morsels and then rolled them in səlu [a powdery sweet made of ground wheat, nuts, and honey]. He went to the suq and began screaming, "Seeds of understanding, seeds of understanding!" A man came up to him and sampled one. At first he tasted the sweetness of the səlu, but then he tasted what was underneath.

"This is shit!" he exclaimed.

"Well," said Jḥa, "You've begun to understand!"

This anecdote not only comments upon the naiveté of the buyer who thought there was such a thing as a "seed of understanding" (ḥabbət l-fhəma), it carries an implicit heed to be cautious of all commodity relations. Though the client gains sagacity from the transaction, it is not in the way he had anticipated.[19] The ambiguity present in all marketplace relations is exemplified here; there is no transaction without some sincerity, but no profit in sincerity alone.[20]

Obliged to lie in order to make a profit,[21] the seller often swears that she or he paid such and such a price for wholesale merchandise and cannot take any lower than a few riyals more. Buyers rarely believe the base price quoted, but the seller's strategy continues to be a viable one since it includes religious oaths that would make the vendor lose face (*l-wajh*) if contradicted. Vendors pivot on the borders of prevarication and truth; they are both tricksters and anti-tricksters. Their invocation of religious language and ideology serves to uphold appearances and sell goods.

This is one rule of the marketplace: recognize lies but do not publicly identify them as such. Accepting the rules of the game is now so much a part of the marketplace mentality that two different individuals told me that lying, which is forbidden (*ḥaram*) in the religious code of ethics, is actually permitted (*ḥalal*) in the context of the marketplace, bending the code to accommodate social practice.

The proliferation of women vendors in the suq the last ten years provides a new perspective on the vendor-as-trickster model. Feminine figures in Moroccan tales and anecdotes have often been portrayed as scheming and untrustworthy (see Dwyer 1978). Involvement in trade relations (other than marital exchange) lends them a new status and power. No longer are women's negotiations with power and authority relegated to behind the scenes.

The Evolution of Worldly Existence and the Loss of Niya

Trickster figures in the marketplace are not confined to sellers. Entering the arena of buy-and-sell relations symbolized by the physical circumference of the suq is like stepping through the looking glass into a world where all consensual ethics are subject to inversion. "Settle your accounts with me as if I were your enemy," goes a proverb, "and entertain me as your brother." Market relations or "settling accounts" are not the domain of family or friendship, but are cast in conflictual terms, as a meeting of enemies.

But if the market is the place of enmity and "evil" (as stated in the opening epigraph), it is countered by an ethic of trust exemplified by metaphors of kinship that extend to society in general. The market has always been a dangerous territory, but if relegated to a physical locus or defined as an extra-familial phenomenon, it could be categorically contained. More than ever, however, commodity relations are exceeding the bounds of the market in the Moroccan imagination (cf. Rosen 1984). With the accessibility of television and its central place in every home, marketplace relations (particularly in the form of advertising) are brought into the privacy of family life. Boutiques and supermarkets are opening in the midst of middle-class housing. In walking out one's door, one walks into the marketplace.

This is not to conflate the suq with commodity relations as they apply in society at large. Although Clifford Geertz maintains that the "rural or 'tribal' market and the urban or 'bourgeois' market are, in analytical terms, the same institution" (1979 : 173), I believe these represent two different social modes of being. The traditional itinerant suq by virtue of its periodicity functions more as a festive "time out of time"[22] than does the permanent and daily market of the cities. The urban market is coextensive with the larger urban geography, while the itinerant suq is still confined to a bounded locale. Within the space of the local suq, prices are negotiated in elaborate verbal dialogue and oratory is still practiced. The urban market, by contrast, is beginning to adopt the policy of prix fixe wherein the exchange of bargaining is silenced. There is a difference between the suq (the market*place*) and the *process* of commodification that permeates society in general (Agnew 1986 : 28, 41). What happens in the local suq ultimately has resonance in the larger market, just as the goods and conditions of the international marketplace affect the bounded itinerant suq. There are different communicative processes at work in each, however; the suq is openly dialogic, whereas advertising and prix fixe stores are becoming monologic. Yet both give reason for suspicion; they are presumed to represent dishonesty.

In Beni Mellal we witness a shift in focus and power from the local suq to the extra-local marketplace of advertising and prix fixe that is struggling to supersede it. When the world becomes a marketplace and deception can no longer be localized and bound, there is little room for either brotherhood or hospitality. The emergent middle class seeks to remove itself from the chaos and dirt associated with the suq in order to constitute itself as a class apart. One consequence of this stratification is nostalgia for a time (*bəkri*, "in the early days") when there was still *niya*, a word that may mean trust, good intention, belief, or naiveté, depending on its context.[23]

Niya and Marketplace Relations

"In the early days (bəkri) there was niya," our neighbor the Ḥajja said. "A woman went, in those days. She said to you,[24] she brought her son to the suq. And he left his mother holding the horse, holding the horse just outside the suq. And one guy came along holding a string of doughnuts.

"He said to her, 'oh woman.'

"She said to him, 'yes?'

"He said to her, 'your son said to you, "take this string of doughnuts and give me the horse."'

"And she gave him the horse. She gave the owner of the doughnuts the horse. Her son came and found her like that with a string of doughnuts." The Ḥajja laughed.

"He said to her, 'Oh my mother, where is the horse?'

"She said to him, 'Oh my son, you see, the owner of the doughnuts took him, the one who gave me these doughnuts.'

"'Oh hell,' he said to her, 'I didn't send anyone to you!' He said to you, she went, the poor woman, into the suq, and she took, the poor thing, that string of doughnuts and, he said to you, she's calling, 'oh owner of the doughnuts, oh owner of the doughnuts, give me my horse!' But the one with the horse was gone. I don't know where he took it. I don't know where he got with it. And that's not niya?"

This narrative pokes fun at an older woman who is naive and vulnerable.[25] The image of a mother with a grown son walking around the suq with a string of doughnuts screaming for the doughnut seller to come back and return her horse is particularly amusing to the Ḥajja. Her laughter denotes both a distance and a proximity with this character, for she freely admits that before her husband's death she hardly ever went out of the house. It is easy for the Ḥajja to imagine herself in a similar situation, though she is now able to laugh at its absurdity.

"And then one day, someone was selling turkeys. This happened right here, right here. And two thieves came and said to her, 'How much, my aunt, did they offer you for this turkey?'

"She said to them, 'That one, my son, they offered me nine hundred for it, and for that one, one thousand riyals.'

"He said, 'that's plenty.'

"She said to them, 'No. This one is one thousand and that one is one thousand.'

"And, he said to you, they bargained for those two turkeys. He said to you, he said to her, 'Close your eyes, my aunt, in order to (. . .) close your eyes [to see if] one is heavier than the other.'

"He said to you, the woman closed her eyes and they went and flew off with those turkeys. And she says to them with her niya, 'Oh my son, oh my son, should I open, should I open [my eyes]?'

"When she finally opened her eyes, she found they had gone and taken those turkeys and left her with nothing." Ḥajja laughed. "That happened right at our own suq!"

These two anecdotes do more than warn against naiveté or blind belief in the context of the marketplace. The first comments on the woman's ignorance about the incommensurability of values (horses and doughnuts) while the second makes reference to the lack of a system of weights and measures in early days, which made it necessary to rely on the fallibility of human estimate in determining worth (weighing the turkeys with closed eyes). In both cases it is a mature woman who is duped at the marketplace because of her niya. These narratives portray niya as a quality of the past that is inappropriate and ineffectual in the marketplace where one must be perpetually on guard.

The coincidence of social nostalgia for niya with the development of the middle class in Beni Mellal is no accident. The fetishization of a conceptual past, a time when there was order and trust, is an attempt to be situated in relation to rapidly changing social practices and their accompanying values. Against this ethic of niya stands the diversity of danger of the marketplace.

Polluting Modernity

The loss of niya is a social theme in Beni Mellal. All age groups from adolescence on bemoan a loss of innocence in society. For marriageable youth, this translates into sexual terms; young men complain about a lack of women who maintain their virginity until marriage, while women, many disillusioned with the institution of marriage and the very high divorce rate, say there's no longer any reason to stay at home and wait for the right suitor.

"A man looked far and wide for a girl who would be a virgin bride," my assistant Si Mohamed told me one day while we were waiting in front of his brother's vegetable stall for his friend Majid to arrive. "He wanted a bride who would be obedient and a good housewife. He traveled all over the country looking for a virgin to wed, but had no success. He finally wound up in a small and secluded village high up in the mountains. He thought sure to find his bride there. He asked her father for permission to talk with her.

"'Do you know [how to] cook?' he asked the girl.

'Cook?' she repeated. 'Is he the one with the Renault 18 or the Renault 21?'"

This joke plays on the homophony between the Moroccan verb to cook (*ṭayəb*) and the masculine proper name Taib (pronounced /ṭayəb/). Even in the most remote of places, the joke implies, women go out with men in cars, the fashionable vehicle for illicit pick-ups. *Ma bqat niya*, "There's no more good intention."

Parents complain that children are no longer modest before their elders. One mother of grown daughters told me, "They go so far as to bring their boyfriend home with them and say, 'Mom, this is so-and-so'!" A boyfriend encountered in the marketplace is not suitable for bringing home. A relationship that is not arranged by the family presents a threat.

An examination of the changing moral fabric in Morocco is a vast enterprise. Despite the important status of the moral canon of deference to authority (*ḥashuma*), this canon is being seriously challenged in *practice*. Davis and Davis (1989:182) allude to this in their study of adolescence in the rural town of Zawiya when they note that "increasing numbers of youth are becoming convinced that broad change is afoot in a world where youth (*shabab*) do not fear to challenge oppression and inequity."

The perceived diminishment of niya is accompanied by an increase in development or evolution (*tatawwur*). In Moroccan dialect this verb also connotes cleverness. A *mra mṭṭuwwra* is not just evolved or developed, but a clever and sharp woman who cannot be duped. She is someone who is keyed into change and this change links her inextricably to the marketplace. Many say that "life has evolved" (*dunya ṭṭawrat*), implying that change is proceeding so rapidly that trust can no longer be taken for granted.

Beliefs About Lies

The admitted prevalence of lies in the marketplace and the salience of lying as a theme in everyday discourse accommodates sentiments of nostalgia for a time when there was truth and trust. But the practice of lying, as well as reflexive talk about lies, also indicates a hierarchy of power relations. In nonmarketplace relations, "the only person who lies to you is the one who is afraid of you or the one who defers to you" (*ma kdəb ʾl-ək ghir lli khaf mən-ək u la ḥshəm mən-ək*, a popular saying). Lying in non-market interactions is motivated by the desire *not* to confront someone higher on the social scale, but to circumvent truth in order to avoid conflict. Lying is a method of avoidance, used strategically in asymmetrical power relations (see Gilsenan 1976).

In the marketplace this ethic is inverted. The vendor lies precisely within a context of confrontation, neither fearing nor deferring to the client, who is considered or hoped to be a dupe. Yet the vendor's profit increases to the extent that she can convince the client of her sincerity despite the ground of distrust in which her utterances are embedded. It is precisely because all intentions are subject to scrutiny that lying becomes a salient theme in marketplace interactions, as in the herbalist's discourse:

"Here, here is real medicine of truth, taken from a book. And whatever is in books doesn't contain lies...

"Don't call me a liar or a bastard...

"Whoever wants some from me give me a hundred. By the truth of God, if I've wasted your 100 riyals, tomorrow next to God — here, you are all more than twelve witnesses — if I've wasted your 100 riyals, tomorrow next to God, you'll take a piece of my meat, from here.

"I gathered them and washed them and ground them and from the book it's copied. Here are the herbs, here they are."

Forging relations of trust becomes a primary market strategy. The herbalist's success depends on her power to persuade the audience of her sincerity. Her socioeconomic standing thus becomes significant: vendors often come from the lower classes or from dire circumstances that have lowered their status and forced them into their profession. The marketplace is no respecter of persons; relations of social hierarchy are equalized if not actually inverted. Power is not solely in the hands of the well-born, the politically influential, or the masculine segment of society. It is for this reason that the suq is a place of the people (*blasa sha'biya*), the domain of the popular and the populace.

Notes

1. Westermarck (1980, proverb #1384).

2. A *ṭajin* is a clay cooking vessel with a conical cover.

3. A *qanṭar* is equivalent to one hundred kilograms or two hundred twenty pounds. It comes from the French, "quintal," a hundredweight.

4. In-city bus service was instituted in 1990 and is an appreciated novelty for residents of Beni Mellal.

5. Building walls to hide what is socially disgraceful has precedent in Beni Mellal. There is a poor part of town where garbage is thrown and sewage emerges every time it rains. Instead of dealing with the source of these problems (no waste

control, no garbage removal), the city has built a wall in front of this section. Some high school teachers who live on the "clean" side of this wall have dubbed the structure *le mur de la honte*, "the wall of shame" (used to refer to the former Berlin wall).

6. Begging is a profession in Morocco, relying on the religious injunction to charity. Several Moroccans have told me that poor families are sometimes happy when a child is born handicapped, as these children are more successful in soliciting alms.

7. Some Moroccan suqs are small and navigable, while others are organized according to a grid structure. The suq in Beni Mellal, being the biggest in the region, is also the most chaotic.

8. In classical Arabic the word *suqiyya* is synonymous with vulgarity. I am grateful to Dr. Hasan El-Shamy for bringing this to my attention.

9. See El-Shamy (1980), "Letter to the Justice," for an illustration of this in folktale. See Fernea (1967) for discussion of women and gold in the Iraqi context.

10. The word for barber (*ḥallaq* [CA]) is built on the same triliteral root as *ḥalqa*. Barbers are found in the same area of the suq as performers in Beni Mellal. They have traditionally cut hair as well as performed blood-letting and circumcisions. Since barbers have an integral role in the transformation of the body (often in the liminal space of ritual), they have the same ambiguous status attributed to performers who facilitate cognitive and affective transitions by addressing themselves to the taboo and the "low" within the public and heterogeneous context of the marketplace.

11. There are some topics which are under no circumstances given free reign. Most notably, words against the King and the political monarchy are censored in every public context.

12. "The 'natural' and 'original' relationship that links man to the use of his goods gives way to *the detour of exchange*. 'In itself, the use-value first translates the individual's relation to nature; the exchange-value added to the use-value, translates his social relations.' Thus the market, the scene of exchange, presupposes a delay in consumption (the enjoyment of possessions) for at least as long as the exchange takes place" (Goux 1990:27, quoting Marx, *Capital*: 58).

13. To say that the ḥalqa performer depends on the ḥalqa is simply to acknowledge the dialogic properties of performance in general, the interdependence of actor and audience. On the audience as co-performers, see Brenneis (1986).

14. Amanda Dargan Zeitlin (1992) uses this term in her discussion of verbal artists in the marketplace.

15. Westermarck (1980, proverb #1138).

16. Westermarck (1980, proverb #21).

17. Caton remarks on the incommensurability of honor with the values of the marketplace when he says that in North Yemen "taking money for verses . . . implies that the act is part of the market rather than a symbolic exchange in the 'glorious deed' of honor" (1990:55).

18. Language and currencies are negotiable; a merchant might quote a price in dirhams, in riyals, or in old francs. Ten dirhams = two hundred riyals = one thousand francs. Moroccans are fluent in all these systems and code-switch frequently,

often with very strategic intent (to make a price sound lower or higher, for example).

19. Waterbury (1972) records a similar tale, but with a different cast of characters. It goes this way:

> A group of *ulema* [theologians] came to Djha one day and said to him, "We have been told that you possess magic seeds that give you intelligence."
>
> Djha replied, "Well, I didn't want to talk about it, but it is true. I have such seeds."
>
> "Can we obtain some?" asked the ulema.
>
> Djha pondered for a moment, "Yes, that can be arranged, but, of course, they do not come cheaply."
>
> "How much?" queried the ulema.
>
> "One thousand riyals each."
>
> "That is a lot of money," said one of the group, "but I will try at least one."
>
> He gave Djha one thousand riyals and Djha gave him a little seed which the man popped into his mouth, chewed, and swallowed. Then he erupted in anger and shouted at Djha, "But that's nothing but a pumpkin seed!"
>
> "See!" said Djha, "you've only eaten one seed, and already you're beginning to learn!"

20. This corresponds to Motif #X77 in Stith Thompson's *Motif Index*. Compare with El-Shamy (1980), "The Quick Ass."

21. See Gilsenan (1976) for an important discussion of lying in the Arab context.

22. This is the title of a volume on festival edited by Falassi (1987).

23. See Chapter 9 for a fuller discussion of niya. See Eickelman (1977) on the concept of time in a tribe in western Morocco. Fabian (1983) critiques the anthropologist's representation of the Other as inhabiting a radically different time and space and calls for an anthropology of coevality.

24. "She said to you," or "he said to you" is a rhetorical phrase that introduces reported speech in Moroccan storytelling, a discourse marker (Schiffren 1987). See Chapter 5.

25. Compare with El-Shamy (1980), "Blow for Blow."

2. Shṭara: Competence in Cleverness

To indicate that the world is topsy turvy, it is said that "the women are going to the market."

—Bourdieu (1966 : 240)

To get to the suq you have to cross three neighborhoods, transverse two empty lots where sheep graze on garbage and shrubs, and cut through the oily streets of the industrial quarter, where black-handed mechanics work on truck engines and repair motor bikes.

I met the Ḥajja and Rquiya, another neighbor, right in front of our house and we set off, my tape recorder in a straw basket on my shoulder. At seven in the morning the streets were already busy — produce-laden donkeys, tethered fowl, pedestrians on their way to and from the marketplace. We made our way through the market entrance, dodging mules, porters pulling carts, the crowd:

"How much is this rooster, oh man (*ah rajəl*)?" asked the Ḥajja when we arrived at the chicken section.

"They offered me 850, that's what they offered me," he answered, picking up the one she had indicated from the row in front of him.

"Shall I pay that price for it?"

"No."

"Oh, which one? That one which has, the one that's sick?"

"Come on! Prayers to the Prophet! All of them are healthy. There's not one that is sick. Here are some roosters [to choose from]. If you offer [a good price] God will help me and help you. If it's worth 600 you'll find it for only 400 [with me]. May God help you and me."

"Deal with us and we'll take this little rooster."

"That's what they offered me for it, those who buy and sell. They offered me 850. I won't swear to you and I won't lie to you. If you want it, you can take it with God's benefit."

"No, no."

"God give you benefit."

"No, no. Shall we pay 700 riyals? That's what's in my power [to pay]."

"'There is no power and no strength save in God'," the vendor said, quoting from the Qur'an. "By God, they offered me 750, those who buy and sell."

"Well, sir, God bring you ease. I, I wouldn't mind [buying it for that price]. Everyone takes what God has written for them."

"Go. Take it for 750 riyals."

"That's it," the Ḥajja said, holding the rooster and feeling its legs.

"Give me that rooster," he told her, taking it back. "Here, here's where to check the rooster."

"Yeah."

"How about the money. There's no problem. By God, I took off 50 riyals, whether you believe it or not. I don't want to keep standing here. This is the one you want?"

"I'm just afraid it's sick," repeated the Ḥajja.

"God forbid! Is this face sick?" asked the vendor, holding up the face of the rooster for the Ḥajja's inspection.

"Put him this way," she told him, flipping her palm over.

"*Aywa!* Prayers to the Prophet! So that he starts to crow?" The rooster crowed, upset with being turned upside down.

"That's it," said the Ḥajja, satisifed and laughing at the commotion. "No, no. He's not sick. God's blessings are upon you."

"Well, shame on you, woman, that [kind of talk]. With that price of 750. And I didn't want to sell it. But when God has something written for you; just take it, like a gift for the faithful. Here are some others if you want another. But if you're convinced about this one, God bring you blessing. Is this your basket? I'll put it here. There's just one sustenance (*rizq*), not four or five. Here, woman, may God give you back."

The verb "to bargain" in Moroccan Arabic is *shṭara*. This verb has two different but complementary definitions; it means both to be cunning and artfully clever as well as to divide into two equal parts. The act of shṭara contains the strategic injunction to be skillful and adroit in the process of the social division of goods.

Bargaining is the most colloquial of marketplace genres and undoubtedly the most dialogic. Within it social identities are constantly negotiated and rhetorically redefined, using oaths, scripture, blessings, and playful speech (*təfliya*). A moral discourse is invoked in the least moral of contexts. "Shame on you, woman," the vendor tells the Ḥajja when she casts doubts on the health of his merchandise. "There is no power or might save in God," he asserts, defining himself as a believer and, by extension, an honest merchant.

The contact that the market facilitates between people of different social strata, ages, and sexes makes it a primary forum for the linguistic construction of social and economic identities (cf. Diouri 1984). This is also true in regard to gender definitions. Only ten years ago there were far fewer women vendors in the Beni Mellal marketplace. Today their numbers are impressive, comprising at least half the marketplace population. And they are not only buying, but they have become vendors of gold, cloth and herbs. In fact, women have cornered the market on items of contraband that they bring from the northern border towns with Spain.

There is a precedent for women involved in smuggling in the north of Morocco, set by women who have done business across the border towns of Melilla and Ceuta (see Hajjarabi 1988; Troin 1975). Women smugglers specialize in women's goods, buying in small quantities. Aided by the taboo on inter-sexual communication as well as by their ability to conceal items under their long jəllabas, they are able to hide these goods from the officials more easily than men. Once back in their villages or towns, these women can sell not only at the suq but out of their own homes. This practice has spread from the north to many other parts of Morocco, notably Beni Mellal, which is about ten hours by bus from Tetouan, the closest big town to Spanish Ceuta.

Several of the women who sell contraband at the weekly market in Beni Mellal spend the rest of the week receiving customers at their residences. Customers even special-order certain commodities and kinds of cloth before the vendors go up north on their weekly routes. The frequency of this kind of long-distance smuggling has resulted in systematized bribes to bus drivers, who in turn pay off the highway police to let their bus pass without inspection (or at least without fines). Women merchants travel together and organize their trips so that they are able to bring the maximum amount of goods for the minimum expenditure.

The high visibility of women in the public sphere of the open-air suq signifies the breakdown of private/public categories that formerly defined the suq as an exclusively masculine domain (C. Geertz 1979; Hart 1976; Troin 1975). Social categories have transformed, as have definitions of social authority and power. The marketplace is an arena where definitions of class and gender are perpetually negotiated. In the examination of the discourse of women vendors in the Moroccan marketplace, the categories and contradictions inherent in the very public speech of these women become evident.

Contraband and Contradiction

> "You didn't use to go to the suq?"
> "No, we didn't go, [not] our generation. We didn't know anything about the suq. Nothing. . . . There were just men who went to the suq. Just men. Women didn't go. Whoever went to the suq…hahaha! [She] got the stick! The stick! *Stay at home!*"
>
> — Hadda

Approaching the Moroccan itinerant suq, it is hard not to make the comparison with the Rabelaisian marketplace Bakhtin so seductively resurrects for us:

> The marketplace of the Middle Ages and the Renaissance was a world in itself, a world which was one; all "performances" in this area, from loud cursing to the organized show, had something in common and were imbued with the same atmosphere of freedom, frankness, and familiarity. Such elements of familiar speech as profanities, oaths, and curses were fully legalized in the marketplace and were easily adopted by all the festive genres, even by Church drama. The marketplace was the center of all that is unofficial; it enjoyed a certain extraterritoriality in a world of official order and official ideology, it always remained "with the people." (1984a : 153–54)

In Morocco there is a word, a category for "the people" as Bakhtin employs the term — *sha'b*. The Moroccan suq is in every way a place of the people (*blasa sha'biya*). But whereas most people with the exception of the urban haute bourgeoisie were "the folk" in recent Mellali memory, the class divisions now developing in this agricultural province have made it so the term is clothed with a certain nostalgia for a world once known, "which was one," and which has been lost. The suq is still a "place of the folk," but to be sha'bi is, for many, to be poor and old-fashioned.

One has to doubt whether the folk or the suq ever existed in the unified simple world that Bakhtin evokes.[1] The heterodoxy inherent in the market breeds stratification and exclusion. But while women predominate in the purchasing scene, women vendors are largely segregated from the men who sell. The women purveying contraband sit outside the northern wall, to the right of the main entrance. Those who sell wool and weaving rags and those who flog old clothes sit outside the eastern wall, to the right of the secondary entrance. Women who sell food are appropriately within the suq walls, in the "belly" of the suq. Nonetheless, there is a definite division of labor here. Women don't sell livestock (sheep, goats, donkeys, mules, cows) and they rarely sell large quantities of vegetables and fruits. Nor do they sell uncut cloth on a large scale. In general, women sell things *en detail*, things that have been separated from their set: a single chicken, clothes collected from various households, cloth cut from its reel, a skein of wool made from the coats of a few goats, a lone television acquired at a good price at the border.

They do sell gold, however, an exception to the decontextualized items mentioned. Because gold is a very important prestige and investment commodity in Morocco, women gold-sellers reflect an important feminine entrée into this formerly all-male profession, expanding the growing numbers of women vendors who are beginning to sell women's commodities to women. They sit under tents with other men and women at the suq, both buying gold from customers in dire straits and selling it, primarily to country women (most middle- and upper-class urban women go to well-known male jewelers in town for their purchases). The presence of gold at the suq juxtaposes the dirt and confusion of the marketplace with the intensified and "pure" value of a metal whose price is set on the international market. Gold incorporates all these values as it is deemed to both pollute an ideal moral world with vain materialism and to embody that world in metaphorical purity.[2]

The market is a place of symbolic exchange and a ground for tangible goods. Because of the license granted to the space of the market and the activities found there, the suq opens the boundaries of the body, indeed the boundaries of the world, for elaboration; gold is found amidst excrement, and all that is low symbolically becomes elevated like gold. The marketplace champions the lower bodily strata and the grotesque (Bakhtin 1984a), where dirt and waste are found in the same vicinity as the vegetables and fruits they help produce. The marketplace "is not a closed, completed unity; it is unfinished, outgrows itself, transgresses its own limits" (26). This breaching of the borders is born out upon examination of the suq's spatial organization and its inhabitants. Tinkers, barbers, and potters—all those who transform material from one state to another—are situated on the inner peripheries of the suq walls, on the edges of an already marginal institution. The cemetery, another liminal locus, is directly across from the suq walls. The borders of the market are thus populated with people whose profession is (or, in the case of cadavers, whose processes are) the transmutation of matter. But the women who have created their own market by catering primarily to other women are quite literally outside the walls, outside the entrances and exits, the orifices, of the suq. Their marginal placement is significant; garbage is burned at this site on non-market days, and the walls of the suq serve as public bathrooms. Women vendors thus sell their goods amidst garbage and human waste, amidst what is rejected from the viscera of the marketplace. These women inhabit the refuse, the graveyard of commodities, where the leftovers of consumption are burned and other commodities are placed on the ashes and offered up as "the new."

For the most part, women vendors are socially marginal characters. Divorced, widowed, or abandoned, often responsible for several children, and dressed in stained and torn jallabas, they do not represent social ideals, yet their impact on society is profound. Not only do they interact with a

Figure 6. Two market women, one with her daughter, outside the suq walls with their displayed goods from the north.

large segment of the population, using the elaborate linguistic and performative genre of bargaining, but they mediate important commodities. In the case of contraband sellers, they actually define the fashionable commodity for the developing middle class by introducing new and foreign items to the market (see Figure 6). What is more, they provide an example of women who have created their own kind of public culture that is inextricable from their class; by stepping into the public sector because of economic necessity, they exemplify self-sufficient women who are nonetheless marginalized because poverty has forced them into the public eye — and public ear as well.

Women in the marketplace understand the power of words and know how to manipulate them to their advantage. An example will serve to illustrate just how complicated and open are the simplest market engagements. Two young men desire to buy a cassette recorder for cost so that they can then re-sell it to their own client. Their interaction is with a woman vendor (in her late thirties) who is in possession of the recorder and a neighboring woman vendor. All four people alternate in the roles of speaker, addressee, and audience (Hymes 1974; Brenneis 1986; Haviland 1986). Although at least three of them are strangers to each other, their talk clearly invokes different social categories, inextricable from their social identities. In the act of bargaining for material goods, negotiation of ideology and values also takes place:

Mohamed[3] squatted near the vendor Aisha's goods, which were displayed on a large piece of dulled plastic on the hard earth. He took the tape recorder that he wanted to purchase in hand.

"Let's just go..."

"I told you [the price]," said Aisha, seated opposite on a section of the plastic.

"But don't you, too, be hard."

"No, my brother, by God, I'm not hard!"

"Take off 200, take it off."

"No, by God, I'm not [being] hard."

"Well I guess that's it [then]."

"If it were sufficient for me . . . look, just look . . ."

"Ah, just take off that 200 and that's it."

"No, there's no profit [in it for me]."

"Ohh, we, too... Waaa..."

Mohamed threw his hands up in frustration and his companion. Ahmed, who was standing near him, squatted down:

"You know…come let me tell you. Come here. Come let me tell you. Umm, he just wants to buy it to sell it again."

"We don't mind," said Aisha.

"It's as if you brought it to your house."

"But I also need a little [profit]."

The adjacent woman vendor, Fatna, then spoke:

"YOU fix it with her," she said, addressing Ahmed.

"We took off 200, but she doesn't want it."

"From what price?"

"Huh?"

"From what?"

"From 4200."

"Just get on with it. Give it [to him], give it. That's what we sold them for."

"We told her 4000, 4000."

"We sold them for even 400!" Aisha then resumed her bargaining.

"I can't send you away. Your face strikes me as dear [and] I didn't ruin it."

"They're taking up space," said Fatna. "Making a performance (ḥalqa) here for me without…Do you have 2000, I mean 4200? Take the recorder!"

"No, I just have 4000."

"That's what we pay for it wholesale!"

"Wholesale, [it's] 35 or 36 hundred," said Mohamed.

"By God, no one would take it for that!"

"Because, he said to you, they aren't made anymore. Why? What's the matter? Don't I go to Nador? They bring them from Nador, but there aren't anymore!"

"Well then," said Aisha, "go to Nador and spend 10,000 on it!"

"Uh…He also brings them. He sells [them] too. There's where his merchandise is. Over there. Now, there's a man who ordered it [from us]. In Nador, there aren't [any more]. There's another brand. But if we have to add 50, we won't buy it."

"What! We swore to you by God [that we wouldn't take that price]. You, too, you think we want to…uh…It's like we're exchanging *riyals* (pennies). Well, there's nothing to do."

"Well, see what you're going to do with *us*."

"That's it, sir. [The price is] what I told you."

"That's it. You'll sell it for 36?"

"36 and decide the price yourself! And see the suq. Here's the suq. You're looking at it."

"We'll [go and] buy it from the store."

"From the store! [What do] we want to sell you, magazines? And that, that recorder is first quality, better than at the store, and the store . . ."

"It's beautiful, beautiful."

"Huh?"

"Everything's beautiful."

"Well, offer a price, sir, and buy. It's not shameful. We're just like the store. What's the matter with us [women vendors]? *Aren't we all Muslims?*"

"No, no, we're all Muslims, one people."

"Well, we too are [Muslims]. Maybe if you gave us one riyal, you'd get back from us much reward."

"Well . . . he knows . . ."

"If we ate that [riyal] with you . . ."

"Here's 26."

"Well, there's 26."

"Here's 28."

"There it is. God brought 28."

"What are you going to do? Let's get on with it."

"You deserve it, my son, ah *shrif.*"

"Well, God help you."

"You merit it, my son, shrif, and there are the owners of the 3400 [riyal] recorder!"

In this quite ordinary bargaining encounter, a young man is not getting the price he wants from a woman vendor. Mohamed, who initiated the exchange, tells the vendor not to be "hard" (qaṣəḥ). In saying this, he implies that there is a group, a category of people who *are* hard: "don't you, too be hard," he says. Who are the others implicated in this statement and why is the quality of being hard so pejorative that it invokes a defensive denial on the part of the vendor?

Being hard means being inflexible, while the premise of bargaining is the flexibility of both vendor and client with regard to price. Without this flexibility there is no reason to pursue purchases at the suq; rather, a potential buyer would and can go to a store where the prices are non-negotiable (prix fixe), a phenomenon that is relatively recent in Beni Mellal but that is becoming more common. The fact that the woman is selling contraband (ṭrabando) further obligates her to negotiate price, as the client knows that the original costs did not include tax.[4] Being hard is thus equivalent to being staid and unmoved by verbal persuasion, closed and single-minded. This attitude is in opposition to the spirit of bargaining, which is the primary currency of the marketplace. A vendor who is hard violates one of the tenets of marketplace behavior.

Being hard has other implications as well. The adjective is most often applied to people who misuse or exploit their power over others. Thus women often talk about their husbands or fathers as being hard: "he was hard with me," people say (*kan qaṣəḥ m'aya*), or "he's a hard man!" (*rajəl qa:ṣəḥ*). By accusing the vendor of being hard, the buyer is implying that she is duplicating the same structures of power and authority as others who are hard. Given both the family and the political structure of Moroccan society, these others are almost unequivocally men.[5] The vendor, by extension, is acting like a man — at least according to the buyer; she is exercising her prerogative of refusal.

Permissible Lies and Strategies of Truth

Mohamed's offer is less than acceptable, it is even unreasonable. Yet the vendor adamantly denies that she is being hard. In fact, she swears by God that being hard is not her intention or motivation. Swearing in the Moroccan context, although extremely common, carries a certain moral impact. It is forbidden in the Qur'an, the equivalent of taking the lord's name in vain. In principle, an oath "by God" is a guarantee of sincerity, a proof against lies. A believer doesn't take an oath unless telling the truth, for this has tangible consequences in the acquisition of rewards (ajər) and demerits in the afterlife. The irony here is that oaths are consciously used and are recognized as a selling strategy in the suq. Swearing by God to make a lie believable is common, as is the public acknowledgement that lies proliferate in the marketplace. Most people will tell you that vendors must lie to make a profit, and some even go so far as saying that lies are ḥalal (religiously sanctioned) in the context of the marketplace. Because lies are an expected medium of exchange in the suq, oaths become all the more significant, asserting that "Even if you think I'm lying, I'm not, and here's the proof *by the truth of God*" (*u ḥaqq llah l-'aẓim*).

But an oath, purportedly a vow of truth, is often a fabrication (Goffman 1974), intentionally misleading the customer about the quality or cost of the merchandise. An oath also implicates the speaker in a dilemma: by using a religious truth attestation as a means of validating a lie, the speaker must either face her refutation and contradiction of religious doctrine (that is, admit to breaking the rules and accept the impending consequences in the afterlife), *or* impute falsity to the dictums of official discourse: "I won't really go to hell for lying under oath; after all I'm just trying to feed my children." Here is an example of the "legalization" of a religious prohibition, an appropriation and recontextualization of the official function of giving an oath.

The contradictions surrounding the use of oaths does not negate their impact. There are times when an oath is used as an expression of complete sincerity (ṣaraḥa) and good faith (niya). This is exemplified in the discourse above. The vendor isn't being hard; rather, the buyers are offering her the wholesale price and Aisha is thus insulted when they don't take her oath seriously.

The evaluation of lying and truthfulness in regard to oaths is context-dependent, calling upon factors such as acquaintance with the seller, knowledge of the going price, and quality of the merchandise. Oaths in the marketplace are not unequivocally lies, but their use in the context of the market unhinges the genre from its official function of assuring truth and recasts it in the interpretive possibilities of falsity. The rules of the marketplace affect the interpretive rules of genre. Oaths in the suq belong to two different orders — official truth and non-official lies — and may be read in either, or in both. This ongoing ambiguity makes the process of bargaining a social challenge, one whose results are discussed as obsessively as sports scores in some sectors of society.

At the end of the exchange the vendor tells the men that if they asked around the market they would find she was not being hard or unreasonable — the market, its prices, and its logic being accessible to everyone. The vendor insists that the price offered is not sufficient to cover her expenses. When the buyer gets exasperated with his failed attempts at persuasion, his companion, Ahmed, begins to speak, functioning in an intermediary and narrative role. The vendor clearly will not bargain with them on the terms proffered so far. Ahmed thus tries another tack, deciding to let the vendor in on "the truth" of the situation. He calls for the seller's complete attention and then speaks in the third person about his companion: "Ahhh, he just wants to buy it to sell it again." The revelation that Mohamed is also in the business of buying and selling establishes an identification between the interlocutors that hadn't existed before. Aisha acknowledges the bond, affirming her acceptance of the situation ("We don't mind"), but this admittance doesn't soften her resolve. Arriving at this impasse, the adjacent vendor, Fatna, becomes a participant in the speech event. She encourages Ahmed to pursue the bargain and the seller to "get on with it," thus facilitating the possibility for a real transaction to take place.

At this juncture bargaining becomes an open discourse. Not only does linguistic indirection make for a variety of possible interpretations, but the dialogue is literally open to the public. There are no limits to the number of people who may add their "two cents" to an exchange. The suq is a noisy place and people must raise their voices to be heard at all. Competition comes from every corner; not only in terms of decibel level, but in terms of gaining credibility with both the buyers and the bystanders — those waiting to buy and those biding their time at the suq. Vendors compete with each other for a favorable reputation among clients. Buyers, for their part, compete to get the best and lowest price.

Hearing the comments of her neighbor, Aisha gives a little ground. She says that she likes the "face" of her client and hasn't refused it, meaning that he has yet to "lose face" in the exchange. But the neighboring vendor has not yet had her say. Perceiving that the negotiation may resume from no better a vantage point, she loses her temper and accuses them of "making

Figure 7. Transacting a sale. The merchant reaches into her jǝllaba to produce change for the client (seated).

a ḥalqa" too close to her own place of business. Those who operate in the ḥalqa are marginal characters in the contemporary Moroccan context, surrounded by a certain moral suspicion largely because their behavior is festive, their language is licentious, and they are known to prey upon the niya of suq-goers.[6]

In comparing the interaction of the neighboring vendor and her clientele to a ḥalqa, Fatna is belittling the seriousness of the speech event, calling it a farce that is cluttering up her space and distracting from her own business. The irony here is that the enterprise of bargaining does indeed share many characteristics with the ḥalqa. Both are multivocalic, open to public participation, and may include anyone whose body approaches the arena of discourse. Buyers and sellers alike habitually draw complete strangers into their verbal transactions, asking for opinions, affirmation, and validation. The opinions of bystanders are important and essential to a potential sale, the words of strangers being doubly valued for their assumed disinterestedness. Whereas the language of the ḥalqa is less commonly accepted as truth (one storyteller was quick to counsel me that his epics are 98 percent kdub [lies]), sincerity is certainly not the guiding principle of a bargaining exchange except when used as a narrative strategy, as is the case above.[7] "You're making a ḥalqa here" is a reflexive remark, drawing attention to the film within the film, the ḥalqa within the ḥalqa, the carnival that, however submerged, is an intricate aspect of the discursive domain of the marketplace.

Open Borders: Feminine Speaking

The dialogue continues, with Ahmed further explicating the details of their story, trying to establish both authority (insofar as he is another vendor who "knows the scene") and identification that he hopes will lead the woman vendor to lower her price. His narrative "truth" tactic doesn't work and the vendor continues to be appalled at the offered price. She reminds him that she has already given oath, making his bids seem more like provocations than sincere attempts at transaction.

As tensions increase, a conflict takes place and categories are exposed. The buyer threatens to go to the store to do his business. Stores are almost always owned by men and many have recently instituted the policy of prix fixe. This phenomenon is a foreign one, representing the international influence of capitalism and the silencing of the shaʿb (the populace or folk).

The refusal of negotiation is significant to both suq vendors and buyers, as it devalues the identity of the consumer and effectively dissolves the genre of bargaining, a discourse of social cohesion in Moroccan society.[8] The woman vendor responds vehemently to mention of the store by implying that stores are only good for buying magazines, which have the price printed right on them.

The expansion and urbanization of this agricultural center and the fact that a university has opened there within the last five years has encouraged the proliferation of book and newspaper stores. As with many new stores, the price of the merchandise is strictly non-negotiable. Her reference to magazine stores also calls on the social distinction between a young, literate generation and an older, illiterate one who now must depend on their children in order to participate fully in an economy which has quickly become reliant on the written word (Eickelman 1992; Wagner 1993). This situation inverts relations of authority in that children become caretakers of their elders.

The vendor is not literate. She does not read magazines or shop in prix fixe stores. Ahmed's mention of the store evokes her disdain because stores represent a world where dialogue is absent (except the silent dialogue of the written word and the individual eye). While magazines open onto various other worlds, they are beginning to replace the world of social discourse that the vendor inhabits. On the other hand, the ravenous hunger for "the new," created in part by international advertising in newspapers and magazines, provides the vendor with a market for the goods of modernity that slip through the Spanish borders and into her possession.

The vendor responds to Ahmed's threat by saying, "What's the matter with us? Aren't we all Muslims?" The phrase "Aren't we all Muslims?" (*wash hnaya mashi kulna muslimin?*) is common in Moroccan colloquial Arabic. It is a traditional saying, a recognizable rhetorical device which has been used historically to assert bonds of community over ethnic and factional differences, in particular between Berber and Arab men in the public domain of post-colonial Morocco. Said by a man, these words pass effortlessly between vendor and client, effecting a minimum of intertextual distance. Said by a woman vendor, however, they evoked the client's laughter and effected a pause in the bargaining, momentarily halting the communicative flow. The laughter of the client registered his recognition that these words, usually limited to mono-sexual communicative exchanges, were being used to effect negotiation of goods across both gender and age boundaries. The woman vendor had *revoiced* the terms of sale by employing a traditional idiom in a non-traditional context and by infusing the phrase with a new pragmatic aura.

Such revoicings reorient the generic conventions of discourse and their interpretive frames. This is not appropriation pure and simple. The vendor did not erase the tradition from this phrase in revoicing it, but deliberately drew upon all meanings inherent in it while adding another important semantic tone of her own — one that jarringly reversed the usual hierarchy of meanings present therein. In revoicing, the semantic intentions of the speaker combine with the semantics of historical precedent to create new venues for relationship — in this case, between speaker and speech community, tradition and modernity, men and women.

The market woman's use of the phrase, "Aren't we all Muslims?" is an example of what Bakhtin calls "hybrid" speech, "a mixture of two social languages within the limits of a single utterance, an encounter, within the arena of the utterance, between two different linguistic consciousnesses" (1981 : 358). Following Bakhtin, hybridization is a "mixing" or "collision" of linguistic *forms* that may be unconscious or intentional (1981 : 358). Its first appearance in *The Dialogic Imagination* is in the context of parodic discourse which, Bakhtin says, is "double-accented, double-styled":

> What we are calling a hybrid construction is an utterance that belongs, by its grammatical (syntactic) and compositional markers, to a single speaker, but that actually contains mixed within it two utterances, two speech manners, two styles, two "languages," two semantic and axiological belief systems. (1981 : 304)

Bakhtin clearly distinguishes between *hybrid* expression, in which two or more voices inhabit one form or "syntactic whole," and *dialogic* expression, which relies upon the relationship (dialogue) of multiple and formally distinct competing voices. It follows that hybridization is a phenomenon of the uniformal — it is perceived at the level of the "primary genre" or the utterance — whereas dialogism works at larger levels of intergeneric dialogue — the polyformal, the "secondary" genre (Bakhtin 1986). Dialogism is hybridization at one remove of (formal) complexity. These two categories are only theoretically separable, for hybrid expression rarely stands alone but is incorporated into large discursive contexts.[9]

The "linguistic consciousness" indexed by this common rhetorical phrase which has been socially authored in history relies on the ability of Muslim fraternity to overcome ethnic difference. However, the consciousness of this woman vendor invokes another "language-intention" and another world view. Her relation to this "we," this "inchoate pronoun" (Fernandez 1986), is different from the "we" represented in traditional Moroccan rhetoric; in saying "we" she invokes women (not men), women vendors (not housewives), and vendors of the marketplace (as opposed to merchants in boutiques and stores). She has introduced new categories into the paradigm, new images into the metaphor, while at the same time evoking all the authority to which the traditional categories lay claim.

The woman vendor identifies herself with a category—women vendors in general—by using the first person plural: "*We*'re just like the store," she says. "What's the matter with us [women vendors]? Aren't we all Muslims?" She is speaking for her gender here in a public discourse that is open to voices other than her own (as attested to by the involvement of the neighboring vendor). Furthermore, the vendor implicitly acknowledges her ambivalent position in the economy of exchange by anticipating her client's judgement and instructing him that there's nothing shameful about buying from her, or from women sellers of contraband in general.

The buyer picks up on the vendor's strategy for establishing legitimacy in the marketplace, one that she uses regularly with her male clientele. He pauses and laughs. He accedes her position in a jocular tone of voice. This is the common response. She nonetheless continues with her strategy of defense. "Well, we too are [Muslims]" she asserts, and she tells him that transaction with her as an equal, a Muslim, will bring reward. The client is thus morally shamed into continuing the bargain, at least temporarily. That he recognizes the "truth" of the vendor's position is evidenced in the defense he offers about his partner: "Well . . . he knows [about that reward]."

No sale is effected; moral discourse does not negate the possibility for choice. It does, however, establish a different value relation *between* choices. This is accomplished, in part, by the hybrid quality of the message, which locates the vendor in two competing systems: the historically male-dominated marketplace where her presence has traditionally been anathema, and the emergent discursive domain wherein her presence is socially and ideologically acceptable. Religious discourse—the invocation of Muslim identity—may be used to locate her in either and she plays with this ambiguity to her own advantage.

When the vendor asks her clients, "Aren't we all Muslims?" the interlocutor is obliged to say yes; but that yes also affirms the unity and rightful place of women in the public domain of the market. It is a yes that says "there is, indeed, no difference between the merchandise of a woman vendor in the suq and a man merchant in a city store." This admission is an uncomfortable one for the male buyers to make, as demonstrated by their laughter when one of them responds, "we're all Muslims, one people." There is a linguistic irony in this response, however, for the expression "one people" is literally, *waḥəd bənadam*, "one *son* of adam."

Examining women's verbal art in the marketplace provides a measure of the rapid changes that are transpiring in the sexual division of labor in Morocco as well as in notions of gender and the economy of genre—that is, who is allowed to speak what to whom (Sherzer 1987).[10] Implicated here is not just the subversion of codes, but a transformation of convention; not just appropriation, but a redefinition of *appropriateness*. This example demonstrates that hybrid utterances do indeed contribute to incremental changes in the expressive and material economies; the utterance situates the woman in both the old system of male-dominated oratory and the new one of feminine revoicing and exchange. Such double-voicedness works like a bridge between novelty and convention, between gender and genre. It does not proceed by radically supplanting one paradigm with another, but takes place incrementally and discursively. What's more, these processes are (politically) inseparable from the marketplace, where norms (generic categories) are negotiated and redefined.

Hybrid Hermeneutics

The repetition of discourse ("Aren't we all Muslims") in particular contexts (the marketplace) and by particular categories of persons (men), accrues authority and receives the label of "tradition." When the notion of genre is reoriented from being a closed and resistant form to an open and mutable one, however, the way is then clear to investigate the transformation of categories that mediate impressions of the world. Revoicings play a critical role in this process as they change the shape of authoritative discourse by introducing a different time-space orientation to words that carry their own historical reality into the present (Bakhtin 1986). In this case, the vendor has appropriated a phrase from tradition and infused it with a new meaning without erasing the traces of the other voices which have historically inhabited the words. She thereby effects an inversion of authorial voice (which here is feminine rather than masculine), a re-authoring of discursive categories and a shattering of monologic metonymy (Muslims as Arab and Berber *men*) into dialogic plurality. "Two edges are created: an obedient, conformist, plagiarizing edge (the language . . . in its canonical state, as it has been established by schooling, good usage, literature, culture), and *another edge*, mobile, blank (ready to assume any contours), which is never anything but the site of its effect: the place where the death of [patriarchal and official] language is glimpsed" (Barthes 1975:6, emphasis in original). Of course, this "glimpsing" of death is just that: an intimation, a momentary loss of boundaries that permits new life into language by displacing old meanings and altering the pragmatic relationships between utterance and context (see Levinson 1983; Silverstein 1976). Contrary to Bourdieu's claims that contextualization *limits* the interpretive possibilities of discourse (Bourdieu 1977a), this example demonstrates the multivocality and multi-interpretability of a single utterance.

Eating Profit

The buyer affirms, however tongue in cheek, that "we are all Muslims." But there is a difference, of course. And the woman vendor is quick to elaborate on it; for if the buyer acquires his merchandise from *her* — if both he and the vendor "eat" the profit of the exchanged riyal — then the buyer will receive *ajər* reward, benefit or recompense). The trope of eating is significant as it expresses not only a transmutation of matter (through processes of ingestion), but an actual crossing of boundaries that, when enacted ritually with others, functions to affirm the body of community in the terms of the individual body; to wit, the "eating" of profit by both the merchant and her client. In this example, money stands in a metaphoric relation to food and the profit that a monetary transaction brings is its nourishment. The first materials of exchange are, of course, verbal — words, money, and food all contributing to the bargain. The sharing of *ajər* through the mutual acceptance and consequent incorporation of the terms of sale, connects both parties in the social body of give-and-take" (*ʿti-ni, n-ʿti-k*). By ritually ingesting food with others, whether the food is material or metaphorical (as in the profit gained from the exchange of money), one participates in a fecund flow of social resources. Some materials go down and back to the market to fertilize the soil, but some go up and become ajər, payback for having broken both bread and borders with another. The shaʿb eat from one plate. (The most elementary lesson of food etiquette that a Moroccan child learns is to respect the "territory" of the tajin, to eat only the sauce and vegetables that are directly in front of her and to divide the meat equally.) This is a negotiation that feeds all parties, not just some to the exclusion or detriment of others. To be of the "folk" is to acknowledge one's place in this food cycle. In the market, everyone is hungry, but only she obtains ajər who acknowledges the preeminence of social over individual provision.

The social body in Morocco is defined between the communal sharing of food at the table and the acknowledgment of profit-seeking (via the circulation of information and favors) that such community affords. This is as true among housewives as it is among college professors or merchants at the market. "Eating profit" is an apt metaphor for social relations which define and affirm the community that emerges in the process of the negotiation of goods. The communal evanescence of social bonds as they are being redefined along new gender lines and class distinctions demands that notions of community coalesce and disperse with equal ease. The permeability of the body as it is constructed in the verbal idiom of the marketplace attests to the open boundaries of the social body by making reference to the porosity and mutability of the physical one.

The buyer in this discourse will receive ajər if he eats the profit of the shared riyal with the woman vendor precisely because she is poor, because she needs that riyal more than the male merchant who can afford to rent a store and have "hard" and fast prices. The vendor uses a traditional unifying concept (Muslim fraternity) to introduce difference. She plays on the moral economy of her client in order to dissuade him from going to the store and to edge him towards the shared dialogue of the marketplace. She uses the official discourse of Islam, its concepts of spiritual reward and charity, to persuade the buyer to do business with her. By calling upon the well-known Moroccan metaphor of ingesting or eating together in order to profit together, the vendor invokes moral discourses of tradition in order to shame the buyer into staying with the sha'b — for the sha'b eat together, they share their meals, even with strangers: Aren't we all Muslims?

The dialogue comes to a close when Ahmed once again offers exaggeratedly unacceptable prices. The vendor sarcastically tells him that he deserves to get the price he is asking for (and that she is refusing) and she calls him by the respectful title of *shrif*, a qualifier which identifies the descendants of the Prophet. The buyer rebuffs with a sarcastic, "God help you," the implication being "because I'm certainly not going to." The buyer has refused the opportunity to gain reward from "eating" with the vendor. The vendor, in turn, tells him that he deserves what he'll get. She points out to him all those who will sell him the cassette recorder for 3400, when she knows that no one will sell it for that price. The bargain ends with a statement of deliberate inversion and contradiction: "there are the possessors of the 3400 [dirham recorder]."

Although the woman vendor swears that she is not being "hard" in the context of this exchange, the mere imputation of this quality to her affirms her ability to be so. She is the "owner of the things from the north" (*mulat ḥwayj sh-shamal*) owning also, to an extent,[11] the terms of sale. In attributing to the vendor the power to be "hard," her male client acquiesces to her public authority and appeals to her not to misuse it. This performative 'bowing' need not be taken as an across-the-board expression of social hierarchical relations; there are times when the client controls the bargain and choice is certainly on the side of the consumer, who is beckoned by a multitude of vendors. But it does attest to the authority of women who now have a firm place in the market.

Within the dimensions of this speech event, not only are the terms of sale negotiated, but the terms of the social gender contract[12] are subtly redefined in the process of their emergence in dialogue. Even traditional bargaining terminology is renegotiated in the context of new power relations — words such as *qaṣaḥ* and phrases like, "aren't we all Muslims" are both meant and interpreted differently when spoken by women. The female vendor opens the borders of traditional genres of speech and inserts the novelty of gender.[13] Borders are, after all, porous for the women who sells contraband. Hers is an open discourse that opens categories.[14]

If people at the market are ingesting profit together, then the mixed company of the suq has a decided effect on the meaning of such eating, especially given the gender polarities that have existed in Morocco until recently. In this speech event, both parties found the other's terms difficult to swallow. Nonetheless, the potential for mutual sharing of nourishment in the marketplace expressed by the eating metaphor embodies the hybridizing process of suq interactions, ones that contradict the monologism of store relations and fixed prices. Mouths, eyes, and ears are open at the suq. Words, like smells, mix indiscriminately. The market is a place of contagion. On the edge of town, it incorporates a garbage dump and all the parasitism that displayed refuse breeds.

Although the life of the suq revolves around the process of acquisition, no one owns the terms, or sets them, except temporarily; ownership passes back and forth.[15] This is the nature of eating together for the Moroccan shaʿb; even if no one gets full, no one remains hungry. But now women have joined the halqa, raising their voices, demanding their share. Hard as they may be, they, too, are Muslims.

Notes

1. See Stallybrass and White (1986) for a critique of Bakhtin's idealism.

2. In medieval Islamic cosmology, gold is the most perfect metal. It represents the combination of harmony of the four principles of cold, heat, humidity, and dryness as well as the feminine and the masculine principles. See Nasr (1964 : 90).

3. I have added names for the ease of the reader.

4. The process of acquisition of contraband is extremely taxing — emotionally, physically and even financially — for the vendor.

5. Eickelman notes that socialization of boys in Morocco requires the diminution of fatherly affection as the son gets older. This prevents the boy from becoming too "soft." He says that "the father increasingly assumes a greater formality with his son and becomes hard (qaseh) with him" (1976 : 139).

6. That ḥlayqi are, for the most part, permanently marginal in Moroccan society, upholds Abraham's and Bauman's assertion that "the same people who engage in license during the festivals are the community agents of disorder during the remainder of the year" (1978 : 195). Festival behavior is present as a constant drone against the official, normative system of Islam; it does not assert itself only periodically and then disappear.

7. See Bauman (1986 : chapter 2) for an examination of the strategic use of expressive lying.

8. A Moroccan friend recounted an anecdote about the time his father, of mountain origins, came to the capital to visit him in college. While at a café, the father began to haggle with the waiter over the price of the coffee. Of course, this was completely inappropriate in an urban setting and my friend was mortified. It does exemplify, however, how linguistic relations are either curtailed or elaborated according to context.

9. Bakhtin further subdivides his concept of the hybrid utterance into the intentional and the unintentional. The former, he asserts, is an "artistic device . . . the perception of one language [consciousness] by another" (1981 : 358, 359), a split subjectivity that is able to see itself. Unintentional hybridization, on the other hand, "is one of the most important modes in the historical life and evolution of all languages. We may even say that language and languages change historically primarily by means of hybridization, by means of a mixing of various 'languages' co-existing within the boundaries of a single dialect, a single national language, a single branch [etc.]" (1981 : 358–59). The mixing of languages and belief systems is an idea with important ramifications; while hybridization affects semantic ambiguity at the level of the utterance, it also influences more complex relations of generic, semiotic, and ideological dialogue. The multivocalic or ambiguous hybrid genre mediates changes that impinge upon both aesthetic and sociopolitical reality.

Hybrid utterances and dialogic genres are double- or multi-voiced and thus resist classification based on principles of internal coherence and unity. There is an inherent reflexivity in the hybrid (cf. Babcock 1980), which like an ethnically or otherwise hybrid individual, is likely to "see" itself because it is more than itself; it is also Other.

10. See also Appadurai, Korom, and Mills (1991).

11. The extent being multiply determined by the price set by the market, the mystification of that price by the community of merchants, the verbal savvy of the interlocutor, and common conditions of economic duress.

12. I call on the insights of Carole Pateman (1988) here. She demonstrates that the "social contract" — the doctrine of civil liberties and democracy in European culture — is based on an unspoken "sexual contract" that insists on the subjugation of women in order to ensure the liberties of men. I use the term "contract" here in a somewhat more loose fashion to mean the spoken and unspoken social agreements that are the bases of the maintenance of the status quo, the premises of the official discourses.

13. As well as that of class. According to the merchant, the buyer would receive spiritual recompense in buying from her not because she is a woman, but because she is a *poor* woman. She is not so poor as to accept his terms, however.

14. Such openness is not without risk. Many are the tales of theft, not only by thieves, but by police who decide to confiscate goods instead of or despite accepting their usual playoff.

15. For other examinations of bargaining, see Bauman (1986); Dargan and Zeitlin (1983); Khuri (1967); Mitchell (1957); Ngole (1988).

3. Words of Possession, Possession of Words: The Majduba

Bargaining is by no means the only genre of marketplace discourse, nor is it even the most dramatic. Other genres that might be called oratory, artful selling, or doom-saying are not delineated in Moroccan terminology except under the heading of *l-hadra dyal suq*, "marketplace talk," a form of discourse that embodies many speech genres much as a novel embodies several literary genres (Bakhtin 1986 : 61–62). Whereas bargaining is overtly dialogic, the genre of marketplace oratory edges more towards the performance of monologue by attempting to subdue the other "voices" in the market.

Women's public oratory in the Moroccan marketplace provides an example of how a speech genre can be appropriated and hybridized — with the result that historically dominant conceptions of "public/private" and "male/female" are put into question. In articulating a verbal genre historically practiced by men, Moroccan women orators challenge the moral and political canon that associates feminine performance with the private realm. Although the establishment of feminine authority in public requires alignment with dominant discourses, the feminine revoicing of marketplace oratory also inscribes a feminine presence into a formerly male domain, thereby expanding discursive space (Frazer 1992 : 124). This expansion is mediated by both the genre of oratory and the marketplace itself. Women's emergence into the discursive domain of the market requires their complicity to the laws of genre, yet it is their expressive hybridization that ultimately transforms the larger public sphere.

Performance in the Marketplace

There is no word that describes the performance of verbal art in the open-air market; it is neither theatrical event (*təmtil*) nor party (*ḥəfla*).[1] There is, however, a designated place for it — the *ḥalqa*. Literally a circle of people, ḥalqa also refers to a part in a sequence, like an episode in a television series. The image is of a storyteller or potion-seller visibly encircled by spectators. Because of the highly interactive nature of marketplace transactions, however, there are often "fuzzy boundaries"[2] — separating performer and audience. This is particularly true in the ḥalqa, where elaborate spiels may be constructed in interaction with one or several members of the circle.

When Aisha says that the neighboring vendor and her clients are "making a ḥalqa" too near her own place of business, she is calling attention to the performance aspects of the bargaining event, denigrating the interaction as "polluting" the atmosphere and possibly preventing further transactions from occurring. In the next speech event discussed, a woman is hawking her own herb-and-mineral incense concoction for getting rid of magic spells. (The text is reproduced in the appendix in a more poetic rendering: line numbers in parentheses refer to this more formal text). The ḥalqa-like qualities created here are more pronounced, moving from a context where performance is negotiated in dialogue (less performer-centered) to one that revolves more around the performer herself.

This vendor is a self-proclaimed *majduba*, or "entranced one" of the saint Moulay Ibrahim, whose tomb and pilgrimage center are located outside of Marrakech.[3] In her sales rhetoric she represents herself as one of his disciples. A majdub (masc.) is someone who has a supernatural magnetism, and thus a certain authority, in regard to the world of the spirit; in contemporary Morocco it refers to someone who has lost care of (and sometimes control over) worldly existence (*dunya*). The most famous majdub in Moroccan history was Sidi Abderaḥman al-Majdub, credited with many wise sayings (*ḥikam*, pieces of wisdom or truisms) that have become incorporated into Moroccan speech. These sayings are printed in chapbooks and are sold at book stalls and the marketplace. The word majdub has now become synonymous with a social outcast, reflecting a lower estimation of roles that do not profit or directly participate in the current capitalist modes of production.

This majduba/vendor is careful to quote Sidi Abderaḥman, thereby putting herself in his "tradition" as a bearer of wisdom and indexing the authority constituted by the reputation of his words — what Bakhtin refers to as "prior discourse" (1981 : 342). She wears large plastic sunglasses (rarely found in Beni Mellal), tucking the frames behind her ears and under her head scarf. Her jəllaba is faded and frayed, displaying an appearance of poverty and a disregard for decorum.[4] Her voice is deep and commanding and her intonation ranges from loud to screaming. She sits under a large sun umbrella outside the western wall of the suq (see Figure 8).

Figure 8. The majduba, disciple of the saint Moulay Ibrahim, selling incense that counter-acts the effects of magic.

There are four other Moroccan women listening to the majduba's spiel. Three are standing about half a meter away and one, the woman who will tell the majduba her tale of woe, is squatting at the very edge of the majduba's display of incense ingredients, under the shade of the umbrella. There is also a boy, about twelve years old, to the left of the women in the audience. My research assistant, Si Mohamed, and I are standing to the right, very much a part of the small semi-circle of the ḥalqa, where some people linger for moments and move on. Her voice is loud and raspy:

"Pray on behalf of the Prophet," she began. "Where are our grandparents? Where are our parents and where is the Prophet? (God bless him and grant him peace.) We want to inherit worldly goods and we want to take them with us? *Wayli, wayli!* The smallest on earth has a meeting [on Judgment Day], that day when your oldest son won't avail you. Come closer, woman, May God have mercy on your parents."

"Whoever wants some blessings [=incense], welcome. And whoever doesn't want any, welcome you, too."

"Yeah," responded a woman squatting down next to the majduba.

"We're just the guides to goodness. I'm just a majduba, daughter of Moulay Ibrahim. That's my state and I'm the owner of it.

"If she's a little virgin, use the 'rocks of redemption'[5] and 'the abolisher.' If she's a woman and there's something between her and her children, [use them] on Friday. If it's something to do with children and their studies, on Monday. If it's [herd] animals, on Monday. If the animals aren't subjugated, the children aren't studying, the [family] gathering is bitter. Here's *maqab*, sea urchin, 'mother of people,' and indigo and coral and *nil l-watqa*, *'ar'ar*, or *dərdar*.

"Every one of these [packets] has a piece of each one of these [herbs], as if you prayed to the Prophet. Who will trust in God with me? And whoever says there's no such thing as magic, go up to [the tomb of] my grandfather Moulay Ibrahim, and my father Hamid. And go up to [the tomb of] my father Omarr.[6] And see how many women and men are shackled by chains by the work of Satan! And how many brides, *lalla* (dear woman), they leave them abandoned. She's shackled, poor thing, and she says, 'I'm begging your protection. Oh Omarr.'"

"Ahh, lalla!" the squatting woman sighed.

"'They burned me with fire, oh Omarr!'"

"Come here, lalla, let me tell you."

"'I'm begging your protection, oh Moulay Ibrahim!'"

"I want to tell you about one girl," began the client.

"Pray to the Prophet," said the majduba.

"She's engaged and she has her marriage certificate."

"Yeah, lalla."

"And she's married and he took someone else who's stuck to him."

"Well, why? That mother of the other one is awake and you, her mother, are asleep, poor thing! Pray to the Prophet."

"Until the act fell and everything and he took someone else!"

"Listen to me, lalla, pray to the Prophet. Yeah! Pure Soussis!"[7]

"She doesn't want him anymore."

"God, God be with you, [and] our grandfather Moulay Ibrahim. No, No, listen to me. Of course, she doesn't want him anymore, because the others have turned around him [with magic]. We women are hard!

"If they love you, they'll feed you and if they hate you, they'll bewitch you."

"She's the first," the client said.

"He who enters the women's suq, beware!" the majduba quoted,
They'll show you a ton of profit,
and make you lose your salary!
　　The ruses of women are their own.
　　From their ruses I came running!
　　Oh, the women belted with snakes
　　and those wrapped with scorpions!

Pray to the Prophet. Yeah, oh woman, whoever is a woman, never hold a[nother] woman dear.

"Use, lalla, the 'rock of redemption.' If it explodes for her lalla, bring me a little dirt from under her right foot. And consider that you're not her mother. I'm her mother. And I'm going to take care of her business. And between us is God and our grandfather Moulay Ibrahim."

"I, now . . . I want . . ."

"This, lalla," the majduba continued, "pound it and light this incense for her for seven days. If it was magic, and it explodes for her, I'll tell you, bring me a little dirt from under her foot in order that I give her the water of seven waves, and the water of seven ironsmiths, and the water of seven wells, and the water of the mill of Moulay Ibrahim, so she can bathe with them."

"I want . . ." began the client again.

"Listen to me! Spare me your words," said the majduba. "Now, you knocked, let me answer you."

"Yeah."

"You want it, welcome, you don't want it, may God make you meet the good thing. {What's straight is straight.[B]}" The client started to whisper.

"I don't tu, tu, tu and don't [you] hide it from me," said the majduba. "Listen to what I'm going to tell you! Pound this in a mortar and pestle of wood. And light it as incense for seven days. And this," she said, wrapping up an ingredient in separate brown paper, "put it in the brazier by itself. If the rock explodes, come and bring me that little bit of dirt that I told you about. Even if they've put the magic I don't know where, with the strength of God and Moulay Ibrahim... Which suq is yours?"

"What?"

"What suq is nearest you? You always come here? Where is your suq? Where?"

"Where?"

"Yeah."

"Thursday's suq [at] Ouled Ayyad."

"Well, I'm also at Ouled Ayyad on Thursdays. You see, I'm at the place where they sell chickens. Pray to the Prophet. If you're in Sebt, I'm also in Sebt. If you're in Hed el-Bradiya, I'm also at Hed el-Bradiya. I don't leave, lalla, a single suq untouched. Bismillah, Bismillah. I'll be the reason [for the cure] and the completion is God's." The client mumbled something in Berber.

"Yeah, lalla," the majduba answered, then said, "They put its seeds in the woods of my grandfather Moulay Ibrahim. This, lalla, pound it and burn it as incense for seven days."

"And the 'seven men'?"

"Yeah, lalla, aaaaaah, yeah, yeah. {There's no might or power except with God, the High, the Great. There's no God but God and Mohamed is his Prophet [CA].} Here, my dear.

"They part brother from his brother. They part the son from his father. You see, they part the youth from his little mother; they part the cow from her buttermilk and aged butter; they part the chicken from…

"Her eggs dry up from under her. She's sitting on them. The chicken dries up on top of the eggs, both she and the eggs. Yeah. Pray on behalf of the Prophet.

"May God scatter their nest [those who bewitch]. God scatter them, may their house be devastated in the afternoon.

"Go, oh woman witch!" the majduba screamed at the absent perpetrator of magic. Her client began to cry. "Go, oh woman cheat!" she continued. "Go, oh woman, who deceives the one who suckled her and her neighbor! She deceives the virgin and she deceives the youth!"

"Plead to God with me," said the client.

"God leave her nest like the suq in the afternoon!" the majduba offered in compliance with her wishes. "In the name of God, Pray on behalf of the Prophet."

"That's the same stuff, right?"

"Yeah, lalla. It's the same. Here. Whoever wants it, take it. Here. Those, those aren't like the others. HERE they are. And you, you're just fighting with your sheet all the time and you say to me, 'He brought someone else to her.' Well, he can bring as many as four! If her mother is like that [you]. Just go on your way.

"Lalla, we don't understand," said the client.

"Here it is, here it is, here. Be the daughter of a lady and a sir. In the name of God. {God help you.[B]}"

"Amen."

"{Put your[B] faith in God.[MA]}

"Amen."

"{Peace . . ."[B]}, the majduba said in Berber, pronouncing a blessing.

"Amen," responded the client.

"Completion is from God the Wonderous."

"Amen."

"My God, a slave [is] your slave. The created [is] your creation. And completion[8] is from you. Pray on behalf of the Prophet. Who will trust in God with me, by God?

"I'm going to come to you in Ouled Ayyad on Thursday Insha'llah. But if you die, May God have mercy. Pray on behalf of the Prophet. Who will trust in God with me, by God? Who will say, In the name of God?" My assistant and I started to leave and the majduba addressed us directly.

"Yeah. Looking won't chill the belly," she said.

"And the camel doesn't nurse the lamb.

And whoever wants to ride, he rides the fattened horse."

Although it is easy to interpret this speech as an example of proselytizing oratory, it is important to remember that a primary motivation behind it is economic. This woman's business depends on the practice of magic. She is selling *tabkhira*, an unblended assortment of plants, herbs, roots, and minerals with a touch of sulfur added for dramatic effect. This combination is wrapped in newspaper and taken home to be ground with mortar and pestle and then thrown on a hot brazier, causing the sulfur to ignite. The act is thought to be sufficient to release the bewitched from the hold of a spell in most cases.

Mixing Goods and Codes

The verbal repertoire of the majduba is obviously different from that of the woman seller of contraband. While cloth and cassette recorders are symbols of status with an uncontested use value, dried sea urchins and indigo only find symbolic placement by reference to a subaltern belief system which attributes chemical and spiritual agency to these products. The place of the contraband items in the reproduction of the status quo is clear; commodities like perfumes, kitchen appliances, and radios display status and act to incorporate a larger population into the homogeneity of the middle-class ethic, setting the middle class apart from the *məskin*, the poor. The contraband items act to unify a group of people by referencing them in the same income range (even if this in-grouping is done by playing on differences in fashion). The majduba's incense, on the other hand, is not a prestige commodity; relatively inexpensive (the "price of a pot of tea," she says in another segment), the tabkhira is accessible to most everyone, rich and poor alike. More importantly, the marketing of antidotes for magic contests the relations of buying and selling by emphasizing that negotiation of power takes place on a more subtle plane than simple "cash and carry." More than money alone determines who "has" and "has not." Magic is also a currency of power and women may accumulate its capital.

The Dialogue of Genres[9]

The recontextualization of genres is an important means of constructing authority in the majduba's discourse and in marketplace speech generally. In this speech event there are several distinct oral genres: *du'wu*, a formal plea for either blessing or misfortune, religious scripture, the recorded wisdoms (*ḥikam*) of Sidi Abderaḥman al-Majdub, and proverbs. The manipulation of these genres in the overall speech event provides keys to understanding the linguistic and cognitive competencies of a woman vendor in the public space of the market. In each case, their use in new contexts — their recontextualization (Bauman and Briggs 1990) — effects a change in the pragmatic dimensions of genre; how genres are used, when and why. The "traditional" authority of genre undergoes transformation as it is appropriated and revoiced.

Religious Aphorism and the Performance of Literacy

Literacy in reading and writing constitutes an important symbolic value in Morocco (see Wagner 1993). At one time being book literate was synonymous with possessing religious authority, as those who could read and write were the *fuqha*, a minority of men instructed in Qur'anic verse with religious responsibilities toward the community. These men are still respected teachers and scholars, though their literacy skills are no longer unique. In Beni Mellal and its environs, the fqih (sing.) often supplements his income by counseling people in the community on personal affairs and by writing charms, which consist of words from the Qur'an written on a small pieces of paper, often accompanied by geometrical designs with metaphysical significance (see Nasr 1964). The fqih writes (*kay ktəb*) charms and magical formulae which are imbued with power. Because the majority of the women who solicit these charms cannot read,[10] literacy maintains its "mystical" significance, particularly for those with ties to the countryside. Although increased access to schooling for both girls and boys has made literacy more common and secular, a majority of women still have an extremely limited knowledge of classical Arabic (Eickelman 1992; Spratt 1992; Wagner 1993).

When the majduba quotes religious text in classical Arabic, she demonstrates her competence not only in religious doctrine, but in another linguistic register as well. Despite the fact that these religious phrases in classical Arabic are now part of the oral tradition (not dependent on book literacy), they are nonetheless marked as a special form of speech due to the fact that they are not spoken in Moroccan dialect.

> lā ḥawla wa lā qūwwata illa bi-llahi al-'ali al-'aẓim.
> There's no might or power except with God, the High, the Great.

> la ilaha illa allah, sayyiduna muḥammad rasūlu allah.
> There's no God but God [and] Muhammad is his Prophet.

The first phrase is from the Qur'an. The second is the *shahada*, the profession of faith required of all Muslims.[11] Although common, the repetition of these phrases in a public setting by a woman has special significance. Speaking these words the majduba draws on religious traditions of Qur'anic education as well as a folk ethic that attributes to religious texts mystical power that may be harnessed to effect changes in personal circumstance (e.g., to keep a husband from wandering or make children successful in their studies). The majduba sells incense, she doesn't write charms. Yet her performance of religious text in the "higher" register of classical Arabic sets her in the same role as the fqih in many respects; they are both religious counselors. The fact that she refers to herself as a majduba means that her discourse, if not her life, is oriented around the communication of a religious ethic, whether in language or embodying the role of a renouncer.

These religious aphorisms are by no means arcane; they are often memorized by children in religious nursery schools run by fqihs, where children spend the mornings chanting and memorizing Qur'anic verses. But the women gathered around the majduba are not repeating the phrases; in all likelihood they are quite familiar with them if only from listening to their children recite them. The significance of these phrases in the majduba's discourse comes from their performative context. Although these aphorisms are in the verbal repertoire of the majority of Moroccans, only those with authority can and do *perform* them in front of a formal audience.[12] Their pronouncement procures social authority and power for the speaker by invoking official ideologies and associations of literacy. By demonstrating her textual knowledge (acquired aurally), the majduba partakes of the status accorded those who understand the power of words and how to use it.[13]

The majduba's discourse is clearly a religious one; her performative role is that of a saint venerator, a self-proclaimed renouncer. Yet the validation of marketplace presence through religious index is not particular to religious figures. Directives like "Pray on behalf of the Prophet" are common fare in this context where sacred language imbues everyday social exchange, permeating even the "secularity" of buy and sell relations. When someone directs an audience to "Pray on behalf of the Prophet" (*salli 'la rasul allah*), the proper response is "May God pray for you, [oh] messenger of God" (*allahuma salli 'l-ik ar-rasul allah*). In this case the response remains unvocalized. Nonetheless, the evocation of such "inner speech" (Volosinov 1973) connects the audience to a religious ethic. A shared moral ground is immediately called up by the repetition of religious formulae.

Da'wa: the Form of Blessing and Imprecation

The repetition of supplications to God (*da'wa* sing; *da'wat* pl.) is another means by which the majduba establishes herself on moral ground. After doing the ritual prayer in Islam the believer may ask God for personal favors or blessings (*da'wa li-llah*). But supplication does not necessarily carry positive connotations. Although it would be foolish to plead for misfortune for oneself, uttering da'wat for others may be unfavorable. A da'wa may be a curse as well as a blessing; it is a multi-functional genre that allows for opposition, providing the form through which both conflict and reconciliation may pass.

Da'wat are often heard in the marketplace, though they can be said by one friend to another in a private context as well. Often the person speaking

the da'wa has her hands together, palms up, in a physical attitude of supplication. Literally a beseeching of God, the da'wa is a formal prayer that begins with the name of God and is often followed by the interlocutor's
response of "amen." They are often said in contexts of commiseration, as
when someone has recounted a misfortune (a responsive da'wa might be
allah y-jib t-tisir, "God bring ease") or may be said in contexts of celebration, as when someone has announced their daughter's engagement (*allah
y-kəmməl b-l-khir*. "God complete [it] with blessing" would be appropriate
in this context). The more formal the occasion (death, marriage, divorce),
the more restricted the da'wa, and the more codified the response.

When the majduba utters the da'wa, "May God scatter their nest" (line
#145), she is referring to those who cast spells on others, those who cause
the eggs to dry up from under the chickens, those who cause the chicken to
come to demise. The interlocutor directs the majduba to plead with her,
and the majduba once again reiterates a da'wa in a more elaborate form,
though continuing with the same image and animal metaphor. "God devastate their nest like the suq in the afternoon," she says (in the afternoon
the suq is empty and littered with trash and flies).

Like the religious phrases already discussed, the repetition of da'wat is
formulaic. It is a native genre of formal speech usually consisting of a single
predicate sentence. As a genre, it has few governing rules except that it begin with the word "God." There are stock phrases for da'wat,[14] but they
may also be created on the spot out of just about any circumstance: to wit,
"God devastate their nest like the suq in the afternoon." The majduba draws
this da'wa out of her own metaphor comparing the bewitched to a chicken
whose eggs dry up from under her even though she's sitting on the nest,
but her words also reference a series of house collapses ("devastations") that
had recently happened in the center of Beni Mellal's oldest quarter (killing
a pregnant woman and her child). They also provide a meta-commentary
on her own place of business, the suq, as a site of devastation.

In the marketplace this genre is used frequently and creatively, depart-
ing from the stock phrases by the introduction of new verbs and images,
new paradigms and tropes. The more frequent function of the da'wa — sup-
plicating God for the blessing of another — shows its Janus face and becomes a curse. In this speech event the da'wa converts from being a vehicle
of blessing to a means for calling devastation upon others. These curses are
plentiful outside of marketplace speech, usually directed from one individual to another (or others) in closed interpretive contexts. In the marketplace, curses take on another life because they are performed publicly in

ritualized speech. Cursing in the suq is not only licensed, but becomes a verbal challenge: "God devastate her nest like the suq in the afternoon" is not common currency (like "God give him the wilderness," or "God give you poison"); rather it is a specialized form of cursing that displays the speaker's verbal creativity, setting her stylistically apart from the crowd that surrounds her. The marketplace in this instance is the ground for the introduction of novelty in verbal genres.

Pronouns and Metapragmatics

Like da'wat, religious formulae are plentiful in the larger text of the majduba's performance and in marketplace oratory generally. They refer to a belief system in which there is a salient canon of appropriate public behavior. Within this system the expression of weakness, especially in regards to matters of male/female relations, takes place in private and usually monosexual contexts. But the majduba must elicit such personal narratives in order to fulfill her role as counselor and to sell her remedial tabkhira. She accomplishes this without losing face by distancing herself from confessional utterances, using direct reported speech (in italics):

She's shackled, poor thing, and she says,
I'm begging your protection, oh Omarr.
The burned me with fire, oh Omarr!
I'm begging your protection, oh Moulay Ibrahim!

The direct quoted speech is clearly in the voice of an abandoned bride soliciting the aid of saints (and by implication, that of the majduba). The majduba embodies this voice of need. In playing the role of someone who's been "burned," she both clears a space for audience identification and participation while distancing herself from the expressed vulnerability, creating an intertextual "gap" between the quoted speech and her own voice (Briggs and Bauman 1992). The "I" in this utterance is a "quoted I," a self-conscious performance of otherness (Urban 1989). The majduba is giving voice to the private discourse of another in a public space. The "I" in "I'm begging your protection, oh Moulay Ibrahim" is an "I" in need of spiritual counsel and magical incense, an "I" that belongs to the "they" of the audience. In her use of reported speech, the majduba creates a discursive space wherein many voices are audible, while at the same time, her multivocal performance establishes her own verbal competency, her ability to author public discourse.

Ḥikam: The Reported "Wisdoms" of Sidi Abderaḥman al-Majdub

The majduba's use of *unmarked* reported speech is more problematic. She quotes a succession of ḥikam ("wisdoms" or counsels) authored by Sidi Abderaḥman al-Majdub, a Sufi teacher during the sixteenth-century reign of Sultan Moulay Ismail. Sidi Abderaḥman became known for his poetic sagacity during a historical period when religious leaders (marabouts) had considerable political influence (see Eickelman 1976).

The majduba appropriates three of Sidi Abderaḥman's counsels in succession, virtually bombarding the audience with rhyming words that have been set apart in the Moroccan verbal canon. This stacking of the words of another produces an affect of heady eloquence, a strong assertion of competence in the oeuvre of Sidi Abderaḥman, an appropriation of his linguistic expertise. The majduba says nothing to indicate that these words are not her own; yet these texts are in the verbal repertoire. Not all people know their author but most would recognize them as frequently quoted sayings. By *not* framing these words as reported speech, however, the pronouns become porous to many identities, they shift. Whereas the majduba begins her litany with "We women are hard," this "we" quickly becomes the third person plural, "they":

> *"If they love you, they'll feed you*
> *and if they hate you, they'll bewitch you."*
> "She's the first," the client said.
> *"He who enters the women's suq, beware!"* the majduba quoted,
> *"They'll show you a ton of profit,*
> *and make you lose your salary!*
>> *The ruses of women are their own.*
>> *From their ruses I came running!*
>> *Oh, the women belted with snakes*
>> *and those wrapped with scorpions!*
> Pray to the Prophet. Yeah, oh woman, whoever is a woman, never hold a[nother] woman dear."

The majduba's voice enters into the quoted words here because they are unmarked for either direct or indirect reported speech, yet they are also renowned as the words of a historical male figure. This does not exempt the majduba from responsibility, but it does add an element of ambiguity to the encoded message. Is she revoicing Sidi Abderaḥman's words? Is she adding an element of irony to his slander against women, confirming the power of women that Sidi Abderaḥman acknowledged in the negative by restatement in positive sarcasm? Or is she simply quoting him? And is there anything "simple" about such a quote?

The majduba is not embodying a male voice when she says, "We women are hard." And yet when she quotes the counsel of Sidi Abderaḥman al-Majdub, women become "they," a marked category. This shifting of pronominal referent is significant because the majduba is indexing a belief system which is subaltern and illicit (magic). By quoting someone else's words, the majduba distances herself from the dishonorability and social stigma of feminine magic. This strategy is not particular to women orators, but since women comprise the clientele for such magical activity, they become their own "other" in the discourse of the majduba. Whereas magical agency is unproblematically projected onto women in male oratory of this kind, the majduba's appropriation of male discourse strategies casts aspersions on her own sex, and by extension, on herself. Yet the theatricality of the event—determined, to a large extent, by the density of reported speech employed, but also by the majduba's screaming intonation and free use of intimidation—puts the voice and intent of the discourse into question. There is a basic irony here: the majduba is a main participant in the "women's suq" (suq n-nsa) against which her words caution. Yet her words, like her near-comical (because unusual) sunglasses, seem to wink at us. Her use of ḥikam is decidedly different from that of the sixteenth-century male Sufi leader who authored them. Such traditional words in the mouth of a woman and in the context of the marketplace produce a transformation of this genre from a didactic to a subtly parodic one. By revoicing these utterances the majduba critiques the world view embodied therein by putting it on hyperbolic display.

Because these quotes are not framed as quotes, their interpretation is open-ended; their parodic value always slightly veiled. Instead of delimiting these voices, the majduba allows the ḥikam to resonate in the diverse consciousness of the now mixed-gender marketplace. The multifunctionality of the pronouns she employs, their ability to simultaneously reference multiple selves (to "shift" their referent) is also an index to the changing functions of women as representations of the marked gender in contemporary Moroccan society. At issue here are not necessarily definitions of selfhood (who "I" am), but definitions of gender (who "we" are).[15] In general, "we" and "they" are more important pronouns in the majduba's discourse than "I" and "you." By carefully, though not necessarily consciously, manipulating the words of others (via reported speech and the appropriation of traditional genres of speech) and infusing these words with her own voices, the majduba calls the hegemony of any one voice into question.

Because knowledge of Sidi Abderaḥman's oeuvre is assumed and not stated, his words *may* be interpreted as hers. They become permeable to her voice, already an intimidating one: "I don't tu, tu, tu (whisper)" she tells her client, "and don't [you] hide it from me":

And you, you're just fighting with your sheet all the time and you say to me, "He brought someone else to her." You see, he can bring as many as four! If her mother is like that [you]. Just go on your way.

The majduba is being "hard," talking like a man, like Sidi Abderaḥman. In assuming a masculine voice she uses the negative stereotype of women to her own advantage, bringing her client both to tears and to a purchase. Yet everything about her performance is exaggerated and visibly contrived: her appearance, her loudness, her free use of intimidation. It is an index of the uneven changes in the Moroccan marketplace that those with niya are brought to tears and those who do not believe in magic walk away from the performance smiling. Some in the audience may have trouble believing in a renouncer who, between sales, buys a zoom lens for her Canon camera from a man who has come precisely for that purpose.

Proverb

Another formal genre the majduba employs is proverb. The last three lines in the cited discourse are comprised of the following three-part metaphorical and rhyming proverb:

> sh-shuf ma y-bərrəd aj-juf.
> u n-naga ma t-radə' l-khruf.
> u lli bgha y-rkəb, y-rkəb 'la 'awd ma'luf.

Yeah. Looking won't chill the belly.
And the camel doesn't nurse the lamb.
And whoever wants to ride, he rides the fattened horse.

These words, exemplifying the majduba's improvisational skills, were directed toward my research assistant and me as we were leaving the ḥalqa. She tells us that looking "won't chill the belly"; specularism (which works by delineating exteriority) cannot make cold what is intrinsically hot (in this case, with thirst). She thereby judges our lengthy observation of her performance as both incomplete and ineffective. "The camel," she says—a strong animal—doesn't nurse what is inherently weak; if the majduba has not provided succor to us (after all, we are leaving without making a purchase), it is because we are not able to digest the potency of her "relief." In these two lines, the majduba judged us as in need of her services, yet unready to make full use of them. The third line offers advice: if you want to ride, choose your vehicle carefully, or more precisely, choose an animal that has been well fed, one that can support you because of the nourishment it has received. The use of metaphors of consumption is once again salient. Strength is incorporated through ingestion. Mere looking or listening is insufficient.

Like the ḥikam, the boundaries of the proverb are unannounced, making the words permeable to the inference that the majduba and her linguistic context confer upon it. The proverb functions as a "transitional device" (McDowell 1985:119), serving both to close her speech as we leave and to open her discourse directly to us, by giving us the opportunity to pick up the dialogue, to engage. We did not accept her challenge, nor did we respond to her humorous insult about our weakness, yet the majduba clearly invited us to do so, while also taking full advantage of the opportunity to comment (to her audience and to us) upon the requisite qualities for those who would "chill their bellies"—satiate the (hot) demands of their thirst. In poking fun at us, the majduba establishes the boundaries of the inside and the outside group: those leaving are on the outside, while those staying will not go thirsty.

The weave of these "simple" genres—religious aphorism, ḥikam, and proverb—into the more complex genre of the majduba's oratory reveals how the formal voices of tradition and authority are strategically and selectively used to carve out a new territory for public feminine discourse. In drawing upon these genres, the majduba establishes her verbal artistry, her cultural and public authority, as well as her sense of humor.

Author(iz)ing Difference in the Public Sphere

The structure of this highly stylized speech event sets up a dramatic tension. The equivalent of a doom-sayer, the majduba is attentive to the pull of differing forces on many levels; the existence and mutual contradiction of varying systems of belief in the marketplace (magic versus money, men versus women) are implicit in her speech, while the schism between social actions in "worldly existence" and the desire for spiritual reward (the tension between temporal pollution and everlasting purity) is explicit. But conflict is exemplified in her manner of speaking as well. Despite the fact that her living relies on the recognition and categorization of social conflict for others, and on making plain what is mystified and revealing the hidden, she is decidedly aggressive in her tactics, eliciting only enough audience participation to feed the almost continual flow of her own discourse. She does not entreat her audience but challenges them to step forward with the full gravity of their problems, going so far as to yell at her client for her timid whispering. The buyer of her incense must either break the performance frame in order to make a purchase or wait for intermission. Those who attempt the former often encounter conflict, as in this speech event. The majduba welcomed only enough information from her audience to provide a dialogic frame for her words. "Who will trust in God with me?" she asks, thereby opening her discourse by offering to include and incorporate the intentions of her audience. But once this frame of discourse was created, she took back the stage, effectively controlling further interruption: "Listen to *me*," she told her interlocutor when she began to speak, "spare me *your* words. Now you knocked, let me answer you" (lines 92–94).

The majduba is not afraid of being authoritative. Her speech is full of directives[16]: "Pray to the Prophet," "go up to the marabout," "listen to me," "bring me a little dirt from under her right foot." As Goodwin notes, directives "are positioned right at the interface between language and social action; they are designed to make things happen in the larger world . . . in which they are embedded" (1990:65). Directives are linguistic expressions of social control.[17] There is nothing indirect about the majduba's act of intimidation as she blames the client for bringing on her own misery: "That mother of the other one is awake and you, *her* mother, are asleep, poor thing." With this one utterance the majduba confronts her interlocutor with evaluative judgement, creating an unequal power differential between them, at the same time that she defines the problem in order to better suggest its resolution.

Although the speech of the majduba uses the call-and-response meta-

Figure 9. The majduba prepares a remedy for her distressed client.

phor ("you knocked, now let me answer"), the embodiment of dialogue is thematic rather than formal in her discourse. Dialogue in this genre of speech has more to do with intergeneric borrowings (the play of formal genres) than it does with the exchange and free-play of utterances. Because oratory is performer-centered, it is more controlled and poetic than the conversational genre of bargaining. This majduba uses regular rhythm, stress, intonation, alliteration, and rhyme to draw her audience into a shared emotional state,[18] one which, in the example shown in Figure 9, was so effective that the purchaser began to cry.

The Poetics of Marketplace Oratory

The co-occurrence of poetic techniques serves to distinguish the formality of marketplace oratory from the informality of everyday speech.[19] Parallelism, internal rhyming, alliteration, assonance, and repetition of words and formulaic phrases all contribute to the definition of this highly marked genre of public discourse. It is by adopting this level of poetic formalism that the majduba aligns herself with her male predecessors in the marketplace.

Forms of Tradition and Authority

The sometimes chanting, sometimes screaming quality of the majduba's intonation is characteristic of marketplace oratory and is intricately connected to the musical meter of the discourse. While the heaviest beat falls on either the penultimate or the last syllable, the larger syllabic structure allows for considerable variation. Although the number of syllables changes, the musical delivery creates an impression of structured form. What accounts for this is the regularity of stress and timing (regardless how many syllables fit into a linguistic "measure") that comply first and foremost with musical demands.

Formulaic phrases are the most salient use of repetition in the majduba's discourse. After mention of the Prophet's name, in accordance with Qur'anic practice, she says, "Prayers and peace [be] upon him" (*salla allah 'l-ih wa səlləm* [MA]). This is an example of what Schegloff and Sacks (1973) have referred to as an "adjacency pair," two sequential utterances that exist in a relationship of codified dependency. The majduba also interjects the imperative: "Pray on behalf of the messenger of God" (*salli 'la rasul allah*), the response being, "May God pray for you, [oh] messenger of God" (*al-lahuma salli 'l-ik ar-rasul allah*). By repeating the first utterance in each pair, the majduba obliges her audience (by habit and moral imperative) to engage in her performance, directing them in no uncertain terms to a religious attitude, much as the words, "Let us pray" or "Let us bow our heads" do in a Judeo-Christian congregation. But the majduba is not in a mosque, nor is she a cleric. Her use of these phrases sets a tone of religiosity that is only seemingly at odds with the context of the marketplace, making the carnivalesque aspects of her discourse evident. In reality, the mixing of the sacred and profane finds long precedent in the marketplace and is precisely the point.

"God have mercy on the parents" (*allah y-rhəm l-walidin*) is another phrase that is said with such frequency in Moroccan conversation and ritual discourse that it is almost spoken under the breath. In deploying these stock phrases the majduba establishes a mainstream credibility with her audience while casting a rhetorical "spell" of obedience. Authority is God's, she implies, but this assertion is precisely the one that effects and actualizes her own authoritative voice. Returning over and over to these words, she brings the discourse back to its "official" center, no matter how far it has strayed. The formulae act as disclaimers, insuring that the majduba's words can always be related back to the praxis of mainstream religious instruction and commentary—a useful device, since she is talking about magic. But although the formulae provide an interpretive frame that can be activated as needed, their semantic presence is diminished by sheer excess. We can almost *not* hear them as meaningful words, as they are so droning in the Moroccan verbal repertoire.

Repetition of words is also frequently used. For example, the majduba says

> *kid n-nsa, kid-hum,*
> *mən kid-hum jit harəb.*

The ruses of women are their own,
From their ruses I came running.

Because of grammatical word endings in Moroccan Arabic, naturally occurring rhymes are frequent, even in conversation. Performed speech is thus easily stylized by breaking phrases at regular intervals, creating parallelism.[20] Here repetition of words and particles (*kid* and *hum*) as well as alliteration serve to lure the audience into the performance. The same monotony of word repetition is found in her listing of remedial prescriptions:

> bəsh n-'ti-ha l-ma dyal səb'at l-mwaj
> u l-ma dyal səb'at l-ḥaddada,
> u l-ma dyal səb'at l-byar
> u l-ma dyal r-rḥa dyal jəddi mulay ibrahim
> t-'um bi-hum.

in order that I give her the water of seven waves,
and the water of seven ironsmiths,
and the water of seven wells,
and the water of the mill of my grandfather, Moulay Ibrahim
for her to bathe with them.

Not only are words repeated in the same sequence but there is a subtle assonance in the syllable of all the ending words: muw*aj* / ḥadd*ad*; by*ar* /

Ibrahim. The syllabic structure is not at all regular, but this does not diminish the strong beat that the speaker imposes on the last or penultimate syllable of each line.

In the following segment of discourse a similar pattern of assonance is observed. The majduba uses the diminutive *mwima* for *umm* ("mother"), thereby permitting an end-of-line rhyme between lines one, two and three (kha-*h* / ba-*h* / l-mwim*a*) and another rhyme within line four (l-lb*an* / s-sm*an*). The majduba is outlining the problems that her tabkhira will assist in reconciling:

> rah, tay-fərqu l-khu ʿla kha-h
> rah, tay-fərqu l-wald ʿla bba-h.
> rah, tay-fərqu sh-shab ʿla l-mwima.
> rah, tay-fərqu l-bəgra ʿla l-lban u s-sman.

> You see, they separate the brother from his brother.
> They separate the son from his father.
> They separate the youth from his [little] mother.
> They separate the cow from buttermilk and aged butter.

These formulae are standard market fare, typical of male oratory of this kind. The majduba employs parallelism to describe a separation that, she asserts, is caused by the magical intervention of witches, resulting in division and pain in a society based upon the patriarchal extended family. The foods she names (buttermilk and aged butter) are staples of the agrarian diet, symbols of the shaʿb—the folk. By invoking these value-laden foods, the majduba draws on a folk aesthetic of community that is threatened by spells. In the next line the parallelism falters:

> rah, tay-fərqu d-djaja ʿla…
> ta-yəbsu li-ha l-biḍ dyal-ha.
> gaʿda ʿli-h d-djaja
> wəllat kərmat fuq l-biḍ,
> hiya u l-biḍ.
> ayyəh. ṣalli ʿla rasul allah.

> Well, they part the chicken from…
> Her eggs dry up on her.
> She's sitting on them,

and she dries up on top of the eggs,
both she and the eggs.

The majduba didn't finish the first of the above lines; the parallelism she has
been employing is halted in mid-sentence, giving the effect of a false ca-
dence. The break in musical measure corresponds with the majduba'a break
from formulaic discourse, as she shifts from parallelism to the more referential language of didactic speech, modulating from a poetic discourse to a
narrative strategy. Such formal shifts often occur at transitional moments,
when a narrator "breaks through" everyday speech into performance, for
example (Hymes 1975). In this case, a divergence in form indicates a break
from rhetorical tradition as the majduba veers from the highly stylized
blame of women witches to an implied identification with women victims.
Here "form and content are so subtly intertwined that no critique can draw
a line between them" (Booth 1984 : xiv).

The Move into Meaning

The majduba's commiseration with her audience is evident in her vivid examples of victimized women:

shhal mən mərrat, məskina, mslukha m'a wlidat-ha
How many times, the poor woman, she's flayed for her children.

shhal mən mərrat, məskina, t'am-ha dh-dhkər
How many times, the poor woman, her food is masculine.

li kay-akl-u kay-nkər.
Whoever eats it, denies [it].

The majduba delineates how natural processes, even those assumed to bring
the most honor (motherhood), can go awry because of bewitchment. Practitioners of magic threaten women in areas where they are most vulnerable — in the honor of their "nests." The theme of social division is brought
up more than once in metaphors that refer to food and the body. The flay-
ing of the mother's body is a striking example of the sacrifice that women
make for their children. The slaughter of animals in the household is a common event in Morocco. Children grow up witnessing it from a very early

age. But the mother here is not sacrificed with prayers and celebration; rather she is flayed, her very skin taken off for the benefit of her children. This dramatic image inverts the categories of animal and human and reinforces the theme of separation present in previous verses. Not only is the woman flayed, however, even her food is "masculine." This is another inversion, for cooking food, the epitome of creative activity in the daily lives of women, is a function imbued with the feminine. Feminine agency in cooking permeates the materiality of the food, even in the digestive stage: the majduba goes on to say that, if food is masculine, "whoever eats it denies it." Such an inversion of categories (masculine food) results in refusal and repudiation by its consumers. Women's bodies as well as the food that comes into contact with their bodies, and even those who subsequently eat the food, are liable to be changed by the volition and spells of sorceresses. The majduba further associates the feminine body with food when she says:

> kayn l-mra, məskina, lli dəggu-ha s-saharat dəggan
> There's the woman, the poor thing, who witches have pummeled twice over

The grinding of herbs, spices, incense, and hənna in large wooden mortars is a frequent feminine activity in rural centers. Here, a bewitched woman is portrayed as being ground up by witches, her very being pummeled and made into powder as if she were a seasoning.

In the discourse examined, the majduba moves from the formality of primary genres to anecdotal warnings whose semantic import engages the female audience members on both a metaphoric and a visceral level. The feminine body is portrayed as being open to disintegrating influences, unprotected from the fragmenting forces that abound in the marketplace. The majduba, of course, has a remedy for these afflictions.

Codes and Lies

The reorientation of genre that the majduba effects is the result of a new audience of women in the public domain. But the indexing of different gendered discourses is only one of the dimensions that contribute to the heteroglossia of the marketplace. The majduba also switches languages in the space of a single sentence.

The use of Berber in the marketplace is common in Beni Mellal. The surrounding mountain villages are almost exclusively Berber, while the city of Beni Mellal itself, like all Moroccan cities, is a conglomerate of Arab and Berber populations who communicate in Moroccan Arabic. Although the majority of Berber-speaking people in Beni Mellal also speak Arabic, the reverse is not true. Because Berber is not a written language (and thus not taught in school), only Berbers learn it.

The code-switching the majduba employs between Berber and Arabic attests to her bilingual sales strategies. Not only is she reaching out to both factions, but she is calling attention to the competition of languages and codes that characterizes the marketplace (Volosinov 1973). "What's straight is straight" (*agharas, agharas*), she says in Berber to her client, who is visibly dressed in a Berber-style sheet. The majduba is counseling the client on the right path of action and is doing so in her own language, establishing a bond of linguistic identity. She again switches codes, this time speaking half in Berber, half in Arabic, when she admonishes her client, saying "Put your {faith [MA]} in God." She continues:

Here's the majduba of Moulay Ibrahim.
Here's who'll give you a treasure from treasures.
Here's who'll give you a charm from charms.
Niya!
{Who will put their faith in God with me?[B]}
That means *Who will put their faith in God with me?* in Arabic.[21]
Welcome.
If you don't have faith in God with me,
God help us and you.

The majduba translates her Berber sentence into Arabic for her audience. "That means *Who will put their faith in God with me?* in Arabic," she says. Her language is literally double-voiced as she discursively embodies the many codes of the marketplace. Layering form with theme, the majduba goes on to speak about the duplicity present in the marketplace:

"The gathering of boys, the gathering of girls, your dinner with screaming, your lunch with screaming, yeah!

"The only ones who take them, lalla, are the brave and the generous, or those whose parents are satisfied with them. It's as if you went and visited Moulay Ibrahim and took from there blessings without lies, without wrong, without forbidden dealings, without your aunt, the Ḥajja, without your uncle, the Ḥajj.

"I'm giving [this to] you, if you still have grief or oppression or if you're sad, whoever has consequences[22] following [them]. Between us, God and the groom of Judgment Day, Muḥammad, the messenger of God."

The majduba clapped her hands. "You're going to give a one hundred! [riyal note] You see, I'm going to take the plane and leave you here on the ground. Today, the older son is no longer useful."

"Some incense," said a woman in the audience.

"Or my money, if it increases," continued the majduba, ignoring the interruption. "This, on the day of Arafat, here it is: the 'rock of redemption,' and 'the abolisher,' and indigo. These, grind them. Burn them for seven days. Give me a hundred, the price of a pot of tea.

"Here I am. I have the wherewithal to lie to you. Here I am. I have the wherewithal to wrong you. Here I am. I have the wherewithal to be a hypocrite to you.

"Tomorrow, next to God, I don't have the dirt of existence to give you. Here's the majduba, the daughter of Moulay Ibrahim."

Here the majduba denies she is lying, inferring that she is prevented from doing so by the supernatural consequences that attend such an act. The majduba calls attention to the proliferation of lies in the marketplace and provides a commentary on the rules of the game. She implies that among those who are oppressed, grieved, sad, and followed by the "consequences" of magical perpetration, only the brave and generous, those whose parents are satisfied with them, will take her incense and advice. These good qualities obviously do not shield the victims from bewitchment, however; values are not remedies. Therefore the majduba asks her audience, "Who will trust in God with me?"

Trust is the first ingredient in the majduba's cure. She mentions niya, and then asks who will trust in God *with her* (not by themselves) in both Berber and Arabic. The Arabic verb here is *tawakkala* [CA], to trust or put confidence in, or to put oneself in God's hands (implying an abnegation of personal responsibility). The majduba calls for trust, mentioning the prevalence of lying, forbidden dealings, and taking advantage of those you know (*ma'rifa* [MA] — referenced by the words "without your aunt Ḥajja/without your uncle Ḥajj"). The premises of the marketplace work against the practice of trust. Although the majduba has the "wherewithal to lie" by virtue of her verbal prowess and her position in the suq, the terrain of untruth, her meta-linguistic commentary distances her from the sinful practices of the marketplace.

The irony here is that she is squarely within the suq. After holding forth on both trust and its counter-forces, the majduba claps her hands and directs her audience to give her one hundred riyals. Then she says, "I'm going to take the plane and leave you here on the ground." Equating "to-day" with the day of Judgment, the majduba uses deictic expressions to conflate the "now" ("Here I am," she repeats) with the "then," the day of reckoning, the day "the older son is no longer useful." She says that she is going to this place by airplane, a symbol of modernity, leaving all her trusting clients on the ground — a trickster image if ever there was one! The essential message is, "I could lie to you, but I won't. But if I did, I'm bound for Judgement Day on my own private plane, anyway." This is an example of what Bauman calls an "emphatic attempt…at validation," which nonetheless "contain[s] elements that subtly undermine the intended effect" (1986:22).

The Terms of Contradiction

Despite the elements of parody displayed in the majduba's use of genre, and the playfulness surrounding the themes of lying and truthfulness, the con-tradictions in her discourse merit further examination. The majduba is a woman of considerable performance ability who breaks with stereotypical roles and challenges categorical definition. This does not mean, however, that her explicit ideology is in any way revolutionary when it comes to gen-der considerations. There is an apparent schism here between form and content. Simply by virtue of being a woman in a male-dominated profes-sion, the majduba opens a space for the construction of new gender iden-tities. The architecture of her discourse embodies this openness, as do the elements of her physical presentation and her representation of herself to her audience.[23] It is thus problematic when we encounter statements that appear to recreate just the boundaries that her personhood challenges. Again, the stacked verses of Sidi Abderahman will serve as an example:

"God, God be with you, our grandfather Moulay Ibrahim. No, No, listen to me. Of course, she doesn't want him any more, because the others have turned around him [with magic]. We women are hard!:
"If they love you, they'll feed you
and if they hate you, they'll bewitch you."
"She's the first," the client said.
"He who enters the women's suq, beware!" the majduba quoted,
They'll show you a ton of profit
and make you lose your salary!

> *The ruses of women are their own.*
> *From their ruses I came running!*
> *Oh, the women belted with snakes*
> *and those oppressed with scorpions!*

Pray to the Prophet. Yeah, oh woman, whoever is a woman, never hold a[nother] woman dear."

This segment is heavy with intertextuality, with words that the majduba has not authored, but appropriated from Sidi Abderahman. Making these words a part of her discourse has predetermined consequences; the words bear their own "history of associations" into the present context, which is precisely why they are problematic (Tannen 1989 : 133). These words are the very ones that have been used in the past by men to define women and delimit the feminine world, as exemplified in the rhyming proverb, "If they love you, they'll feed you. If they hate you, they'll bewitch you." The message is simple and simplistic: good women are nurturers, bad ones are witches. The majduba also draws on another well-known aphorism of Sidi Abderahman that equates the feminine world with a woman's marketplace and counsels against entrance:

> ya d-dakhəl suq n-nsa rəd bal-ək,
> y-biynu-lək mən r-rbəḥ qanṭar
> wa y-khəsru-k f-ras mal-ək.

> He who enters the women's suq, beware!
> They'll show you a ton of profit
> and make you lose your salary!

By speaking these words the majduba indexes the spiritual authority of a man whose tradition she continues. Although part of oral tradition, its history is easily traced: these are the reported words of Sidi Abderahman al-Majdub. And if there is any doubt, one need only buy a cheap copy of his sayings at a nearby used-book tent.

Sidi Abderahman is not known for his progressive views on women. In another rhyme he says, "Women are fleeting vessels / Whose passengers are doomed to destruction."[24] These sayings, more like warnings, are often used in cynical contexts — spoken by one male friend to another in order to cure the latter of the "blindness" of romantic love and longing, for example. The implication is that in the "women's market," women promise a lot and then rob you blind.

The majduba continues to employ poetic speech that describes women as "belted with snakes and oppressed by scorpions." The segment culminates with advice: "Whoever is a woman, never hold a[nother] woman dear." In other words, women should not trust other women. This sets up a linguistic paradox (Bateson 1972), for the majduba is a woman who requires the trust of her audience in order to do her business. In the final analysis, she manages to circumvent this paradox. She does not directly say, "trust me" (although she does go a long way in order to convince her audience that she is *trustworthy*); rather, she asks, "Who will trust in God with me?" Trust is required, but the majduba channels it toward God, thus making hers an enterprise in league with God's. If you trust God, then you will buy this incense and it will work for you. This is the premise of niya: Trust in God equals trust in the efficacy of the tabkhira equals trust in the seller of the incense. The result is money in the majduba's pocket. This creation of co-identity in the face of contradiction and through the confluence of categories is very subtle and thus successful.

We are still left with the disturbing associations of the recontextualized discourse, however, and the apparent contradictions these recycled utterances create between the openness of the majduba's poetics and the restricted interpretations inherent in the traditional and generic speech she employs. These words have traditionally been in the mouths of men, but when a woman calls down women in the manner of men, in the public context of the marketplace, there is reason for suspicion. She is metapragmatically calling attention to her own use of stereotypes, employing them and creating distance from them. Only members of an in-group have this license. Calling attention to stereotypes says in effect, "Women, who are you? Are you this, what they say you are?" Even if the majduba affirms that, yes, women are "hard," she is also noting the schisms in the feminine community, providing a social critique of the competition and lack of cohesion that exist there and—insofar as she acknowledges that the consequences are detrimental (which she does)—condemning both.

The majduba defines women as agents of considerable influence, using images of animals that are powerful and dangerous, animals that live in the wilderness and are undomesticated. If women are not to be trusted, it is because they have the ability to both nourish and devastate. The tendency to attribute to Moroccan women the power to overturn civilization unless their sexual appetite is socially controlled is well documented (Mernissi 1987; Rosen 1984). Women are not constructed as powerless in Moroccan society, but powerful women are often constructed as dangerous and "low." The majduba alludes to this body of belief by setting up the dichotomy between feeding and bewitching. But her categories are not rigid, nor are they monologic. After all, she says that the perpetrator of the magic was "awake," whereas the mother of the abandoned girl was "asleep...the poor thing!" What the majduba implies here is that the victim's mother should also be awake, that she should be alert to the power of magic and not naive. It is doubtful whether the majduba would qualify herself as asleep or powerless. In this context, being awake means being powerful and active; and although the majduba invokes the popular saying "completion is God's," she is not reluctant to be the agent who begins: "I'm going to take care of her business, and don't consider yourself her mother; consider that *I'm* her mother." These implications come through what Brenneis, following Searle (1975), and other speech-act theorists have referred to as "indirection"—a mode in which "listeners are...compelled to draw their own conclusions" because the literal function in the speech event takes a backseat to a multiplicity of implicit and covert messages that are coded in form, function, and meaning" (Brenneis 1986:341).[25]

The majduba's speech is more than literal, it is pragmatically overdetermined; its meaning depends on its situatedness in any one of a number of possible interpretive frames. In marketplace speech these frames are various and constantly shifting. "Trust God and don't trust others," is one of the messages. "Be cunning," is another. Mix genres, appropriate language, turn categories on their heads. "He [or, in this case, she] who enters the women's market, *rəd bal-ək*," literally, pay attention. This is one of the only consistent messages of the majduba's discourse: pay attention, beware, and be wary in a market of mixed messages.

Despite the vertigo that the mixing of associative worlds creates in the majduba's speech, she ultimately offers at least a veil of resolution to conflicting interpretations through the mediation of her "goods"—her good words serve to gather people around her and around common social topics, while her good goods undo bewitchment. If spells divide people, her incense takes away division, abolishing contradiction also, even if only in the momentary smoke and smell of burning incense.

Notes

1. A party (*ḥəfla*) is a context where performances are shared between professional performers and audience, given and received by different people throughout the collective event.
2. Charles Briggs uses this term to call attention to the often ambiguous demarcation of performative and non-performative modes of speech (1988:17).

3. The worship of saints, or marabouts, is the main defining characteristic of North African Islam. According to Eickelman (1976:6–7), marabouts are "persons, living or dead, to whom is attributed a special relation toward God which makes them particularly well placed to serve as intermediaries with the supernatural and to communicate God's grace (*baraka*) to their clients. On the basis of this conception, marabouts in the past have played key religious, political, and economic roles in North African society, particularly in Morocco." The majduba in this study calls herself a disciple of the saint Moulay Ibrahim, though she spends more time in the market selling goods than she does at the pilgrimage site.

4. I saw this majduba buy a camera lens from someone who came to do business with her personally, belying her apparent poverty.

5. *ḥajrət l-fək* can be translated as the "rock of redemption," or the "rock of severing."

6. Buya 'Omar is a saint (now-dead) whose tomb is a sanctuary and pilgrimage center. He is known for his powers of healing mental illness. See Naamouni (1993).

7. The Soussi Berbers are known for their expertise in magic.

8. *kamal*, meaning both completion and perfection in completion.

9. Bauman (1992) also speaks about the "dialogue of genres" in his discussion of the interplay of two genres, verse and story, in a narrative context.

10. Many girls are still not sent to school (their parents judge it unnecessary and a threat to the inculcation of obedience). Literacy rates for girls continue to be lower than for boys. In 1985, 78 percent of Moroccan adult females but 56 percent of males were illiterate (see Spratt 1992, quoting World Bank 1990). Many girls drop out after grammar school, and many more along the way in high school.

11. It is the phrase that effects conversion to Islam.

12. The exception to this being children's often halting recitation in Qur'anic school.

13. The recitation of the Qur'an by men trained to do so — *ṭulba* — accompanies rites of passage in Morocco, including naming ceremonies for newborn children, weddings, and deaths.

14. Some examples of stock da'wat are
allah y-kəmməl b-l-khir, "God complete [it] with blessing"
allah y-jib t-tisir, "God bring [you] ease"
allah y-stər 'l-ək, "God protect you"
allah y-'t-ək s-sam, "God give you poison."

15. See Singer (1989) and Urban (1989) on pronoun use and conceptions of the self in linguistic analysis.

16. "Directive" is the term Austin uses to refer to a speech act whose intention is to get the listener to do something (1962).

17. Brown and Levinson (1978).

18. See Besnier (1989), Ochs (1986), Ochs and Schieffelin (1989), Haviland (1989), and Lutz and Abu-Lughod (1990) for an elaboration of the intersection of emotion and language.

19. See Irvine (1979) on formality in language use. On formal poetics, see Jakobson (1960, 1966, 1968) and Johnstone (1987).

20. See Jakobson (1981) on parallelism.

21. The majduba translates what she has just said in Berber into Arabic, demonstrating her fluency in both languages and thus identifying herself as a Berber. (Only Berbers know Berber — Arabs have no reason to acquire it.)

22. *tab'at* (literally "followings" or "consequences") names the illness that results from witchcraft. It is very difficult to diagnose in scientific terms.

23. The majduba uses kinship terms to describe her relationship to her saint, indexing the malleability of definitions of Moroccan kinship and the potential to create close ties outside blood relations.

24. Fatima Mernissi (1987 : 43) translated this one from the book, *Les Quatrains de Mejdoub le Sarcastique, poète Maghrebin du XVIième siècle*, collected and translated by J. Scelles-Millie with B. Khelifa (1996 : 161).

25. "Indirection joins together *form*, how something is said or, beyond that, staged; *function*, both individual intentions and the audience's definition of what is taking place; and *meaning*, the overt and covert content of what is being said" (Brenneis 1986 : 341).

4. Words About Herbs: Feminine Performance of Oratory in the Marketplace

> Nothing to be done: language is always a matter of force, to speak is to exercise a will for power; in the realm of speech there is no innocence, no safety.
>
> — Barthes (1977:192)

The frequency of oaths, proverbs, blessings, and scripture in Moroccan oratory make it a formal or ritualized language like those historically associated with tradition and rhetorical power.[1] Yet despite its highly stylized form, the pragmatic revoicing of this oratory by women opens the interpretive possibilities of traditional speech events. Formal language in the informal setting of the suq does not limit meaning; rather, by embodying words and gestures customarily performed by and for men, women orators create a multivocalic and hybrid discourse in a context of heteroglossia. By appropriating the authority vested in public discourse, women marketers challenge traditional notions of who may exercise the powers of coercion and for what ends.

The Renegotiation of Codes

Explicit discussion of sexuality, impotence, magic, and prostitution has long been popular in the Moroccan marketplace. The new wrinkle in the history of marketplace activity is that women are emerging as key players in these social performances. The enactment of artistic license by women orators brings the negotiation of gender, and definitions of honor and shame regarding gender, into public focus.

In the following discourse of an herbalist (ʿashshaba) there is a direct confrontation with the honor code. Like the majduba, the ʿashshaba uses religious aphorism to temper the immodesty of her words, including quoted scripture in the high register of classical Arabic [CA]. Also like the majduba, she sells a commodity that purports to rid the client of spells perpetrated by women, although these goods must be ingested, not just burned as incense. But unlike the majduba, the herbalist uses very explicit language in her attempts at persuasion, broaching topics that have until recently been spoken about only in monosexual gatherings.

The herbalist is located in the ḥalqa, which overlooks the suq proper. Middle-aged and corpulent, she stands under a makeshift tent awning projecting from the side of a light-green Peugeot. A microphone in her hand periodically emits a loud and piercing screech of feedback and gives her voice a static quality. She is talking to thirty-four men and twelve women about problems of induced impotency, magical agency, and spiritual and sexual worth. Her language is bawdy and humorous. She is not talking to individuals, however, but rather to gender categories — you [men], we women. It is these categories that are in the process of discursive negotiation in her speech:

"God gave you [men] five liters of blood and us [women] seven liters of blood, the blood of menstruation and the blood of childbirth. Why are you [men] beautiful with three [appetites] and we're beautiful with four? Why has God given you [men] one desire and us ninety-nine? You see, you just have one desire. If it's gone, you won't have honor in your house any more. The man will appear like a donkey next to his wife. Nothing enables or honors you except bodily desire (*nafs*). If it goes so far as to be lacking, you can count your soul (*ruḥ*) as having no value. You see, even religion and medicine are not ashamed [to address these issues]!"

The herbalist's mention of the blood of childbirth and menstruation in a public and mixed-sex gathering is considered inappropriate by most. Perhaps more important than her daring is her discursive reconstruction of metaphysical assumption. In Muslim religious thought there is a consistent duality between the carnal, desiring self (nafs) and the transcendent soul (ruḥ), as well as between desire and the world of the intellect or wisdom ('aql). In the sufi practice of soul purification, nafs is considered the "beast" to be subdued (see J. Anderson 1985:203–11, 1982:397–420; Boddy 1988: 5; Mills 1991:248–49; Rosen 1978; Schimmel 1975). Yet in the herbalist's discourse this relationship is inverted, the soul's value depending upon an active desire life:

You see, nothing enables or honors you except desire.
If it goes so far as to be lacking,
you can count your soul as having no value.

As a woman, the herbalist breaks with social convention by talking about restricted topics both to men and in a public context. The reference to sex is implicit, but understood: men have "one desire" because they reach orgasm only once, their desire is singular and exhaustible. Once spent, honor is in jeopardy, as a man is likely to be cuckolded if he doesn't exercise his nafs by servicing his wife. Women, on the other hand, have the possibility of multiple pleasures, "ninety-nine" according to the herbalist. Although nafs here refers to sexual desire, the term is commonly used as a synonym for "self" and the conflation is not arbitrary; sexual potency (and particularly its ability to draw bride's blood) is an important element in the constitution of manhood, or men's selfhood in male rites of passage in Morocco (see Combs-Schilling 1989). But the correlation between desire and personhood is not restricted to the male sex; the malleability of the term nafs in this regard expresses a general equation between physical desire and personal identity.[2] Without nafs there is no self, and selfhood is often mediated through the expression of sexuality.[3]

This is a convenient philosophy for someone who is selling an herbal remedy that counters spell-induced impotence, as it asserts that honor is only accessible through restoring carnal desire, first by buying the herbs, then by embracing women. But this is more than a sales strategy. To assert that honor is only accessible via sexuality is not new, but women in the herbalist's discourse are not just passive vehicles through which men construct their honor; rather women have the power both to take away a man's honor (by casting spells of impotence) and to constitute a man's honor and their own.

The herbalist's speech is a self-conscious breaking with social conventions of honor (cf. Naaman-Guessous 1990). She acknowledges the shameful (hshuma) quality of her speech by justifying it, saying that both religion and medicine also address these important topics publicly and with impunity. The herbalist thereby enacts a common religious attitude, captured in the axiom "there's no shame in religion" (la hya f-d-din), a phrase often repeated by marketplace orators in order to deflect the embarrassment evoked when mentioning genitalia or referring to sexual acts in public — subjects that in other contexts would be considered immodest.[4] By consciously calling attention to her verbal license in such regards, the herbalist puts herself in the same category as a spiritual advisor or a medical doctor — customarily both men. She also defends her right to speak the taboo: "By God, I won't be ashamed before you!" she declares in another segment (*wa-ḷḷah, ma n-ḥashəm ḥda-k*).

Like the majduba, the herbalist employs religious aphorism, direct reported speech, and quotation of scripture in classical Arabic to establish authority and credibility with her audience. It is often difficult to distinguish what and whose voice is being asserted. For example, she states:

"Be careful you're not deceived by a woman. And she'll tell you, 'all right, you're my husband and are dear to me and if you died tonight I would mourn for you.' Don't trust [it]! By God, we're being hypocrites about that! Because these four, they eat and don't get full. Count with me: One, the eye eats and it doesn't get tired of seeing; two, the ear eats and it doesn't get tired of hearing news; three, the earth eats and isn't content with water and rain and the fourth... finish it with your mind. May God honor your standing, my gentlemen."

In this passage the herbalist calls down her own sex using facile stereotypes of deceitful and insatiate women whose intentions (niya) are judged by the way they will ultimately mourn their husbands.[5] But once again a paradox is presented, for, although the quotation marks serve to distinguish the herbalist's voice from the quoted utterance, that distance is immediately spanned when she follows the quote with the inclusive pronoun "we": "Don't trust [it]/ By God *we*'re being hypocrites about that," she asserts. The irony here is that the herbalist is dressed in mourning clothes (a white jəllaba, white *bəlgha* shoes, white socks, and a white scarf draped around her head and tied under her chin). She informs the audience later in her discourse that her husband has just died and that her father died two months before him. So either she is mourning her husband, providing a counter-example to the assertion that women are hypocrites, or she is also acting outside the canon of honor, in which case she undermines her own course — "Be careful you're not deceived by a woman!" And although she will assert that she is about to go to Mecca, she is now in the marketplace doing business, clearly in breach of the prohibition for mourning women to have social intercourse (verbal exchange or even eye contact) with men during the four months and ten days following their husbands' death.

There are different messages encoded in the many levels of semiotic communication occurring here. The herbalist is drawing on a publicly recognized discourse, common in marketplace oratory, that constructs women as deceivers and hypocrites. While the herbalist seems to accept this familiar gender characterization in her condemnation of women who break the rules, she nonetheless defies the same norm in her own dress and demeanor. It is precisely the herbalist's presence in the marketplace in mourning clothes that alerts us to women's transition from the private "feminine" realm to the public, working, "masculine" one, for men are not required to mourn their wives, but are expected to continue in their public life with no visible reminder of mourning. They do not suffer dishonor thereby: "May God honor your standing, my gentlemen," the herbalist asserts, as if to ensure her own.

The herbalist is both enacting deceit and critically commenting on it. But there are other themes of violation in her discourse besides that of trust, a salient one being transgression of the boundaries of moderation, the theme of insatiateness: the eye does not get tired of seeing, the ear doesn't get its fill of news, the earth (which regularly suffers from drought in Morocco) never gets enough water, and sexual appetite is never (permanently) appeased. There is a regenerative aspect to these expressions of excess, referred to as acts of ingestion: the eye, ear, and earth eat, and do not get full. It is the limitlessness of appetite (echoing the ninety-nine desires of women) that threatens stability, that makes the husband a cuckold or the unmarried daughter come home pregnant, winding up a shikha, a performer with loose morals[6]:

"By God, if you lack desire, your wife will sleep with the shepherd of the forest. Wake from your stupor and be a man! You men, why do you want us? What is beautiful about us that you want us for? Why are we near paradise and near hell and near Satan? The Prophet said, Prayers and peace be upon him: 'A woman that is obedient to her husband [CA]...' There are those of you who marry an adulterous woman. Women are the only thing that can make you men's value fall. If your wife doesn't make your value fall, your daughter will make it fall — she'll come [home] pregnant and end up a performer (shikha). If your wife or daughter doesn't make it fall, your sister or mother will make it fall. You see, my words are with those whose reason ('aql) is in their hearts. My words are not with him that eats and gets full and lies down next to you like a sack of cement and begins to piss half on the ground, half on his thighs. God give you, sir, blessing, to wake up from your stupor."

The herbalist uses two instances of direct reported speech to construct her own authority in this passage. First she quotes an example of fallacious speech, introducing it with, "she'll tell you, 'all right, you're my husband and are dear to me and if you died tonight I would mourn for you.'" The herbalist's authority here comes from her ability to distance herself from the quotation and to judge it as a lie, saying "Don't trust it." The quoted utterance carries no socially recognized or inherent authority; it is simply speech that was either overheard or authored by the herbalist. The utterance thus stands apart from its speaker, but is also permeable to her "voice." She may very well be its original author — the words are imbued with her own authority (especially given the fact that she is visibly in a state of mourning) while, at the same time, they provide the context for her meta-linguistic commentary.

The second instance of reported speech is also direct, but the citation is in another register [CA] and purports to be a documented utterance of the Prophet. Consequently, this utterance carries its own innate authority and is therefore more resistant to the herbalist's commentary. In fact, she gives none, for the utterance speaks for itself: "The Prophet said, Prayers and peace upon him: 'a woman, that is obedient to her husband'..." Here again the herbalist invokes the social authority already invested in these words and appropriates it. The first instance of reported speech is embedded in commentary; here, in contrast, the herbalist employs religious text more for its effect than for its meaning. This is evidenced by the fact that she does not even complete the Prophet's saying, but relies on the associative world it calls up. In so doing, she creates a collage of religious sentiment while calling attention to themes of deception and contradiction.

The herbalist warns against immoderation, using examples of women who step outside the bounds — a female performer and an adulteress. Yet she gives a discomfiting image of male satiation, which induces stupor of the most incontinent sort. The mere mention of incontinence in mixed company is a serious infraction of social etiquette. Her messages are thus conflicting: in the act of breaking the rules for acceptable speech for women, the herbalist condemns the transgressive. Her language, which is dually gendered and vacillates between several associative worlds, "takes up its menacing stance in the forum itself, and, as it were, dares the representatives of order to grapple with it" (Turner 1986:75).

The potency and import of transgression are at issue here. Being obedient is not a passive role, but a predictable and social one. Creative agency, by contrast (an enactment of the individual), is constructed outside the bounds of social ordinance, pointing to lines of tension between the extended and the nuclear family, the community and the individual, men and women. Like the marketplace, transgression exceeds itself, breaking open the cocoon of license until it becomes the larger practice (*l-qaʿida*), the way things are done.

The herbalist's discourse on taboo subjects is consistent with the general ambience of carnival that reigns in the marketplace. As Bakhtin notes, carnivalized speech is characterized by the inappropriate word — "inappropriate because of its cynical frankness, or because it profanely unmasks a holy thing, or because it crudely violates etiquette." Because the "scandals and eccentricities" of the herbalist's discourse breach "the stable, normal ('seemly') course of human affairs and events, they free human behavior from the norms and motivations that predetermine it," thereby opening a space for the creation of new social identities (1984a:117).[7] Yet such violations are not free of shock value. My companion at this event, a divorced woman who by no means lives a sheltered life, walked away from this performance shaking her head and repeating, "Damnation, that's shameful!" Although men have broached the topics of sex and bodily functions before in the marketplace, these same words in the mouths of women are qualitatively and pragmatically different. They introduce issues of appropriation and the problematics of difference. The sexually charged language of the herbalist entices people to linger for the duration of the performance, which often spans more than an hour. The audience is in awe of a woman speaking to a mixed crowd as if she were a man, yet without sacrificing her feminine voice.

Words and Currency

The words of the herbalist identify a changing ideology regarding gender and articulate tensions arising from the rejection of the mobile and dialogic marketplace of negotiated exchange in favor of the "permanent" and extra-local one struggling to supersede it. It is not surprising to find that relations of capitalism, even in this most commoditized space of the marketplace, are being put into discursive question. As diviner, healer, and saleswoman, the herbalist discursively removes herself from the short-term monetary exchanges of the capitalist marketplace to better establish her spiritual authority in the public realm. Holding what looks like a miniature hourglass filled with water in her hand, she says:

"Here. Now I am going to lift this scale,[8] here it is. I'm going to use this scale, like I'm doing here. The sickness that you have, I'll show it to you. Don't complain to me, complain to God. Give me just your hand and be quiet. I'm going to tell you about every sickness that you have. If this scale works for you in your hand, God, it won't move from its place. If you pay me for it or give me something for it, God burn you with it [the money]. Or if I put out my hands [for the money] and am paid, God burn me with it. The payment I want to hear, I didn't hear [you] say, 'God have mercy on the parents.'"

"God have mercy on the parents," repeated the audience.

The herbalist maligns monetary transaction, defining it as inappropriate to the present context of healing. In so doing, she distinguishes the rhetoric of long-term reciprocity (indexed by blessing the parents) from the rhetoric of commodity relations ("God burn me with it [the money]!"). These discourses occupy two different places in the Moroccan imagination. Although both mediate paternalistic values, long-term relations of obligation resist commodification and price assignment,[9] being intricately connected to the personal identities and reputations of those involved in negotiation. The rhetoric of commodification, on the other hand, based on "free exchange," carries no obligation, extending only to the actual transaction. Negotiation in this realm takes place between players — consumers, sellers, producers — and not actual or fictive kin.

The construction of the herbalist's public authority is of primary import in her oratory, as she is holding forth in a territory that has historically been a masculine domain. Not only is she engaging in a new genre of speech, but she is addressing an audience of men whose co-presence has a determining power of its own, demanding that she prove herself by persuading them that her power extends beyond mere rhetoric to the realm of healing and the body.[10] The herbalist speaks in the voice of the healer as she divines the illness of her clients with the aid of a "scale" whose sensitivity to body temperature registers illness or health.[11] Such powers may be worth a lot, but the herbalist does not ask for money, only the repetition of the common blessing, "God have mercy on the parents" (*allah y-rḥəm l-walidin*).

"God have mercy on the parents" is an example of a formal daʿwa, a "primary" or unmediated genre of speech (Bakhtin 1981) which may be appended to virtually any request, especially in polite conversation with elders. Indexing the system of filial piety and long-term reciprocity in which

Figure 10. An herbalist, with her children, warns a mixed-sex audience about the dangers of magical spells.

obligation (*al-wajib*) is immanent (Eickelman 1976; Rosen 1984),[12] the daʿwa functions to draw the audience into an emotionality of religious performance based on shared moral sentiment and socialization. Such dialogicity is further evidenced by the verbal response that such a blessing elicits — either ratification (saying *amin*, amen) or repetition of a corresponding blessing. The herbalist uses this formulaic blessing strategically, engaging her audience in a call and response that employs a rhetoric of reciprocity in order to better disguise the terms of commodity. She thus distances herself from the vulgar exchange of the marketplace at the same time that she situates herself and her audience firmly within its performative economy. By invoking the parents, the herbalist reminds the audience that payback is incumbent on the receiver, whether to parents, ancestors, or whoever proffers a gift. Whereas the group recitation of blessing creates social cohesion, money is portrayed as injurious. There is continuous and intricate interplay between these two ethics and their dialogue is particularly salient in the marketplace where people often try to frame commodity relations in the more comfortable terms of kinship.[13]

The herbalist asserts that she wants to be paid in a currency found outside market relations, one that seems to be incommensurable with the context that solicits it. But she does not acknowledge this contradiction; rather her verbal performance so backstages the marketplace setting of her monologue as to virtually disguise any economic motivation on her part. By invoking the system of filial piety and honor, she attempts to sanitize processes of commodification.

In evidence here are the contradictions inherent in hybrid genres which talk across differences (Hanks 1987). This oratory draws upon two ideological discourses — the moral discourse of kinship and obligation, with its inherent conceptions of the sexual division of labor, and the discourse of individualism and capitalism, which sometimes challenges and sometimes upholds these divisions. The mixing of these ideological realms serves to loosen the weave between signs and their historical meanings, thus opening a space for the transformation of conceptions of gender.

Challenging all kinds of limits is one of the emblematic strategies of the herbalist. In the following stretch of discourse, she declares herself outside the law of propriety, while condemning the impropriety of others:

"These four, avoid them, God give you blessing, sir. The first of them, if you pray to the messenger of God..."

"Prayers and peace be upon him," the audience responded.

"First of all I want you to avoid making friends with just anybody. If you want to make a friend, make friends with those better than you, not worse. The second thing, God give you blessing sirs, I want you to avoid the vagina. All that follow those [girls] of the street, that one is no longer considered a man. Because a woman, what is she called? By God, I won't be ashamed before you! A woman, what is she called? A well, and a man is called a bucket. A woman is called an ink well and a man is a pen. A women is called a field and a man is the irrigation. A woman is called a mattress and a man is a cover."

These metaphors are considered risqué because they allude to anatomical differences between men and women. They are certainly not original in their tendency to equate women with nature (a "field") and men with culture ("irrigation"). In all of them men are characterized as instrumental (active) and women as material (passive). More significant than the metaphors themselves, however, is the statement that precedes them: "By God, I won't be ashamed before you!" This declaration "keys" the entire discursive scene as one that self-consciously flaunts social convention (Bauman 1977; Hymes 1974). Despite the fact that similar things have been spoken in the marketplace before, they have always been spoken by men to men. The herbalist is calling attention to the taboo of mentioning these topics in public and heterogeneous company, while asserting her intention to break the rules. Thus although she appears to adhere to thematic modes of male/female relations, she rhetorically violates the rules for mixed-gender interaction and appropriate speech. The market *is* a place of license, but women are in a continual process of acquiring their "papers" in this domain, with forceful voicing of their intent and right.

Pollution and Porosity

The herbalist is concerned with delimiting the sources of pollution that can affect health and nafs detrimentally. She talks about water that is drunk at an inappropriate time, as well as water that is emitted in sweat and water that is not emitted but that "dries up in… [the] kidneys" because of inattention to the body's perspiration. Men supposedly catch "bad smells" from women of the street and are "poisoned" by sexual contact with a menstruating woman:

"There is a man who is attacked by the 'bad smell' [14] just from women. And third, God give you blessing sir, don't drink water in the public bath, you see, it's like embers that were hot and [then] put out. Don't drink a bottle of soda in hot weather when you're sweaty, your nafs won't live. Don't drink water from the refrigerator, your health won't last. Don't breakfast with black coffee, it kills nafs. Us women, even if we eat rocks, they leave because we have wide cans. [15] Men have livers like 'scarves of life' [a transparent and thin material]. Don't be sweaty and then lean on a wall, that's the sickness of the spine. Don't be sweaty and get out of a car when you're sweaty, that makes your sperm dry up in your testicles.

"My Lord said in the Qur'an, because of His word He is most high, after {'God save us from the cursed Satan, Man should look from whence he was created.' [CA]} Did the Prophet say this verse or is it counterfeit? {'Man should look from whence he was created. He was created from water flowing between the loins and chest' [CA]}

"That drop of water that comes from the spinal cord of the back, where does it pour into?[16] Half of it goes to this kidney and half of it goes to the other kidney. What do you ejaculate, blood or pus? Whoever is sweaty and gets out of a car, his sperm dries up in his spinal cord.

"The fourth [one] to avoid, God give you blessing, don't get together with a menstruating woman. God has advised against periods. The Prophet said, Prayers and peace be upon him, 'Whoever looks upon a menstruating woman, is like someone who has eaten a viper with its poison.' If you want to stay a clean and beautiful man, the first thing, I'm going to show it to you. I didn't hear you say, 'God have mercy on the parents.'"

"God have mercy on the parents," followed the audience.

The "pollution" in this segment refers to liquids that leave and are taken into the body, which is a thoroughfare for properties or values that may take up temporary or permanent residence. It is just this ability for giving passage that both pollutes and purifies the individual; for not only filth, but also blessing (*baraka*) may be incorporated through bodily contact and ingestion.[17] Clearly certain sites of the biological body (particularly its entrances, exits, and organs of transformation) provide experiential and symbolic access to the social categories that shape conceptions of the world (see Douglas 1982; Laquer 1986; Mauss 1973; O'Neill 1985). But where the body is open, it is also vulnerable. Thus the herbalist warns men of the dangers of ingesting cold substances when the body is hot: "don't drink water in the public bath," she says, "it's like embers that were hot and [then] put out." "Don't drink water from the refrigerator, your health won't last." But the herbalist constructs the male body as vulnerable not because it is open so much as because it is permeable and frail. If a man drinks black coffee for breakfast, "it kills nafs"; women, on the other hand, have a hardier constitution. The fragility of the male body is poignantly rendered and is not contested by anyone in the audience. In underscoring the vulnerability of the male body, the herbalist feminizes it, for weakness and vulnerability are characteristics of the feminine, and not the masculine, world. Women's bodies, by contrast, are constructed as strong, their experience with crossing boundaries (as preparers of food and givers of life) making them more "masculine" than men themselves.[18]

Three of the dangers the herbalist warns about have a relation with commodities that have become extremely common in the last ten years—soda, refrigerators, and cars. The herbalist draws on traditional notions of bodily contagion and applies them to the relatively new situations created by the encounter with commodification and the world economy.[19] The herbalist has a cure not only for magical spells, but for the illnesses of modernity. Before she offers it, however, she wants to make sure that the audience knows her credentials.

"With Authorization, with Papers": The Public Construction of Authority

"Come here, Mister Khalid [a generic name]. Whoever gathers his hands together with me, I never want thorns to enter his bones. Whoever is too proud to do it with me, his hands are paralyzed at his sides. Put your hands like this with me. Put your hands with me. Gather them together with me, God give you sirs blessing.

"You see, it's now a month that I've been here with you. I'm going to pass out a copy of my address to all of you. I have a residence in Casablanca and a residence in Marrakech. My residence is in Doukala [the region of Casablanca].

"Whoever lies to you, may he go blind in both eyes. I have a shop in l-Qri'a, in Casablanca. I buy and sell medicine, herbs. I have an herb that is worth five hundred thousand francs a kilo, with authorization, with papers. And I'm a daughter of veins, not a daughter of diapers. Do you think just anyone can follow this profession? Well, I'm following my grandfather's grandfathers."

The herbalist defends herself against the criticism that a woman in the marketplace might encounter. She refers to her grandfathers and, in the following segment, to her sons. There are men backing her, she asserts, delineating a male genealogy of influence. Furthermore, she is a pious Muslim, a woman in mourning who does not indulge in genres of speech, like lying and gossip, that are inappropriate and informal[20]:

"Stand just next to me. Don't tell me what's ailing you. The sickness that you have, I'll tell you [what it is], just with my eyes, without putting this scale in my hands. I've gone to Medina, to the tomb of the Prophet five times. Seven times I've done the minor pilgrimage (*ḥajj*) to the tomb of the Prophet. Here I am wearing mourning clothes. A month and fifteen days ago I lost my husband. He wasn't sick a day or two or an hour or two. He slept and the owner of his faith took his faith. Between his death and my father's, two months. God remember us in his rulings. He said to you [*gal-lək*]: When God wants something, he says 'Be' and it is. Now, he's dead and he's standing here with me. I don't know [if he's] with you or with me.

"And whoever is wearing these [mourning] clothes mustn't speak foolish words. She mustn't gossip. Because she's in the time of mourning. I have ten children, Praise God and thank him. I have men [that are] lions. I can't show them to you, where they are. But if you want me to show them to you, I'll show them to you.

"You see, people with reason say, 'the [splinter of] wood that you laugh at is that which will blind your eyes.'"

When the herbalist refers to her children as men who are "lions," she is defending her honor. The need for self-defense arises because she has crossed the symbolic line of male-gendered space, both with her (feminine) presence in the (masculine) market and in the thematic space of her discourse, wherein she charts new territories of the permissible in feminine speech. At first she says that she cannot show these "lions" — they are, after all, a symbol of the hidden dimension (and may even be fictional). But in keeping with her practice of opening boundaries, she reconsiders and says, "if you want me to show them to you, I'll show them." She asserts her right to be in the market and offers to bring what is usually left at home and hidden (children, food, sexuality) to public attention.

The herbalist is engaged in her own validation in the marketplace. Not only does she assert her honesty and honorability,[21] but she makes herself accountable to her audience by passing out slips of paper with her address on it, a written guarantee that recalls the practice of charm writing and similarly invokes the symbolic power of the written word (Spratt and Wagner 1986; Eickelman 1992). But if the audience have any doubt about her legitimacy as a healer and public speaker, the herbalist warns them with a proverb, an "official" (because traditional) genre, which she frames as reported speech[22]: "You see (*rah*),[23] people with reason say, 'the [splinter of] wood that you laugh at is that which will blind your eyes.'" Something considered small and inconsequential (a splinter of wood) is often quite powerful. Thus the herbalist implies that underestimating women's power in the marketplace may have unexpected and detrimental consequences for those who choose to deny its agency. Indeed people with reason (*l-'aqlin* [MA]) would never deny it. Of course, those with reason (*'aql*) in traditional Moroccan ideology are thought to be men; women and children are inherently deficient in this characteristic (Eickelman 1976; Rosen 1984; cf.

Abu-Lughod 1986). Her comments thus assert that men with reason do not scorn women's new position in the marketplace.

Embodying Difference: The Ritual Ingestion of Herbs and Words

At the same time that the herbalist is asserting her genealogical claim to male authority, she is also positioning the bodies of her audience. She places her hands together, palms up, in the common attitude of supplication when speaking a daʿwa. She circles around the audience, placing her hands before them and instructing them to assume a like posture. It is a posture of submission and vulnerability. After several men have complied, she begins distributing samples of her herbal morsels directly into their open palms. She refers to these morsels as gold:

"Praise God and thank him. A doctor has never examined my health. And a doctor has never come to my house. And a needle has never entered my flesh. God give you all the health that I have.

"A piece of gold…" She distributed some morsels. "I'm going to buy my acquaintance with a man or a woman. I want him to ask for me here on Tuesday. I'm going to give this mercy to all of you. Here's a piece. A piece. A piece. I didn't hear anyone say, 'God have mercy on the parents.'"

"God have mercy on the parents," the audience repeated.

The herbalist draws on notions of pollution, equating them with the "modern" medical system: "A doctor has never examined my health," she says using the verb *kashafa*, which also means "to open up," or "lay bare" [CA]. These words construct her as inviolate to an institution that is invasive of both home and body; being healthy means being closed to this system. Indigenous health practices work more in sympathy with the body's natural boundaries than in conflict with them. They are based on a system of "hot" and "cold" designations where sickness (most often considered on the cold end of the spectrum) may be treated either by quickly tapping the skin with a hot iron (performed by a *kuwway* practitioner) or by eating herbs. Although both practices admit of the body's permeability and responsiveness to outside influences (especially those dealing with temperature), they do not pierce the skin as injections or operations do.[24] The herbalist refers to this intrusion in her previous remark as well: "I want never for thorns to enter his bones." Thorns (*shuk*) are synonymous with needles or injections.

This is a clear message about modern medicine; not only is it equated with invasiveness and disease, but its practitioners are strangers. When you go to a European-trained doctor you take a number (*shəd n-nuba*) and wait your turn, sometimes for the better part of a day. There is a factory-like feeling to state-run medicine in Beni Mellal, aggravated by overcrowding of hospitals and lack of funds. These western-modeled institutions are also extremely patronizing; patients are given written prescriptions (that most cannot read) for large quantities of expensive drugs as well as oral directions for their use, but are usually offered few explanations of their condition.[25]

In delimiting what is and should remain "outside" the body and the home, the herbalist defines modernity — its commodities and institutions — as a source of pollution. This applies particularly to money, which by virtue of its ability to establish general equivalence makes possible the radical inversion of the social hierarchy. Yet the herbalist says that she is going to buy her *ma'rifa*,[26] her "acquaintance" or connections. This purchase is not made with money, but with a sample of herbs that she literally *feeds* to her audience. What's more, she refers to the herb morsels as "gold," the universal equivalent par excellence.[27] The ingestion of "gold" effects a relationship of reciprocity between the herbalist and her public. She not only bribes her way into a sale, she explicitly combines a capitalist vocabulary with the terms of reciprocity: while the audience is receiving a "gift" that incurs obligation to them, the herbalist "buys" her influence with her clientele, an inversion of customary buy and sell relations. By giving the gift of the gold-like herb morsel, the herbalist utilizes the system of obligation and reciprocity (indexed by the word *ma'rifa*) in order to reinforce the asymmetrical relations between herself and her audience. She refuses monetary payment (at least in this transaction) but exacts it in obligation, the same obligation that is evoked by the da'wa, "God have mercy on the parents." What the herbalist is giving to her audience is, in fact, "mercy," the value that is passed on to the ancestors. What she is getting in return is their obligation to come back next market day. She thus enacts a system of clientelism customary in Morocco wherein "big men" (*l-kbar*) support dependents by obligating them either financially or morally.[28] But the herbalist frames this newly gendered clientelism within the boundaries of buy-and-sell relations. She will not be beholden, but consciously purchases her influence in no uncertain terms. Using the verb "buy" in this context amounts to unmasking and implicitly challenging the rules of the game: it asserts that capitalist relations exist even within the moral economy of reciprocity.

Redress: Speaking the Body

At this point in her discourse, the herbalist begins a much more interactive phase with her audience, eliciting their verbal response and instructing them with words and gestures to assume different bodily postures.

"This little bit that I'm going to give you, what is it useful for? By God, I'm not going to tell you what it's for unless you ask, 'Why?'"

"What is it used for, lalla?" several in the audience asked.

"By God I didn't hear you."

"What is it used for?" more people repeated.

"Listen to what I'm going to say. And remember my words. If you don't go in here, you'll leave by there. First, give me those that are going [she puts her hands on her lower back, as if in pain] and those that rest their hands [here] because of a [sick] liver. He complains of his spinal column. He screams about these. Half of this [she points to the groin] had died for him. He's lame with them. Desire is dead. You're no longer a man. Remember what I say. You see, I'm talking to you!

"You get up four or five times a night. You can't hold your urine. Go ask for me on Sundays in El Ksiba. You see, lines from here to there. He spends the night going in and out. A woman with a stinking uterus. You're no longer a man.

"If I let some doctor yet examine your body, between me and you, he that we all share is the Prophet."

"Prayers and peace be upon him," the audience said softly.

"You're a witness of God [she points to individuals in the audience]. You're a witness of God. You're a witness of God. You're a witness of God. You're a witness of God. You're a witness of God.

"If I give you my herbs and you drink them, you've washed the kidneys. And you've straightened the spinal column. And you've given life to your self with your children. And you've gotten rid of asthma in your chest. You see, I'm talking to you with doing and saying.

"I've beautified your stomach. And I've enlivened your nafs. And I've opened your desire to eat. And I've strained off the heavy blood. And I've washed the woman's uterus. And I've left the man like an illumined diamond. And I've left the woman like a diamond. Do I merit some recompense [ajər] or not?"

"You merit it."

"By God, I didn't hear you."

"You merit it," the crowd repeated.

In outlining the symptoms of her audience, the herbalist uses a kines-
thetic and deictic vocabulary, one that points to particular people and body
parts and depends on the unchallenged attention of her audience in order
to be effective. She actually performs the experiences of pain, holding her
back, placing her hands "here," and motioning to the genital area instead of
speaking the taboo. Insofar as she is demonstrating not her own state (*ḥal*)
but theirs, her communication includes and activates the sensations of her
audience, being based on sympathetic energies. "To attend to a bodily sensation," says Csordas (1993 : 138), "is not to attend to the body as an isolated
object, but to attend to the body's situation in the world. The sensation
engages something in the world because the body is 'always already in the
world.' Attention *to* a bodily sensation can thus become a mode of attend-
ing to the intersubjective milieu that gives rise to that sensation." The herbalist draws the bodies of her audience closer to her, activating both their
verbal and physical response. It is by engaging this embodied aspect of experience that she effects her cure with both "doing and saying." Her speech
is not just "empty talk" (*hadra khawiya*); rather her words, like her herbs,
are performatives: they enact cure.

Her testimony is also an enactment that she verifies by pointing to
individuals and declaring them "witnesses to God" (*shahadat-llah*), thereby
making them accountable to the rest of the audience, "the intersubjective
milieu." Islamic law requires twelve official witnesses for an act to be validated legally. By designating members of the audience as "witnesses to
God," the herbalist guarantees the indelibility of her testimony and the efficacy of her goods. She does not say this twelve times however; her designation is an abbreviated one meant only to index the official discourse of
Qur'anic law and thus partake of its authority. This official validation continues with the repetition of religious supplication and the assumption of
bodily postures equated with worship and subjugation (hands together,
palms up, the posture taken at the end of the prayer sequence, when the
supplicant is asking personal favor from God).

The herbalist's embodiment of the role of a healer of men challenges
social practice by setting new precedent for women's public "dispositions,"
the axiological beliefs expressed in the body. Following Bourdieu (1977),[29]
dispositions of the body are acquired habits — gestures, social stances, and
discursive practices that make up one's *habitus*, the physical and social
environment of a person's upbringing, inseparable from class. In admin-
istering cure to men, the herbalist not only performs a new authoritative
role for women, but challenges the physical and psychological attitudes

that circumscribe them in particular domains of discourse and not in others.

"Whoever helps me with this word, I never want a doctor to examine his health. My God, if you're not in agreement with me on one word, all together, this supplication (*fatḥa*)[30]: Whoever has splintered bones, God weld them."

"Amen."

"Say Amen," directed the herbalist, unsatisfied with the lack of unanimous response.

"Amen," more people repeated.

"How many people are grilled by their pain? Burned by their pain? We don't know [how many] are here. We don't know if they're in the hospital. We don't know if they're in their homes. God teach us. If you send these prayers for blessing, [because] even you don't know if what is supporting you is going to bend [and break]. If you don't say this fatḥa with me: Whoever has splintered bones, God restore them. [He who has] his head lying on a pillow, God raise it and help him. That the healthy never show themselves frightened with their health. The parents, God cover them with mercy. My father and your father, God renew their mercy. Our King, God put him on the narrow path and make his enemies friends. We want our king to come and go preserved. Whoever has something beautiful in his heart, God make him attain it. If you won't put your hands like this with me and say bismiḷḷah ('In the name of God')"

"Bismiḷḷah."

"I also want a blessing from *you*. Agree with me on it, all of you. I also have given you my blessings. You see, I'm away from my children, and away from my relatives. I've taken my leave and am going to the tomb of the Prophet."

"Prayers and peace be upon him," said the audience, responding to mention of the Prophet.

"If you won't say with me a word, all together, this fatḥa: God give me death at the Prophet's [tomb]."

"Amen."

"Whoever doesn't say it, I won't forgive him."

"Oh God, Amen."

"God bring my death at the messenger of God's [tomb]."

"Oh God, amen. Amen."

"By the dignity of the Prophet and Ali. By the dignity of Bokhari and the Prophet's companions.[31] By the dignity of those who believe and trust in him without having seen him. And he is the groom of the nation, our master, Muḥammad. Put your hands [she demonstrates] with me and say "bismillah."

"Bismillah."

"I'm going to give you this mercy piece by piece. And I didn't hear anyone say, 'God have mercy on the parents.'"

"God have mercy on the parents."

"Here's a little bit. Come a little closer to me, those who are over there. Whoever comes close, I know he submits to God. I won't say another word until I see who submits to God. Sit, sir, on the ground, take a rest, woman, on the ground. Are you married?" the herbalist asked one man.

"Yes," he replied.

"Stay. By God, this past night you mounted her! Well, stay." The crowd laughed at the herbalist's bawdiness and someone asked a question [inaudible] to which she responded, "Insha'llah (God willing). Come here by me," she instructed her interlocutor. "Come next to me, you there, move [closer]."

"These men, why did I bring them here? God bring about your integrity for them. What is God going to teach them? But wait until I ask them [this], If you die, will God forgive [me]?" the herbalist said. A man nodded in the affirmative.

"You, too. Will God forgive?" she asked. Another man gave his affirmation.

You, do you still covet worldly existence?" she asked pointedly, making the crowd laugh.

"You don't want to get better? You too, God will forgive? You too, God will forgive? That is... did they say that from their hearts? They said it just from here [points to her throat] to here [points to her tongue]. May God make them die on Sunday. Say Amen."

"Amen," the audience repeated.

"And may God favor you, too, with waste and nakedness and emptiness.

Say Amen. You don't want this?"

"We don't want it."

"God favor you with addiction," she continued. "God give you nakedness. God favor you with the wilderness."

The herbalist withholds information in this segment, asking her audience didactic questions whose response serves to make them co-participants in the performance (Brenneis 1986; Duranti 1986). As Goody notes (1978), asking questions is often a means of asserting status and power. In this case, such question and answer techniques function to construct the herbalist's position as the master of ceremonies (Besnier 1989a; Brown and Levinson 1978). She manipulates her audience into compliance by conflating obedience to her instructions with deference to God: "Whoever comes close, I know he submits to God. I won't say another word until I see who submits to God."

The herbalist has given her blessing to the audience and, in the spirit of reciprocity, clearly wants them to give her a blessing as well. Her supplication that she might have the fortune of dying at the Prophet's tomb is said in a context of communion, or "communitas"; for as the people are holding their hands towards heaven, the herbalist is dropping her herbal remedy into their open palms, beginning a ritual of communal ingestion. But even as the audience is putting the herbs into their mouths, the herbalist asks them if they will forgive her if this ingestion results in their own deaths: "If you die, will God forgive [me]?"

Playful sarcasm is the modus operandi here. The herbalist is making the niya (both the naiveté and the intentions) of her audience visible both to themselves and to each other. Introducing this level of reflexivity, the herbalist calls attention to the unspoken trust, the principles of sincerity, that underlie "the doing and saying" taking place.[32] But while she indirectly condemns the naive trust of her audience, who are, after all, ingesting what could be harmful to them, she also points to their own untruthfulness. She says that their response was only from their throats to their tongues, not from their hearts, a more profound place in the body. Their insincerity (the principle of marketplace communication) is then rejected by the herbalist, who uses common curses to catch the audience up in ludic dialogue: "May God make them die on Sunday. Say Amen.... And may God favor you, too, with waste and nakedness and emptiness." These are common-fare curses that the herbalist has the audience ratify by eliciting their repetition of "amen." By making them reflect on their willingness to follow her rhetorical ploy and curse themselves, the herbalist draws attention to the strategies of interaction at work in marketplace performance, ones that are quite different than those employed in daily social enactments. This meta-pragmatic act further convinces the audience of her authority by making plain its power over them.

Having established her voice and position as an orator and bestower of blessings, the herbalist is at liberty to engage in təfliya, a genre of teasing and playful joking common in the marketplace, especially among equals.

The artfulness of this playful speech lies in her ability to turn her sarcastic curses into sincere blessings, as if demonstrating the transmutability of base metal into gold:

"God addict you to the stars and the dawn. God leave our hearts and your hearts without envy. God make us naked from the failings of worldly existence. God make our faces red on the day our faces are black [Judgment Day].[33] God make us pass where our relative, the Prophet, passed, that no misfortune or bereavement befall us. God take us out of this house of fault without fault."

What is this "house of fault" if not the marketplace itself? A place that the marketgoers are condemned to inhabit, by default to a power larger than their own. She then begins a ritual communion, with humor yet with all the traditional elements and postures of a high ritual—the giving of remedy into hands open in supplication, the crowd sharing a communal cup, the written words of guarantee distributed.

"Here's one morsel that I'm going to give to this man. Bismillah. Open your hand, God give you paradise. I'm going to make conditions with you sir, and they're lawful conditions. You see, I'll be with you next Tuesday. If you conceal [your state] from me, God clothe you in a cloak of leprosy. I'm here with you every Tuesday. On Sundays in El Ksiba. Friday in Bilminsimtah. Saturday in Ouled Said. Tuesday here in Beni Mellal. Wednesday in Zouia Cheikh. Monday in Tadla. Those are the official markets.

"But there are ten days left with you [before I go to Mecca]. God part us without sin. Here's my address. I'm going to give it to this man. Bismillah. This is it [she holds up the herbal remedy]. It has three names. The first name is 'stone-breaker.' The second name is 'wood of communion.' The third name is 'life of desires.'[34] Whoever wants to be a man, make conditions with me. I'll accept your condition and you accept my condition."

Holding up a golden chalice, she continued. "Here's a drinking vessel of gold that I'm going to give to this sir. Here's my handwriting above it. Here's my handwriting above it. Here it is.

"I'm giving my work [address] and I'm giving the address of my house. Drink this medicine and bring this to me and ask for me with it."

The herbalist stipulates that reintegration to manhood depends upon conditions, inherent in all relations of reciprocity. Although the herbalist doesn't make her condition explicit, it is clear that her legitimation in the public realm is predicated as much upon her audience's response as upon her own verbal artistry and herbal savoir-faire. This is demonstrated by the high frequency of turn-taking in this phase of her discourse. One "condition" is that this response be an embodied one; not just a formulaic response, but an acceptance and incorporation of feminine presence into the larger social body. The herbalist offers to accept the conditions of her clients as well, provided they return to her and tell her if the herbs worked or not. She facilitates this return through the written word: a piece of paper with her address on it.

When the herbalist distributes her remedy to her audience, she is not affirming the bonds of a traditional community, since her audience is comprised of both men and women. Rather, by calling upon the rhetorical genres of marketplace oratory, the herbalist is facilitating the emergence of a new community, one which accepts the place of women in the marketplace. In a sense the act of ingestion in the mixed-gender marketplace works to incorporate new notions of what constitutes the social body of community, a body that recodes honor and shame, holy work and secularity, outside and inside, center and periphery.

The herbalist goes on to distinguish women's from men's herbs, implying that there are substances that are appropriate exclusively for women's or men's consumption. The "masculine herbs" are too strong for female ingestion, being as potent as they are economically valuable:

"This has feminine and it has masculine. If a woman goes as far as eating the masculine [herbs], she'll have two hundred on her odometer turning around. This masculine of yours, men, we can't eat it, us women. Here it is.

"This is worth twelve thousand riyals, this masculine [stuff]. Tonight, tonight, Insha'llah, when you want to go to sleep, throw this pill in your mouth like this." The herbalist demonstrated, eating one. "Eat this. Come here. You, too. Do you have some teeth?" The audience laughed.

"Let's go. Chew them. Eat this, chew it up. Be careful that you don't think it's a sweet and begin to suck it." The audience laughed again. "I'm going to give you all a little bit. And say, 'God have mercy on the parents.'"

"God have mercy on the parents."

"You don't have money? God blind me if I give you credit!"

Here commodity relations break through into the performance. The herbalist refuses to give credit—not exactly in keeping with the principles of clientelism. Earlier in the dialogue, she asked, "Do I merit recompense (ajər) or not?" To which the audience replied, "You merit it." Ajər is often associated with spiritual recompense, *ajər-lḷah* being "the recompense of God," but it also means payment in the secular sense. Using euphemism, the herbalist indexes the necessity for cash payment in veiled phrases that minimize the contradiction between reciprocal and commodity relations.

Market Play

Once her rhetorical power has been established, the herbalist's dialogue moves from the formality of call and response to the informality and humor of personal inquiry. She begins by eliciting religious formulae and blessings from the entire group, words that no Muslim would ever refuse to speak aloud, such as the repetition of "Prayers and peace be upon him" after mention of the Prophet's name. The frequent elicitation of the da'wa, "God have mercy on the parents" in the beginning of the performance also contributes to this tone of religiosity, evoking a mood of faithful submission. This accomplished, the herbalist relaxes into a more personal style, directing her questions to individuals and making jokes at their expense:

"When Tuesday comes along, bring me this. Here it is. If you conceal [the truth of the results] from me, God clothe you in a jəllaba of leprosy. Eat this. Throw it in your mouth. Come, you, too. Throw this little bit in your mouth. Come forward, you, too. Are you married or not?"

"No."

"Tonight, by God, you'll have an accident [a sexual encounter] in the harvest field."

"God save us!" the man laughs.

"By God, this night, you [could] put a van between your thighs. Eat this. Open your hand. Do you have some teeth or not? Do you think it's candy? Just put it in your mouth and start to suck it?"

"Just give it to me."

"But I'm giving it to you to CHEW."

"Just give it."

"The moment that you put this morsel in your mouth... God give you blessing sir. Chew it now, next to me, here. The moment you put this morsel in your mouth, you're going to take this herb after it—what I'm going to give you. Here it is. It has three hundred and sixty-five herbs.

Open your hand. Did you eat it?" The man acknowledges that he has ingested the herbs.

"Well, open your hands and eat this little bit. Pour some water. Come here, you, woman! Here." The herbalist motioned to a woman who was leaving the ḥalqa.

"If you go, you'll find that your husband's fled." The crowd laughed.

"And if she doesn't have a husband?" asked one man.

"She doesn't have one," another responded.

"And you see her, frightened that her husband will flee?"[35] exclaimed the herbalist. "Because she knows that men have begun to diminish and women have begun to increase! Follow it with this bit of water," she resumed. "Here it is. Open sir, your hands. God inspire you, sir. Bismillah. Eat this bit. Bismillah. Eat this little bit. Bismillah. Put this little bit in your mouth. Wait and I'll give you a sip of water. Let's go. Get up. Go on your way. On Tuesday, whoever likes his friend will come and look for him."

The herbalist's monologue breaks into dialogue at this point, as the members of the audience accept her herbs, ingest them, and begin to give lively responses to her provocations and sexual innuendoes. The herbalist swears that the herbs will facilitate sexual activity on the very day they're ingested. The herbs are, among other things, "enliveners" of sexual desire. In metaphorically comparing the sexual organ to a van—a symbol of modernity and "big" status—she also hyperbolizes women as possessions that need to be driven well.[36] She is talking to an audience that is about seventy percent male, demonstrating her ability to joke like one of the guys, using language that is overtly transgressive. After teasing a woman who was leaving the ḥalqa, the herbalist also says that men are becoming fewer and fewer—a worrisome thought to women, but an interesting one for men to ponder, as scarcity implies an increase in value.

Her authority achieved, the herbalist cajoles her audience, playing with the boundaries of humor and transgression. Her propositional force is evident (Austin 1962); she performs a new feminine identity and makes it palatable, indeed acceptable, by embedding it in traditional oratory that carries its own authority and power. In continuing the increasingly festive and celebratory ceremony, she finds another opportune moment to mention money:

"Open your hand. Follow it with this little [sip]. Open your hand. Did you eat that little bit? Did you ever eat anything like it? Did you ever eat its twin? By God, this night!

"You see [put] your hands with me like this. I'm going to give you a little. A little. No one said, 'God have mercy on the parents.'"

"God have mercy on the parents."

"Come closer, pay for them."

"God have mercy on the parents."

The mention of payment here is sandwiched between two formal blessings that invoke obligation to the parents. Although the sentence is a directive to produce cash, it is disguised in an intonation and rhythm that aligns it with the parallel blessings that precede and follow it. The fact that the last da'wa is not elicited by the herbalist points to the presence of a shill—a collaborator—in the audience. Complicity notwithstanding, however, the effect of repetition is achieved: the reference to money is hidden in religious formulae, accompanied by the command to "move closer." The herbalist's denial of cash transaction is even more explicit in her finale:

"If you stay, God give you a clean death. I never want a doctor to examine you. Put your hands like this with me. Here's a little bit of what I have. I weighed it with a scale [used for] gold. How much is here? Fifty grams. How much do I sell this gram for and sell this piece for? By God, I won't tell you how much until you say, 'How much?'"

"How much?"

"By God, I didn't hear you!"

"How much?"

"These, this morsel and this, I sell them for one thousand francs. I'm not going to give it to you for this price. I didn't hear anyone say, 'God have mercy on the parents.'"

"God have mercy on the parents."

"I want a man to call me, 'Oh Ḥajja Fatima, give me your goods! Give me the address of your house!'"

The herbalist asks the audience to call on her and express their desire for the herbs and written guarantee. The audience do not need to ask for her address, since she is handing it out with the herbs. At this point, the rhetorical spell has been broken. People are either reaching into their pockets or beginning to move away from the circle. The herbalist continues to talk, giving individual buyers precise instructions on how to use the herbs, finishing by again disacknowledging the monetary transaction:

"Look for me with that address. On Tuesday I'll look for you here. This is what I'm going to give you. If I go back on my word, my faith is sin. These men, how much did they eat? One morsel. Here, sir, you. Here are two. Eat them tonight. Here are two. Eat them this night. Drink this [herb] with them and follow them with a glass of hot tea.

"Here, tomorrow, Insha'llah. Here, tomorrow, Insha'llah. Here are two. Eat these two. Follow them with this. Follow them with this and drink a glass of hot tea afterwards. Here, take this on the third day. Here it is. Here's the third day. Eat these two and follow it with this and drink a glass of hot tea afterwards.

"Here, here's the address of my house, so I know you took the medicine. Hit your hand in your pocket and give me one thousand francs from the sweat of your shoulder. But I want you to close your eyes and open the eyes of God. You are blessed, sir, you are blessed."

In the final play, the herbalist exhorts her clients to "hit their pockets" and pull out one thousand francs (ten dirhams or about $1.25) using a colloquialism expressing familiarity with her audience and equating money with the physical sweat of the labor that produced it. But she asks this payment be made with their eyes closed, a final refusal of the terseness and impersonality of commodity relations. "I want you to close your eyes and open the eyes of God," she says. Do not look at the monetary exchange. Open, rather, the eyes of the spirit, and thereby receive blessing.

The herbalist's explicit disacknowledgement of money even within the context of market exchange is as much a reaction to her own commodification (as a new woman player in the marketplace) as it is to the contradictions that result when one value system is infiltrated by another. Recourse to a common moral ethic is necessary to validate the herbalist's claim to tradition and authority.[37] In this sense, an opening in the performative economy is also a re-inscription into institutionalized convention. Yet the herbalist uses the generic discourse of tradition to create a very untraditional event: the construction of female authority in encounters in the public sphere. She employs the powers of persuasion inherent in the genre of marketplace oratory to reposition the embodied attitudes of a community toward what is appropriate to do and say in this realm. Not only does she assert her bodily presence in the marketplace, but she effects a transformation in the physical and psychological attitudes of her audience (their habitus), "submitting" them to the ingestion of herbs and words that challenge conventional notions of womanhood.

Oratory as Ritual

The carnival ambience of the suq allows for the relaxation of interactional norms which reign in the more private segments of life, providing a fertile ground for the emergent expression of new social identities.[38] But the marketplace is not an all-out carnival. Not all rules are suspended, but all may be contested. Contestation enacts movement, which in turn effects changes in social order.

Victor Turner ventures that all cultural performances bear within them a meta-communicative and explanatory function that attempts to make social sense of schism, ambiguity, and division through "public reflexivity" (1990:11); society sees and knows itself through its enactment of ritual, including the ritualized language of oratory. Such social dramas, he asserts, consist of four stages: "breach, crisis, redress, and reintegration or schism."[39] Like the discourse of the majduba, the oratory of the herbalist is intricately connected to ritual by way of thematic structure; it is concerned with "redressing" a crisis through "divination into the hidden causes of misfortune, personal and social conflict, and illness." Although marketplace oratory does not enact cure on the spot, it does define/divine social conflict and offer a remedy.

Within the herbalist's performance the entire drama of social change is enacted. By breaking the social custom of topical taboo she enacts a breach; by introducing contradiction (exemplified not least by a feminine revoicing of a male speech genre), she identifies a general crisis of social pollution, of gender and genre boundary dissolution; by consequently manipulating the bodies and postures of her audience, the herbalist enacts a redress, a re-attainment of equilibrium; and by literally feeding the audience her herbs — creating a ritual of group ingestion — she enacts re-integration. The herbalist then guarantees the reintegration of her clients' state (*ḥal*) by handing out pieces of paper with her address written on them so that they may come and hold her accountable if the herbs do not work, the written word here symbolizing the link of community.

The herbalist employs the same four stages of social drama in her thematic discussion; she identifies a breach between the sexes that is also a breach between "man" and God; this results in the crisis of losing one's selfhood, exemplified in the loss of one's desire life; this crisis is then redressed by the ingestion of remedial herbs, which, in turn, effect a reintegration of the self with the body, soul, and spirit.

Oratory as Politics

Although not explicitly political, the oratory of the herbalist encodes notions of power and status. As a woman orator she is obliged to justify her presence in the marketplace, tracing her genealogy along male lines and putting herself in the company of religious and medical authority figures. She blesses the King and makes frequent and appropriate bows to the ancestors. Yet the herbalist is neither humble nor self-abasing (cf. Bloch 1975; Keenan 1975), going to elaborate lengths to publicize her talents and validate her approach. She revoices the highly codified genre of oratory to instantiate her legitimacy in the marketplace.

The architecture of the herbalist's performance moves from a monologue containing quoted scripture to a dialogue of ribald joking (*təfliya*). Throughout, the herbalist makes her rhetorical and curative expertise evident to her audience, blessing and cursing them and manipulating their verbal responses and bodily postures. The fact that a woman is enacting a ritual ingestion and communal blessing in the marketplace effects a shift in gender relations. Employing the gestures and stances of a man — and eliciting the verbal and bodily responses *due* a man — the herbalist uses her rhetorical powers to transform the embodied attitudes, the actual habitus, of her audience in regard to gender.

The oratory of the herbalist is motivated by the desire to sell a homemade concoction that restores a man's potency and well-being. As commodity her herbs have a particular social life[40]: not only do they facilitate a discourse across gender boundaries, but they actually cross the boundaries of the body as they are ritually ingested in a performance context that literally incorporates new notions of value into the individual and social body. More than herbs, what is being sold is a changing value for the feminine presence in the public sphere. In offering remedies for illness and spells — something male herbalists also offer — the herbalist provides a verbal antidote to the feminine stereotypes that dominate the marketplace. What's more, her bodily presence desegregates the public realm of the market, reorienting relations between gender and genre. In this case, a discourse analysis that does not take the body into consideration is one that fails to grasp the import of change and exchange in the expressive and material economies.

The saliency of issues of honor and shame in women's marketplace oratory in Beni Mellal is a clear indicator that definitions of these codes are in flux. The multi-referentiality of pronouns and the porosity of quoted speech contributes to this state. The contradictory logics at work in marketplace oratory reflect the ambivalent status of women who, in their appropriation of a male role and an often misogynist rhetoric, are also voicing a feminine presence into the public realm. While the herbalist is in breach of the mourning prohibition, she rationalizes her presence in the marketplace by publicly announcing the death of the male family members who might otherwise support her. Whether or not her audience notices the discrepancy between what is said and who is saying it, however, there is one reaction that is common to the herbalist's oratory: *a wayli, ḥshuma hadək shi*, "damnation, that's shameful!"

In contemporary Morocco "the boundaries of the community within which communication is possible [as well as] the boundaries of the situations within which communication occurs" are changing (Hymes 1964 : 3). These changes are not only discernible in the discourse, but are enacted by it. Although women marketers employ conventional speech patterns, drawing upon an established tradition of multivocalic performance, they are also appropriating strategies, expanding repertoires, and putting the functionality of linguistic codes, bodily dispositions, cognitive categories of gender and conventional moral evaluation into serious discursive question. If the embodied words of marketplace women are still somewhat shameful, their discursive practices are nonetheless creating an honorable position for women in the general marketplace by stretching the limits of the permissible in the public domain.

Notes

1. On formality and oratory see Bloch (1975); Brenneis and Myers (1984) Irvine (1979).

2. This is not the only equation operative in Moroccan conceptions of selfhood, of course.

3. The crisis described by the herbalist is the actual disintegration of the man who, lacking desire, loses both his woman and the value of his soul. In this state he appears as a donkey, the animal on the lowest end of the value scale in Morocco, an animal that bears other people's burdens and is subjected to their will. The herbalist goes on to emphasize that a man without nafs (by which we understand a man who is impotent in both a sexual and a social sense) is not a man at all. There are two elements that must be taken into account here. The first is that illness, in general, is equated with femininity, as it exemplifies weakness and vulnerability. Crapanzano notes that "The symptomatology of many of the illnesses—paralysis of the limbs,

pinching bones, impotence — suggests an inability to play the male role; barrenness and children's diseases prevent the continuation of the male line. Illness, especially for men, is conceived at some level of consciousness as an inability to live up to the ideal standards of male conduct. That is, illness is associated with being rendered a woman. Feelings of inadequacy, weakness, and impotence are symbolized by the female" (1973:224). The second is that, given the system of filial piety and the dominant social definitions of man and womanhood in Morocco, sons are always constructed in a feminine relation to their father: "In order to obtain his father's baraka — to live up to the male ideal — the son must play the passive role before the father (and identify with the mother). He must be as woman to the father" (Crapanzano 1973:224). This situation creates very poignant conflicts for Moroccan males, conflicts that are all the more aggravated given the presence of alternate systems of relationship (the reification of the nuclear over the extended family on television, for example, or the related paradigm of commodity relations which grants power to whoever possesses capital, not honor). The third and equally vital fact necessary to the interpretation of the crisis the herbalist is invoking is that the most frequent bewitchment of men by women (called *tqaf* "closing") results in the man's sexual impotency, that is, in his emasculation. This carries the subject to the heart of the complicated discourse on magic. The herbalist is referring to a very real and multidimensional crisis (or set of crises) that everyone in her audience is subject to. While this section of her spiel is not so reliant upon ideas of magical intervention, its importance surfaces elsewhere.

4. I am grateful to Dr. Abdelaziz Abbassi for calling my attention to this.

5. It is an acknowledged truism that women outlive their husbands, often because men are older than their wives at the time of marriage.

6. Abu-Lughod's remarks concerning the Egyptian Bedouins are relevant here: "Because men's positions in the hierarchy are validated by the voluntary deference shown them by their dependents, withdrawal of this respect challenges men's authority and undermines their positions. In the eyes of others, a dependent's rebellion dishonors the superior by throwing into question his moral worth, the very basis of his authority" (1986:158).

7. Bakhtin illuminates the qualities of the mennipean satire, as it diverged from epic, legend, tragedy. Although there are many differences between marketplace discourse and the mennipea, there are also some marked similarities. For example, Bakhtin says, "Very characteristic for the mennipea are scandal scenes, eccentric behavior, inappropriate speeches and performances, that is, all sorts of violations of the generally accepted and customary course of events and the established norms of behavior and etiquette, including manners of speech. These scandals are sharply distinguished by their artistic structure from epic events and tragic catastrophes. They are also different in essence from comic brawls and exposés. One could say that in the mennipea new artistic categories of the scandalous and the eccentric emerge which are completely foreign to the classical epic and to the dramatic genres. ... Scandals and eccentricities destroy the epic and tragic wholeness of the world, they make a breach in the stable, normal ('seemly') course of human affairs and events, they free human behavior from the norms and motivations that predetermine it" (1984b:117).

8. *Mizan*, literally "measure." This object resembled a small hourglass filled with clear liquid. By holding the bottom globe in one hand and the hand of her client in the other, the herbalist purported to divine the illness of her subject by examining how much liquid rose to the top globe. She did not use the device in this performance except as a prop.

9. See L. Abu-Lughod (1986); Bourdieu (1966); Caton (1990); Meeker (1979) and Peristiany (1966) for discussions of honor in Arab and/or Mediterranean societies.

10. On the audience as co-author of a performance see Brenneis (1986); Gumperz (1982); Haviland (1986); Hymes (1974).

11. The belief that sickness is often "cold" is part of an Islamic medical canon with origins in the Middle Ages, see Nasr (1964).

12. Morocco is a commodity society in terms of its material economy, but its moral economies are overwhelmingly concerned with prestations and the long-term reciprocity characteristic of gift societies. *ʿti-ni, n-ʿti-k*, "give to me and I'll give to you," is a common expression in Morocco. Obligation inheres in sociability and does not end with the acquisition of either goods or services. The elaborate discourse of bargaining—its blessings, oaths, and artistry—reveals this clearly: not only is a chicken being purchased, but a social value system is being recognized and continually reauthorized. Applied to the Moroccan context, Rosen (1984:) has gone so far as to say that "every relationship implies an obligation. To be related in a particular degree of kinship, to another's neighbor, to be the client of a merchant in a bazaar carries with it certain expectations of potential recompense. Indeed, every act requires some form of reciprocation as an aspect of its very nature: every act creates an obligation or expresses a right asserted."

The concept of obligation has been given much consideration by students of Morocco. Both Eickelman (1976) and Rosen (1984) explicate the term haqq in referring to a system of uneven reciprocity and negotiated power relations. To have haqq "in" or "over" someone means that one maintains a position of dominance over a person with an outstanding debt of reciprocity. As Eickelman notes, "If a person repeatedly asks for a service to be rendered but is incapable of full reciprocation, then he falls into a client relationship with the other person. The dominant partner in the relationship is said to hold an 'obligation over' (*haqq ʿala*) or "word" (*kalma*) over the other" (1981:182). These debts may be incurred even in such mundane actions as social greetings or invitations to meals. Because of its relation to issues of power and control, haqq plays a role in definitions of honor: honor accrues to those who are not obligated, but who have the power to obligate others (see Bourdieu 1966).

The concept of obligation also includes that of duty, especially in regards to notions of filial piety, the duty one owes to one's parents. In this context the term used is often *wajib*, from the classical Arabic meaning "obligation" or "necessity." It is an index of the influence of literacy that wajib is coming to replace the more colloquial haqq to express relations of obligation and duty. Children learn poems about wajib in grammar school. One such poem is the following, in which debt to one's mother (al-wajib) is clearly distinguished from what she has a "right" to expect (al-haqq):

awjabu al-wajibāti ikrāmu ummī
inna ummī aḥaqqu bi al-ikrāmi.

I owe generous duties to my mother
as my mother has a right to generosity.

Political rhetoric also employs this distinction between al-wajib and al-ḥaqq. With the advent of the war in the Sahara, political slogans rallied the populace around nationalist issues and encouraged young men to enlist in the army by talking about one's duty (wajib) to the country. One such slogan, which clearly dichotomizes "duty" towards and "rights" over is the following:

Fi waṭanika, ʿalay-ka wājibāt (pl.) wa ʿalay-ka ḥuqūq.
In your country, you have duties and rights.

In these contexts, as in others, ḥaqq may be said to index one's rights or power over others, whereas wajib expresses a moral sense of obligation to people and institutions that are higher in the social hierarchy.

This study employs the term wajib to refer to an aspect of the Moroccan moral economy that values the notions of duty toward one's parents (and one's nation) and obligation in social relations of reciprocity.

13. Intricately involved with *l-kəlma*, the "word" of the father, the system of obligation has historically been perpetuated with the exchange of women. Although a means of measuring equivalence exists in this system (for example, when the son embraces paternity and, himself, acquires l-kəlma) actual relations of equality are never fully attained, even when the father dies (Crapanzano 1973). Capitalist relations, on the other hand, represent the possible subversion of this hierarchy by introducing another measure: money. The privileging of monetary relations makes the (oedipal) usurpation of l-kəlma a matter of revolutionary immediacy instead of a lifetime process. Autonomy is bought, not bartered. The potential ability of women to participate in this acquisition of capital gains (an arduous process with many adversaries) adds yet another wrinkle to an already fraying social fabric.

14. *Al-khnəz*, literally "the stink"; this refers to sexually transmitted infection and disease.

15. This euphemism for women's bottoms elicited laughter from the primarily male audience. This laughter does not diminish the serious implication of the herbalist's following statement. Men "have livers like 'scarves of life'," a transparent and thin material; they are not able to pass rocks. Not only are their organs incapable of handling rough materials, but their very skins do not protect them from disease. ("Passing rocks" is a pertinent metaphor in Beni Mellal, as there is a lot of calcium in the water and many people are afflicted with kidney stones.)

16. In his discussion of the concept of baraka, Crapanzano notes that "It is rumored that some saints and their descendants cure sick women by having sexual relations with them; they give them their baraka directly. Semen is, according to the Moroccans of the Ḥamadsha's background [a Moroccan sufi sect], produced by a

"vein" in the man's back that extends downward to the lumbar region. This vein converts blood into semen; blood itself is said to contain baraka and is frequently employed in Moroccan cures and magical practices" (1973:49–50).

17. Crapanzano documents the transference of baraka through the drinking of endowed bodily fluids in the legends of the Ḥamadsha (1973). Ingestion of baraka, however, is evidenced within the discourse that we have already examined, as when, for example, the majduba says that one of the herbs in her incense was grown in the woods of the tomb of her saint, Moulay Ibrahim, or, in a segment not examined here, when she encourages a woman in the audience to come to the tomb so that she may drink the water from the well there. Both the herb and the water are held to embody the baraka of the sacred ground of Moulay Ibrahim.

18. Brandes (1980) has suggested that similar inversions in San Blas, Andalucia are actually psychoanalytic "projections" of characteristics that are inherent to one sex and not the other. The portrayal of men's bodies as weak and vulnerable may be seen as a projection of feminine state onto a male role, but there is good reason to believe that this is not what is happening in the case of market women in Morocco. Rather, discourse such as the herbalist's articulates a subordinate belief system that need only be spoken aloud to be communally recognized.

19. In the same segment, the herbalist warns about social intercourse with those who are worse than oneself. "Make friends with someone better than you, not worse," she says, calling attention to social hierarchy. Note that she does not say someone "richer." In fact, richer is not necessarily better in the herbalist's estimate. Capitalism and commodity relations are at odds with the hierarchy based on adherence to the predominant moral canon. Commodity relations divide the shaʻb; people with money become snobs (sh-shiki), losing their relation with the humble people (n-nas d-drawsh) to whom the herbalist is speaking. The division between common people and "the sons of money" (ulad l-flus) is emotionally charged, especially when unemployment is widespread and "the sons of the bourgeoisie," (ulad l-bourgeoisie) get the few jobs that exist because of their connections (maʻrifa).

20. On the genre of gossip see Abrahams (1970); Bauman (1986); Besnier (1989); Brenneis (1984a); Haviland (1977).

21. See Bauman (1986) for a discussion of the "public fiction" of telling the truth in narratives that accompany transaction in the marketplace.

22. See Lucy (1993); Volosinov (1973) on reported speech.

23. Rah ("you see") is a discourse marker that calls attention to the speech which follows it, much like "that is," in English; see Schiffren (1987).

24. The practice of bloodletting or siphoning is an exception to this. Although it is no longer a prevalent medical practice, it is still done.

25. Some Moroccans believe that institutionalized medicine is deliberately mystified, to the benefit of physicians who, they assert, have pre-arranged percentage agreements with pharmacists. Some Moroccan doctors are themselves beginning to bemoan a loss of wholism found in more traditional systems (see Akhmisse 1985).

26. It is pertinent that two of the terms discussed here — maʻrifa, and ḥal — have sacred as well as secular semantic dimensions. Maʻrifa in the sacred Sufi realm means "gnosis"; a state (ḥal) of knowing (in terms of being one with) God. In secular usage, however, it is equated with a system of mutual aid based upon "know-

ing" or acquaintance with others. To say that someone got a job or a promotion because of ma'rifa means that "connections" played a big part. Ma'rifa in the secular realm is a system of networking, and, of course, it is successful to the extent that the people involved are "high power."

27. Goux (1990:16) notes: "Now the world of commodities converges towards this exclusive form (historically, gold), relating unanimously to this 'universal equivalent' that functions in its 'social monopoly' as money; the manifold world of commodities becomes centered, centralized around what confers a value—a fixed worth, or price—on each commodity." He also discusses the conflation of gold with other terms of hegemonic power.

28. Both Rosen (1984) and Brown (1977) note that client-patron relations are not exclusively controlled by the patron in Morocco; rather, they depend upon interpersonal negotiations. In the marketplace, this is also true.

29. Bourdieu follows Mauss (1973) in his delineation of the bodily aspects, or "techniques," of social practice.

30. A *fatha*, literally an "opening," is very much like a da'wa except that a fatha cannot be a curse; it is restricted to "good" supplications to God and the invocation of blessing.

31. Bokhari compiled one major edition of the *hadith*, the collected sayings and deeds of the Prophet.

32. See Grice (1975) on sincerity and intention in speech acts.

33. In this context, a "red" face is a proud and blameless one, whereas a "black" face is associated with the sin that is brought to light on the Day of Judgment.

34. *hyat an-nufus*. Nufus is the plural of nafs.

35. The herbalist laughs at her own ruse; for despite the fact that the woman isn't married, she was intimidated by the herbalist and stayed in the halqa.

36. See chapter seven for a further discussion of women as vehicles.

37. See Bauman (1992) on "traditionalization."

38. As Abrahams (n.d.) notes, the market is a world "in which openness and the possibility of transformation become normal expectations. From this perspective, markets operate in parallel with ritual time-spaces in important ways." Agnew has examined the historical interrelation of the marketplace and the theater, noting that as "religious drama gradually extricated itself from the confines of the church, the medieval market square became the site where actors and spectators—the roles were interchangeable—could mime, mum, and mock the hierarchical principles of the surrounding society" (1986:33).

39. Although "crisis" is a strong word in the context of the marketplace, it serves to call attention to the potentially radical changes that are affected there, however incrementally.

40. See Appadurai (1986) and Kopytoff (1986) respectively for an exploration of the "social life" and "biography" of things.

5. Reporting the New, Revoicing the Past: Marketplace Oratory and the Carnivalesque

In 1935, Roman Jakobson noted that all art is influenced by an overarching principle, what the Russian Formalists called the "dominant" (1971:82), a structuring orientation characterizing a work or even an entire epoch. Although a narrative may have many functions and embody several forms, an internal hierarchy exists which determines the relative value of its components. The dominant of poetic language is the aesthetic function — its form. Poetry is oriented toward the sign, while prose narrative is directed toward the referent.[1] "Poetic evolution," says Jakobson, "is a shift in this hierarchy."

Marketplace oratory is only sometimes poetic. It is also prosaic[2] and conversational, embodying official discourses of scriptural citation as well as colloquial cursing and blasphemy. Where then, is its integrity, its "dominant"?

The expressive forms examined here are characterized by their relation to the carnivalesque, which Bakhtin defines as an oral or written literature whose subject is present experience (rather than history), and whose forms rely on "free invention." Carnivalized genres contest their own bounds, resisting dominance; they are anti-genres,

> multi-styled and hetero-voiced. . . . They reject the stylistic unity (or better, the single-styled nature) of the epic, the tragedy, high rhetoric, the lyric. Characteristic of these genres are a multi-toned narration, the mixing of high and low, serious and comic; they make wide use of inserted genres — letters, found manuscripts, retold dialogues, parodies on the high genres, paradically reinterpreted citations; in some of them we observe a mixing of prosaic and poetic speech, living dialects and jargons (. . . direct bilingualism as well) are introduced, and various authorial masks make their appearance. Alongside the representing word there appears the *represented* word; in certain genres a leading role is played by the double-voiced word. And what appears here, as a result, is a radically new relationship to the word as the material of literature. (Bakhtin 1981:108)

This "radically new relationship to the word" comes about through double-voicing and revoicing the words of others, often in parodic or reflexive language. Carnivalesque expression enters the domain of the ludic, playing with multiple forms and meanings to ensure that neither a genre nor a subject can be circumscribed or fixed, that both are always in a state of "unfinalized transition" (Bakhtin 1984a: 164; cf. Berrechild 1977, 1993; Mniai 1990; Saddiki 1991 on Moroccan festive theater).

Marketplace oratory makes contradiction its dominant, the obligatory open text. To this end, it combines religious discourse with the most bawdy of innuendoes and is not ashamed. The very law of marketplace genres is the breaking of the law of combination — genres which, separately, have an indexical relation to the serious (scripture, oaths), the transcendent (proverb, axioms), or even the comic produce a different pragmatic aura when

Figure 11. Moulay Omarr, a storyteller in the marketplace, recounts the wondrous deeds of 'Antar in Moroccan Arabic. The yellowed book in his lap is in classical Arabic. He uses it as proof that he's not just making up "lies."

juxtaposed or mixed together. Thus notions of both genre and the subject are fractured; and ideals of wholeness and impermeability are mocked. The confounding of boundaries characteristic of the carnivalesque relies on semantic excess; in marketplace oratory, this is evidenced in the use of reported speech.

Strategies of Reportage: The Recontextualization and Revoicing of Genres

> The way discourse is ordered in a given society is the most sensitive and comprehensive register of how all its other ideological practices are ordered, including its religion, education, state organization, and police. Cultures can be classified as open or closed according to the way in which they handle reported speech. (Clark and Holquist 1984: 237)

The use of reported speech in the discourse of all of these market women provides important keys to understanding not only how new meanings emerge from received knowledge, but how different meanings and time-frames become co-inhabitants of familiar or traditional forms. At stake here is not the radical act of supplanting one meaning or paradigm with another (commodity relations have not replaced those of reciprocity); rather the impact of the two systems results in hybrid forms of social interaction wherein the values of one infiltrate the discourses of another.

Reported speech plays an essential role in Islamic theology and exegesis, especially as far as the *hadith* is concerned. Hadith, which literally means "report" or "narrative," refers to the oral record (now transcribed) of the utterances and deeds of the Prophet. These reports contain two parts: the *isnād*, or genealogical chain of witnesses responsible for transmitting the narrative, and the *matn*, the account itself (Humphreys 1991; Juynboll 1983; cf. Spellberg 1994). Three types of hadith are recognized: (1) true narrative (*hadith sahih*), (2) good narrative (*hadith hasan*), and (3) weak narrative (*hadith daʿif*). The first is actually attributable to the Prophet through a traceable lineage; the second depends on a lineage that has a few links missing; and the third is unreliable (though not necessarily dismissable) because its genealogy is faulty. These chains are less reliant on the degress of harmony between the texts than they are on whether the links in the chain actually knew and spoke to one another; the importance of oral transmission is primary.

Reported speech is thus at the very foundation of theological thought in Islam, while authenticity is equated with authority. The importance of witnesses as validators of authority has already been noted. Not only do witnesses attest to the truth of an utterance but truth is constructed via their attestation. Personal knowledge of what is already reported speech constitutes the claim to authority. Not only is narrative reified here, but so are the narrators. Narrative is the material of tradition and cultural practice, while narration is its perpetuation. The inability to authorize narrative (literally to identify its author) is the inability to distinguish the true from the false. This prevents transcendence; the singular "word" of authority (l-kəlma) is lost in dialogic speech (l-hadra), which is plural, multivocalic, mutable, and moving. And although the authority of discourse is questionable, it is the means by which "the word" is circumscribed and constituted in the social imagination. The authority of "the word" is known through its contextualization in citation.

The historical dimension of reported speech has bearing upon contemporary marketplace practices. The ability to choose and fuse different forms and genres is the very basis of marketplace expression; it is composed of reportage, whether of oral or textual discourse, and assumes the ability to manipulate ("decontextualize" or "decenter") varieties of formal and colloquial speech. Any use of reported speech is an example of entextualization, exemplifying the process whereby discourse is rendered extractable from some former context only to be recontextualized in another (Bauman and Briggs 1990). What I have variously referred to as the "dialogue of genres," "feminine speaking," and the "words of others" are all examples of fused-form speech employed strategically for pragmatic purposes.

Recontextualized speech, however, ceases to be "itself" as soon as it is embodied/embedded in the pragmatic relationships of its surrounding discourse. Here the notion of organic hybridization becomes useful in empirically describing the way linguistic forms mutually influence and change each other as they infiltrate and alter larger "orders of discourse" and asymmetrical power relations (Foucault 1981; see also Hanks 1990; Lindstrom 1992). "Hybridization" captures the continually emergent quality of expressive forms and genres as they meet, merge, transform, and perhaps separate.

As the bargaining exchange examined earlier exemplifies, the repetition of a generic phrase ("aren't we all Muslims?") in a new context changed not only the referent of the pronoun (from we-masculine to we-feminine), but the indexical relations of the utterance to its habitual context.[3] The double-voicedness of this saying is intricately related to the somewhat new placement of women in the material economy. Women's physical presence in the marketplace grounds them in a new domain of discourse, while their speech indexes their emergent status in the public realm (cf. Hanks 1990). Such revoicings change the shape of recontextualized speech by introducing a different time-space orientation to genres that carry their own historical associations into the present (Bakhtin 1986; see also Ben-Amos 1976; Holquist 1986). The sayings (*ḥikam*) of Sidi Abderaḥman al-Majdub, for example, express a certain social ethic (characterized by chauvinism) which is in the process of being challenged in some realms of contemporary Moroccan thought and practice. The relation between genre and gender here becomes salient: stereotypical notions of gender find expression in a genre like ḥikam, while novel expressions of gender (exemplified in women's presence in the market) appropriate and transform genres by altering the habitual relation between context and utterance, content and form. Women verbal artists in the marketplace make the politics of difference palpable by infusing tradition with a newly-gendered poetics. Their embodiment and revoicing of public speech genres makes their audience *see* what is usually only recognized[4] (or misrecognized) the power of words to effect social change.

Speaking Tradition: "He said to you": "Gal" as Quotative and Discourse Marker

Fluctuation in the sum total of reported speech provides a means for comparison among the public discourse examined. Bargaining, for example, is a relatively informal genre employing conventional rules for interruption and turn-taking, wherein oaths provide a main vehicle for the establishment of authority. Citation of actual persons is kept to a minimum in this genre, which is composed largely of formulaic openings, oaths, and closings. Like English, however, Moroccan Arabic employs both direct and indirect reported speech.[5] One way of introducing reported speech is by the quotative verb *gal* and its use in the expression gal-lək, literally "he said to you."

Gal-lək is perhaps one of the most frequent and ambiguous forms in Moroccan colloquial speech. In some contexts it functions as the equivalent of the English "they say," marking the speech that follows as a proverb or another type of traditional wisdom. For example:

gal-lək,
ṣḥab l-məllali
mən ṣbaḥ ḥətta l-a'shiya

he said to you,
Mellalis [are your] friends
[only] from the morning until the afternoon.

The speaker, an emigré to Beni Mellal who does not associate himself with the region or its people, made it clear to me that these were not *his* words, but were socially authored. By introducing the phrase with gal-lək, he distinguished it as a "saying" in the local repertoire, a much-reported utterance.

In other contexts gal-lək functions much like the English discourse marker, "y'know," its referential function suppressed in favor of a rhetorical one,[6] serving to gain "attention from the hearer to open an interactive focus on speaker-provided information" (Schiffren 1987:267). This usage is found in the bargaining event described in Chapter 2, when Ahmed says, "he said to you, they aren't made any more":

> "That's what we pay for it wholesale!"
> "Wholesale, [it's] 35 or 36 hundred" said Mohamed.
> "By God, no one would take it for that!"
> "Because, *he said to you*, they aren't made any more. Why? What's the matter? Don't I go to Nador? They bring them from Nador, but there aren't any more!"

Ahmed employs gal-lək to mark what follows not as reported speech but as information that is vital to the transaction: Ahmed is not responsible for the fact that the cassette recorder has been discontinued, yet he would not be pursuing the bargain otherwise. By using gal-lək the buyer introduces essential background information to the vendor, implicating her in his predicament by simultaneously personalizing his form of address (he said to *you*) and de-personalizing the conditions of the speech event (the passive construction, "they aren't made").

In the Ḥajja's narrative about belief (niya) in Chapter 1, gal-lək reports both speech and action (cf. Urban 1984b), the several functions of the quotative verb gal emerging side-by-side:

> Wa gal-lək, tshaṭru 'la juj bibiyat. Gal-lək, gal-li-ha, səddi 'ayn-ək, akhalti, bəsh…səddi 'ayn-ək, ila waḥda tqila 'l-ukhra.

> And, *he said to you*, they bargained for those two turkeys. *He said to you, he said to her*, "Close your eyes, my aunt, in order to…close your eyes [to see if] one is heavier than the other."

The first two uses (he said to *you*) provide accent to the utterances that follow and mark them as words that have been socially authored, whereas the last use (he said to *her*) is a quotative that introduces the reported speech. The indirect object (you, her, him, me) here determines the rhetorical function of the quotative verb (cf. Munro 1982).

That gal-lək is a discourse-marker is especially clear in instances where the pronoun referent is not only absent, but irretrievable and unnameable. Again, the Ḥajja's narrative serves as an example:

> "In the early days there was niya. A woman went, in those days. *She said to you*, she brought her son to the suq. And he left his mother holding the horse, holding the horse just outside the suq. And one guy came along holding a string of doughnuts.
>
> "He said to her, 'oh woman.'
>
> "She said to him, 'yes?'
>
> "He said to her, 'your son said to you, "take this string of doughnuts and give me the horse."'
>
> "And she gave him the horse. She gave the owner of the doughnuts the horse. Her son came and found her like that with a string of doughnuts." The Ḥajja laughed.
>
> "He said to her, 'Oh my mother, where is the horse?'
>
> "She said to him. 'Oh my son, ara, the owner of the doughnuts took him, the one who gave me these doughnuts.'
>
> "'Oh hell,' he said to her, 'I didn't send anyone to you!' *He said to you*, she went, the poor woman, into the suq, and she took, the poor thing, that string of doughnuts and, *he said to you*, she's calling, 'Oh owner of the doughnuts, oh owner of the doughnuts, give me my horse!' But the one with the horse was gone. I don't know where he took it. I don't know where he got with it. And that's not niya?"

Throughout the narrative the quotative verb is used to introduce direct reported speech. Three times, however (see italics), the Ḥajja uses it to report action — once in the feminine form (galt-lək, she said to you) and twice in the masculine (gal-lək). These phrases create referential ambiguity; the implied person ("she") did not tell the addressee ("you") anything; in fact "she" perhaps did not even tell the speaker, nor is it guaranteed that "she" will not become a "he" later on the the discourse. Gal-lək functions metapragmatically (Silverstein 1976:48–51), resisting semantic interpretation, yet balancing on the line between the literal and the rhetorical. It erases the locus, or boundary, of accountability, allowing possible disclaimer if necessary. At the same time that a limit is created, it is also made to disappear. By placing the addressee directly in the action and by implicating her (indirectly) in the reported event ("he said to *you*"), the addressee is virtually catapulted into the pragmatics of discourse (cf. Lucy 1993; Sherzer 1983).

Appropriative Speech: The Majduba

The majduba does not preface any of her discourse with gal. But its absence is conspicuous, as several of the aphorisms she uses were said by Sidi Abderaḥman al-Majdub, an important cultural figure whose life still remains in social memory. Despite the fact that the words are not her own, nor socially recognized as her own, the majduba "possesses" them by *not* calling attention to their reported status, thereby governing the interpretive frame more directly.[7] This does not solidify the boundaries of the utterance so much as it opens them to different interpretive frames, making possible the implicit meta-communicative commentary of the majduba. According to Hélène Cixous, this is an example of linguistic "stealing."[8] Volosinov refers to this process as one of infiltration:

> Language devises means for infiltrating reported speech with authorial retort and commentary in deft and subtle ways. The reporting context strives to break down the self-contained compactness of the reported speech, to resolve it, to obliterate its boundaries. (Volosinov 1973 : 120–21)

The dissolution of authorial boundaries allows the majduba to revoice an utterance with an established interpretation. In this sense, reported speech, although seeming to bid for closure and monologic status, actually opens the interpretive possibilties of discourse, renegotiating the circumstance and position of its speakers. Whereas the quotation of authoritative language may be an explicit strategy to establish intertextual proximity[9] with prior discourse, the majduba's revoicing of these quotes leaves this relation ambiguous. She neither identifies with these words nor critques them explicitly; rather, she does both implicitly.

Bowing to Authority: (Sub)Versions of Social Ritual

Unlike the majduba, the 'ashshaba (see Chapter 4) is careful to preface all examples of recontextualized speech with phrases that mark them as such, drawing on the most conventional sources of authority for her validation. Yet her parodic revoicings and feminine embodiment of this discourse subvert the very authority that her surface structure invokes.

The herbalist uses a range of registers to index formality. The most informal register that she employs is the dialect of Moroccan Arabic, which comprises most of her discourse. There are times when she peppers her dialect with a word or two of classical Arabic, for example, when she says, *li'anna, al-mra' ash kat-tsamma?* "because the woman [CA], what is she called?" [MA]. This is an intermediate register. The other extreme is her use of high classical Arabic as in the Qur'anic citation:

> rabbi gal f-l-qur'an,
> li qawli-hi ta'ala
> ba'd {*a'ūdu bi llāhi mina ash-shaytāni ar-rajīm,*
> *fal ya-nzuri al-'insānu mimma khuliqa*}
> wəsh had l-'aya qal-ha rabbi u la mzawra?
> {*fal ya-nzuri al-'insānu mimma khuliqa*
> *khuliqa min mā'in dāfiqin ya-khruju min bayni aṣ-ṣulbi wa at-tarā'ib*}

> My Lord said in the Qur'an,
> Because of his word, He is the most high,
> after {*God save us from the cursed Satan,*
> *Man should look from whence he was created.*}
> Did the Prophet say this verse or is it counterfeit?
> {*Man should look from whence he was created.*
> *He was created from water flowing between the loins and chest.*}

The herbalist contextualizes the didactic citation in another quote, thus elaborating her performance of religious text while making the audience its judge: "Did the Prophet say this or is it counterfeit?" This question effectively puts the audience in the role of hadith-critic. If the verse is familiar, then its authority, and that of the audience, is validated. If it is not familiar, only the reputation of the audience is in jeopardy.

By making salient the theme of the counterfeit and the false, the herbalist brings together both marketplace and religious issues, introducing a corpus for religious scrutiny. What exactly did the Prophet say or not say? What narratives can we invest with authority and which ones are, indeed, counterfeit? When she purportedly quotes the Prophet's words, half in

Moroccan dialect and half in Classical Arabic, is this as an authoritative quote (*ḥadith saḥiḥ* or *ḥasan*) or a faulty one (*ḥadith ḍaʿif*)?:

> qala rasulu ḷḷahi, ṣalla ḷḷahu ʿalay-hi wa səlləm
> "man naẓar mra b-dam-ha
> bḥal ila kal l-fʿa b-sam-ha."

> The Prophet said, prayers and peace be upon him,
> "Whoever looks upon a menstruating woman
> is like someone who has eaten a viper with its poison."

Given its register and rhyme, there is reason to doubt the quote's genealogical purity. Regardless of its official categorization, however, the verse expresses a strong cultural taboo which the herbalist publicly authorizes with the words, "The Prophet said."

Authority is also constructed in the quotation of anonymous persons. Here authority is constituted outside the question marks, in the ability of the herbalist to distance herself from the quoted utterance, as she does earlier in the discourse on p. 106:

> "Be careful you're not deceived by a woman. And she'll tell you, 'all right, you're my husband and are dear to me and if you died tonight I would mourn for you.' Don't trust [it]! By God, we're being hypocrites about that!"

The herbalist uses reported speech in order to comment critically on insincerity, a theme pertaining to the discursive domain of the marketplace. (The herbalist can be subjected to a similar critical scrutiny, of course—not always with results that point to her genuineness.) Reported speech is a way of disguising voices as much as it is a means of illuminating them. Whose voice is it that speaks within the quotation marks? Is it the anonymous hypocrite or is it the herbalist herself who has created both the character and her words. The porosity of these boundaries permits a (en)textual polysemy, a manifold meaning, that defies circumscription.

These examples suggest that any quoted utterance may contain multiple voices, whether these "words-of-others" are marked or unmarked for reported speech, announced or silently usurped. The appropriation of what "they say," the discerning of what "we say," and the creation of what "I say" or what "she" or "he says" is all of a piece. Subversive messages are coded in subtle ways in the Moroccan suq. If marketplace women sometimes employ negative stereotypes of feminine gender, it is in order to situate themselves in a domain which has always been inhabited by men. Their intermittent construction of their own sex as "low" (exemplified by the adulteress, the liar, the sexual insatiate, the perpetrator of magic) does not necessarily construct men as "high," however. The categories of "low" and "high" are too facile to be applied to the thematic construction of gender being renegotiated in the contemporary Moroccan marketplace. Rather, these terms pertain to the linguistic realm wherein "high" (religous and formal) language is pragmatically brought low and "low" (colloquial and immodest) speech becomes a "high" ritual. The vendor of contraband, the ʿashshaba, and the majduba, are not elevating women, but are publicizing feminine power and multiplicity. Their speech draws upon categories of masculine authority while undermining all that is closed, compartmentalized, and impermeable. The presence of women in the marketplace puts traditional definitions of womanhood into question, and everything is subject to question in their language. They are the anti-heroes, the carnivalizers, the sanctioners of Babel.

Notes

1. The poetry of one era is characterized by rhyme; in another, meter is dominant. Although both types of poetry have rhyme and meter, these qualities act differently in each work, according to the operative canon.
2. Although this word often refers to written language, I find it useful in describing oral discourse that focuses more on reference than on poetic form.
3. See Duranti and Goodwin (1992) for a review of the literature on context.
4. Shklovskij (1914) in "The Resurrection of the Word," makes this distinction between recognition and artistic seeing (as quoted in Ejxenbaum 1978:12):

> We do not experience the familiar, we do not see it, we recognize it. We do not see the walls of our rooms. We find it very difficult to catch mistakes when reading proof (especially if it is in a language we are very used to), the reason being that we cannot force ourselves to see, to read, and not just "recognize," a familiar word. If it is a definition of "poetic" perception or of "artistic" perception in general we are after, then we must surely hit upon this definition: "artistic" perception is a perception that entails awareness of form (perhaps not only form, but invariably form).

5. Gal-liya, "Bghit n-mshi." He told me, "I want to go."
Gal-liya bi'anna-hu bgha y-mshi. He told me that he wanted to go.

6. In American usage the word "like" functions similarly as both a quotative and a discourse marker.

7. "The question of how much of the other's meaning I will permit to get through when I surround his words with my own is a question about the governance of meaning, about who presides over it, and about how much of it is shared" (Clark and Holquist 1984 : 237).

8. "Stealing is woman's gesture," says Cixous, playing on the double meaning of the French *voler*, which means both to steal and to fly, "stealing in language and making it steal. We have all learned the art of stealing and its numerous techniques; for centuries we've been able to possess anything only by stealing" (Cixous 1986/75 : 96). Cixous plays on both of these meanings, though I have chosen to emphasize one over the other here.

9. Briggs and Bauman (1992) assert that, since all notions of genre rely on an implicit or explicit relationship to some prior discourse, genres may be considered in light of a measured "gap" between genre and text:

> The process of linking particular utterances to generic models . . . necessarily produces an intertextual *gap*. Although the creation of this hiatus is unavoidable, its relative suppression or foregrounding has important effects. On the one hand, texts framed in some genres attempt to achieve generic transparency by *minimizing* the distance between texts and genres, thus rendering the discourse maximally interpretable through the use of generic precedents. This approach sustains highly conservative, traditionalizing modes of creating textual authority. On the other hand, *maximizing* and highlighting these intertextual gaps underlies strategies for building authority through claims of individual creativity and innovation…, resistance to the hegemonic structures associated with established genres, and other motives for distancing oneself from textual precedents. (1929 : 149)

When intertextual distance is contexualized in the space of market encounters, the results are usually hybrid in kind; that is, discursive strategies may employ both "minimizing" and "maximizing" techniques at once. Marketplace women authorize their place in the public realm of performance by drawing upon a "traditional" rhetoric of oratory associated primarily with men. On the other hand, they distance themselves from that tradition by exaggerating it with subtly satiric intonation and gesture.

PART TWO

Gender on the Market

Only the imagination is real.
— William Carlos Williams

6. Women on the Market: The Subversive Bride

The increased earning power of women in the economic market is introducing fundamental changes in ritual life and the social values it expresses. The Moroccan bride negotiates between relations of reciprocity (between two families who are merging their destinies by mingling their bloods) and relations of commodity, expressed in the bride's ability to "make good" and goods in the material economy. Ritual, in representing an intensification of social relations and values, provides a potent example of social change. The bride may still be considered a gift between families, but her packaging has changed considerably, and the packaging affects the contents, just as the mirror image affects the self image (cf. Ossman 1994).

Imagining Tradition

"I'll tell you about the *real* Moroccan weddings," Fadela said one evening as we sat on sheepskins on the balcony of her fourth-floor apartment; our children played a few feet away. The main boulevard below was already thick with pedestrians and café-goers breathing the cooler air of dusk. We watched a wedding procession move slowly down the streets: a mule-drawn cart laden with bags of flour and sugar, bottles of oil, blankets, clothes, a tethered ram. About forty men and women followed the cart, singing, clapping their hands, and hitting small drums. The sound of the *ghaita*, a small double-reed instrument, sang out above the other noises.

"Not the 'evolved'[1] weddings of today," she continued, aware of my interest in ritual. "The [traditional] weddings are still enacted in the countryside but hardly ever in the cities any more. Though sometimes you find them in the cities among the very oldest inhabitants.

"Seven days before the wedding of the bride is ḥənnaed from head to toe. They cover her under a large piece of cloth, like a tent. Only her mother and sisters may see her. For seven days they put ḥənna everywhere. It removes sunspots and blemishes and purifies the skin. Her skin becomes really beautiful, like new.[2] After the ḥənna has been on for a while each day she goes to the public bath and washes. This is repeated every day for seven days.

"On the day of the wedding celebration someone or some people from the bride's family try to steal her. They take her somewhere and hide her. The groom's family must find her. This makes the bride into something very desired. When she is finally found and brought to her husband's house, she must be carried. Her feet must not touch the ground.[3] This makes the bride 'proud'; she is unspoiled. The groom's brother or cousin carries her. She is covered completely with veils and cloth.

"The day of the wedding, the groom is also dabbed with ḥənna. There is a party for him. Of course there is a procession in the streets with the *ghaita* and singing and dancing when they bring the bride's things to the groom's house. *Bien sur*, after everything, the bloodied panties are displayed and celebrated. The next morning the bride's mother brings breakfast to the bride and to everybody in the new husband's house.[4] The bride's mother helps her to put on kohl and lip rouge (*'akkar*) for the first time. She mustn't put on a belt, though. Not for another week. Seven days after consummation there is another celebration for the belting of the bride."

"Why is this done?" I asked.

"I don't know the exact reason for the belting. My mother was married this way. Before her wedding day she had never seen my father, nor had my father seen her."

Fadela's description of a "real Moroccan wedding" (*'ars maghribi ḥaqiqi*) as it was enacted in her mother's generation is distinctly different from contemporary practices, which she says have "imported the traditions of Andalucia" and are not authentically Moroccan.[5] Fadela is well placed to discuss Moroccan tradition. As an educated working woman struggling to maintain extended-family values in her own nuclear family, Fadela is concerned with questions of authenticity and Moroccan identity.[6]

Fadela's family is originally from Marrakech, though she grew up in Casablanca. Both she and her husband are college educated. They now reside in a recently built apartment and have two young children. Both have left their natal regions and families to work in Beni Mellal. Fadela is an accountant and her husband is a high school teacher.

Fadela's life epitomizes what Hoschchild (1990) has called the "second shift"; she works fulltime while also performing all the responsibilities of a

Moroccan housewife. She prepares breakfast and lunch before leaving for work in the morning, walks half a mile uphill to her office, returns home for lunch, serves and cleans up, returns again to work, comes home, and prepares dinner. Her husband brings the children to and from school, but does not cook, clean, wash, or do any other traditionally female tasks. Although Fadela has a maid who comes for about four hours a day to help her with housecleaning and washing the clothes, Fadela is still overtaxed and usually exhausted. She takes great pride in her apartment—the banquettes are stuffed with expensive wool and covered with a rich brocade. There are always homemade Moroccan delicacies on hand for guests—sweets made with almond paste, dried meat, hand-pressed olive oil and wild honey from the countryside and, of course, an impressive tea set. Fadela takes the business of tradition, the "real" Moroccan ways, very seriously.

The terms for "real" or "authentic" (*ḥaqq*) and "tradition" (*taqalid*) are semantically related. Haqq is "something that exists in the public world, an authenticity made tangible by the acts and covenants that engage those capable of understanding to one another" (Rosen 1984 : 120–21) Although the concept of authenticity carries connotations of a metaphysical and permanent truth, it exists in relation to social practice; its tangibility establishes its value. Taqalid is also thoroughly entwined with social practice. Loosely translated as "tradition," etymologically it is the plural of *taqlid*, which in classical Arabic means "imitation," "copying," "blind, unquestioning adoption (of concepts or ideas)," and "uncritical faith . . . [as in] in a source's authoritativeness" (*Hans Wehr Arabic-English Dictionary*). Taqalid is constructed non-intentionally by imitation, just as authenticity emerges out of tangible and public acts. As Hobsbawm (1983) notes, the notion of tradition takes shape and is "invented" in the face of rapid change.[7]

If tradition is construed in the Moroccan context as an unselfconscious copying, then the deliberate eclecticism or bricolage of contemporary weddings makes them nontraditional. But in her description of the real or authentic Moroccan wedding, Fadela asserts that contemporary weddings are *evolué*—evolved forms of tradition—western-leaning and fashionable; she thus objectifies tradition as a separate historical process, while establishing a relationship with its materializations. Weddings in Morocco rely on imitation and adaptations reaching across class divisions and boundaries of ethnicity. The symbols of the Moroccan wedding are traditional in the literal sense—they are mimetic—but are appropriated from several cultural practices, increasingly used to create a new, over-arching, and hybrid form.

The nostalgia for a real or pure tradition is evident in contemporary ritual life. Fadela laments the passing of countryside weddings, which have not borrowed anything from either Andalucia or Europe. Her comments register the threat of hybridization posed by contact with other ethnic groups,[8] and mirror a larger social preoccupation with the reconstitution of Moroccan custom. Tradition as she defines it is "unspoiled," like the virgin bride. Just as there are fewer virgins on the marriage market, so are there fewer weddings that do not evidence the Western white wedding dress or other "imported" customs.

Spatial mobility from region to region and economic class mobility have facilitated similar transitions in custom (*l-qaʿida*). Leaving the village or the extended family means taking responsibility for either the reconstitution of tradition in new contexts or the dissolution of tradition in the face of new circumstance. In such periods of social transition, concepts of tradition are up for grabs — especially in a society as pluralistic as Morocco's. In response to such diversity, Fadela describes tradition in terms of an ideal purity, untainted by foreign influence. But tradition in practice is an intensely hybrid affair. Although Moroccan weddings differ from region to region, they nonetheless are in the process of becoming standardized. This trend, a form of nationalization, combines elements from Berber weddings, European ceremonies, and in particular the marriage customs of the Moroccan *haute bourgeoisie*. The resultant mix is now called a traditional wedding (*ʿars taqlidi*), a codified celebration that is accessible at some level to all Moroccans.

Ritual Transformations

The bride Fadela described is seen to pass through the three phases of a rite of passage as defined by Van Gennep (1960). The removal of the bride from all but her mother's and sisters' eyes seven days before the marriage begins the rites of *separation*. She becomes a *liminal* entity — a woman in transition — virtually living under a tent of cloth and covered with an earthy substance. The abduction of the bride by her own family and eventual retrieval by the groom's family continues the separation rites, while the breakfast brought to the groom's family by his mother-in-law the day after consummation and the ritual painting of the bride with kohl belong to the *aggregation* rites that incorporate the bride into her new life as married woman. She begins the separation rites seven days before the wedding/consummation and is not wholly incorporated into her new role as a woman and wife until seven days after, when she is ritually belted, or bound, to her new self.

These days the rites of separation rarely begin seven days before the wedding; two or three days is now the norm. Working people cannot spend a week in celebration, nor can the families afford the expense of extended entertaining. Modernity and the marketplace put a higher premium on time, with contemporary weddings usually taking place on the weekend. For the bride this involves three days of ritual: the day of the bath (*nhar l-ḥammam*), the day of ḥənna (*nhar l-ḥənna*) and the formal wedding celebration (*l-ʿars*), which culminates in consummation (*ar-rwaḥ*).

Ḥənna: The Objectification of the Bride and Her Body

Khadija was twenty-one years old and had just spent a year in Paris visiting her brothers. She was now preparing to marry a Guadalupan man she had met there, a supervisor in a small Parisian supermarket. Since he didn't speak Arabic, he conversed with Khadija, her brothers, and her father in French. The couple planned to return to France and live in a suburb where they had already bought a house. Although it is customary for a spouse to convert to Islam before marrying a Moroccan woman, this did not take place. Khadija's family defended this decision by asserting that her groom was a hybrid—that is, his genealogy already contained Moroccan blood. Yet the groom did not consider himself a *beur*, a second-generation French citizen of North African descent. Indeed, he had no family residing in Morocco. The discursive creation of his Moroccan bloodline, however, allowed the marriage to stay within the contours of this provincial capital's mores.

On Friday morning Khadija came home from the hairdresser and was driven to a rented villa on the outskirts of Beni Mellal where her ḥənna party was being held. By the afternoon, all Khadija's female peers and women folk had arrived, gathering in a large room lined with couches and borrowed rugs covering the floors. Khadija, two close friends and I sat in a side room with two professional bride adorners—a mother/daughter team. The daughter, Aisha, was a ḥənna artist (*nəqqasha*, literally an "engraver"). Divorced, she lived with her mother, father, and four younger brothers and sisters. Her mother, Fatima, the *nəggafa* (the bride's paid handmaiden), was charged with dressing the bride. The two of them had made business cards which said *n-naqsh l-biḍawi*, "Casablanca Adorning."

Aisha squatted on the floor, rapidly mixing the ḥənna powder with

Figure 12. A ḥənna artist at work on Khadija's hand.

orange blossom water until it formed a smooth paste. She then wiped her fingers on a towel and placed the bowl of ḥənna paste on a silver tray next to another Chinese ceramic bowl containing milk. There was also a plate of dates and a cup containing a beaten egg, all three foods symbols of good luck and fecundity. Fatima helped the bride pull on her qaftan and touch up her makeup. When everything was ready, the nəggafa escorted the bride to her pillowed "throne" in the other room. We all chanted loudly: "Prayers and peace to the messenger of God. There is no power but the power of our master, Mohamed. God be with the Higher Power."

Khadija's feet were propped on more pillows while the nəqqasha scooped some ḥənna paste into the body of a new syringe. She held this just above the surface of Khadija's skin and, with the concentration of a surgeon, began to decorate her feet with fine filigree lines of ḥənna (see Figure 12). The other women in the room were served tea and cookies. Soon the performers would arrive.

Ḥənna and the Inscription of Subjectivity

Transformation of the physical body effects changes at all levels of the Moroccan social corpus. In Fadela's description of an authentic wedding, the bride is not painted with ḥənna so much as she is washed and smeared with it. Ḥənna, in her account, does not have a decorative function, but draws on popular belief in its prophylactic and apotropaic properties. The bride is covered with ḥənna because it imparts divine blessing (baraka) and protection at a critical moment of life transition.

The ḥənna plant is the nexus of a rich folklore; its power to evoke both historical and dynamic meaning is indelible. By virtue of its baraka, ḥənna possesses many of the curative and prophylactic qualities traditionally attributed to tattoo, whose capacity to change the physical appearance effects the physical and mental body as well (Westermarck 1926a; see also Eickelman 1976; Geertz 1971 on baraka). Like tattoo, baraka works through the physical body to affect the metaphysical one. These two bodies are not antithetical (as in the Cartesian dichotomy) but rather sympathetic, representing two parts of a larger whole whose state they both partake of and contribute to — the social body.

Baraka as a noun corresponds to the Christian notion of grace; it is a state of being possessed by people of virtue. Baraka, in the Moroccan idiom, exists in degrees. The baraka of saints is of sufficient magnitude to heal and bless others and is thus solicited at their shrines. In one sense, the baraka of saints survives the body in that it is an effective power for healing and blessing even after death; in another more pertinent sense, baraka is inextricably linked to the physical body in that its power "resides" (in popular belief and practice) in the actual place of entombment. In life, as in death, baraka may be said to inhabit the body; being both material and ethereal, it is able to permeate the porosity of the skin.

Ḥənna's status as a bearer of baraka reinforces its connection to the body. Ḥənna paste is an earthy substance that penetrates and stains the top layers of skin. It is a botanical agent that acts, in popular belief, to purify the body from the outside in. The skin is not a seal to the self; it allows baraka to pass through and infuse the psychological, the social, and the spiritual bodies.

Although ḥənna coloration is temporary,[9] its status is somewhere between the indelibility of tattoo and the superficiality of commercial cosmetics that may be removed with water. Even substantially, ḥənna is ambiguous; when applied, it is a viscous paste, neither liquid nor solid.[10]

Ḥənna transforms the body in subtle ways; because of its baraka, it has the potential to change the nafs. Ḥənna acts as a tonic, inducing feelings of well-being in the individual.

As Douglas has shown, concepts such as baraka are needed to balance social conceptions of pollution, particularly salient in ritual moments and in circumstances of transformation such as marriage (1988:112). Like baraka, polluting substances can also permeate the organism via the skin. Ḥənna is often applied when "impure" female blood is an issue: during wedding celebrations (before consummation) and shortly before delivery of a child. Both transitional events involve a dynamic engagement of self with another at the borders of the skin and change the status and identity of the woman engaged. In the case of birth, what is inner becomes outer; from one skin, another emerges, bringing prestige to the mother (especially is she has a son) as a fecund and useful member of society. In the case of marriage, the blood of the broken hymen externalizes what the bride has internalized: the social acknowledgment of responsibility for a sexual life that must be controlled and hidden. No longer a virgin, a married woman presents a threat to social order should her sexuality go unchecked (Mernissi 1987). She is potentially a pollutant to society and must come to terms with the power ascribed to her.

Baraka fortifies the initiate with prophylaxis against the stigma of pollution ultimately linked to these rites of passage. Through ḥənna, baraka enters the skin from without, purifying what is within. The boundaries of the self are here conceived as porous, the body permeable not only through its orifices, but virtually through its skin. But whereas the bride in Fadela's narrative is covered completely with ḥənna and then hidden under a full-length veil, contemporary ḥənna ceremonies involve the application of ḥənna in painstaking detail, creating an artistic display of decorative virtuosity. This move from hidden to displayed object parallels women's social movement from the private to the public sphere. In this case Khadija's worldliness, evident in her marrying a Guadalupan immigrant to Paris, disinclined her to any sort of veiling whatsoever. Yet she was very concerned to have a traditional Moroccan wedding in her natal region of Beni Mellal, in which ḥənna played an integral part.

The high visibility of ḥənna and the fact that it remains on the skin for two to three weeks is an important factor in its definition. The lace-like designs draw in the gaze of the observer yet repel it by establishing a decorative boundary, a reflector, between gazer and object. The designs also permit the subject to see herself and in this sense they become reflective—

they mirror the subject. A relationship exists between the artwork (the ḥənna design) and the subject of the work, the woman herself.

The ḥənnaed woman becomes a double subject, forming the essential substance of the publicly visible artwork and constituting its very theme; she is both form and content, word and image. Although the reflection that results from the process of ḥənna application is not consciously acknowledged in the native discourse, the talk around the ḥənna ceremony—talk concerned with major life issues such as marriage, divorce or widowhood—reveals what is at stake. In the ḥənna ceremony women not only confront the marking of superficial boundaries, they are involved in the recognition and renegotiation of personal and social boundaries as well.

Moroccan art has traditionally avoided the re-creation of the physical form in the public realm (thought to be reserved for God alone), yet body-marking draws attention to the human form, making it a living icon of human representation. The designs themselves are floral and geometric, but the total depiction is of the feminine body, highlighted and elaborated—and thus objectified and eroticized. Ḥənna application is forbidden during the holy month of Ramadan, for example, as it conveys vanity and self-conscious sexuality. It is this aspect of body design that imputes ambiguity to its symbolism, for according to Islam (and most religions), a sexually alluring woman and the promiscuity that she can incite are of a highly polluting nature (Mernissi 1975) and can pose threats to social concepts of patriarchal honor (Abu-Lughod 1986). Ḥənna thus empowers its wearer, protecting her, but also making her potentially "dangerous."

Ambiguity is echoed in the designs themselves, which act to both reveal feminine sexuality and to hide that sexuality in layers of other socially significant meanings, like that of "tradition." On the most superficial level, body-marking can be seen as both an elaboration of the human form and as a covering or disguise. This reversible quality is especially evident in ḥənna design, whose patterns cover the hands and feet like gloves and stockings.

The cosmetic use of ḥənna predates Islam, yet there is little evidence to suggest that contemporary ḥənna decoration was practiced by any but an elite urban minority as recently as three to four generations ago (Kapchan 1993a). The popularization of ḥənna decoration and its central status in the definition of Moroccan marriage tradition reveals its role in the contemporary re-creation of tradition. It has become so emblematic of wedding tradition that brides who want to be "modern" (évolué) often refuse to wear it.

Dressing the Bride

A similar transformation from hidden to displayed is witnessed on the third and final day of the wedding ceremony. Just as ḥənna practices have become more elaborately patterned, so have practices of dressing the bride. At this final and official celebration, the bride's clothing is changed numerous times by a nəggafa (professional attendant) and she is displayed on a throne-like chair throughout the evening. Male relatives are often present and the groom eventually takes his place beside the bride after the ceremonies have begun. The bride is no longer cloistered from either the male or female view; she is neither veiled nor guarded from the male gaze.[11]

Supervising both the gaze and the gazed upon, the nəggafa is not new to the cast of wedding characters, though her competitive professionalism is, reflecting the larger social trend towards commodifying services that were once rendered by kin or exchanged in community barter. The proliferation of nəggafat (pl.) is an example of the burgeoning service sector in the feminine population, with market competition among nəggafat becoming a source of the corruption of tradition noted by Fadela. In holding responsibility for the traditional costuming of the bride, nəggafat are also using decorative innovations in new materials and design in order to attract customers. Fierce competition governs the feminine service realm as nəggafat attempt to protect their professional secrets. On one occasion when I ran into Aisha and Fatima at an herbalist's shop, they explained that a young woman they had taken on as an apprentice had parted company with them and was now appropriating some of their business. Thinking this the work of a spell cast by the apprentice, the nəggafat were purchasing a counter-potion. New techniques and ideas in bride decoration are coveted as nəggafat become the brokers of "tradition."

The relationship between the nəggafa and the bride and her family is one of commodity: payment for services is made by the bride's parents with no obligation incurred by either party. What used to be owned by the bride — costumes and gold — is now leased: the nəggafa brings suitcases packed with cloth she will drape and veil over the bride, who will be arrayed in anywhere from three to eighteen different ensembles throughout the night, depending on how many the bride's family can afford. The cloth is untailored, draped loosely over the bride, pinned at the shoulders and belted at the waist. The looseness of the fabric allows the nəggafa to use the same material on all brides, improvising the costuming according to the bride's physique, making her dress "custom-made." This element of free play creates a space for the nəggafa's artistry, which serves to establish her professional reputation.

Both the act of clothing the bride and the ritual change of clothing during the wedding ceremony express the bride's transition from girlhood to womanhood, much as the seven-day covering with ḥənna did in Fadela's description. But the "traditional" bride was covered with ḥənna and hidden from view to effect her purification and transformation, while today she is adorned and on view to the public, a virtual inversion of the ritual.

Most Moroccans have their own version of "the real Moroccan wedding"; yet traditional ceremonies all embody rites similar to those described above. Moroccan wedding ceremonies and their accompanying customs vary from region to region and have changed considerably since Khadija's parents were married, bringing more standardization. The wedding customs of the Fes "aristocracy" have trickled down to the larger society; differences in weddings now denote class distinctions more than regional ones. The children of well-to-do parents, for example, may be taken to a four-star hotel in order to consummate the marriage instead of to a room in the groom's parents' house. The upper classes, I am told, are less concerned than other sectors of society with the public proof of virginity. Honor here is not invested in one girl's "virtue." Virtue, in fact, may be a secondary issue.[12] As élites marry only élites, the honor of the families is assured — determined by hard currency and social status.

Shifting Liminalities

Weddings in contemporary Morocco embody the display — the proclamation — of social and familial power. Taking on the dispositions of the elite, in both dress and demeanor, the bride represents the possibility of upward mobility. Via her marriage, she has a role in establishing or maintaining a family's status in the community, and her ritual behavior affects the larger social imagination.

There are basically two parallel ceremonies at the Moroccan wedding: one for the guests and one for the bride and groom. As noted, all historical and present accounts of Moroccan weddings qualify the bride as an initiate in the classical Gennepian fashion (see Combs-Schilling 1989; Maher 1974; Westermarck 1926a). The fact that the bride is hidden and then abducted in Fadela's description of a traditional wedding underscores the loss the bride's family is symbolically trying to prevent. The bridewealth (gifts to the bride from the groom's family) is repayment for that loss, but is never so complete as to facilitate total independence on the part of the new couple. It is acknowledged that the bride's emotional ties and support will always remain with her family of birth. Sheep are sacrificed and blood is spilled to commemorate the future fertility, the first fruits, of the bride's labor in childbirth. The bride is a gift, reciprocated for with bridewealth (gold for the bride, sheep for the wedding guests), and the bride's first child is the second phase in the gift exchange between the bride and the groom's families, whereupon the bride enjoys a higher status.

The semiotics of gender and culture make for differences in the way ritual is both experienced and perceived by others; liminality has many guises (see Bynum 1984). Because the bride is a gift, she incorporates the qualities of liminality Turner describes as accompanying rites of passage. As "gift-in-motion" she leaves girlhood and her parents' home to enter a new life. The bride's performative role is that of the initiate. She speaks little, if at all, during the wedding preparations and celebrations (Maher 1974). Her face is placid, showing no emotion whatsoever. She eats and drinks little while all around her people feast in her honor (see Kapchan 1993a).

Although the contemporary bride still shares much with the traditional "liminal entity," she exhibits marked differences, particularly with regard to the symbolic pinnings and underpinnings of her dress and adornment. She even displays attributes that run counter to those Turner ascribes to the liminal state ("nakedness or uniform clothing," "minimization of sex distinctions," "disregard for personal appearance," and "no distinctions of wealth"), contrasting sharply with the bridal comportment of only a generation ago. The modern bride is an ostentatious object of display, highly marked as a sexual being (despite her supposed inexperience in these matters) with elaborate and expensive decoration. She wears as much gold as she owns or can borrow. This marks a shift from the display of her family's honor (symbolized by the modesty of the full veil) to the display of family wealth (both her own and her husband's). The process whereby an intangible symbol of the moral economy (honor) is translated into a tangible symbol of the material economy (gold) is occurring at all levels of Moroccan life.

Historically, other Semitic traditions involve the bride's display and elaboration (see notably Weir 1989), but it is usually after the marriage consummation that this ostentation is evidenced. The Moroccan bride is decorated and displayed a day or two before the presumed consummation of the marriage. This display is not performed in one set of prescribed "coming-out" clothes, as in the Palestinian example (Weir 1989), but uses an array of dress determined by the bride, and in part by the nəggafa. The bride's autonomy in taste and distinction is expressed before her transformation from girl into woman, before she is "belted" into her role as wife and mature woman.

The liminal phase where the bride is ḥənnaed and adorned has undergone the most noticeable change. Credited with embodying the potential for social transformation, this phase is characterized as the "seedbed" of cultural creativity, where new symbols arise and eventually integrate into normative life (Turner 1974). Sutton-Smith sees liminal phenomena as "the source of all culture" (1972), having "earnest" connections to the symbolic work of the community. Liminal activity has consequences even outside the ritual frame, enacting "la vie sérieuse" (Durkheim, quoted in Turner 1974:64), thus heralding the transformation of girl into woman in what is still a socially validated rite of passage.

Turner juxtaposes the liminal phase in tribal and early agrarian societies with what he calls the "liminoid" phase in post-industrial societies. Liminoid phenomena, he argues, are more concerned with play for play's sake, and while liminality may invert social structure symbolically, it cannot *subvert* it. Yet liminoid phases *do* subvert the status quo by "lampooning, burlesquing or subtly putting down the central values of the basic, work-sphere society, or at least sections of that society" (Turner 1974:72). Is the behavior of the Moroccan bride liminal or liminoid? Is she faced with serious enactment or merely play? Is the suggestion of subversion a real and threatening one? What is the bride's actual power in the wedding ritual?

Morocco is a complex society, having inherited the great literary and religious traditions of Islam, and withstanding colonization the longest of North African countries while tolerating it the least (Combs-Schilling 1989; 'Arawi 1982). Since Morocco is not a post-industrial society, the term "liminoid" as defined by Turner may not apply here. But as a liminal nation in transit between complex and post-industrial, Morocco is rife with semantic diversity. Both liminal and liminoid apply, though neither term adequately describes the transformations in Moroccan ritual life. The bride both acquiesces to and provides a critique of the social structure, a critique which brings symbolic resources from the public sphere — especially the market — and places them into what had been a primarily private realm.

The Commodified Gift

The bride, presented as gift, is clothed as a commodity, a site for the display of consumer competence and commodity relations. The cloth and gold she wears may indicate purity and honor, but actually represent economic status and her potential for earning money. As inflation climbs steeper and more "respectable" women enter the workforce, a higher value is attributed to the woman with a potential of working for wages. No longer hidden beneath veils, she is displayed in brocaded velvet and gilded synthetic. Her qaftans and dəfinas (long overblouses) have been elaborately prepared at the tailor's with fine thread work meticulously sewn on the edges of silk-like material. A single qaftan and dəfina ensemble may cost as much as 10,000 dirhams (about $1,200.00), but the true cost may double and triple with the bride's several changes. Compared to the average upper-middle-class income, this represents an exorbitant sum, borne primarily by the bridewealth but sometimes subsidized by the bride's family. The clothes symbolize the bride's worth in the estimate of the groom's family; they represent the capital that the groom has seen fit to give her. But they also represent the actual worth of the bride; for no matter who has provided the money for her clothes, it is her worth on the marriage market that has brought the price. The clothes remain with the bride and will be worn again at future festive occasions.

The aesthetics of cloth have great importance in display. Authenticity is not at issue here. It doesn't matter who made the cloth, or whether it was woven by hand or by machine; what matters is its distinction in color, texture, and design from other imported materials. These are sometimes delicate and floral, sometimes garish, and always synthetic. The glossy materials refract light, and, much like ḥənna, attract and yet deflect the gaze that never quite settles upon them. Except for the western wedding dress that has become one of the Moroccan bride's required changes, her clothing is undistinguished from that of the other women present. The cloth of her qaftans and dəfinas expresses her individual taste in color and pattern, as bridal qaftans are not marked as wedding gear. Festive dress is remarkably similar for brides, the guests at the wedding, and even for *shikhat*, the female performers. In fact, the bride and the *shikha* (sing.), who usually represent two opposing poles of purity and pollution, are here linked in their mutual display of large quantities of decorative gold. What differentiates the bride from the other lavish dressers at the wedding are not the gold bangles but the materials that are draped over her qaftans by the nəggafa, as well as the tiaras, the headgear, the face paint, and the ḥənna that is applied to her.

When Khadija, the bride, first appeared at the *mixte* wedding (the culminating celebration occurring after the day of ḥənna, where both men and women were present), she was ushered in with a blessing chanted by the nəggafa and the bride's female peers. The guests then applauded as she was paraded around the room, a practice unknown only a generation or two ago. Afterward, she was seated (always by the nəggafa) on the "throne" of pillows and draped with shimmery cloth.

A group of young musicians with amplified ʿuds (lutes, string instruments) played as the girls started dancing. This was their opportunity to obtain exposure to older males or to mothers of eligible young men (adolescent males were gathered on the periphery of the wedding celebration, outside or upstairs in the room where the musicians retired between sets). Self-display is given license in this context (T. Joseph 1980). Only after the night really warmed up did the older woman lose their inhibition and join in.

After a while the groom took his place beside the bride on the throne, where they sat for the rest of the night, with Khadija occasionally retiring to the dressing room to be changed and primped by the nəggafa. After a fairly long span she would reappear and parade before resuming her seat. The guests meanwhile left in shifts of about twenty to thirty at a time to be served a late dinner. When everyone had dined and returned to the main salon, music and dancing provided entertainment for a few hours. The music was electrically produced (the fashion these days) and extremely loud. Everyone was taken up by the ambience, either in dancing or in observation. Khadija's clothes continued to be changed throughout the performance.

Some of the different costume changes have names, the "big outfit" (*l-ləbsa l-kbira*) being the most important. Its Moroccan origins are found in the customs of the Fes elite. The ləbsa l-kbira, heavy and awkward with its large head fixture, was once worn by the bride all the way to the groom's house as a trial to see whether she was patient. Although the bride no longer wears it for more than a couple of hours, its weight and unmaneuverability still try the bride's patience (see Figure 13). When the bride appears in the "big outfit," her most elaborate and constrictive costume, she is put on a pedestal and carried around on the shoulders of the nəggafa and others (see Figure 14). The same thing is then done to the groom, though

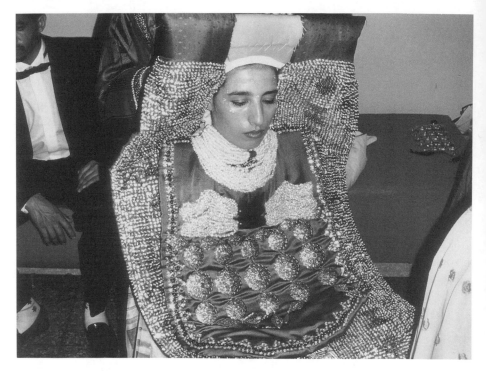

Figure 13. The bride harnessed with the "big outfit."

he does not carry the burden of an awkward costume, but is dressed in a Western suit or a jəllaba. The ləbsa l-kbira includes costly gold lamé fabric and a "golden" crown. The adoption of this tradition by non-élites via the mediation of the nəggafa raises the status of the bride, who is confined under heavy regalia as she is mobilized and borne into society. Both the bride and the groom are objectified here; they are paraded above the heads of the guests as the bridewealth is paraded before the community on its way to the couple's new home.

The nəggafa also dressed Khadija in a Middle-Atlas Berber outfit, putting on her large amber-colored beads and decorative pins that held a hand-woven cloth around her shoulders (see Figure 15). These items are common in depictions of what Moroccans refer to as "folklore" — that is, representations of Berbers for tourists. The pins, beads, and cloth have acquired a metonymic quality, standing for Berber identity before the advent of urbanization and cultural hybridization. The beads, once real amber, are now

Figure 14. The nəggafa and her peers carry the bride around the room in the ləbsa l-kbira.

made of plastic and sold in urban shops, as are the other elements of the costume — long-fringed and colorful scarves and silver-blend jewelry. The significance of such ethnic representations bears on a process of essentialism common in the context of modern hybrid culture. These costumes are seldom worn today except in national performances of "folklore" — in televised festivals that celebrate different tribal identities via music and dance performance. Berbers in urban areas are often so removed from these symbols as to become nostalgic about them, even to the point of parody.

The last costume of Khadija's evening was a version of the western white wedding dress. This addition has become popular among the middle and lower classes only in the most recent generation of brides, and exemplifies the process whereby novelty emerges in conditions of change.[13] Like western women, the Moroccan bride participates in marketplace culture to a much larger degree than ever before. The marketing of goods on televi-

Figure 15. The bride dressed in a Middle-Atlas Berber outfit, donning large amber-colored beads and decorative pins common in depictions of what
Moroccans refer to as "folklore" — that is, representations (in this case, of Berbers) for tourists.

sion exposes her to international symbols of status. In donning the white
wedding dress, she becomes a symbol of purchasing power, a modern
woman consumer.

Other changes Khadija's nəggafa did not employ, but that are quite
common in Moroccan weddings, are both local fashions (the folk dress

characteristic of regions like Tangier, Tetouan, Marrakech, or Oujda) and imported ones, like the Indian sari. Just as Moroccan ḥənna artists draw on Indian and Pakistani ḥənna designs for inspiration (one ḥənna pattern is called "the Indian design," *l-hindiya*; cf. Kapchan 1993a; Slyomovics and Dargan 1990), so professional adorners have adopted traditional Indian dress into their repertoire of bridal changes. This self-conscious appropriation of foreign fashion makes the bride an icon of internationalism, employing symbols of the urban elite and of the mountain nomad, of the "authentically" Moroccan and of the "authentically" Other, the Western as well as the Indian. The Moroccan bride becomes a trans-ethnic personage, expressing a fast-becoming-universal category of "bride."

The combination of local and transnational symbols is not limited to adornment, but is expressed also in the social relations displayed between the bride and groom. Because the two are seated next to each other for the complete duration of the night, they exchange words, smiles, perhaps even hold hands. In traditional weddings the bride rarely saw her husband until they were about to consummate their marriage. This informal behavior between bride and groom is relatively novel,[14] a result of the diminishing number of strictly arranged marriages and of an easing of the taboo that kept women's and men's spheres completely polarized. This, in turn, reflects the increased presence of women in the workforce.

The elements of display in the contemporary Moroccan wedding are especially striking. The bride and groom, their families, the guests, and the nəggafa are all involved in performances of finery, taste, and economic power. The ambience emerges out of an abundance that verges on excess. For the guests this means consumption of large portions of freshly slaughtered meat; it means dancing, sweating, seduction, tolerating a bombardment of sound, and losing at least one night's sleep.

The bride also undergoes a trial of excess, one of patience (ṣ-ṣbər, "long-suffering" is a more appropriate translation in this context). The bride gives herself over completely to the nəggafa, who dresses and arranges her as if she were an infant. The bride symbolically gives up her volition to a female who is not of her family, just as she may have to relinquish her freedom to her mother-in-law after marriage. Yet the growing importance of the nuclear over the extended family is changing these relations of dominance. Khadija will not be under her Guadalupan mother-in-law's tutelage in France. Nonetheless, she did demonstrate an infant-like passivity while being clothed in the ornamentation of mature womanhood, taking no initiative to remove or put on even an article of clothing. This passivity was not in relation to her family or future husband, but in relation to a profes-

sional whose job it is to make the bride a desirable object. Thus liminality
is played out in relation to a paid ritual specialist and contracted employee,
the nəggafa, rather than to family members, marking a new relationship
between women and commodity culture. The bride's ritual encounter is
with the stranger, one whose goods and services she is buying, ultimately
manifest in her own commodification as a saleable good, a beautiful bride.

The Loosening of Reserve

If the bride seems to be more free in her movements now than she was a
generation ago, it is because she is more relaxed (*maṭluqa*) and less bashful
(*ḥashshumiya*) than the traditional bride. These two qualities are always in
contest at Moroccan festive events. To be maṭluq is to be open and "free-
flowing" (from the root *ṭalaqa*, which means to cause to go free, to release),
while to be hashshumi is to be respectful, reserved, and somewhat shy. To
dance, you must be maṭluqa (fem.), but to function in the hierarchy built
on respect for elders and the maintenance of the status quo you must be
hashshumiya. To be maṭluq is a characteristic of the marketplace (market
women are rarely shy and diffident), demanding performances of identities
otherwise veiled in codes of honor and deference.

A wedding where people are bashful is no fun, but a bride who is too
exuberant runs the risk of losing face and respect for herself, her family,
and her husband. Traditionally, unmarried girls, who are still finding their
position "in the market," had license to be moderately open at weddings,
whereas the bride had to be completely diffident. These polarities are now
breaking down; contemporary brides eat, talk, and sometimes even dance
at their own weddings.

The relaxation of the canons of deference (*l-ḥshuma*) is greatly facilitated by the expanded repertoire for female behavior presented by the media, particularly television. Appadurai refers to the vocabulary of images
presented by the media as "mediascapes," which he says, "provide large and
complex repertoires of images, narratives and ethnoscapes to viewers
throughout the world, in which the world of commodities and the world
of news and politics are profoundly mixed" (Appadurai 1990:9).

As in many places outside the ambit of the West after colonialism,
Moroccan women are bombarded with images of powerful and overtly se-
ductive women, whether in Egyptian movies inspired by Hollywood where
Arab women, dressed in western garb, are feisty and sexy, and manipulate

their husbands, or in the American women of *Dallas* who embody similar attributes. Moroccan television mixes images of veiled women going to Mecca with advertisements for mineral water featuring svelte Moroccan-looking women in leotards doing provocative aerobics. Although two opposing ideals are here represented — the veiled and the revealed — the onslaught of advertising targeting the women's market tips the scales heavily in the direction of the modern image.[15] An index to this is the changing ideal of women's sexual attractiveness. Corpulence, once appreciated as a sign of affluence, is clearly out of fashion. Despite the real disjunctures between the images on the screen and daily life, women are beginning to imagine the Other as themselves; they are embracing European styles, western values, and the culture of commodification (Ossman 1994 : 114).[16]

Most brides still don't dance much at their weddings, but they are paraded around, move about, talk to their husbands, laugh, and smile. Yet in the dressing room they are patient while an ordeal is endured, a rite expe-

Figure 16. How to interpret the wink of a bride?

rienced, a ritual performed; the same patience was exacted of the traditional bride. Liminality is not absent, but it is also not constant, visiting by moments. Separation is enacted in the ritual changing of clothes; liminality, in the passive stance of the bride towards the nəggafa, and reincorporation in the eventual consummation of the marriage and return to the groom's house. The feasting, dancing, and nearly deafening music go on all night (sometimes for three consecutive days), until both the bride and the groom are exhausted from being on stage, and guests from sensory overload and lack of sleep, and the mother of the bride or the groom hosting the wedding is, as they say, *aplatie* (flattened).[17]

The Bride: A Hybrid Nation

As an object of display, the bride shows more than the symbolic capital of her new husband's family or her own material worth. She constitutes a new notion of tradition as mediated by the nəggafa. Now dressed as a bride of the Fes elite, now as a Berber from the Middle Atlas mountains, now as a western bride in white chiffon and lace, her eclectic bridal repertoire is intricately related to the diversity of the marketplace. What is created in the bride's ceremonial change of costume is a national identity drawn from many ethnicities and social strata of Morocco. She models these fashion commodities and embodies them, becoming part western, part nomad, part élite. She is a commodity on the market and, like the market women of the ḥalqa, a hybrid being. Her increased autonomy (her potential to earn and spend money) encourages her to fetishize herself and her liberated state as items of consumption. Her own identity as an object, a piece of property, is expressed in a playful wedding song the nəggafa sings:

> l'rusa mərhuna, ha hiya mərhuna
> 'and ba-ha mərhuna, ha hiya mərhuna
> 'and um-ha mərhuna, ha hiya mərhuna
> 'and 'am-ha mərhuna, ha hiya mərhuna
> 'and khal-ha mərhuna, ha hiya mərhuna . . .

> the bride is pawned, [here] she is in hock
> before her father she is pawned, she is in hock
> before her mother she is pawned, she is in hock
> before her paternal uncle she is pawned, she is in hock
> before her maternal uncle she is pawned, she is in hock . . .

Every time the nəggafa calls a relative's name, that person approaches the bride, kisses her and places a gift of money, usually in one hundred-dirham bills (about $12.00) on the tray of dates and milk before her. The bride is put into hock, she is *mərhuna*, until sufficient money is gathered on her behalf. She is pawned like a piece of jewelry at the marketplace, traded temporarily for money, but still somehow belonging to the original owner. There is a clear relationship expressed here between the bride and her monetary worth. Commodity exchange takes place in the most familial of contexts.

Hospitality and the Transformation of the Commodity

Marriage is always an exchange; one exchanges a solitary status for a shared one, or a life in one's parental family for a life outside of it. Marriage customs in Morocco historically result in one person or family incurring obligation (*ḥaqq*) to another, serving to cement social relations within a community. Lévi-Strauss commented on the role of women in this social exchange, saying that "the likening of women to commodities, not only scarce but essential to the life of the group, [must] be acknowledged" (1969a:36). Whether women are considered gifts or commodities, the issue of gendered exchange is still central to understanding changes occurring in the ritual and nonritual life of contemporary Moroccans.

In Moroccan society, unlike that of Melanesia or among Native North Americans, there is no tradition of prestation or potlach where one may refer to a gift's gender or the act of giving as gender-marked (see Strathern 1988). There is instead a tradition of extravagant giving where value is placed upon the range and intensity of hospitality (*ḍiyafa*, literally "guesting"). As changes in marriage ritual indicate evolving gender roles, the transformation of hospitality is likewise a fecund ground for sensing these new roots and growths.

Hospitality is the act of transforming the commodity into the gift. There is no Moroccan who would deny the obligation that is incurred thereby: "If you eat another's chicken, begin to fatten your own," a proverb goes, for reciprocity is imminent. Hospitality given is undeniably community received. This is exemplified in the hospitality offered at wedding celebrations. Men may provide the capital that buys the sheep, but it is only in the hands of the women that the livestock becomes the nourishment of gift. Although men as well as women concur on the priority of hospitality as a Moroccan value, its performance has been the responsibility of women, for whom it is a display of competence and artistry. Men slaughter the sheep, but women clean it, often butcher it, prepare the skin (turn it into a rug), and finally change the raw into the cooked. In this sense, women become agents for transforming nature into culture, while men are associated with the live and the dead animal.

Whereas not too long ago all the women in the community aided the bride or groom's female family members in the cooking, baking, and other preparations for the wedding, these responsibilities are now frequently allotted to hired employees. This is found especially among the new middle class, now struggling with fulltime maids who are hard to come by and no longer reliable or obedient.[18] Women in the community are busy with their own lives and families, so preparations for festivity fall to a class of women who hire themselves out (usually cheaply) to do work that was heretofore parceled out among friends and neighbors. Mutual aid among women — long-term reciprocal relations — is being replaced with the more short-term commodified relation. What was once given as a gift of labor (with expectations of reciprocity) is now sold by women so that guests at the wedding may enjoy labor-free celebration. This corresponds to the transition in Moroccan society from generalized reciprocity in family matters to relations dramatizing a new class hierarchy.[19]

The enactment of hospitality has likewise changed. No longer do the women of the community rally their communal efforts in order to provide hospitality for the guests; rather employees, often strangers, are engaged so that men and women may both enjoy the benefits of hospitality. Respected guests, whatever their gender, need no longer get their hands greasy with fluffing couscous or their arms tired with kneading bread for a hundred or more visitors.

Stratification and urbanization in Beni Mellal create a feminine labor force in need of capital. Clifford Geertz has remarked on the proliferation of middle men in marketplace relations in Morocco (1979). Women are now exploiting this cultural tendency by creating a service economy within their own feminine world, the domain of hospitality. The talent of turning commodity into gift is the same talent that permits a woman to accommodate herself to the commodity realm, objectifying herself as an adorner, a cook, a ḥǝnna artist, a market woman, or an herbalist and orator.

A working wife is now a source of income in a very inflationary economy where two salaries are necessary in order to attain (or maintain) the lifestyle advocated both in children's textbooks and in television advertising — that is, an ideal middle-class lifestyle. Yet it is also possible that in

becoming commodities for others women are actually giving a gift to themselves. In playing with the boundaries between motivated gift and "free"
commodity, women find a social space they can control, a space where tradition is being redefined.

The Subversive Bride

Women are socialized into the realm of hospitality, enabling them to transform commodity and gift relations, and to effect this transformation within
themselves as well. Yet it is naive to think that the realms of hospitable reciprocity and commodity are amicable partners. They co-exist with difficulty:
witness a working mother like Fadela who sells her skills for income eight
hours a day but is also expected to be the gifting nurturer at home in the
foyer (see Mernissi 1988). But this conflict, sometimes grueling in everyday
life, provides impetus for the rejection of old categories, generating consciousness and anger. "Men and women's differential participation in public
wealth transactions is   a principal locus of the difference between them"
(Strathern 1988:4). A change in this participation, however subtle, generates changes in gender awareness and in the placement of anger concerning
power inequities.

Women are not imitating men so much as they are embodying their
own masculinity, culturally defined, by bringing formerly private discourses
into the public realm. But the realm of hospitality does not evolve into the
realm of the commodity; reciprocal relations do not necessarily give birth
to those of prix fixe. The co-existence, or hybridization, of the two realms
is a more acceptable explanation of change than an evolutionary and hierarchical continuum. If mutual aid is giving way to buy-and-sell relations, it
is because of the hegemony of commodification and not the irrelevance of
friendship.

The expansion of the service economy into the female sphere is changing definitions of obligation, hospitality, and gifting. In this light, the service sector is diagnostic of a modernizing culture. New expectations from
women and by women in the marketplace and at home are straining traditional roles and values. Women are (often subversively) finding an ever-
larger niche for themselves in the new moral economy, one in which they
amplify choices by commodifying themselves. Although there is nothing
demeaning about a bride being a gift as long as the husband is likewise
considered, women's changing positions as commodities in the work force

is having a definite impact on their roles as gifts (brides) and gift-givers in traditional society.

The Moroccan wedding is a paradigm for much that is meaningful in Moroccan culture, providing the model for social interaction and cohesion in a system of regulations that juggles prestations with commodities in rather deft fashion. Disentangling the gift from the commodity is not easily done. Although the modern wedding contrasts dramatically with the wedding of only a generation ago, it still functions as a rite of passage and an important ritual moment in the lives of families. Within the process of commemorating the union of a woman and a man and their respective bloodlines, the symptoms of social transformation with its disequilibriums, tensions, yawns and sighs of relief, are evident.

Notes

1. Words in quotation marks were spoken in French.

2. This practice runs counter to another, which is to keep the bride from the sun in order for her skin to become white (Y. Stillman 1995; personal communication).

3. Westermarck (1926a: 239) notes that blessing (baraka) "may be spoiled by contact with the ground and its impurities." Thus both brides and returning pilgrims are carried over the threshold of the house.

4. This is usually the groom's parents' house.

5. Andalucian influences have been present in Morocco for more than five hundred years. What is significant in Fadela's statement is not its factual validity, but the importance of constructing an authentic and pure Moroccan tradition.

6. The near-revolutionary changes in Moroccan women's definitions of self and gender identity are evident in their increased visibility as they begin to appear in certain public milieux previously denied them: as merchants in women's cooperatives, high school teachers, or tellers in urban banks. But as Moroccan scholars have noted, increased visibility makes practices of inequality all the more salient. Mernissi (1988) discusses the large number of women who are paid less than the minimum wage because they are categorically denied working papers, and who are thus not accounted for in the percentages of women in the Moroccan work force. Belarbi (1988) reveals the plaintive voices of women working fulltime jobs while also fulfilling the traditional expectations of caring for home and children. Yet despite the struggles inherent in social transition, statistics support the fact that "the Moroccan woman is progressively breaking with certain traditions of subordination and is forging a not negligible place among other animating factors of economic life" (Rahmouni 1988: 107). All this qualifies the perception that roles and categories are in the process of reorganization and reformation. The weave of society is loosening and consequently what Appadurai calls the "ethnoscape" is affected: "This is not to

say that there are no relatively stable communities and networks, of kinship, of friendship, of work and of leisure, as well as of birth, residence and other filiative forms. But it is to say that the warp of these stabilities is everywhere shot through with the woof of human motion, as more persons and groups deal with the realities of having to move or the fantasies of wanting to move" (1990:7). In this case, the movement is from private to public sphere and from familial duty to economic responsibility for the family. Women are a "moving group" in Morocco and this relatively new mobility is changing the landscape of society.

7. "It is the contrast between the constant change and innovation of the modern world and the attempt to structure at least some parts of social life within it as unchanging and invariant, that makes the 'invention of tradition' so interesting" (Hobsbawm 1983:2).

8. There are many ethnicities in Morocco: Soussi Berbers, Berbers of the Middle Atlas, Berbers of the Rif (all with different languages), Saharans, Arabs, and Arabs who consider themselves related to Spain, thus Andalucian. Depending on the social context, a Berber may identify her or himself by regional, ethnic, or national identity (see C. Geertz 1976 on the phenomenon of *nisba*).

9. Ḥənna has a longer-term coloration effect when used on the hair and nails.

10. Thus ḥənna as a substance is difficult to categorize. For a discussion of the ambiguous nature of viscosity, see Sartre (1943:696) and Douglas (1984:38).

11. Like the west, Morocco is a specular society that privileges sight over the other senses in the establishment of the parameters of valuation.

12. This is documented in a well-known, albeit off-color joke in which people of the upper class are rumored to have loose morals. The joke goes as follows: Three friends, a Berber, an Arab from the plains, and a Fessi, were all to be married on the same night. The next morning they got together and asked each other how things had gone. The plains Arab said, "I worked at it for two hours before I got in." The Berber said, "that's nothing, I was at it all night. She didn't open until the morning call to prayer." Both friends then turned to the Fessi and asked how things had gone for him. "Me?" he said, "I found her wide open!"

The "openness" of the upper classes may be mocked, but it is not mimicked. The petit bourgeoisie selects only the more "closed" customs (for example, the adornment of the bride with gold chains or heavy headgear) in their construction of tradition.

13. The tradition of the western wedding dress has a longer history in other parts of the Middle East, particularly among the upper classes. See Graham-Brown (1988:chap. 5).

14. I have observed a gradual relaxation of bride-groom demeanor at many weddings over a thirteen-year period.

15. This was true in 1990–91. In 1995 I noticed a much larger proportion of advertising showing women in traditional jəllabas.

16. This is not a new phenomenon in large cities like Casablanca, Fes, Marrakech, Rabat, or Tangier.

17. It is another index of the transformation of tradition that the wedding may be hosted by either the bride's or the groom's family. Although holding the celebration (customarily held at the home of the groom's family) at the bride's family's

house may be a bit embarrassing, financial circumstances or a divorce between the groom's parents may provide reasons for doing so. In either case, it is the host mother or mother-in-law who takes responsibility for the details of the affair. The father receives people and presides over the men's celebration, his function largely ceremonial.

18. Because of public schooling accessibility and the increased attendance of girls, poorer families are more reluctant to send their children to middle-income or rich families to be socialized and kept. For similar reasons, young girls are less willing to be subservient in exchange for upkeep; they have more choices and are thus more autonomous.

19. The institution of the professional female cook (*tabbakha*) is not new; however, the service economy among women is burgeoning. In large cities, weddings are often catered.

7. Catering to the Sexual Market: Female Performers Defining the Social Body

Nothing illustrates the recent changes in the relative status of women and men in Moroccan society so fully as the altered position of the shikha, the female performer. As women who commoditize their voices and bodies in contexts of public celebration (both outdoors at saint's festivals, and indoors at wedding celebrations) shikhat (pl.) are often associated with the marketplace. In fact, women without moral scruples may be compared to shikhat who are "lost in the suq."

I first met Mouna at Khadija's wedding. She was the lead singer in a group of four women and two men. These women all wore qaftans made from an expensive peach-colored satinet material, complemented by gold bracelets, necklaces, and earrings. Mouna, in particular, displayed an impressive amount of gold on her limbs. She was an ample woman with fair skin and blue eyes. Because of her eyes, she was called "the blue one" (az-zərqa).

Mouna initiated the first song, cueing the man who played fiddle (kamanja) and joining him with a steady beat on a clay-bodied hand drum (ṭaʿrija).

"Tell me about my lover,"[1] she sang, "who has gone away, oh bachelor!"

"If I'm gone, I will be back," the other shikhat answered.

"The sleep of my mind has flown away," Mouna continued, "and I worry all night. Everybody has his lover

'awd liya 'la grin-i lli msha 'azri
ila mshit dəba n-wəlli.
n-n'as ṭar mən ras-i
u n-bat n-khamməm.
kula u ḥabib-u.

Over the course of an hour the beat got faster and faster, the words more difficult to distinguish. Mouna and the other women in her troupe circled the room, dancing close before the guests seated in the audience or drawing them up and into the dance. In the middle of the last song, Mouna unfastened her hair, curved her back, hung her head in front of her chest, and swung it from left to right, eyes closed, hair waving. Another woman in the group did the same. The music of the fiddle was now in pace with the quick beats of the drum. Several women from the audience were dancing. Mouna resumed an upright posture. She nodded to the man playing the bandir and he immediately began a different beat. The shikhat stamped their feet in time to the new rhythm and then the set was over.

During the break I followed the performers upstairs. Two brothers of the bride were also there. One shikha lit up a cigarette, as did the men, while the brothers poured wine for themselves and for the group. Mouna looked at me inquisitively. I was also dressed in a qaftan and gold and she didn't understand why a wedding guest had approached her. I explained interest in recording some of her songs.

"*Məskina*, poor thing" Mouna said, using a term that expressed both pity and endearment. She held my hand for the next twenty minutes, asking me questions about my life — why I was in Beni Mellal, where I lived, who my family was.

"This is my friend," she told the others when they were preparing to return downstairs for another set. "She's going to come to my house."

I visited Mouna regularly for the next two summers. She lived in a poor section of town, but in a brand-new house she had paid for with her own earnings. She had two daughters from different fathers, one seven, one fifteen. Her elderly aunt sometimes lived with her and there were usually friends, other shikhat, who came to visit in the afternoon.

Going to Mouna's place was always a bit risky. I had to keep my visits a secret. My in-laws would never approve and I feared that my middle-class friends, although usually very encouraging of my research, would be embarrassed about my visits to women with reputations for licentious living.

On my visits to Mouna, I would usually find her seated on the floor, plucking a chicken or preparing sweets. Apart from a wooden hutch and a bed in the bedroom, there was no furniture. We sat on blankets on the cool ceramic tiles and leaned on pillows propped against the wall. Mouna's youngest child made brief appearances, drinking the soda and eating the cookies Mouna would set out for me, before disappearing into the neighborhood again. Her teenage daughter did chores around the house; she ran to the grocer to buy soda for us and then sat on the doorstep while the older women talked inside.

Loose Words and Loose Women

Mouna was a very successful shikha. Her group were constantly asked to perform at weddings and had already recorded their music on audio cassette and distributed it to cassette vendors in the region. A video for home distribution was in progress. Not all Mouna's friends were so fortunate, however. I met Fatiha in Mouna's house one afternoon. She was a strikingly beautiful woman, especially by western standards, with dark hair, large brown eyes, high cheek bones, a gruff voice, and a quick sense of humor. We took to each other immediately and she invited me to her house, promising to sing for me.

Fatiha lived several streets away from Mouna in two rooms that she shared with her elderly mother, two grown sisters (one divorced, one never married), a grown brother, her sister's two year old daughter, and her own six-year-old son. The rooms were dark and sparsely furnished. Fatiha's "monsieur," a married landowner in a neighboring town, paid the rent. She told me he was crazy about her, and she tolerated him. (He showed up one day when I was there, a balding man with a generous smile, and was eager to discuss American politics.) Fatiha's younger sister was very thin and ill, possibly with parasites. She did embroidery work for other women to make some money. Fatiha had recently stopped performing in compliance with her man's wishes, but was getting bored sitting at home and wanted her own money. She was thinking about going back to work.

One afternoon Fatiha took me into the back room, where a picture of a regal-looking man in a white robe and a turban—her boyfriend's grandfather—hung on the wall. She sent her son to buy two cigarettes from the corner store. When he came back I noticed that he had only four toes and four fingers on his left hand and foot. "I'm crazy about him," she told me. He smiled at me and left. We lit up the cigarettes, I put the tape machine on "record," and Fatiha recited:

> If you're going to the heights
> Come here first and I'll give you some advice
> If you get there, show good will [to the local saint].
> Don't talk to the city or its people.

If you talk about them, you'll regret it.
Show good will.
Don't scorn the heights.

wa l-ghadi l-ʿalwa
aji n-waṣṣi-k baʿda.
ila lḥagti səlləm.
l-ʿalwa la tkəlləm.
ila tqawlti t-ndəm.
səlləm, səlləm.
f-l-ʿalwa la tkəlləm.

And you, who are leaving, what's your business?
And you who are coming, what's your business?
Those town people are all crazy;
Those going scorn you
And those coming scorn you.
But you, you followed the entranced ones
And forgot your family.

wa l-ghadi wəsh mgabl?
wa j-jay wəsh mgabl?
l-ʿalwa gaʿ b-bahəl.
wa l-ghadya ʿayb ʾl-ik.
j-jaya ʿayb ʾl-ik.
u tbʿati nas l-ḥal
ura nsiti walidi-k.

The movements of the shikha trace the patterns of propriety and impropriety in Moroccan culture. Her body is a socially designated site of shamelessness in that her social mask requires a refusal of deference rules and moral norms. By artistically publicizing the intimacies of private life in the public sphere of ritual and secular celebration, the shikha sets cultural definitions of public and private domains into relief. She does this by over-stepping social boundaries in a performance mode designated for such activity. By assertion of sexual liberty in heterosexual company, expressed in song lyrics, physical postures, and provocative dance movements, the shikha commoditizes sex, becoming a fetishized commodity occupying the margins of Moroccan society.

The "inseparability of conceptual and bodily activity" (Jackson 1983:137) is exemplified in the case of the shikha. An exponent of the "relaxed" (*matluq*) in Moroccan conceptions of the body, the shikha is also categorized as "loose": her freedom of physical expression in dance is tied to an assumed licentiousness in the moral realm. The performance of shikhat articulates the tension between the reserved and the open—the ḥashshumi and the maṭluq—in Moroccan cognitive categories.[2] These expressions are displayed in postures (lowered eyes, bowed head or, by contrast, direct gaze, rhythmic gait) and may be used to circumscribe individuals who exhibit one quality more frequently than the other. In the colloquial context, someone who is maṭluq is flexible and easy-going, while someone who is ḥashshumi is shy and formal. These physical postures are inseparable from their moral character. As Combs-Schilling notes, "experiences of the body build categories of the mind" (1989:xv). What Mauss spoke of as the "techniques of the body"—stances, postures, physical habits of body use that are acquired like language and that are equally communicative (1973)—are learned as culturally interpreted "physico-concepts"; they are the terms of embodiment (what Bourdieu 1977 refers to as "dispositions" of the body). Thus the ḥashshumi, the shy and reserved, denotes respect and deference to the "pervasive male discourse"[3] in Moroccan society, while the maṭluq, the open, the free, asserts liberty from this discourse and is tolerated only when it is unthreatening, as in the case of a lovable drunk.

Infamy has often preceded fame for the woman artist. As Jones has noted, "The link between loose language and loose living arises from a basic association of women's bodies with their speech: a woman's accessibility to the social world beyond the household through speech is seen as intimately connected to the scandalous openness of her body" (1986:76). The "loose" language of the shikha is both linguistic and corporeal; these two expressive aspects cannot be divided. The shikha opens her mouth in public—singing words that discuss sexuality, inhaling and exhaling cigarette smoke, imbibing wine—and uses her body to draw others to the dance. Often a "meaty" (*mlaḥma*) woman, the shikha enacts the carnivalesque body of plenty, moving her hips rhythmically and displaying a minute control of the musculature of the "lower bodily strata"[4] at close proximity to her audience, whether they are male or female. Waving her loose hair back and forth before her face, her feet beating the floor in regular rhythm, the shikha

Figure 17. The performance of a Moroccan shikha.

may even approach trance (Figure 17); indeed, her dancing makes salient
the permeable boundaries between the sexual and the sacred, drawing
upon a vocabulary of movement similar to that used to commune with the
spirit world in Moroccan esoteric practice (see Crapanzano 1973; Fernea
1978). The performance of shikhat at annual festivals celebrating local saints
(*musəm*s) reinforces the intricate and often inseparable relationship between the sacred and the profane in Moroccan expressive culture.

Just as the shikha is associated with secularity, she is also aligned with
the subaltern and the disenfranchised. Her community is with other shikhat. They perform collectively, often in groups of three or four women,
playing an array of small drums (the *darbuka*, the *ṭarija*, the *bandir*), singing and sometimes drumming with their feet on an overturned metal basin
(*aj-jafna*). They are usually accompanied by two or three male musicians

who play the *kamanja* (the fiddle, a men's instrument), the *lutar* (a three-stringed small-bodied instrument also played by men), and the drums.

The physical centrality of shikhat in the majority of Moroccan celebrations and their explicitly erotic physical attitudes make them metonyms for the festive body. But although they are central in their artistic function, they are marginal in society. As representatives of boldness and excess, they position themselves beyond the borders of social restraint, beyond ḥshuma, or shame. Stigmatization thus becomes society's means of controlling them.

Legends of Resistance

The subversive power of shikhat song (particularly the complex genre of *l'aita*)[5] is documented in oral legends that recount its political role in resistance movements against the French, as well as against certain Moroccan officials who conspired with them during the Protectorate. One such controversial figure was the governor, or qa'id, 'Aissa ben 'Mur, who had a conflict with the Oulad Zaid, a dissident tribe under his jurisdiction in the region of Safi. There are varying opinions regarding the character of this governor. Although some people praise his justice, others say he was a tyrant, an "artist in torture and murder," and a pawn of the administration who collaborated with the colonialists (Kharraz 1995; cf. Bouhamid 1995). He was also, however, a connoisseur of popular music, known for his nights of artistic revelry.

Qa'id 'Aissa bən 'Mur was particularly fond of a shikha named Hadda, a religious woman and tribal poet who performed for him whenever she was summoned. Legend has it that the Ouled Zaid tribe persuaded Hadda to criticize the qa'id in song so that other tribes would be aware of his wrongs and would rebel against him. Hadda did this, singing verses such as

'aissa ya d-dwib
ya ujah l-klib.
'aissa l-qatəl khut-u.

'Aissa oh you little fox
oh dog-face.
'Aissa, the killer of his brothers.

When the qa'id heard about this, he commanded Hadda to sing these songs in front of him and, upon hearing them, ordered his servants to kill her. First, however, she was allowed to do her ablutions and pray. Some say that when doing her ablutions, she found a baby crying in a room of his house — the qa'id's grandson, the son of Moulay Hamid. Hadda nursed him and consequently Moulay Hamid forbade his father's servants to kill her, instigating a conflict between father and son. Others say that 'Aissa bən 'Mur either buried or burned her alive. As Kharraz notes, whatever relation this legend bears to history, it attests to the role ascribed to shikhat song in political conflict; l-'aita was not just sung at harvests and weddings, but had and continues to have a socio-political function in the Moroccan historical imagination.

> dar s-si 'aissa khlat.
> qbalt-ha l-m'ashat.

> The house of Si 'Aissa was devastated.
> [Because] It was opposed to the M'ashat [a powerful tribe with holy
>   lineage].

> l-'badi ṣaila⁶ 'l-ik
> mzaida walidi-k.

> The 'Abadi [tribe] rioted against you
> and also against your parents.

A parallel figure to Hadda in western coastal Morocco is Mbaraka l-Bihishiya in Beni Mellal who, during the protectorate, sang songs against the French, and particularly against a captain named Bironi who went on to write a book about the possibilities of civilizing the land and population of the region (see Juwiti 1995). As Juwiti notes, the history of the pacification of Beni Mellal can be read as a dialogue between the colonialist writer and the illiterate but inspired artist who defied him in song, an exploration of "two sides of a single historical wound" (Juwiti ibid.).

When France invaded by air and the population was chased to the hills, l-Bihishiya encouraged the fighters, and criticized the deserters, singing:

> shaft l-ḥakəm jay-ni rəjdad
> b-nfaḍu jdad.

t-bqai b-khir ya l-blad.
hada ma ktab.

I saw the governor coming after me
with new weapons.
Stay well oh my country.
That's what's written.

After the fighting was over and the French had established themselves,
l-Bihishiya sang vitriolic songs about the French and those who accepted
and worked with the colonialists:

ḥətta ʿriwa ʿraf l-biru.
ḥətta ʿriwa dayr ksiwa.
ḥətta ʿriwa ʿad ifari.
shad l-iyam l-məṭluba.
shi ʿṭat-u shi gəlʿat l-ih.

Even a little nothing⁷ knows bureaucracy.
Even a little nothing is wearing a little uniform.
Even a a little nothing has become a conciliator.
He is holding on to borrowed days.
They are given to some, and taken away from others.

As a consequence of her songs of protest, Bironi exiled her to a small town
in the mountains (*fum l-ʿanṣər*), but her tribe went to get her and she
returned to Beni Mellal, continuing to sing songs about the evil that was
afoot, citing by name the people who died in conflict with the French.

tkəlləm l-kur qbəl l-fṭur
kif r-rʿud l-kharfiya.
shabət kul mən hiya dərriya.
ṭharqat l-khayl u r-rəjliya.

The canonball spoke before breakfast
like the storms of autumn.
All the young girls have turned grey.
The horses were burned with the foot soldiers.

bki ya l-məllaliya.
bki b-d-dmuʿ s-skhiya.
l-qaṣba tgəlʿat li-ya.

Cry oh Mellali woman.
Cry with generous tears.
The fort has been taken away from me.

Centrality and Anomaly

For a large majority of contemporary Moroccans, shikhat continue to be an indispensable part of religious and national festivity: "If there aren't shikhat, there's nothing" (*ila ma kaynsh sh-shikhat, ma kayn walu*). They are called upon to entertain at saint's festivals, wedding celebrations, circumcisions, naming ceremonies, and ḥənna parties. These social occasions are for the most part ritual times as well as festive events. Shikhat divert attention from the private dimension of family rite to a festivity that is created for the express enjoyment of the guests. Although a bride may be taken up in the seriousness of ritual or a little boy may be having his foreskin removed at the center of a rite of passage, the guests engage in a more secular celebration whose success is predicated upon gazing at and dancing with the shikhat. "Gazing" in this context is not a passive activity, nor is it confined to men. Initially seated on long couches or mattresses, the guests are approached by the performers, who proceed to dance and sing at high volume directly in front of their spectators, inviting participation as well as soliciting ten- and fifty-dirham notes (about $1.25 and $7.00) to be tucked into their belts (Figure 18).

The clear visibility of money in the festive context demarcates the shikha as a commodity, set apart from the rest of the audience. And yet there is little in the shikha's dress and adornment that separates her from her female public. She wears elegant and expensive qaftans much like those of the guests at the celebration, also displaying considerable amounts of gold. The physical identification of the audience with the shikha is thus easily facilitated once the party gets going and the guests allow themselves to be drawn into the dance.

Different rules of behavior apply in festive contexts, as the ordinary and quotidian gives way to the extraordinary and exceptional (Abrahams 1986). Events such as weddings inevitably provide counter-performances to

Figure 18. The shikhat sing and dance in close proximity to their audience, often playing with them and pulling them up to their feet to dance.

everyday norms and conventions by putting them into differential and experiential relief. Shikhat provide this "relief," yet their marginality in the larger society acts to further instantiate the very moral codes they challenge. Because they blur the boundaries between ordinary and extraordinary experience, between private and public genres of expression, they become the social representatives of transgression (from the Latin *transgredi*, "to step beyond or across").

Codes of propriety are an extremely important aspect of Moroccan culture and of the circum-Mediterranean world in general (see Abu-Lughod 1986; Bourdieu 1966, 1977; Brandes 1980; Herzfeld 1985; Perestiany 1966). The enactment of these codes is context-dependent, relying on notions of social position, status, and discursive role negotiation (Rosen 1984). Within the dominant "moral economy,"[8] one way that women access limited honor and respect is by "distancing themselves from sexuality and its antisocial associations." Yet, as Abu-Lughod has made clear for the Bedouin women of Egypt, normally hidden emotions (such as love and desire) are permitted expression in private and monosexual contexts (1986:165). Likewise in Morocco, the unconstrained expression of emotion and all activities associated with pleasure are socially curtailed except when given deliberate license during periods of festivity (*n-nashat*) or monosexual intimacy.[9] Expressions of sexuality and personal emotion through music, dance, or poetry, are manifest mainly in particular performance contexts due to their potentially subversive power.

Shikhat embody this subversion as they cross the boundaries between acceptable female and acceptable male behavior; they smoke, drink alcohol, and may have several sexual partners, while capitalizing on their femininity. Because of this, shikhat are presented as everything respectable women are not. A popular joke recounts the reaction of a man from Fes when, on arriving home, finds his wife in bed with another man. "All you need is a cigarette," he tells her, "and you'll be a shikha." The shikha becomes a metonym for female transgression. She is a free woman and anyone who exercises freedom beyond the socially defined limits is a shikha. Maher notes that shikhat "are popularly defined as 'women who do not want men to tell them what to do'" (1974:111, cf. Graham-Brown 1988).

Yet shikhat serve a role in the inner thoughts of honorable women insofar as they are licensed in performance to publicize the private desires and disappointments of the majority of Moroccan women. As many as 50 percent of all village women may look forward to divorce, while the statistics run about 28 percent for the "urban employed class" (Maher 1974:110). Divorce is easy and abandonment is common.

> Beg of the one who cauterized you
> If he will take you.

> The love that I'm used to
> Took the bus and went.

> Oh one going to Beni Mellal, put me in mind
> The route to Chaouia is between my eyes.

> zawgi f-l-kawi-k
> ila bgha y-ddi-k.

l-kbida lli n'tad
shad l-kar u zad.

l-ghadi l-bəni məllal dir-ni f-l-bal
ṭrəq sh-shawiya bin 'ayniya.

The lover here is he who heals by burning—cauterization. The image comes from a traditional healer (*kuwway*) in Moroccan society who cures all manner of sickness (considered "cold") by quickly tapping the body with a hot iron rod. The shikha has been abandoned by the one who both healed and burned her and the route of his departure is seared into her bodily memory, "between her eyes."

The Performance of Openness

Shikhat divulge their own and other women's secrets in public (extra-familial) celebration and sometimes in bawdy language. The potential subversion of this act is felt by society as a whole. What applies to Bedouin society applies also here: "to express sexuality is... an act of defiance" (Abu-Lughod 1986:157), an assertion of power that has no place in social hierarchy. Because enacted in a festive mode, it is tolerated and enjoyed; a defiance but also a source of social renewal, permitting the social ideation of alternate wells of power within the individual. Despite the unreality created by the performance frame, "both rituals and festivals enter into the process of self-authentification" (Abrahams 1987:177). There are times when play is dead serious. The shikha says, in essence, "I am playing, but I am playing at what I am; I am this mask."

Shikhat have the license to play with gender boundaries and with what is socially permissible during performance time. But shikhat are threatening precisely because they extend the license of public performance to their private lives as well. In a real sense, their livelihood lies in transforming their private selves into public display, hypertrophizing themselves. Their sexual liberation and licentiousness becomes symbolic of their selfhood: the sex stands for the whole.

Being without closure, however, they are also without defense. The poetic publication of privacy in song lyric and bodily movement establishes the shikha as public property; that is, her commoditized vulnerability serves the purpose of society as she is appropriated as a symbol of immodesty and becomes an emblem of shame. Yet the performance of shikhat exposes the values of the dominant culture to challenge by speaking a different attitude — physical, emotional and moral — into being. They "reflexively comment upon those patterns and alter a society's awareness of itself" (Babcock 1980:5). Poesis, bodily and lyrical, becomes a means of self-revelation, social reflexivity, and subtle resistance (see Abu-Lughod 1986, 1990a; Boddy 1989; Caton 1990; T. Joseph 1980).

Socio-Sexual Reflexivity and the Limitation of Chaos

The altered awareness that shikhat bring to society in their bodily poetics is imbued with social and political import. Shikhat illustrate a reality that they actually live and by so doing they draw attention to both the disjunctures and the congruences between the real and the fictional in society's definitions of the feminine. The shikha's unabashed expression of sexuality in song, movement, and lifestyle comments upon and, in a limited sense, reveals what is usually clothed, veiled, and preferably dismissed among those who are modest:

> Beer and red wine
> she blamed it on them.

> They made you drink whiskey
> and you spent all night [pining and] crying.

> l-birra u r-ruj
> dart-hum ḥujuj.

> sharbu-k l-wiski
> bayt 'a t-bki.

But this same forthrightness also accounts for her designation as the diseased member of the social body who must pay for her libertinism:

> Oh one who bought me
> Put me next to you.
> Now you'll begin to need me.

You sold me and I bought you.
My heart is your property.

ah wa ya sh-sharini
wa dir-ni ḥda-k.
daba təḥtəj-ni.
bə'ti-ni u ana n-shri-k
qalbi rah məmluk l-ik.

Or,

I fear that you will become addicted to love.
No doctor will be able to cure you,
even with pure faith.

n-khaf 'l-ik mən l-ḥub la y-bli-k.
u ḥətta ṭbib ma y-qdər y-dawi-k
wakha b-n-niya ṣ-ṣafiya.

The commodification of desire is here eloquently if ambiguously stated.
The body is bought and sold by both men and women, while a piece of it
(the heart) is singled out and appropriated. Love infects the body with
incurable addiction. Desire becomes a commodity that can be controlled
by women as well as a disease that spreads like a virus, uncontrolled. The
lyrics sung by shikhat attest to the power of feminine desire to change lives
and circumstance. But they are also rife with the painful consequences of
taking responsibility for that power. The shikha is ultimately "burned" because she rejects the boundaries that are socially prescribed for her emotional
and physical lives and breaks "the silence of women [which is] one of the
bases of Moroccan civilization" (Mernissi 1989 : 1). təḥragt b-l-kabrit, u 'mr-
ni ma nsit: "I was burned with sulfur," intoned Fatiha, "and I never forgot."
    The shikha enters into dialogue with many and all. She is a female
rebel, a dialogic entity[10] who by her very being questions the validity of the
monologic and prescriptive place designated for female desire by the "pervasive male discourse."[11] Ironically, she also dialogues with the belief that,
unchecked, women's sexuality lures men (and thus society) to fitna, "chaos"
(from the root fatana which means to seduce, or to tempt).
    The fear of fitna is described by Rosen as underlying the construction
of all social relations in Morocco. Because social status is negotiated rather

than hierarchically prescribed, he argues, personal and social identity in Morocco take shape in a "web of relationships" that is perpetually transforming and indeterminate (1984:8). Power and position in Moroccan society are discursively constructed and thus subject to the vagaries and instabilities of interpretation by both kin and strangers. "And over (or under) all this uncertainty," Rosen asserts, "resides a sense—indeed a fear—of chaos, a belief that the orderliness of the world is contingent on many factors and that the tendency, or at least the strong possibility, exists that this uncertain physical and social environment might well give way to utter disorder" (1984:8). Ludic behavior like singing and dancing is particularly subversive in such a climate, threatening to destabilize and decenter the serious and canonical aspects of the quotidian.

This fear of the contingent and inchoate in social relations is certainly not confined to Moroccan culture. Trickster figures in the folklore of many societies attest to the fear and fascination with which humans regard the boundless.[12] But while male performers are also marginal to Moroccan society, conceptions of disorder are clearly gendered; fitna is also a synonym for a "beautiful woman."[13] Insofar as the shikha threatens "the orderliness of the world," her social presence provides reasons and reinforces the axiom that "women must be controlled to prevent men from being distracted from their social and religious duties."[14] Her very being proves that women who are not controlled turn to temptation and sedition—to fitna (economic motivations are not taken into account in this argument). Because shikhat enact their own autonomy, society institutionalizes their freedom and circumscribes the concept of fitna in social stigma. The irony, of course, is that shikhat perform a very codified set of social behaviors, their roles prescribed and anticipated. It is the contradiction of being victimized for representing a freedom that they are not at liberty to enjoy that leads the shikha to lament:

> The clairvoyant is the mistress of prediction.
> Your tomb is in hell.
> Where are the brothers and sisters
> Who will be present on the day of death?

> shuwafa mulat l-'lam.
> qabr-ak fi jaḥnnam.
> fin l-khut u l-khwatat
> y-ḥadru l-ik yum l-mamat?[15]

The Competent Body

Despite their rule-governed disorder, shikhat are nonetheless artists, taking responsibility for the voicing and interpretation of social disjuncture, caused, for example, by the competing forces of family expectations and personal desires.[16] Indeed, their lamentations (referred to as *bəkiya*, crying) on themes of lost love, abandonment, and sexual longing define feminine crises as they are experienced in the everyday world. The thematic sadness that is registered in the song lyrics, however, is countered by a joyousness of delivery as the words are vigorously drummed and intoned (often around the triad of a minor third and a lowered seventh note). The juxtaposition of mournful words, festive voicing, and sexualized dancing acts both to define and, at least momentarily, to resolve crisis. Contradiction, whether of semiotic codes or of social and evaluative roles, is not bemoaned in this context; rather, the plurality of messages in different symbolic venues acts to integrate and renew the community. Lamentation sung as celebration may be said to have therapeutic effect, the benefits of intersemiotic dialogue finding resonance with evidence from other Islamic rituals and crises (see especially Boddy 1988, 1989). Contradiction is thus celebrated, embodied, and made into strength.

Once they have the stage, shikhat dominate and dictate the emotional tenor of celebration. Through the provocative movements and loud singing of the shikhat, the audience is drawn up and into a collective state of celebration, their bodies literally pulled into the dance. Like other systems of signification, the body is inherently reflexive,[17] calling attention to itself as the primary symbol for self-designation in the performance. For although the shikha's semi-improvised song lyrics delimit social stress points, they are often inaudible under the percussive noise and near-screaming quality of the voices. It is the body that imposes itself upon the audience, making the most permanent impression both in the moment and in memory. Regardless of the audience's gender, the shikha approaches and demonstrates how to "lift the belt" (*haz as-səmṭa*), an undulating movement that rolls the lower abdomen up to the waist. If, as Bourdieu asserts, "competence implies the power to impose reception" (1977:649), then this is definitely a performance of both competence and power. In performance, the shikha is engaged in an intense demonstration of physical and artistic prowess. The audience expects it and the shikha is responsible for communicating it (Bauman, 1977). To the extent that the shikha successfully lures her audience and captures the attention centered on her, a state of "communitas"[18] may be momentarily achieved, facilitated at times by musical climax or by the loss of self-centeredness that transpires in shared dance. The shikha, in this instance, becomes a liminar, a facilitator of transition from one state (*ḥal*) to another.

In delimiting the competence of the shikha, it is impossible not to speak of the shikha's body, for the shikha is not only a professional dancer, but is understood to be a professional in other physical matters, as a shikha has illicit sexual relations (*kat zni*). As one Moroccan novelist describes her, a shikha can smoke a cigarette with her sexual organ (Khatibi 1983); she is an adept. Because of the high value traditionally put on virginity in Moroccan society, a number of young men were first "initiated" by shikhat. Shikhat may provide an introduction to sexuality, both literally for young men, and symbolically for young women, for it is through the physical liberty displayed by shikhat at times of celebration that the limits of the feminine "techniques" of the body are socially explored; shikhat present to the public the various ways that women may "use their bodies," thus codifying a possible repertoire of feminine movement into the social canon (Mauss 1973:70). Moroccan girls learn to dance at a very young age in the company of their female kin, but it is only during times of celebration when this competence is displayed outside the family situation. Shikhat provide the model for competence in this regard as they call the body to a remembrance of its earliest joys in movement.

Shikhat master the moves of the dance. They are maṭluqat, "free, unlimited, unrestricted." They are also fun, garrulous, and outgoing. Someone who is maṭluq, is also often *nasht*, an adjective which carries connotations of becoming intoxicated. If one is nasht, one is "lively, animated, spirited," but if one is *na:sht* (drawing out the vowel), then one is really in the spirit of things, high on wine or dance or love. A common comment made about a shikha is that she is *na:shta m'a ras-ha*, "spirited in her head," celebrating and jubilant. When I remarked that a particular shikha was so spirited, a young woman was quick to tell me that shikhat *always* embody this quality of exhilaration and flowing movement.

Women who are maṭluqat are often appreciated in public and scorned in gossip or the reverse, depending on the intimacy and gender identity of the group. This duality articulates two opposing values: the hegemonic system of deference condemns the maṭluq as potentially subversive of the dominant value system, whereas the "subordinate discourse of women"[19] applauds the maṭluq as courageous and entertaining, though not necessarily discursively safe:

The gossipers, what are they worth?
Oh my hell, oh my hell.
They're worth the wind
Those who say disgraceful words.

u lli hadru ash kay swaw?
wayli wayli.
y-swaw r-riḥ
ya lli y-gulu klam l-'ar.

Traditionally, unmarried girls have had license to be moderately matluqat at celebrations such as weddings, as this is their chance to exhibit themselves to mothers of prospective young men. Yet there is a limit to their exhibitionism, since they are amateurs playing at "the dance." Although they may be seen as imitating the movements of shikhat, resulting in an inversion of roles (virgin as prostitute), their display is not taken seriously.

Shikhat, on the contrary, are disgraceful precisely because they have no shame (*ma kay ḥashmush*). They extend the license granted by the performance situation to their lives in general. They are licentious in taking authority into their own hands and deciding to author their lives outside the socially admonished roles. But their role is nonetheless socially prescripted; they occupy the margins of society in order that the center may be more clearly defined. Because they carry their performative role into their quotidian lives, they open themselves to social ostracism and marginalization.

The Nonsense Body

Shikhat express and create the festive body by making public a repertoire of movements and emotions, embodied in dance and lyric, that are otherwise limited to familial and monosexual occasions. They also embody the carnivalesque in that they are at liberty to publicly indulge in wine and in cigarettes, a license that is not in general open to women in Moroccan society.[20] Wine is thought to be an integral ingredient for stimulating their verbal improvisation and artistic style. When I asked what shikhat sing about, several Moroccans told me "they drink wine and they begin to make nonsense." The lyrics of their songs may be considered nonsense by some, but they are a very serious nonsense as they refer explicitly and allusively to a body of cultural tenets that—apart from the Moroccan novel—are not given artistic expression in any other form:

> Please Mr. Fqih
> Make me a charm for him
> In order to make him crazy and mad
> And take him away from his parents.
> Oh my days.

> 'afək as-si l-fqih
> dir-liya shi ḥjiyib 'li-h
> bəsh n-ḥamq-u u n-səṭṭi-h
> u n-fərq-u 'la walidi-h.
> ay-yam-i.

> Bring the blood of sacrifice
> And we'll put it on his motorbike
> In order to make him crazy
> And leave him to turn in circles.
> Oh my days.

> jibu dam l-mghdur
> n-'alq-u l-ih f-l-muṭur
> n-ḥamq-u
> u-n-khall-ih y-dur.
> ay-yam-i.

> Bring the whiskers of the mouse
> So I can hang them from his door.
> My love has become a cheat.
> Oh my days.

> jibu zghibat l-far
> n-'alq-hum fi bab d-dar.
> ḥabib-i ulla ghaddar.
> ay-yam-i.

Here a folk ethic that is associated more with the feminine than with the masculine world[21] is evoked: the belief in charms, in potions, and in illicit magic. Although this world is known and accepted in Moroccan culture, it represents an alternate power system to that of orthodox Islam. The speaking of these words at a public celebration gives credence to this alternate and feminine power system, thereby challenging more dominant beliefs that classify these practices as shameful. In this, shikhat speak directly to people whose origin (*aṣl*) is rural and whose belief system resembles that documented by Westermarck in 1926a. Although much of the folk mentality has changed, just an hour spent at an herbalist's shop is enough evidence that sympathetic magic and herbs are still solicited on a large scale.

Also at issue in these lyrics is the tension between love and family. Shikhat side with the former:

> For years I've loved him.
> [Now] a woman came and wants to take him.
> By your mother, you won't win him
> Even if we make his life fall.
> Oh my days.

> sinin u ana n-bghi-h
> jat uḥayda bghat t-ddi-h.
> u llahi ya mmu-k la fəzti bi-h
> wakha n-ṭayḥu r-ruḥ 'l-ih.
> ay-yam-i.

> His old wrinkled mother came.
> She told me, "let go of my son."
> He's your son [but he's] my love.
> Oh my days.

> jat sh-shərfa taʿt mm-u.
> galt-liya ṭalqi wald-i.
> nti wald-ək u ana ḥubb-i.
> ay-yam-i.

This theme is common in shikhat song, considered a genre of Moroccan popular music (*musiqa shaʿbiya*). The tension between romantic love and the assignment of partners by family and social pressure echoes the shikha's own dilemma: in choosing the former, a young couple attain their own prerogative but lose the support of their families. Likewise for the shikha:

the same freedom that allows her to live fully in her senses also imprisons her in social stigma. Most all shikhat are also divorcées or women who have had to fend for themselves and their children. Many refuse to be dependent on an already impoverished family and decide to work as performers. Categorizing the lyrics of shikhat's songs as nonsense is a way of masking the issues of class, poverty, and female autonomy, perpetuating their social "misrecognition" in the larger community (Bourdieu, 1977b).[22]

The Exiled Body

As shikhat choose against shabby indigence with respectability and for marginality with "independence," their choice is not without regret. "They say this work ruins us," Fatiha told me. When I asked another young shikha if she chose her work willingly, she said, "I do it by necessity, sister, just by necessity." Another friend of Mouna's told me, "we're not like you, we're not going to paradise." These comments indicate that social attitudes towards shikhat are indeed incorporated into their own view of themselves; shikhat become the object that society says they are. There is little resistance to romance here;[23] shikhat internalize the dominant value system which degrades their material and spiritual worth.

The shikha's discourse of victimization rationalizes her social position with arguments about fate and financial necessity (Gilligan 1982). Pity is among the most frequently elicited reactions to her plight. As Si Mohamed told me, "I don't judge them, as you never know what circumstances made them become what they are." Shikhat are well traveled in tribulation:

> If you're going to the heights
> Come here [first] and I'll give you some advice . . .

Although "the heights" in the context of this song is a metaphor for "the city," its use is not wholly arbitrary. Shikhat enjoy a freedom not only of bodily movement, but of geographical movement as well. But if they see summits that average women do not, they are made to pay dearly for the privilege. Because they embrace unlawful "heights," shikhat are socially constructed as the epitome of all that is low and base in society. As one college-educated working woman put it, shikhat were *dégoûtantes*, "disgusting."

Shikhat are usually associated with a particular place (the shikhat of

Khenifra or of Beni Mellal, for example), though many have migrated from their village or town of birth to cities or provincial centers. A majority have been rejected by their families: "They live alone or in groups, having in common the characteristic that they have left or been repudiated by their kin, and have thus forfeited lineage and male tutelage," says Maher (1974). The rootlessness of the shikha's existence contrasts starkly with the sense of origin (*aṣl*) and belonging in normative definitions of selfhood in Morocco. "To Moroccans, geographical regions are inhabited spaces, realms within which communities organize themselves to wrest a living and forge a degree of security. . . . To be attached to a place is, therefore, not only to have a point of origin—it is to have those social roots, those human attachments, that are distinctive to the kind of social person one is" (Rosen 1984:23).

In this light, shikhat are uprooted personages with no claims to an identifying geography; they are free-floating bodies in social exile.[24] The Moroccan proverb, "There is no good in a woman who roams about and no good in a man who does not" emphasizes the masculine characteristics of the shikha and her repudiation by normative society.[25] In another song, the shikha is portrayed as spending her "days touring cities and the country." By following in the footsteps of the shikha, one loses not only a sense of place, but one's family as well. In Moroccan society, this is the greatest hardship possible. Without family or sense of place, the shikha's subjectivity must necessarily take roads less traveled. It is not then surprising that the bonds of friendship and mutual aid between shikhat are profound.[26]

The Metaphoric Body

Linguistic metaphor functions as a means for constructing identity at all levels of society. Whether women are referred to as horses (*l-khayl*) or deer (*l-ghzal*) in the Moroccan idiom changes the interpretive context of a conversation. "[O]ur experience of the world… rests upon choices of metaphor" (Fernandez, 1986:x), providing a rich base from which to appreciate the shikha's self-conceptions and society's conceptions about her:

> If I were a porter, I'd carry him.
> If I were a carrier [of children], I'd pick him up.
> I'm afraid! I'm afraid that I'll make him fall.
> If I make him fall, I can handle it. Yes.

ila kunt ḥammala n-ḥaml-u.
ila kunt rakkaba n-rəkb-u.
khaif khaif la n-ṭayḥ-u.
ila ṭayəḥt-u n-qad bi-h. Hah.

What's the matter with him?
What's the matter with him?
What is it?
He looked at me
And then lowered his eyes.
And seared me yet again.

wa ha mal-u hah?
wa ha mal-u hah?
wa ha mal-u?
shaf fi-ya
u ḥdər ʿayn-u.
zadn-i kiyya tani hah.

Here's my arm for a pillow.
Easy, easy
don't break it.
And even if you break it,
the bone-setter is nearby. Yes.

hak draʿi twəsd-u.
kays kays
la t-hərs-u.
ila hərəsti-h,
ha j-jabbar ḥdaya hah.

The first impression in this lyric is that of support: "if I were a porter (*ḥam-mala*)." The verb *ḥməl* [MA] means to carry, to bear, or to support. Professional porters are called "the owners of the carts" and may be hired cheaply to carry goods from the marketplace to home. They are often humble or homeless people who sleep in their carts at night near bus stations or empty stalls. A ḥammal is a carrier without even the distinction of a cart. This poem mentions a ḥammal*a*, a female porter—an anomaly in Moroccan culture.

The verb "to carry" is also used to express the state of pregnancy: to carry a child. A *mra ḥamla* is a pregnant woman. The verb ḥmǝl has psychological connotations as well, used colloquially in the expression *ma kan-ḥamlush* "I can't bear it/him." Thus a hammala is someone who bears both physical and mental burdens.

The second line is also predicated on the act of carrying, using the verb *rakǝb* [MA], which means to ride or mount. In Morocco a child rides on her mother's back (*rakba ʿla dhar um-ha*), held by a large piece of cloth secured about the mother's waist. This line thus continues the support imagery: if I were a rakaba — one who provides a ride — I'd pick him up.

One also rides or mounts animals; in the following stanza a woman is compared to a horse who carries both armor and its owner. It is no ordinary horse, but a show horse displayed at national or religious festivals where "they play the horses" (*kay-laʿbu al-khayl*).

And whatever the fair-haired woman does, she merits.
Like the blue-speckled horse armored by his owner
Who took him to the running grounds to be proud of him.
It's for him that I've come.

u z-zaʿra ila dart-u t-stahǝl ila dart-u.
kif l-bǝrgi sǝnh-u mul-ah
u dda-h l-ʿalfa y-tʿanna bi-h.
u ʿla qubl-u jaya.

The French translation of this event (the running of Arabian horses) as "fantasia" no doubt comes from the classical Arabic word for imagination (*khayal*),[27] built on the same triliteral verb as horsemen (*khayyal*). Although Moroccans associate the word khayl primarily with horses and their impressive performance, there is a semantic interplay between the two realms. The fantasia is a dramatic event that engages the spectators as well as the actors in agonistic play, involving the promenade and racing of Arabian horses with elaborate saddles, mounted by riders elegantly dressed in white jǝllabas and carrying long rifles. From five to twelve horses and their riders line up, the horses biting at the bit and prancing, while spectators gather at the borders of a long field. At the signal, the horses take off at full speed down the dusty terrain for about 300 yards and then stop abruptly in unison right before the edge of the crowd while the riders shoot their rifles into the air. It is a game of dare that is played with the audience, who try not to leave their places, though occasionally they are forced to move aside. Before the performance, people stroll around and view the horses tethered to stakes throughout the vicinity. Tents are set up for the riders, as these events may last for as long as a week.

The comparison of women and horses has special significance. Horses are animals of prestige in Morocco, and their owners take great pride in them. Not only are the horses monetarily valuable, the owners must enjoy enough leisure to be able to stop their work lives several times during the year to show and perform. The government requisitions them without payment on national and religious holidays, conferring on them a certain status but also incurring resentment on the part of the owners who are obliged to participate. The source of their pride carries a social and economic obligation that pulls the reins on their increased social status.

Throughout these lyrics, women are portrayed as being "armored" as horses in their raiment; they are displayed and owned, a source both of pride and of financial obligation. They must be trained to proceed carefully and in close proximity to others while knowing how to stop at a moment's notice. When they are not being ridden, they are tethered or within guarded bounds. Women are also represented as supporters and carriers of men who ride on them in the capacity of both owners and children, or rest on them as if they were pillows. Such responsibility requires great strength and is not without risk, so the refrain asserts, "If I make him fall, I can handle it. Yes." And even if arms get broken, "the bonesetter" is never very far away.

Metaphors can be either an instantiation of identity or a reorientation of it (Fernandez 1986). These lyrics express the predominant cultural mappings that construct women as subordinate instruments of men's employ. Yet there is a subtle anomaly in this instrumentality: implicated is a feminine agency that is not afraid of taking risks and that is strong enough to bear the results. Her final admission is ambiguous:

> Love, love
> We didn't have our fill of it.
> It's for that [him] that I'm here.

> l-ḥub, l-ḥub
> ma shab'anash mənn-u.
> u 'la qubl-u jaya.

Is it for him that she is here? Or for the sensation that love leaves in her body? For whom and for what is the shikha?

Concluding to Change: The Embodied Nation

Shikhat bear witness to the extreme ambivalence that any loosening of the definitions of womanhood may incite. In interviews, upper-class Moroccan women are not particularly interested or affected by the aesthetic of shikhat—they find them rough-hewn and peasant;[28] bourgeois women find them vulgar and try to disassociate themselves to the furthest degree (though in their homes many gather around the VCR to watch and talk about the songs, clothes, and behavior—on and off screen—of their favorite shikha); women of the lower classes, the majority, do not approve of them either, but have a more profound understanding of their situation and their choices or lack of them. As shikhat can be considered both artists and symptoms of social malaise, they serve a complex and controversial function. In publicizing some aspects of femininity's private side in song and movement, shikhat define the feminine while disenfranchising themselves from the "respectable" community.

Shikhat have several functions in society: in breaching the world of male power they become anomalous and as anomalies they become scapegoats—they epitomize the "fallen woman." On the other hand, they exemplify feminine potential as embodiments of independent and brave women, albeit outcasts. The fascination of the majority of Moroccan women with them bears this out. They are admired and feared, spoken of with both awe and a conditioned disgust. They are women who, by virtue of their physical expressions of emotional and physical liberty, transgress the social codes of modesty. But although their performance is socially sanctioned, their personhood is not. Society both employs and rejects them. They stand for what women can do and for what happens to women who choose to do—namely, social exile.

The exile of the shikha is not based solely on her refutation of moral codes, however. Such codes are often violated with impunity by other sectors of society. For example, the behavior of shikhat parallels the behavior of upper-class women in many ways. Both categories of women may smoke cigarettes, drink wine, and have casual sexual liaisons, and often display large quantities of gold. The behavior of the shikha, however, breaks sharply with the bodily dispositions fostered among *nas sha'biyin*, "the folk," her *aṣl* or origin (Bourdieu 1977b). A rich woman can obtain her freedom both with money and through an established identification with western culture, which sanctions such behavior. A poor woman has no such alibi. The shikha's sin is not that she drinks and dances in heterosexual company, but that she commodifies her talents and participates in her own fetishization as a prurient object of male desire. Her sin is her unmediated affiliation with the marketplace.

This affiliation changes radically, however, once her relationship to the economy is mediated. The status of the shikha is quickly changing largely due to her reorientation to the market. Successful shikhat save their money, buy gold, and eventually buy their own land and homes. In becoming land-owners, their social exile is lessened as they resituate themselves in social and symbolic space, buying themselves place names, as well as new social categories.

A year after I met Mouna, she had sold her first house and bought another one in a very fashionable part of town. Visiting a few days after the Great Feast (*l-'id l-kbir*), I found her on her roof with her daughters and younger married sister visiting from the Sahara. There were several big plas-tic tubs, with Mouna washing clothes in one tub, her daughter rinsing in another, and her sister rinsing them once again. The water overflowed onto the red tiles, cooling our hot feet. There were sheep intestines drying on clotheslines strung near the walls of the roof. I sat on a wooden stool, get-ting up occasionally to hang the clean clothes on the remaining lines.

Mouna told me that she and her group would soon be performing at a saint's festival (*musəm*) in Settat. "There will be shikhat from all over the country," she told me. "We all sing and dance during the day. Then at night we're in the tents. We eat and drink." I expressed my disappointment at not being able to attend.

"You should come and live in Morocco," Mouna told me.

"There's no work for me here," I answered, adding "But I could work with you Mouna, couldn't I?"

"You don't know how!" her sister told me.

"She can learn," Mouna replied, going along with the joke.

"There's no shame in it, is there?" I said. "It's not like it used to be."

"No, it's not like it used to be," her sister said. "Now everyone wants to be a singer (*mughanniya*)."

Mouna's sister's use of the term mughanniya rather than shikha is significant. Oum Khaltoum, the famous and loved Egyptian singer, was a mughanniya; the term carries little stigma. This change in name, though not inevitable, attests to the shikha's increasing centrality in Moroccan consumer culture as well as to her own acquisition of cultural capital therein (Bourdieu 1984). When shikhat begin to record their music on audio and video cassettes (often done themselves by renting studios in Casablanca) their agency as social performers is affirmed. If the cassettes become popular, their value as artists is perpetuated. The very association that has stigmatized shikhat in the past (their unmediated relationship to the marketplace) is now providing them with a certain social standing precisely because of the intervention of the media.

Perhaps even more significant than the shikhat's use of the media is the media's use of shikhat. State-produced television broadcasts air performances of regional shikhat groups in an effort to give voice and body to the different regions of an ethnically diverse nation—the shikhat of the Souss (a Berber region), the shikhat of Tetouan, the shikhat of Taroudant. In this context, shikhat are no longer emblematic of shame, but metonyms for ethnic and regional identity. Their artistry has been highlighted and their social history suppressed in the service of rallying the "populace" around sentiments which valorize the heterogeneity of the one nation. The shikha has become an item of folklore in the Monarchy's construction of national identity.

How can we interpret this re-evaluation of the shikha in Moroccan popular culture? How can a cultural symbol of shamelessness be transformed into a symbol of national diversity?

The appropriation and exploitation of the shikha by national television obviously pays tribute to her extant popularity with the majority of Moroccans. It is an official acknowledgement of an unofficial art form—one with the power to rally intense sentiment and interest in viewers. But this appropriation depends upon a "disacknowledgement" of the shikha's libertinism. Her appearance on television as well as at festivals and folklore spectacles "launders" the shikha's image, purifying it sufficiently to become a symbol fit for regional and national identity.

Metaphors have transformed, but so has the personhood of the shikha. No longer a social pariah, the shikha finds herself a valued, if appropriated and still somewhat anomalous, symbol of nationalism. If successful, she may effect not only a personal transformation from the habitus of "the folk" to the legitimizing domain of landowner, but may also embrace the status of the mughanniya and thereby embody the transcendent state.

Notes

1. "Lover" here is the word *grin*, from the Arabic *qarin*, meaning "companion," or "peer."
2. These words are not opposites. It is not immodest to be maṭluq. A shikha often exceeds the maṭluq, and is characterized as immodestly bold: *ujə-ha mqazdər*, tin-faced. Such behavior constitutes a breach of honor.
3. Mernissi (1989).
4. The terms are Bakhtin's (1984a).
5. Many shikhat song genres are defined by region; namely *l-gharbawi, l-hasbawi, l-ḥawzi, j-jəbli, jʿaidan, l-mərsawi, az-zaʿri,* and *z-zayani.* Other genres include *l-ʿlawi* (song by the Beni Iznesan tribe, near Algeria) *r-rwais* (from the Souss region) and *s-sakən.* Of these, only *l-hasbawi, l-ḥawzi* and *l-mərsawi* are considered *l-ʿaita,* which are *l-ʿanmaṭ l-murakaba,* complex genres (Bouhamid 1995).
6. This verb in Moroccan Arabic refers to the uncontrollable behavior of a vengeful camel.
7. *ʿriwa,* literally a little cup handle.
8. I use the term "moral economy" with caution, taking into account that it is an analytic category, originating with E. P. Thompson (see 1991). There are several moral economies in Morocco. All of them, however, recognize, even if they don't enact, similar rules for what is considered proper female and male behavior.
9. Lortat-Jacob (1980) notes that codes of modesty in the Berber tribes of the High Atlas mountains in Morocco do not generally allow the enjoyment of music in public places unless specific circumstances of festivity and certain conditions of hierarchical relations prevail.
10. I invoke Bakhtin's notion of dialogism here (1981). In the glossary of *The Dialogic Imagination,* Holquist defines this term aptly when he says, "a word, discourse, language or culture undergoes 'dialogization' when it becomes relativized, de-privileged, aware of competing definitions for the same things" (Bakhtin, 1981: 427). A dialogic entity, then, is an agent of dialogism.
11. Mernissi (1989).
12. See Fernandez (1986) for the relation of the "inchoate" to metaphor. Carol Pateman (1989) offers a critique of the association of women with disorder in western political thought.
13. Mernissi (1987:31).
14. Mernissi (1987:32).
15. This is an example of the genre of *s-sakən.*
16. See Appadurai (1990) for a discussion of the concept and phenomenon of disjuncture.
17. Babcock (1980:4).

18. Turner (1977) uses this word to denote a state of being in which status, hierarchy, and structure disappear and are replaced with a bond of community.

19. Messick (1989:217) defines "subordinate discourse" as "a form of expression characterized by its power relation to a dominant ideology with which it coexists. A subordinate discourse must be distinguished from an alternative or competing ideology (or model, theory, subculture), which would entail an explicit elaboration of an oppositional conceptual order, and might give rise to efforts at suppression by upholders of the dominant ideology."

20. This is changing. Because it was once morally prohibited for women to smoke, it has now become a symbol of liberation among young students or women of the upper or middle classes. In Beni Mellal smoking in public is done infrequently, except by shikhat, who make of it a display of transgression, smoking even in public places like post offices.

21. As Dennis Tedlock (1983:240) notes, "I mean 'world' in the sense that Paul Ricoeur does when he says that the task of hermeneutics is to reveal the 'destination of discourse as projecting a world,' or when he says that 'for me, the world is the ensemble of references opened up by every kind of text.'" These quotes are found in Ricoeur (1976).

22. Shikhat do not characterize their lyrics as nonsense. Although they rarely valorize their work, they are acutely aware of the socioeconomic dimensions that have forced them into it. They do not misrecognize the issues.

23. See Abu-Lughod (1990) for a critique of the anthropological literature on resistance.

24. See K. Basso (1988) and Feld (1990) for recent discussions of the symbolism of place and place names in expressive culture.

25. Rosen (1984:24).

26. Shikhat not only provide emotional support to their "sisters," but also organize childcare and food cooperatives (buying large quantities to be distributed among themselves).

27. Also translated as phantom, phantasm, fantasy in Hans Wehr, *A Dictionary of Modern Written Arabic*.

28. This attitude represents what Scott calls the "public transcript" — the story as it is wont to be told, either by the dominant powers that be or by those who pay lip-service to those powers. He contrasts this with the "hidden transcript," a discourse that employs the "politics of disguise and anonymity" to effect "a double meaning or to shield the identity of the actors" (1990:19).

8. Property in the (Other) Person: Mothers-in-Law, Working Women, and Maids

When Khadouj was still pre-pubescent (in the early 1920s), her soon-to-be mother- and sister-in-law came to her house for a tattooing ritual. The sister-in-law held Khadouj down while the mother tattooed her wrists, ankles, and chin with a needle dipped in ashes to enhance her appeal. She was thus made the domain not only of her husband but of his entire family, and most particularly of his mother. The tattoo, meant to beautify, also marked her as property long before the consummation of the marriage. As a promised article of exchange between two families in a tribal village in the northeast section of Morocco, she learned everything—cooking, cleaning, and childcare—from her mother-in-law. She was, for all intents and purposes, her adopted child.

Such occurrences are rare in contemporary Morocco due, in large part, to changes in the social estimation of what constitutes symbolic capital and who possesses it. The shift in relations of social authority and power is exemplified in women's narratives about mothers-in-law and maids, where the discursive construction of gender and class takes place.

Women in Morocco have never lacked power in relations with daughters-in-law.[1] Traditionally, nothing less than complete obedience to the mother-in-law in the early years of marriage was acceptable (Lacoste-Dujardin 1985; see also Davis 1983; Maher 1974). One reason stringent behavior was exacted from the daughter-in-law is that she presented a threat to the household's social balance. Not only was she an outsider (a "good" from the marketplace if the marriage is not endogamous), but she represented the awakened sexuality of the son. This sexuality, if unchecked, could easily give way to fitna, disorder or chaos (see Mernissi 1989). It was the responsibility of the husband to keep the assumedly boundless sexual appetite of his wife, as well as his own, within limits. In this sense, the construction of women's "impropriety is the guarantee of man's proper reign over them" (Gross 1986 : 137). If, for example, the son were to become obsessed with his wife's charms, he might begin to make inappropriate requests on her behalf. The daughter-in-law was thus kept very busy and made to know her place — the lowest one in the family hierarchy.

Mother-in-law relations are never simple, but are changing rapidly, especially in the middle class — those aspiring to the ideal of the nuclear family. These changes epitomize the shifts in relations of dominance, intricately related to the bride's status in and on the market. Hadda described it this way:

"*Bəkri* [in the early days], the mother-in-law was in the house. She never left the house; [it was] as if the bride was hers. And she'd hit her and rule over her and teach her and tell her, 'Do this, do that.' And she'd hit her.

"The husband would come home and she'd tell him, 'She did this to me and said that to me.' And the husband would get up and he, too, would hit her. He'd tell her, 'Why did you talk like that to my mother?' And the wife would stay put and be patient and that's it. Patient. She was silent. She didn't say anything.

"If that woman went... if she went unhappy to her parent's house, they would say to her, 'What's the matter with you?' And she would tell them, 'My mother-in-law had words with me.' They would hit her and return her again. Her people would tell her, 'Your mother-in-law has to speak [harshly] with you, to teach you housework and to teach you...'"

"And now, the mother-in-law, [the power] is not in her hands?" I asked.

"The mother-in-law is outside!" Hadda laughed. "The mother-in-law doesn't have anywhere to go anymore. That's it, the mother-in-law used to rule over the bride like her mother or more. Now, no. If she talks, that's it! If the mother-in-law talks, the door (*la porte*)!

"Now the bride is knowledgeable. She doesn't need the mother-in-law to show her. That's it. She no longer shows her. In the olden days, the mother-in-law used to show the bride because the bride didn't know."

"And the bride married young?"

"Ahuh. Even though she's young now, this generation, this present generation knows everything. They know how to do housework and cook. They know how to make salads. Now, those modern ones that are coming up now, they know it all from their education. They study that stuff. It's from their studies. Everything is written for them."

The bride in this scenario is noticeably defenseless; she is hit by her mother-in-law, her husband, and also her parents if she dares return to her natal home for refuge. She has no refuge.[2]

The presence of the mother-in-law in the conjugal home maintains the son's role as son and the daughter-in-law's as daughter. Children remain children in the eyes of their parents, but also in the hierarchy of deference rules. The son is often torn between his allegiance to his mother and to his wife; if he buys a scarf for the latter, he must buy a scarf for the former. Because social convention has privileged the role of the mother-in-law, the son is out of his mother's favor, and possibly outside the social canon, if he sides with his wife during domestic disputes. This no-win situation for the bride meant she was simply to be patient, obedient, and subservient to both mother-in-law and husband until she became a mother-in-law herself.[3]

Today the young middle-class couple in Beni Mellal often do not live with the groom's parents, as doing so bespeaks economic difficulties. If the mother-in-law lives with the couple (as a widow, for example), it is often in the couple's apartment. Although the mother-in-law does not usually have any trouble making herself at home, it is still not *her* home; she is not the woman of the house, the *mulat d-dar*. Furthermore, the young bride is often more educated than her mother-in-law. She knows how to read and write, she is savvy in her purchases, she reads recipe books and consequently has a larger repertoire in the kitchen, one that includes European as well as Moroccan dishes. The young bride also wants more time-saving appliances in her home: a refrigerator, an oven, even a washing machine. The mother-in-law may find herself being instructed by the daughter-in-law in domestic "literacy"—including the latest fashion in serving, the newest recipe of a sweet, or where to find the best tailor in town. Young brides not only know more about domestic fashion, but they are often more experienced in public life than their elders, familiar with the goods and services of the marketplace, with prescription drugs (rather than home, herbal remedies) and with cities and towns other than their place of origin.

The new brides are also more demanding. Those that work outside the home have more or less bought their clout. But even those who do not have outside jobs know that the social ideal of the nuclear family has replaced that of the extended patriarchal one as the model to be aspired to. This idealization and marketing of the nuclear family is especially evident in television advertising, where small families with one or two children are portrayed in dreamlike hazes of bounty and happiness. Mothers-in-law or any other extended family members are rarely present in these scenarios.

Their absence from the ideal picture facilities the disempowering of the mother-in-law in actual family relations.

The Commodification of Literacy

Just as ideals of the nuclear family have diminished the dominant position of the mother-in-law, book literacy has reversed the roles of dependency between the generations. Whereas a great deal of symbolic capital used to reside in the honor due to the male elders of society, and to parents generally, changing literacy demands have made non-literate elders dependent upon their children's reading and writing skills in order to participate in a society which relies more and more on the comprehension of the written word (Wagner 1993; see also Eickelman 1992). Elders need the younger generation to interact with the civil system in their stead. This dependence has been a gradual development with significant repercussions in the symbolic realm.

The younger generation speaks for or represents the authority of the elders — in courts of law, in civil offices, and in the "modern" marketplace of credit transactions. This "speaking for" shifts authority from the oral voice of the elder to the literate hand of the junior, whose networks may be based more on literacy and professional friendships than on kinship. Literacy is a commodity in Morocco that the younger generations possess and may exploit to their benefit. In conferring upon the literate young the *power to report the speech* of their nonliterate elders, a permanent shift of social authority takes place. It is not enough to simply honor mother and father, one must be able to represent that honor to others in indelible language. The permission to do so (which is a social exigency, in any case) involves a transaction of generational power and a redistribution of that power along less strictly patriarchal lines.

This is not to say that filial piety does not remain a strong and determining value in the Moroccan consciousness; rather it is just one of many factors determining how dominance is translated into the realm of practice. Not only may a son or daughter be richer than his or her parent (and thus more powerful), but the parent may have to rely on the child to interpret the signs of commodity culture and write his or her oral voice for the social "authorities" that demand permanent records.[4]

Given the privilege of male voice over female in civil relations in Moroccan society, it is often the voice of the father that is represented in writing by the son. But because of the high divorce rate in Morocco, there are also important numbers of women heads-of-household who call on their children for acts of secular literacy (Wagner 1993).

The Narrative Construction of Feminine Objects

In addition to the power that mothers-in-law have traditionally exerted over their sons' wives, relations of dominance among women are also evident between housewives and their maids. Narratives about maids reveal the tensions among literacy, power, and social stratification in the feminine community as well as the process whereby words create their objects (cf. S. Stewart 1984).

"When the children come home from school they need someone to take care of them," Hadda told me. "My daughter has a maid, but that maid isn't good. She's mischievous. She hits the children."

"Really?" I said.

"Yeah. She hits them. She keeps herself a mess."

"Who is she?"

"The little girl is a Berber."

"From your family?"

"No. From Agadir. Us, from our family, no one works. From our family they don't want to. They don't want to work. They say, 'No, we don't need it.'"

"She hits the children?"

"She hits the children and she scratches them. They pick up those pillows and they hit each other with them. [My daughter] comes home to find the house upside down (*dunya magluba*)."

"Really?"

"Ahuh. That maid of hers is rough. She's not good. She does work. She sweeps. She washes the dishes. She does everything. Cooks. Everything. But as soon as my daughter leaves to go to work, you'll find the world upside down. The pillows are all over the place. They strike out with whatever they find. And her head is naked [no scarf]. Her hair is a mess. She comes home [from work] and hits her and hits her children and hits and hits and hits."

"Then she's not good with the children. She's only good for housework."

"No. She's jealous of the children. If she sees them studying, she messes up their work and grabs their notebooks."

"Why?"

"She wants to. She tells them, 'Me, too. Get up and show me also how to write.' She doesn't want to work any more. She—my own daughter—goes to work and they come home [from school] and study and revise their lessons. And the maid puts their notebooks there, and she looks for her papers and she comes and sits next to them. And she tells them, 'What you're doing, do it for me.' And they tell her, 'No. Let us study. Let us write. We, we want to pass our tests.' And she tells them, 'No.' And she puts her hands on their notebooks and they get up and fight." Hadda laughed. "By God! Well you see, maids, they're not good. My daughter, she… the poor thing, she faints and she falls and faints and she tells you, 'That maid will do me in. See, she's going to let my children go without their studies.' And she pays her four thousand riyals.⁵ And she clothes her. And she eats and drinks. She stays with her. And she's young, not old."

"How old is she?"

"She's… she must be about sixteen."

"She's still young."

"Young, young," Hadda repeated.

"And she sleeps at their place?"

"She always stays with them. She clothes her, like, like her [own daughter]. She gets her skirts and sweaters for working and that stuff. And she washes her hair and cleans her. She does this. Zohra will tell you. My daughter understands a lot. She's educated, knowledgeable. My daughter was a teacher in a nursery school. She went through civil service and all that in Rabat. She did her training there. Like you. She takes care of the wives in the army [now], and the wives of those who've died. She goes in the morning. She leaves at eight and comes home at twelve. And goes back at two and comes home at six in the afternoon. Then that other one [the maid] has made disorder for her in the house. You see? She tells the children, 'Get up and study and me, too! Write for me.'"

"She reads?" asked Zohra.

"Well yeah," Hadda laughed, and explained. "She swore one day to Aisha [one of the children]. And she said to her, 'Write a letter for me to my boyfriend.' And she wrote it for her."

"She has a boyfriend?" Zohra asked, surprised.

"It's true. And she wrote it for her. My granddaughter wrote it for her. The maid told her [what to write] and she wrote it. She dictated it to her.

And she gave her the letter and she went and gave it to a boy. She said, 'Deliver this letter to that boy standing there.' He, also, was a little bug [just like her]. Just young. I don't know who told it to Atiqa, my daughter. They said to her, 'Suad wrote this letter.' And she hit her daughter. She whipped the hell out of her daughter (*qətlat-ha b-l'aṣa*). She said, 'Why did you write that for her? What's the matter with you? What do you know about that stuff?'

"Then she hit the maid and she said, 'Why do you teach my daughter that?' She's just sixteen years old and she wants to eat her head [get herself into trouble]."

"And the maid's still with them?"

"She's still there. They're used to her. She can't leave them."

"Why don't they let her study with them?" I asked.

"This maid, her parents are poor. They have nothing. And they gave her to us to work in order to bring them money, in order to be paid and bring them money. Well, he has a lot, the poor man, he has a lot of girls. He has one boy that studies. He has just one boy that studies. He says… [doesn't finish]. Those Berbers of Agadir, they don't educate their girls. They educate just the sons. Just the boys. He says, 'those, those girls don't study.' They just give them to work at other people's [homes]."

Several cultural identities collide in these words. The woman of the house, Hadda's daughter, Atiqa, is a high school graduate with two years of post-graduate training. She is a "modern" middle-class working woman, "educated, knowledgeable," and, her mother asserts, she is much like me, the American ethnographer. The maid, on the other hand, is uneducated, poor, and from a traditional family that doesn't believe in sending girls to school. Although both are of Berber origin, the wife grew up speaking Arabic in Casablanca, whereas the maid grew up in the country speaking a Berber dialect.

The maid is a symbol of disorder in this narrative. She succeeds in turning the house "upside down" as soon as the children come home from school. She prevents them from studying by insisting that they teach her to read and write. Whether the maid's jealousy is justified or not, it is clearly inappropriate in maid/employer relations, and instigates family disorder. The larger problem that this narrative brings up—that "those Berbers of Agadir, they don't educate their girls. They just give them to work at other people's [homes]"—is treated as a given, a social consequence rather than the valid cause of the maid's distress.[6]

Not only does the maid interfere with the children's studies, but she also exposes them to behavior that is damaging. She persuades the young daughter to use her literacy skills to further her own romantic (and, by cultural standards, shameful) interests. She thus corrupts or pollutes the insularity of this nuclear, dual-career family by introducing an example of transgression to the children and by luring them to participation in such behavior.

The maid in this narrative lives with her employer's family, who "clothe and clean" her; she is a live-in servant, called an apprentice (*matᶜalma*) if she is a young girl, a housekeeper or "worker" (*khaddama*), if an adult. Many Moroccans, from the elite mercantile class down to the barely comfortable, have live-in female domestics, often poor girl children that wealthier families agree to raise (see Ennaji 1994). One such child whom I knew lived with an upper-middle-class family in a Casablanca apartment and had near full-time responsibilities for an infant. She received neither education nor money, but simply her keep. She went to visit her divorced mother and younger sister in the countryside two or three times a year for a day or two (when her mother received a small compensation for her child's services). She seemed to have no playmates.

This situation is especially common among upper-class families in metropolitan areas such as Fes, Rabat, Marrakech, Tangiers, Meknes, and Casablanca. The families these youngsters serve vary in their generosity, with some bringing up the child as one of their own, even arranging and financing her marriage. Others are only interested that the girl do her work and not cause trouble. When these girls are poor relatives, they enjoy a better status. Most often, however, their parents receive a nominal compensation for hiring out their children. An important benefit the children receive for their services is *tarbiya*, proper "upbringing," consisting of good manners and etiquette. That is, they get to see "how the richer folks do it."

The tradition of the servant arose in a social climate where there was a very polarized sexual division of labor and consequently the woman of the house was always present in the home, an omnipresent supervisor. The servant was under the tutelage of the woman of the household much as the bride was under the gaze and direction of her mother-in-law. The goal was eventually to produce a worker who would fulfill the desires of her mistress without being constantly instructed to do so.

It is more difficult to acquire young servants these days, primarily because girls have equal access to public education and their poor parents want them to be able to take advantage of it in hopes of breaking the cycle of poverty. Yet the increase in the number of working adult women in the emergent middle class also augments the need for domestic service. Working women in Morocco are expected to continue fulfilling their fulltime responsibilities in the home. The increased need for domestic and childcare help coincides with an expansion in the female service economy such that large numbers of poor women are marketing themselves to middle-class, two-career families as maids (*khǝddamat*, as opposed to *khadmat*, or servants). Unlike servants, maids do not live with their employers and are often mature women.[7]

The introduction of the stranger, the maid, into the private realm of the home and nuclear family is causing such a social disruption that gossip (*l-hadra*) about maids is prevalent. This discourse reflects a change in the status of working women, whose roles are "normalized" through the discursive acknowledgment of their needs, but it also indicates major shifts in power relations between women in general. Because of economic hard times, women employing maids often pay minimal wages for maximum service and are obliged to drive a hard bargain in negotiating the maid's salary. Yet with maids very much in demand, they too are able to make demands of their employers, and no longer accept salaries that are incommensurable with their services, or the verbal abuse and degradation that have often accompanied their profession. In the realm of service relations between women, we perceive the nascent struggle not only for personal independence and identity in the labor force (for both maids and their working employers), but for the social recognition of rights in the face of gender and class prejudice (cf. Mernissi 1982b).

I learned about these struggless from spending time with the women in the afternoon, listening to gossip that they told about each other.

L-hadra

Gossip in Morocco may contain any number of oral genres such as proverbs, jokes, or longer narratives. It is a *forum for* speech rather than a *form of* speech, moving freely between conversational turn-taking and uncontested monologue. Defined as much by its setting as by its content, gossip takes place in small groups of two or more, much like many other folkloric events (Ben-Amos 1972). Gossip is a personal representation of the characters and circumstances that comprise community life, reflecting and affecting the way people perceive each other, with both positive and negative results (see Abrahams 1983; Besnier 1989a, 1990a; Gluckman 1963, 1968; Haviland 1977; Spacks 1985). But because malicious gossip is feared more than complimentary gossip is desired, "talk" (*l-hadra*) is a pejorative descriptor that acts to marginalize and devalue any speech that may threaten recognized authority. To say that an account or speech event is l-hadra is to trivialize its sociopolitical import.

One evening, a week after the death of the Ḥajja's husband, a number of women paid her a visit. The Ḥajja sat in mourning clothes (white jəllaba and scarf), while her daughter brought us cookies and tea. The conversation turned to the afterlife and Rquiya recounted:

"There was a man who prayed and fasted and was charitable and went to Mecca. There was little to prevent him from going straight to paradise. But he used to talk (*kan kay hdər*). And that gossip sent him to hell. One arm records the good, the other records the bad.[8] His bad accounts added up and he got fire on the spot."

It is interesting that the admonition not to gossip is exemplified with a male character. Despite the fact that gossip is associated with women, everyone recognizes that men gossip just as much as women do, although their subjects are by custom more restricted. Rquiya herself is renowned for her proclivity for gossip. Approaching middle age, she is becoming very cognizant of her "record" (kept not only by her peers, but stored in the body itself). Her story asserts that even a man who is a model Muslim in every other way can go to hell for the weakness of talking about others.

"They say, if there are three or four gathered and they start gossiping," she continued, "you say, 'Be quiet, God have mercy on your parents.' And if they don't want to be quiet, you get up and go on your way. Don't stay with them if they're gossiping."

Despite the fact that the stigma of gossip is incorporated into the social imagination and associated with sin, its social importance is nonetheless understood. The most vital desires and poignant fears of society — anguish, hope, anger, worry, love, excitement, humor, disillusionment, and nostalgia — are expressed in this register, which is marked by intimacy, informality, and a requisite display of trust between the individuals present. Because gossip depends upon the complicity of its participants, it takes place in small gatherings and is usually facilitated by "closed" or private contexts such as tea visits, outings to the public bath, or celebrations such as weddings or naming ceremonies[9] that permit the coalescence of small groups in an atmosphere of leisure. The context of gossip problematizes the notions of private and public domains, for although it relies on an audience that is exclusive (especially of the person being talked about), l-hadra functions to publicize what was formerly private knowledge (cf. Grima 1992 on categories of public and private in a Middle Eastern context). In other words, gossip makes the private realm public in an atmosphere that is always both semi-private (exclusive) and semi-public (a gathering at a wedding).

Gossip is often characterized by social themes.[10] One story about a divorced relative will being up another story about divorce. Every woman has a story to tell about a bizarre phenomenon that happened in a public bath (ḥammam), just as everyone can contribute her own narrative about the uses and practice of magic (shur) or the consequences of interacting with spirits (jnun). In this way, thematically related narratives are stacked and evaluated in light of each other. The frequency of a particular theme as it is discussed in l-hadra and the degree of emotional involvement attached to such a theme signifies its importance in the life of the community. In the summers of 1990 and 1991, I was struck by the large proportion of talk about maids in Beni Mellal.

The Marginalization of Threat Through Discursive Categories

In gossip, many voices and genres meet; it is a discursive domain where reputations are negotiated and values redefined. From a non-native perspective, gossip spans a continuum from non-serious joking to very serious "news," from lies to truth and legend. Personal memorates, or first-person narratives that are based on experience, are an important aspect of gossip, where values and relations of dominance are renegotiated discursively in the feminine community. Analysis of personal narratives reveals how middle-class women in Morocco are constructing the maid as a threat to the purity of the home, an agent of disorder and an embodiment of the "low." Casting the maid in such marginal terms disguises her actual centrality in the maintenance of social and family order. Working women, who have only recently established their place in the "outside" realm of the marketplace, situate themselves higher on the social scale than women who market themselves *into* the family unit.

The following narratives were recorded one afternoon when Saadia, Zohra's closest friend, came to visit. The Ḥajja's daughter, Aisha, was also present, as was my youngest sister-in-law Amina. We were five women in our late twenties and early thirties: two divorcées, two married, three with young children. These stories illustrate the almost mythic quality that the character of the maid is acquiring in Moroccan female society:

"The wife of Amrouch had a girl, see, who was working for her. She brought her when she was just young. And this housekeeper got up and made friends with a guy.

"And when she got to know him, when she'd stayed a while, it wasn't long after, he told her, 'Tomorrow I'm going to marry you. I'm going to marry you.' On that day, she got up and messed up the house. And the wife of Amrouch had bought her some gold [jewelry]. She'd bought [it for her] because they were bringing her up. She treated her like her daughter. She could call her 'mama' and the other would call her 'my daughter.' But they didn't understand each other very well. Recently [her employer] had begun to express doubts about her."

"To her husband?" I asked.

"I don't know. Well, she told her. And she went and made a date with that guy [anyway]. Three o'clock or something. It was Friday then and she took her [gold] chain with her."

"Ahuh…"

"The chain was around her neck and she took it off. And she took off her bracelet. She said (galt-lək) that it scratched the wall when she was doing housework. And when she went to El Ksar, or wherever, she said (galt-lək) she stayed with him and all that. And he promised her. He said to her, 'I'm going to marry you, to marry you.' And she said… And he did it [he made love to her]. And he said to her, 'And this necklace, we can't wear it a little while?' And she told him, 'No,' she told him. He said to her, 'you're not putting your trust in me.' She said, 'There is trust. There is and there isn't. But this necklace, I'm not going to give it to you.'

"And he took it from her, from her neck. He told her, 'Until tomorrow, at ten o'clock. Come and I'll give it [back] to you." She [the woman

of the house] said (galt-lək) that the maid kept on cleaning, kept on cleaning, until a certain time and she just went crazy. She went running to the
place where they had decided to meet. She didn't find him and came back.
She went and came back. And the wife of Amrouch said to her, 'My heav-
ens! What's the matter with you? You just keep going back and forth.'

"She said to her, to the wife of Amrouch, this is what happened to her.
This is what happened: 'The man that I told you about wants to come and
marry me. See, I gave him the necklace. He took it from me.'

"Well, that's it. They went looking for him. They went to his sister's.
She knows, I guess, his sister or one of his friends showed her [the house]
or whatever. He wouldn't give her the necklace or anything. Well, she came
home from where she'd been. The wife of Amrouch—we asked her and
everything—she said (galt-lək) that the girl became bad. She started to
do… that is, she did her own thing. [As if] she was the mistress of the house
and she would do what she wanted. She didn't care. She said she would
leave you like that, sitting with people, and get up. She said she would jump
up, go to her room, put on pants and makeup and fix herself up and leave."

"Even pants!" said Zohra.

"Hey Hey! You think she's… You think you're going to stop her?"

"Where is she from?"

"Ah, she's from the region of Boujad."

"Is she a relative?" I asked.

"There's some relation between them," answered Saadia.

"And she's still with her?" asked Zohra.

"Still there! She kicked her out. They told Amrouch [the male head of
household] about it and all that. They told him what happened to her. He
told them, 'It's not my business. She went and told the police by herself.
She managed and got up by herself.' He told them, 'It's not my business.
She should have consulted me and told me what happened, said, "someone
took me and did this to me and that to me." I'd know what to do, that's my
work. But now she's managed, managed by herself. God help her. It's not
my business.'

"That's it. And she left. She went. That's it. And she stayed away longer
than, longer than a month. And they knew where she was."

"They did?" I said.

"They knew. That's it. They no longer… Their hands were cut off
[with so much work]. You know, she was carrying a lot [of work]. She was
doing a lot for them. And so she came back. She [the employer] said, 'She's
necessary and I have to have her back.' But the wife of Amrouch is ugly

with her sometimes. She scolds her. She abuses her and she scolds her and she's not very kind to her. Well, that's what I know about her."

A breach of trust occurs in this narrative, symbolized by the improper circulation of gold. Gold is consistently associated with the enhancement of both femininity and feminine power in Morocco. The maid's gold necklace was her own; but it was given to her by her female employer in a gesture of inclusion in the family. It was a gift that incurred an obligation in the form of obedience and good faith. By allowing the gold to leave the family network and enter the hands of a stranger, the maid not only incurred a personal loss, but dishonored her family of employment. The misuse of gold, its recontextualization in shameful circumstances, transformed the status of the maid from a "daughter" to a "bad," albeit independent, woman. The more serious transgression, however, was in not seeking the mediation of Amrouch, the male head of household, after the gold had been taken. She was too independent. The really scandalous part of this story is that the girl "managed her affairs by herself" (*dabrat 'la ras-ha*), going so far as to make a show of her independence: jumping up, putting on pants and makeup, and leaving at will.

The maid's transgression is emphasized largely because the narrative is told from the perspective of the maid's employer. There is a thick embedding of direct and indirect reported speech here. Saadia employs the rhetorical phrase, galt-lək (she said to me) frequently, as when she says, "The [the woman of the house] said (galt-lək) that the maid kept on cleaning, kept on cleaning, until a certain time and she just went crazy." The quotative draws attention to the voice of the wife of Amrouch within the narrated event, while drawing the listener into the narrative by using the second person: she told *you*. But Saadia also quotes the heads of household directly, embedding one quote within another:

"He told them, 'It's not my business. She should have consulted me and told me what happened, said "someone took me and did this to me and that to me." I'd know what to do, that's my work. But now she's managed, managed by herself. God help her. It's not my business.'"

Saadia quotes Amrouch, who in turn gives voice to the maid's persona, though he does not quote her actual words, only those that he thinks she should have uttered. The maid's subordination is thus doubly embedded in the text, her voice appropriated and her actions condemned.

The demand for maids is great. When this maid left for a month (to sow some wild oats), her former employer was overwhelmed with work. Because of this, and because of some kind of relation between the maid and her employer, she was taken back into service. Yet her untrustworthy behavior had set a precedent for all future relations and she thereby subjected herself to future abuse by the *mulat d-dar*, the woman of the house.

The sexuality of maids is reason for concern among their female employers. They present a threat to monogamous relations between husband and wife, especially because polygamy is religiously allowed and concubinage socially tolerated. These facts, combined with the reality that many maids are divorced (sexually experienced) women, makes the presence of the maid in the private realm of the home problematic.

"She said to you," Aisha said, adding a narrative of her own, "One woman, she was well off. Her husband also had a good job. She had a good job and he, too, had a good job. And they had a maid. He's disgusting, the one who falls for maids, and all that."

"In those days, he was bathing and he called her. He said to her, 'Come here, you.' She said, 'What?' She went into the bathroom and he said to her, 'Hold this, your dear one [his penis].' And he's bathing!" Aisha laughed.

"Well, [his wife] she stayed like that, poor woman. Whether she employed beauties or ugly ones, he fell for them!"

An even more serious scenario takes place when the husband wants to marry the maid. In a narrative I did not record, Hadda told me a purportedly true story about a couple with children who hired a maid to help them out. Soon after, the husband married the maid, the first wife moved out and the "maid" became the woman of the house. In this story, power relations were actually inverted: the original outsider became an insider, while the original wife was out the door and "in the street." There are numerous stories of this type. They are Cinderella stories, in the sense that they transform the status of the maid, as if by magic; however, the female "heroine" does not always trade in her rags for riches. In fact, she often remains victimized:

"And when people leave [leftover] food, they eat it," said Saadia. "They eat all that and then they leave the children hungry. You see there are a lot of problems with them. They... maids are the daughters of sin[11] (*bnat l-ḥaram*)."

"Tell her about the teapot," said Zohra.

"Oh, the story about the teapot. There was this woman who also had a maid, who took care of her house and her children. Well, her husband wanted to marry the maid. And when she knew that the maid was pregnant, she emptied a teapot of boiling water on her. When the child was born, with his luck, she gave birth to a blind child. He can't see anything."

"Well, it's her fault [the maid's]," said Zohra.

"By God! You see, the poor wife! He's the disgusting one [the husband], the bastard. And that's it. She kept the maid. She came back again and she beat her. How many times she beat her! How many times she hit her! Well, that's it. She threw her out and she has the child now."

"And the child?" Zohra asked.

"And the child is still at Mahjuba's. So he won't pay her alimony."

"And [the child's] mother?"

"His mother, they threw her out. The child is with the wife of his father, with her."

"That's why I always see her [the former maid] at the lawyer's!" said Zohra.

"You see, he, too   he's strange. He goes up the stairs [to the lawyer's office] and he's talking [to himself] and he 'crr crrs' [laughs out loud]."

This narrative refers to real places and times; it is grounded in the life of the community.[12] The lawyer's office, where I have gone to accompany Zohra in her efforts to obtain alimony payments, is not far from the center of town. The characters are also known community members. And yet the story as told takes on a mythic dimension in its representation of gender and class identities. This story is not only about a singular and unique incident. It is being told to illustrate the general assertion that maids, as the "daughters of sin," suffer the consequences of their actions; the sinner's illegitimate child is blind, and "with his luck," cannot "see" the shameful circumstances of his birth. He is adopted by the father's wife, while his birth mother is thrown out and left to fend for herself. The story is not without consequence for the father-adulterer, either, who is publicly perceived as someone who has lost his mind: he talks and laughs out loud to himself while ascending the stairs to the lawyer's office.

This narrative is an example of l-hadra (sometimes referred to as *l-hadra u l-klam*, talk and words). Yet it embodies the characteristics that Stahl (1983) attributes to personal experience stories, providing an implicit commentary on social norms and what happens when they are transgressed. In the next narrative in Saadia's discourse the maid is not only a stranger introduced into the privacy of the home, but an agent of the disintegration of that home through her evil activities; she is both a threat to conjugal relations and a dangerous perpetrator of social harm.[13] The anxiety expressed here has to do with relinquishing control of one's charges, especially one's own children, to someone outside the kinship network, a representative of the marketplace:

"But the maids that stay, they pound up the children," said Saadia.

The women laughed at Saadia's choice of words. "You're not bashful!" Zohra told her.

"The mistress of the house would always leave her child with her," she continued. "He would always scream. He would always cry with her. She waited for the mistress to leave and she would take a needle and she would start to put it in the child's soft spot of his head. And she paralyzed the child.

"The important thing is that she kept doing it and doing it. She continued to do it every time, every time to him. Until the child died, poor thing! Just like that. And they didn't know why he died.

"But then the family reconsidered and took the maid and put her in prison. She confessed. But this operation, she didn't do it just once. She repeated it not just one time or two. Waaa! Wherever she worked and there were small children, they would die."

"They would die?" I said, incredulous.

"They put her in prison. They said to her, 'What do you do to young children?' She said to them, 'I take a needle like this or a straight pin.'"

"Where did this happen?" asked Zohra.

"This is in Rabat," answered Saadia. "This is reality. This [story] about children's death is real in Rabat. And she would do this in the soft spot of their head. They were just young and they would die and she was at ease!"

Here the maid takes on an absolutely sinister character. She is a murderer of infants without a conscience, violating the very realm that she was employed to protect. This symbolic inversion of caregiver to lifetaker represents the most extreme example of threat, the existence of disorder (fitna) embodied in an uncontrollable, yet socially prescribed Other.

To Eat or Not to Eat with Strangers

A major index of maid-employer relations is whether the maid is invited to eat with the family. Until recently there was no question of the maid participating in family meals; she ate in the kitchen, by herself or with the children.[14] Now, however, some employers are ambivalent about this practice, self-conscious about their codes of hierarchy and discrimination. The act of eating at the same table involves a leveling of categories, a dissolution of boundaries through the act of dipping one's bread in a communal sauce and ingesting in the company of others (see Buitelaar 1993). Since eating together is an act that bonds, a ritual which enacts humility (a primary quality of the *sha'b*, the people), the situating of the maid at mealtime is significant. Although gender-bonding across sexes is now part of the picture being sold to middle-class Moroccans (especially in television advertising), women bonding with other women *across classes* finds no precedent. To the contrary, the stranger — or anyone who represents difference — violates the image of the safe and pure middle-class nuclear family.

Eating with others is a forum for the display of etiquette and culture (Elias 1978; Lévi-Strauss 1978; Bourdieu 1984). Inviting the maid to the table, then, is both an opening for the redefinition of cultural categories and a test whose results are largely fixed. Though employers may make a gesture towards the equal status of the maid, they also point out why she is not culturally competent enough to share in the status that is proffered. "She would begin to clear the plates as soon as she was through," Fadela recounted about her maid, "even though the children weren't finished. And she would tell us stories about her ex-husband!" This was more than the family wanted to find out about over dinner.

Even if invited to share a meal, most maids decline in an act of deference to their employers. Yet the ability of the maid to cross over the boundaries of social hierarchy contributes to the ambiguity of her status. She is a stranger who nonetheless has intimate access to the secrets of the family's life. She has the power to disseminate what is literally "class-ified" information to other segments of society. Though the need for domestic help permits the maid to be demanding, their demands are received as affronts to the class that employs them.

At one social occasion, we gathered as three couples for dinner and a game of poker. One of the other guests, Mina, told me about engaging a maid for the care of her home and children. The first day the maid arrived she discovered that there was an infant in the house. "No," she told her potential employer, "the price we agreed on only took account of an older child. I don't want to care for a small child." This independence on the part of the maid incensed the woman of the house, who thought the maid had a lot of nerve to make stipulations! In the past it has been the lack of ability to make stipulations that defined the live-in servant. A maid who does not live with her employers threatens the marked difference between house-wife (*l-mra dyal d-dar*) and domestic worker, which lies precisely in the fact that "the housewife is the owner [of her domain], while the maid, poor thing, [has] nothing" (*l-mra dyal d-dar mulat sh-shi, u rah l-khəddama, məskina, walu*).

"They come to you young, dirty," Mina told me. "They don't know anything. They don't even know, let's say, what a television is. And little by little they learn how to do things. They go to the public bath, they clean themselves up. They get themselves together and, before you know it, they're giving you lip! [*kay ḥshi l-ik l-hadra*]."

Although said about maids, these words could have been said by a traditional mother-in-law describing her daughters-in-law. Talking back to one's employer (not unlike talking to one's mother-in-law) is considered grounds for dismissal. In this sense, obedience is a primary value; the maid dutifully performs errands and chores. Paying lip service to one's "oppressor" is an essential aspect in the reproduction of social relations.[15] In a long story about the employment of a forty-five-year-old divorcée, Fadela quoted her maid as saying, "If I had had an education, I'd be a state employee like you." Fadela laughed with disdain at what she considered an audacious statement by the maid who dared define access to education as the only difference between the two women. The maid's mistake was not in recognizing the symbolic and economic capital gained through education, but in articulating the rules of the game to her employer.

Maids are not only portrayed as embodying physical dirt, but, as in the examples already cited, they are morally dirty and threaten to contaminate the family they work for (precisely why shikhat are estranged from their natal families). The body of the maid becomes a symbolic site for the construction of moral discourse. Though she is washed and clothed by her employer, even adorned with gold, she may persist in distracting the children from their studies, giving away the gifts given to her, or sleeping with the man of the house. As represented, the young maid is easily lured to the street, while the older maid is either divorced or has been a prostitute in the past. The behavior of the maid necessitates her subjugation.

Not only does the maid transgress sexual norms, but she is feared as someone without ethics. Because of her symbolic marginality in the home and her centrality in the economic marketplace, the maid is always suspect. She is often portrayed as a thief. In fact, thievery is the most common complaint of female employers; the maid might siphon the flour, take milk home for her own children, or steal the cooking oil. "Maids like to work for rich people so they can eat and drink well," Mina told me; the rich don't notice if small amounts of food are missing, but lower-middle-class house-holds keep track of every gram of flour.

"Before this maid, we had five," Mina explained. "But they never stayed. They used to steal. One used to siphon the flour. At that time it was just me and Ali and a sack of flour would last only fifteen days. Now we have two children and it lasts a month. Another maid used to steal milk to nurse her children with, and another took coffee. It all comes from 'need' (*le besoin*)."

My friend Fadela recounted this story: "I bought a bottle of oil. That night we made about ten pancakes with it. The next morning a third of the oil in the bottle was gone. I asked the maid about it and she said that it all went in the pancakes. Damn! A third of a bottle of oil for ten little pancakes?"

Eventually this maid left of her own accord, tired of defending herself against accusations. This was the exact response Fadela was hoping for:

"At the end of the month the maid said, 'Find someone to look after the children. I'm going on my way.' I said to her, 'That's it?' 'That's it,' she said, 'I thought I was going to find a house where I could play and laugh.' 'Not this house!' I said. 'Go find somewhere else to play and laugh!'"

To say that "we played and laughed" is to affirm that successful social ex-change and hospitality took place in the feminine community. While the expression indexes a degree of openness in social relations, it is also a way of defining a household. Women admire the ability of other women to cre-ate a jovial ambiance, even when it is only with other family members. The maid's expressed desire to find a place where she could laugh and play is equivalent to asserting that she wanted to be an insider, someone who could relax, be maṭluqa. To Fadela, however, playing and laughing are inappropriate in the work context and she had no intention of letting the boundary between domestic work and simple domesticity dissolve.

Maid and Mistress

The development of an educated middle class in Morocco, defined by two-career couples and the proliferation of service-sector jobs in the domestic realm, is contributing to a reorganization of power relations as played out between the mother-in-law and daughter-in-law and between educated working women and their less-educated domestic employees. The mother-in-law has lost status, while the working woman is trying to gain it — often at the expense of the maid, who is represented as constituting all that is low and shameful. In carving out their new domain as respectable workers in the public realm, middle-class women are distancing themselves from their lower-class "sisters" whose labor has long been in both the public eye and private household domain.

Because of the maid's physical proximity to the nuclear family, the middle class finds it necessary to exclude her psychologically. Yet the maid may become an object of desire or envy insofar as she is made to represent the transgression of prescriptive laws of feminine social behavior. She is the exotic other, the outlaw, a woman with license. This joint fascination and disgust with the character of the maid is evidenced in women's gossip: she is discursively excluded from the middle-class body by virtue of her low status, yet it is this very exclusion that helps define the emergent categories of both the working woman (*muwaẓẓafa*) and the nuclear family (*z-zwaj dyal daba*, "today's marriage"). "A fundamental rule seems to be that what is excluded at the overt level of identity-formation is productive of new objects of desire" (Stallybrass and White 1986 : 25). The maid's ability to be both an insider and an outsider with access to private secrets as well as to a public in which to divulge them, makes her a threat to the sanctity of the nuclear family which employs her. Yet this threat is "naturalized" and diffused by delineating the maid as an agent of pollution and disorder which must be held in check.

Much like the newlywed under her mother-in-law's jurisdiction, the young maid is subject not only to social stigmatization but to physical abuse. She may be hit by her female employer: *kat-akul l'aṣa*, "she is made to eat the stick." The use of corporal punishment is not shocking in the Moroccan context where there is historical precedent for the physical reprimand of children, servants, and wives. Even when physical discipline is not practiced, however (it is never a means of correcting an older woman), maids are either portrayed as evil women or pitied as disenfranchised souls with questionable pasts. They are the *bnat l-ḥaram*, the daughters of sin, presenting an explicit sexual threat to the woman of the house. Discursive categories such as this one permeate the social imagination and actively constitute the division of social classes.

Notes

1. The tyranny of the mother-in-law in North Africa is well documented. She has been criticized for perpetuating the very roles of subservience she had to endure as a young bride (Lacoste-Dujardin 1985).

2. Traditionally, the bride was married very young. Physical reprimand was not considered abusive, but rather a way of instructing a child in proper upbringing (tarbiya).

3. Davis notes that in Morocco

"The mother-in-law is deeply attached to her son and sees the new bride as a competitor for his affection and his loyalty. In an extended family, the two women are also in competition for resources, the bride desiring to channel goods into her nuclear family, while the mother-in-law attempts to distribute them to her family, the extended kin group. The new bride is also expected to take over much of the housework, relieving her new mother-in-law of all duties except criticism of her daughter-in-law's performance, which she usually relishes. (1983:37)

4. Fine (1984) calls this "intersemiotic translation." The situation is endemic in any modernizing society in which schooling is the agency of intervention.

5. Four thousand riyals is equivalent to two hundred dirhams, or about thirty dollars a month.

6. This is Hadda's opinion and cannot be taken to represent general reality.

7. The institution of the khadəm (masc. sing.) has much in common with Western notions of indentured servitude. Yet since the faithful in Islam consider themselves 'ibad allah, "servants (or slaves) of God" ("Your slave, oh God / your slave, oh God / they become Muslims from among your slaves," said the majduba), this concept does not have the same negative connotations that it does in English. The same word for slave, 'abd, when made into a verb means "to worship" and is so intertwined with the positive value of obedience that exploitation is easily disguised and rationalized. This is often the case with a live-in domestic who is "prise en charge," taken care of by her employers, much like a child dependent on her parents, or like the new bride in her husband's family. She is not a possession of her husband or her mother-in-law, but is their domain, as they exercise dominion over her.

8. This makes reference to the folk belief that there is an angel on the left arm that records all one's good acts, and another on the right arm that records the bad.

9. Seven days after the birth of a child, a naming ceremony (sbuʿ) is held for relatives and friends. This may be a very festive event, with professional dancers and elaborate offerings of food, or a simple serving of tea and sweets to commemorate the new birth.

10. Given the historical mutual exclusivity of feminine and masculine gender spheres, there are some themes which are more common to men's or women's gossip. In general, however, women are free to discuss any topic — including the more "male" subjects of politics and economics — whereas men are more restricted: they almost never talk about their wives, for example. Customarily, a man will avoid even referring to his wife, using metonymic phrases like "the house."

11. Although haram means "forbidden," not "sin," this translation best corresponds to the English connotations of illegitimacy; if said of a man, wald l-haram, the translation would be "bastard."

12. See Webber (1991) for a discussion of how hikayat (historical narratives) function similarly in a Tunisian community.

13. Urban legends are defined by Brunvand as "stories in a contemporary set-ting... that are reported as true individual experiences but that have traditional vari-ants that indicate their legendary character" (1986 : 165). According to Brunvand, "Basic modern anxieties often lie behind popular urban legends" (167).

14. The phenomenon of a family meal — a meal where both men and women are present — is not a practice that extends to all sectors of society. There is a pro-hibition on eating in mixed-sex company among some older generations in Beni Mellal. One woman in her late sixties told me that her husband, with whom she had four children, never saw her in the act of eating: "he never saw me lift a glass next to him," she asserted.

15. The Arabic verb used to describe the duties of a maid is *sakhkhara*; *l-khad-dama kat sakhkhar* means that the maid does errands and chores. In classical Arabic this verb has other connotations as well. *a'mal s-sukhra* [CA] is "slave labor" and the word for "oppressor" in Arabic (*musakhkhir*) is a derivation of the same root.

9. Terms of Talking Back: Women's Discourse on Magic

It was a hot day and the sellers in the cloth market were standing around with nothing to do. They began yelling at the few women who were in the market gossiping, saying that if the women didn't shut up, God would give them a "women's war." Well, one woman present didn't like the attitude of the man who said this and she decided to show him what female revenge was.

She went to a cemetery and waited until a family came to bury their dead child. When the mourning family left, she unburied the child and put it in a basket. Then she went back to the vendor in the market who had offended her.

There she bought lots of cloth. But when the time came to pay, she pretended to have left her money at home. She told him that she would take the cloth home and leave the covered basket with him until she returned with the money. She took the cloth home but returned to the market without any money. She told the merchant that, after all, she had left the money in the basket. When she opened the basket she began screaming, "I left a basket full of goods with you and when I return there is a dead child in their place!"

The merchant was very upset and offered her everything in the store if she would be quiet. She accepted on the condition that he take responsibility for burying the dead child. He agreed.

The next morning he was a very poor man on his way to the cemetery and it happened that he met the woman who had played the awful trick on him. She looked at him and said, "Now you understand what a women's war is!"

This story was told to me by a man selling traditional medicines in Beni Mellal in response to my questions about women who came to buy herbs, incense, and ingredients for magical potions. The story represents the antagonism between women and merchants (traditionally male), men's derision of women for their gossiping, as well as the "no-holds-barred" stance of women in combat for power with men. It also emphasizes the power of women's talk (l-hadra). The man knew he was not responsible for the contents of the basket, yet he feared the scandal the woman's testimony would create. Although the woman in the tale ultimately discloses herself to him, she does so without witnesses and only after she has "won the war."

This story is told from a male vantage point where women are portrayed as gossips and ruthless avengers, while men are victims of their ruse. Aspects of the power struggle described in this traditional tale find contemporary correlation in women's magical practices and in the narratives that surround them. Magic in this context is about taking control; talk of magic becomes discourse about empowerment in the face of polygamy, social impotence, and lack of choice in one's conjugal destiny. The reasons women employ magic usually relate to heterosexual gender conflicts. A woman frequently engages in magic (shur) to (1) make a man love her, (2) make a man love *only* her, (3) control the movements and actions of a man, (4) win the attentions of a man by inflicting harm on a female rival or (5) harm a man physically for reasons of revenge or jealousy.

Quite apart from the motivations of shur or its reputed results, narratives about magic are also about boundaries. In discussing magical practices, women are exploring the furthermost limits of social behavior, vicariously entering into possibilities offered by acts of transgression. As in the discourse of the herbalist examined earlier, talk of magic stretches the limits of moral license by exercising maximal liberty in verbal performance; what is said clearly has an impact upon the moral evaluations of the subcommunity. The terms in which magic is discussed delimit the fluctuating domains of the permissible (*l-ḥalal*) and the forbidden (*l-ḥaram*).

One afternoon Zohra when to visit a friend of hers, Fatna, who was well versed in magic. Knowing my interest in women's narratives, she asked to take the tape recorder with her, telling me that she would engage the women in conversation about magic. Although I expressed interest in accompanying her, Zohra encouraged me to stay home, assuring me that the women would be less inhibited if I were not there. This proved to be the case.

Fatna, whom I met only later, was a plump woman, her head always wrapped tightly with a white silken scarf. That afternoon Fatna's divorced younger sister Aisha fixed tea and the women sat on a low sponge mattress eating sweets. Fatna's husband was away and her younger children were playing outside in the stone alley.

When Zohra asked her to talk about magic, Fatna laughed, amused that the "wife of Yahya, son of Mason Hmid" wanted to know about such practices. Her voice took on a tone of authority as she held forth on her area of expertise:

"Now if a woman wants a man to want her, she goes to a fqih or to a woman,"[1] Fatna explained. "Well then she gives her that cloth—the one she cleans herself with after she has intercourse with her husband. That water that he ejects, women put it on that cloth. And she takes it to the fqih or to the woman. They put herbs on it. Well then!"

Fatna drank her tea, which had been placed next to the tape recorder on a low wooden table.

"Well," she continued, "she begins to fix things for her. Either she tells you 'right now' or she tells you that for seven days you should keep putting [the semen] on that cloth: 'Every day sleep with him until seven days have passed and bring the cloth and I'll fix it for you.' Now everyone has what they will say.

"The important thing is, she takes it to her. She fixes, she fixes. There are those who fix it and he begins to want her and all that and there are those who fix it and only then does he begin to fight with his wife![2]

"And she goes to the fqih. Either she tells him, 'that which you did for me was good' or she tells him it wasn't good. He again writes charms for him, or something.

"And there are some fqihs that tell you, 'Wait, I won't fix anything for him until I see his star…' There are those who keep count and read the lines on their palms. Or they look at his star when it is in the sky. Because we, everyone… that's what they say, and God knows. Do you understand? His star. Because we all have those stars. Like now, someone… Like now you see a falling star. The fqih says to you, 'Someone died.' You're sitting like this and you see a falling star. He tells you, 'Someone died.' Now he tells you, 'I'll look and I'll count and I'll see when his star rises.'

"He says that if he's brown, if the man that has taken you is brown, we'll make him… You go like that to the fqih and buy a sea onion ('aṇṣla). And they do that to him. And if he's white, they use eggs. Understand?"

"What do they do with the eggs?" Zohra asked.

"The cloth, you straighten it out, with the eggs and with dates and all that. And she always tells you 'the cloth that you use with your husband has to be new ḥayati[3] cloth.' And for the brown man, you put that sea onion that you bought from the druggist. Remember? Now if you want to fix the cloth, you… you use it seven times and you put three eggshells in it. Right? And you buy a ḥayati glass — and don't bargain for it! Just go and ask: 'How much is this? This glass?' Pay for it and come home and take honey and trace three lines on it — over here on this side and over there on that. And put it in the brazier and put dates and eggs around it and light it. There has to be fire. And bury it in the ashes. Right? Bury it in the ashes."

"And sea onion?" asked Zohra.

"And sea onion. Bury them in the ashes and light the fire for him. For seven days you light the fire for him. That's good, I know by experience!"

If maids are considered "daughters of the forbidden" in social discourse, women who practice magic and, particularly specialists in magic (*s-saḥ-ḥarat*) like "the woman" in Fatna's narrative, constitute the furthest bounds of transgressive behavior. When Fatna explains what she knows "by experience," she is identifying herself as a participant in a power struggle whose means are covert and subversive. Although magic, like charm writing, is not always illicit, women's practices take important steps away from the traditional and "sanctioned" magic practiced by men. The astrology that Fatna equates with the fqih has its roots in medieval magic and does not contradict Islamic cosmology; indeed, the two systems are complementary (see Nasr 1964).[4] The fqih uses written verses from the Qur'an as amulets which are meant to persuade the supernatural forces to comply with one's wishes. The practices of the sorceress, on the other hand, are more coercive and less formally religious. Though built upon the magical practices used for centuries in North Africa, women's use of magic represents another historical trajectory.[5]

Magic and History in Morocco

In 1926 Edward Westermarck, a Finnish scholar who taught at the University of London, published a two-volume study called *Ritual and Belief in Morocco* in which he provided exhaustive description of the folk beliefs and practices of Moroccans, both Berbers and Arabs, from all regions of the country.[6] His descriptions of the folklore and life of Moroccans have yet to be surpassed, for any time period. Consequent studies, particularly in America, seem to ignore the very "thick descriptions" (C. Geertz 1973) of belief in magic that permeate Westermarck's writing, and focus instead on socioeconomic structure (C. Geertz 1979), the intersection of history and politics with religion and social structure (C. Geertz 1971/68; Eickelman 1976), the construction of social identity (Rosen 1984), kinship structures (H. Geertz 1979), and Moroccan society as seen through the eyes of note-worthy Moroccans (see Crapanzano 1980; Eickelman 1985). Although these studies have illumined much about Moroccan culture and society—as well as about the ethnographic enterprise itself (K. Dwyer 1982; Rabinow 1977)—they largely give the impression that the magical practices which Westermarck described over half a century ago comprise a world that has vanished with the advent of modernism (for exceptions see Buitelaar 1993; Crapanzano 1973; S. Davis 1983; D. Dwyer 1978; Hart 1976; Maher 1974; Rosander 1991).

In fact, s̲h̲ur, which can be translated as magic, sorcery, or conjury, is very much alive in Morocco today. Most of the studies that do not take account of it rely on male testimony or sensibility.

According to scripturalist Islam, religion (din) and magic (s̲h̲ur) are exclusive categories, with magic being forbidden according to the Qur'an: "I seek refuge in the Lord of Daybreak from the mischief of His creation; from the mischief of the night when she spreads her darkness; from the mischief of conjuring witches" (Qur'an, 113). But what Scott (1990) calls the "hidden transcript," a veiled discourse of resistance, tells a different version of the story, where religion and magic are inseparable. An example of this was provided in the market discourse of both the majduba and the herbalist who authorized their dealings in the business of magic with religious phraseology and invocation.

Westermarck made reference to this hybrid phenomenon when he said that "the relationship between magic and religion is... intimate. [M]agical practices may become genuine acts of religious worship, or acts of worship may become magical practices, or the same act may simultaneously be magical and religious, coercive and propitiatory... In the ancient religions of the East magic and religion are indissolubly mixed up together" (1926: 24, 33). Westermarck's words reflect a preoccupation with defining the terms "magic" and "religion" as they were used at the time, particularly by Frazer, who defined religion as a propitiation of spirits or god(s) and magic as the coercion and control of the same (Frazer 1911; see also Doutté 1984[1908]; Hubert and Mauss 1950; Lévi-Strauss 1966: 11). As Hammoudi notes, colonial scholars mapped categories such as these onto different Moroccan populations (Berber "paganism"/Arab orthodox Islam) with strategic intent (1989). In this light, Westermarck's observations seem to construct the "ancient religions of the East" not only as syncretic, but also as "indissolubly mixed up."

Yet the division between magic and religion becomes salient when regarded as a distinction between good and bad, and sometimes between men's and women's belief systems in the Moroccan imagination.[7] Magic as it is practiced in Morocco today is about controlling forces — *taking* control rather than relinquishing it to a higher power, whether that be the secular power of the patriarch or the sacred power of the religious code of ethics. Magic presents a third force and another choice. Discourses about magic contest both the dominant notions of what constitutes honorable and shameful behavior and capitalist practices which define value in terms of material wealth.

A Market for Magic

The subject of magic and its importance is particularly evident in the marketplace, which abounds with herbalists selling potions and their antidotes, men orating on the dangers of witchcraft, and women holding forth on the efficacy of their herbal mixes to get rid of or placate spirits (*jnun*). As we have seen, the suq is a place where otherwise private discourses emerge into the public domain. This is largely due to the ambiguity of all marketplace discourse, which may always be interpreted as "lies." Nonetheless, advice about what kind of magic to use under what circumstances is solicited in the marketplace. Not only are potions sold, but knowledge about how magic is employed, its symptoms and its consequences, is disseminated.

Outside the licensed arena of the marketplace, magic, like gossip, is either publicly demeaned or ignored in an effort to disavow its centrality in the lives of a substantial number of Moroccans. In formal interviews, many women distance themselves from the practice of magic, equating it with the "backward" ways of the country. "I don't go along with that stuff," many women told me, "haram, it's forbidden," they said, shaking their heads. Often the same women who denigrate the suq also remove themselves from discourses on magic. Yet denial of magical practice, even among women, is a sign of its symbolic importance. No one denies the *existence* of magic in Morocco and its threat to family and community order; what is denied is their own personal practice. Resorting to magic means "buying into" a socially stigmatized belief system; even women who are specialists in magic know enough not to advertise their talents among an unappreciative audience. Thus a veiled discourse is born and perpetuated.

Magic combines commonplace materials with abnormal motives to create a state (*ḥal*) that is both "frightful" and powerful. Items such as kitchen utensils (clay pots, frying pans, and pressure cookers) are combined with ritual foods (milk, dates, and honey), mixed with corrosive cleaners (bleach or caustic building materials such as lime), then added to bodily emissions and weaving materials. The result is a mixture that acts both to bind and to disintegrate, to "give" life and to "close" it. The efficacy of magic relies on the collision of otherwise non-compatible elements and the mixing (actual and metaphorical) of distinct cultural categories such as dogs and men, food and dirt, and women and social agency.[8]

The very terms of magic are thus hybrid, a semiosis that employs signs from various facets of Moroccan life — from the religious invocation of the fqih and the power inherent in his once-coveted literacy skills to the manipulation of polluting materials such as semen (whose emission renders the subject ritually "unclean") and dirt. Yet sḥur entails no dialogue or negotiation with its object, but rather seeks to appropriate power covertly and often violently. In this sense, the system of magic shares much in common with the commodity relations of the marketplace, exemplified in the phenomena of prix fixe and advertising: bargaining is silenced and desires are controlled through the covert manipulation of images and signs.

Magic and Secrecy

> That which women do here! The wonders of God!
> They have that way… just women do that. They do it to a man so he'll
>   want them.
> He finds that something's been done to him; he's sick or something.
> Or else she wants him not to love his mother anymore.
> She does something to him.
> And then it ruins him.
>
> — Karim, a traditional druggist in Beni Mellal

There are many degrees of attempted coercion in Moroccan magical practices, ranging from the socially condoned visits of women to a fqih in order that he might "write" them a charm,[9] to the highly secretive solicitation of witchcraft from women who specialize in the field (*s-saḥḥarat*). Somewhere in the middle is the traditional druggist (*'aṭṭar*), a man who sells the necessary ingredients for both herbal remedies and magic (including rare spices, coveted bird feathers, live scorpions and lizards) and who knows how much is needed, for what purpose, when and why.[10]

Figures 19 and 20. Herbalists in their shops.

The 'aṭṭar has access to the secrets of women. Indeed, he knows more about the collective secrets of the community than most. This might put him in a powerful position in the circulation of "news," but he does not "talk" (*hdər*) about women and their magic with anyone who might pose a threat to their magical activities. These subjects are inappropriate in mixed company, and are disdained as "women's talk" among men. Yet over and above the fluctuating rules for topical conversation, the business of the 'aṭṭar relies on his ability to keep secrets and his perpetuation of the belief system that fosters consumption of "magical" goods.

Although the practice of magic in Morocco is no secret, it was only in spending many hours at the shops of two traditional druggists to record bargaining discourse that I became aware of the extent of such practices. These young men, Hassan and Karim, who had inherited their knowledge and their livelihoods from their fathers, offered me a perspective on the "business" of magic. Many hours in their company convinced me of the real need for secrecy regarding magical practices, some of which would be considered criminal in the context of official society.

Magic is forbidden according to the official discourse of religion in

Beni Mellal, but accepted as a reality of daily life. Unlike the Bocage population in France that Favret-Saada describes, a victim of magic is not shut
out by "criticism and scorn" or deemed "superstitious, backward, raving ...
[by the] priests, [and] the other villagers (1980:15; cf. Stoller 1989a; Stoller
and Olkes 1987)"; rather, he (or she) is pitied by women and treated by
priests (the fqihs), the condition often eliciting a wary silence from other
men.[11] European-trained medical doctors in Beni Mellal, representing a
hard and empirical approach that comes from "outside," deny the validity
of magical intervention. Moroccans rarely go to medical doctors for afflictions of magic, except in cases of being poisoned, when they are treated for
food poisoning.

The Poetics of Herbalism, the Stance of l-ʿaṭṭar

Most of the magic that the ʿaṭṭar sells works on the principle of sympathetic
energy. Body substances of hair, spittle, sperm, sweat, or even dirt scraped
from the victim's shoes are mixed with druggists' supplies such as candles,

herbs, and caustics. The manipulation of these ingredients affects the nafs of the person being bewitched. These bodily emissions, collected without the victim's knowledge, symbolize a link between inner and outer life and constitute the most powerful (because polluting) ingredients of magic.

While the 'attar provides the ingredients for magic and the woman provides the substance that links the magic to the victim, the efficacy of shur depends on the one principal factor of niya, in this context, best translated as "belief." "Religion by belief; magic by belief; everything by belief,"[12] Hassan told me. Niya makes magic work.

The necessity for belief in the activity of magic is acknowledged frequently in the discourse. It is a major theme in the following excerpt of a playful bargaining dialogue between a Sahara woman buying a potion from the 'attar Karim and his assistant, Abdellatif. Also illustrated here is the importance of the "sounds of words" in magical discourse (Stoller 1989a). Karim has run out of *ḥarmal*, an odiferous plant that is used as incense to remove the effects of the evil eye.

"I joke with your father so much. Add some ḥarmal [to the incense]."

"Ḥarmal so that he comes seeking protection," said Karim, "There's no one who'll give you ḥarmal. You won't find ḥarmal. There is none. There is none. There's some in the Sahara. There's none here. Forget the ḥarmal, God give you ease."

"Leave the ḥarmal for another time, oh shrifa,"[13] said Abdellatif. "No one has any here. It all disappeared at once. Ḥarmal so that he comes seeking protection."

"God bring you ease," offered Karim.

"God bring what is good," followed Abdellatif.

"Amen," said the client.

"And lichen moss for cheating (*ashan 'la l-ghərshan*)," said Karim as he opened a large plastic bottle of powdery green moss and poured some onto the piece of newspaper where he was assembling the potion. "Without the ḥarmal," he told her, "Just have faith and you can sleep with the snake" (*ghir dir niya u bat m'a l-ḥayya*, a rhyming proverb).

"Sleep with the living," corrected Abdellatif, playing on the homophony between the words snake (*ḥayya*) and living (*ḥayin*).

"With the snake, not with the living," Karim returned, gesturing to include the people before him, "HERE are the living, HERE they are!"

"The living are plentiful and the dead are next to God," added the client. "I just want the approximate [amount of herbs], my son. I'm just the envoy."[14]

"By God, I prepared this stuff without [need of] your talk!" Karim returned, his intonation subtly challenging the boundaries of respectful speech to elders. "I won't give you anything! If you just have niya, I'll give you an empty paper and you and your niya will attain your objective."

"You see," said the Saharan woman, offering her own wisdom, "there was a man and some other people, and they passed by an old woman. And that old woman, the poor thing, her eyes were in pain. And they [the men] were going our way, the way to Moulay Bouazza.[15] And she and her niya, the niya of God, that old woman said, 'Please heal my eyes, they're hurting me.' And he spit in her eyes. And when they started on their way back from Moulay Bouazza, she found her eyes as if they had never hurt. With niya."

"Ah! Just niya!" said Karim.

"Everything is a matter of niya."

"Ahuh. 'Niya is worth more than action.' (an-niyatu ablaghu mina l-'amal)"[16]

"Ahuh. If you attain niya everything comes."

In this exchange, the 'attar employs poetic devices and proverbs to describe the assemblage of herbs, minerals, and spices that they are preparing for the Saharan woman. The 'attar and his assistant are enacting təfliya, a conversational genre which involves joking and teasing in a performative mode. In this speech play,[17] the druggist and his assistant are having fun, both with each other and with their client. They are at special liberty with her as the client is an older woman, a status allowing her a certain degree of license in social interactions.

Within this performance of təfliya, multiple meanings break through the surface structure of their speech in the use of alliteration, rhyme, and pun. The first three letters of the herb ḥarmal, for example, are used to construct a predicate, tḥarəm, which in Moroccan colloquial Arabic means "to seek protection," especially in the feminine domain of the home.[18] Ḥarmal, which becomes a metonym for magic in general, makes a man seek protection in his home (the verb connotes "running for shelter" or "taking cover"). As most magic is an attempt to gain either the love or the physical presence of a man, the phrase "he comes seeking protection" (y-ji kay tḥarəm) is especially pertinent. Likewise, in listing the diverse ingredients he is placing in the newspaper for his client, the 'attar also mentions lichen moss, for "cheating" (ashan 'la l-ghərshan).[19] Through the use of rhyme, the 'attar delimits the ingredients of the incense and their uses, increasing the buyer's knowledge about the essentials of magic by performing his own verbal competence. The word play continued as Karim, Abdellatif, and their Saharan client brought the transaction to a close:

"This moss, so she gets attention," said Abdellatif, reaching into the plastic bottle and pinching a powdery substance into the newspaper.

"So she can raise her status," said Karim.

"She gains status," the Saharan woman said.

"And *ḥalḥal* and *shdəq j-jmal* and ghoul eggs," said Karim.

"And ginger so he comes even if he's in a well."

"Blue iron, blue fire, and 'sauce of colors'."

"He said 'sauce of colors.' By God, they use this sauce of colors in prison!"

"Sauce of colors?"

"Sauce of colors."

"So he comes in many colors! He turns red and yellow."

"Put *ḥab l-məshak* so he becomes ensnared."

"And *shṭarṭar* so he comes broken-down and exhausted."

In Arabic, the play with rhyme is evident:

Ass't:	Had *ashan* bəsh t-*ban*
'aṭṭar:	Bəsh t-waqəf *shan*-ha
Client:	T-wəlli b-*shan-ha*
'aṭṭar:	U l-ḥalḥ*al* u shdəq-j-jm*al* u biḍat l-*ghul*
Ass't:	U skinj*bir* bəsh y-ji wakha f-l-*bir*
'aṭṭar:	l-ḥdida z-zərqa, l-'afya zərqa u mərq-lwan
Client:	Gal-lək "mərq-lwan" U aḷḷah, had mərq-lwan kay st'amlu f-l-ḥabs.
'aṭṭar:	Mərq-*lwan*?
Client:	Mərq-*lwan*.
'aṭṭar:	Bəsh y-ji kay t-*luwən*.
Client:	[laughter]
'aṭṭar:	y-wəlli ḥm*ər* u ṣf*ər*.
	Dir ḥab l-məsh*ak* bəsh y-shb*ək*.
	U *shṭarṭar* bəsh y-ji kay *ṭaḥṭaḥ*.[20]

What is striking in these rhyming phrases is the consistent manipulation of the male "victim." The man is always referred to as "coming" to the woman in various states of vulnerability. He comes, or is made to come, in any circumstances and against all odds, "even if he's in a well." He loses his will and becomes *mshəbbək*, "ensnared," a pawn.[21] He turns "red" with embarrassment and "yellow" with fear. The woman, on the other hand, only gains standing from these activities; her status is "raised up."

These phrases of the ʿaṭṭar are not spontaneous improvisation. To the contrary, the young druggist has heard his father repeat them many times. They are formulated upon folk interpretations of *materia medica* that have existed in Morocco and the Middle East for centuries (Hamarneh 1984). The verses are memorized in the course of the ʿaṭṭar's apprenticeship; having learned them, the young ʿaṭṭar plays with them in an almost mocking fashion. This quality of təfliya serves to distance the ʿaṭṭar from the potential threat his goods pose to the honor (autonomy) of manhood, and from the entire system of magic that these verses define.

The ʿaṭṭar manages to be in the business of magic without being subject to its marginal status by publicly asserting that all magic relies on belief. He is thus seen to place responsibility for magical intervention not with his commodities, but with the belief of those who use them. "[If] you just have niya," he told his client, "I'll give you an empty paper and you and your niya will attain your objective." After the client left, Karim explained it to me this way:

"For example, [let's say] I gave her an empty paper. Now she tells me, 'Give me something.' I come and I give her an empty paper and tell her, 'that's it, the thing that you want is there.' She had niya, the poor woman. She takes that paper and goes. Perhaps that niya will work for her, in truth. That objective that she wants, she finds it, even though I gave her an empty paper. For her, that goal was attained. She comes back to me and that goal was attained. You, now, [let's say] you don't believe. And look! I was joking with her and she had niya and she got what she wanted. It's for this that niya plays a role."

These words establish Karim's relation to magic as one of business; the incense he is selling is a commodity which is only activated by the belief of its procurer. On the other hand, the verses he recites, albeit playfully, serve to reinforce the belief system of his clientele and the success of his business. It is only in intimate conversation with Karim that his stories about "the bewitched" betray his own belief, and indeed wonderment, at the results that are possible with magic:

"There's one guy, a son of Casablanca. He must be about fifty years old. He was living in Casablanca. And you know there's a Jewish quarter in

Casablanca. There are a lot of Jews there. Well, he liked a Jewess. And she liked him too. And the magic of her [angry] parents still happens to him, even here [in Beni Mellal]. He feels himself to be no longer 'normal.'[22] And when he feels like that, he goes and drinks. And he said (gal-lək), 'I gave this charity with God: I made her enter Islam.' And he's still with her today. That makes twelve years. And she doesn't give birth or anything. His parents said to him, 'It's either [our] blessing or [our] indignation; she doesn't give birth. What do you want to do with her?' He told them, 'Now she's converted and my help is with God.' He saw that his parents didn't understand and he came to Beni Mellal to live."

"With his wife?"

"With his wife."

"When he goes to buy tomatoes, they both go. Even when he just wants to buy cigarettes she goes with him. They understand each other. They come to buy candles from me. They just laugh and laugh. She likes candlelight. I don't know why. Even though she has electricity, she illumines [their rooms] with candles. He has a connection who got him work in the Ministry of Transportation. He earns, I don't know, sixty thousand riyals and the house is given to him [for free]. And he still feels that magic. It finds him even here [in Beni Mellal]. And look at the Jews, there they've gotten to! They went all the way to America. When I got to understanding him he said to me, 'Her family, if they could find a way to get her back, they'd pay even two hundred million.'"

"But that [magic] comes from where? From her parents?"

"From her parents, that magic. Because, they say, it's as if she's kidnapped. They say he enchanted her. But he hasn't enchanted her or anything. He just wants her and she wants him. And he brought her to prayer. She's started to pray. And she knows how to read. And when that magic hits him, he comes to me and I give him a little "rocks of *fasukh*" so that he [can] breathe again."

The 'aṭṭar's belief in the effects of sḥur is implicit in this narrative and finds resonance in the testimony of a middle-aged man who believes himself to be a victim of magical perpetration. He is a client of the 'aṭṭar, and in these matters a confidante. The man believes himself to be bewitched by his wife's parents, who are opposed to the marriage.

In Morocco, both Jews and Berbers from the Souss region are known for their prowess in magic. In fact, there is still a Jewish "sorcière" in Beni Mellal, a regular client of Karim, whose powers are both solicited and feared by the community. This story attests to the 'attar's belief in the powerful force of Jewish magic which has been affecting his client for more than twelve years. The account is a warning against interfaith marriage, a testimony to the possibility of conversion, and a commentary on the ambiguous success of such conversion (the final hybrid form — a child — is ultimately not conceived). It also provides an "outside" cause, or excuse, for behavior that challenges prescriptive definitions of social boundaries: interfaith marriage, the gender bonding displayed by the couple (who are portrayed as virtually never leaving each others' side — a very unusual situation given the gender polarization in Beni Mellal) and the drinking into which the husband escapes when he feels the effects of the magic coming on. Anticanonical behavior is easily attributed to shur; in fact, both the woman's parents and the woman's husband blamed each other for the social (and in his case, physical) malaise brought about by the marriage, which they all relate to the effects of magic.

If sympathetic magic is efficacious only when there is accompanying belief, magic ingredients that are ingested (t-tukal)[23] become less dependent upon such belief factors. Here, Karim clearly had no reservations about admitting the existence of magical practices:

"There was a guy who used to work in this company and a girl was working with him. That girl prepared some magic in a glass for that guy. She [also] put it in his food. So that when he comes, she'd tell him, 'You see, I brought you some food from my house.' But that guy was kept busy with his work. No one came [to eat] except another boy who was working with them. [That boy] he said [to himself], 'Hmm... give me that food to eat and if she comes, I'll tell her.'

"She came and she didn't find the food. She said, 'the [intended] guy must have eaten it.' But she saw that he hadn't taken it and she called the boy who ate it. And he told her. She just opened her mouth and just... and she just stared at him.

"He said to her, 'I'll bring you some food [to replace it], don't worry.' And she grabbed her jəllaba and left.

"He started throwing up, poor guy, for a week. And from that night on, he hasn't been able to sleep, either at night or during the day. He's left with nowhere to go. Seven months and he's still in agony. And when he comes to me, he shows me his arms. It's as if he's not human. Those arms are blue, like... I don't know. If you saw him, by God, you'd cry! Seven months and he hasn't slept. And he shows me those arms. Sometimes they have pimples, sometimes they're blue, sometimes they're yellow. And he's gone relentlessly to the fqihs. Nothing. They just take his money!"

In this scenario, nothing is said about niya or about the motives for the poisoning. The story highlights the ultimate threat in bewitchment: namely, being an innocent victim. In this story, the victim is a boy, the one with niya, translated here as an unsuspecting naiveté. The boy in this narrative trusted, and his trust led him into unfortunate circumstances. Someone else, older or more experienced, would not have eaten a plate of food intended for another. As Rosander acknowledges, "men do not dare eat the food or drink the tea or coffee prepared by women they do not trust. For food, drink and sex — three of the most essential physical needs of a human being — men are dependent on women and at the mercy of their magical potential" (1991 : 250). Just like the women who had their goods taken from them at the market, niya, as naiveté, can be injurious in a world of tricksters and witches.

The ingestion of magical potions presents a threat that even the fqihs cannot counter; although they offer help, they do not alleviate the suffering of the poisoned boy. They only "take his money." As evidenced here and in much of the discourse to follow, fqihs who write charms and prepare amulets are losing credibility in the eyes of both women and men.[24] Their supernatural practices are not considered efficacious and their literary skills are no longer unique in the community.[25] Fqihs are also poor, relying on donations or living on meager salaries gained through running Qur'anic nursery schools (see Wagner 1993). Because of their low economic status, some people assume that they — like the other persons in the ḥalqa — must rely on ruse to earn their living.

But if the fqih is unable to help the afflicted boy, neither does the 'aṭṭar offer a remedy; as he said, "there's nothing... to cure. They [would] now have to... change all his blood." Women via magic manipulate both the soul (ruḥ), of the victim and his very blood-life. In this sense, magic is physically contaminating, potentially threatening even the innocent with permanent disability.

Terms of Talking Back:
Control and the Construction of Identity

The meaning of magic is discursively constructed by women themselves on occasions, such as visits, when magic is a common topic of gossip. As

Fatna asserted, "the ocean [of magic] is vast [and] there is much to say [about it]."

In delimiting the social function of shur for Moroccan women as a means of "talking back," a counter-hegemonic discourse, the terms are clearly contestative. The question remains, however, does this practice challenge the male power that it seeks to manipulate or does it actually reproduce an official discourse that defines women as evil agents of disorder?

In Fatna's opening narrative, she mentions the purpose of the magic, to make a man desire a woman, and the vital ingredient for the spell—a cloth with the man's semen on it. Referred to only as the *kəttana* (from the word "cotton"), this cloth has an important role in magic, representing the nafs, the desires which comprise the self of the intended victim. Like other bodily emissions (blood, urine, breast milk or saliva), semen[26] traverses the body's boundaries and carries the power of the "internal" to the outside world. By virtue of its procreative function, semen has a direct relation to honor, which is increased by having many children, a source of symbolic capital. It also represents a man's nafs which, as we have seen in the discourse of the ʿashshaba, finds direct correlation in definitions of manhood. Nafs, here, becomes a commodity of sorts; it is an essential aspect of the self, which can nonetheless be appropriated by another, or lost in dissipation.

Belief in the ability to control the soul-life of another testifies to permeability in native concepts of personal boundaries. For example, when someone does not control his words, it is said that "his tongue is not his own." In not controlling his words, he has not appropriated them; even his own "tongue" does not belong to him. By contrast, a man who is "the master of his word" (*mul l-kəlma*) has recognized authority since he wins out over, or conquers, his carnal soul (*kay-tghalləb ʿla nafs-u*). The equation is simple: assertion of control is an act of appropriation, even in the realm of one's own speech. A person who does not control himself is "wide open" (*məhlul*).

The possibility of controlling the nafs of another must first be seen in relation to self-determination and identity. If Moroccan men and their honor have been defined by what they control (evident in relations with patron-client relations and dependents), the same is true of women. This is historically evident in relations between mother-in-law and daughter-in-law, and between the woman of the house and her servants. But with the breakdown of power relations in the extended family, women in particular have less of an opportunity to control anything or anyone.[27] Thus we witness the transference of this mode of domination from the feminine/familial and masculine/tribal realm to the larger scale of class stratification.[28] Implicit in the notion of class is the premise that holdings in the material economy determine one's identity vis-à-vis the larger society. Under such a system of classification, power to effect change in the social realm is directly related to economic mobility. Of someone who is poor in Morocco, it is said that "it [power] is not in his hands" (*ma f-id-ush*). Moral control through the code of honor and shame has taken a back seat to the material control of others.

Throughout history status, power, and self-identity were attained through relations of obligation. But magic, in seeking to augment personal status through the control of others, is outside the system of either market-place or kinship reciprocity. Magic requires little cooperation; it controls others not by obliging or shaming them, but by subversively inverting power relations. Magic must be covert to be successful. It does not involve rhetorical persuasion, but a form of guerilla warfare.

The sorceress is involved in a power struggle. The disorder she represents is specifically the breaking down of the patriarchal value system, which gains its identity in part through the control it asserts over women. But unlike the social manipulation of women, manipulation of men via magical practices is not socially sanctioned.

Discourse about boundaries and codes always involves negotiation. Yet it is pertinent that the spell outlined by Fatna prohibits bargaining for the hayati glass that will be the receptacle for the "cloth." The buyer is silenced, the social relations of bargaining eclipsed. In purchasing the "my life" glass, the price is fixed and the woman must be willing to pay.[29] In this sense, the process of obtaining the glass is emblematic of the process of power appropriation in general. The person with the most capital — whether that be money or magical power — is the one who controls the transaction and owns its terms. Attempts to control the nafs of another do not involve a dialogic interaction. To the contrary; incantation is a monologue and manipulation must be secretive if it is to be successful. Despite the dialogic properties characteristic of women's discourse about magic, its enactment is a more violent and appropriative activity.

"Here is one about candles," Fatna continued. "You have seven candles. You buy seven candles and you take the cloth of your man, that has his "water" on it. And you put it in wild honey and herbs. And you take those pieces of cloth and you shred them into small pieces. Every night you twist [a piece] around a candle, until it reaches the head [of the candle]. At night. And you light it with a match. But before you do that, before you light the fire on it, you take the cloth that you're going to wrap around the candle and you put it on your thigh, on your right thigh, and you start saying,

> ftəlt-ək 'la fakhdi limən
> t-na's bi-h
> t-fiyq bi-h
> t-nsa khu-k shqiq bi-h
> t-nsa l-qəḥbat d-day'at f-l-swaq.

> I twisted you around my right thigh
> to sleep with it
> to wake up with it
> with it to forget your full brother
> with it to forget the prostitutes that are lost in the marketplaces.

"You say this seven times, until the last time and you turn it around that candle and light it with a match. Every night, every night, until seven days have passed. As the candle melts, the husband melts too."

Unlike the Qur'anic recitations of the fqih, these words are not religious, they are words relating to the body. In sleeping and waking with her "thigh," the man is made to forget his brother, even the prostitutes that are lost in the marketplaces, everyone except the woman whose thigh is touching the cotton cloth. The woman winds the cloth around the candle as she winds the man around her "thigh." After seven nights, the candle is burned and melts, as does the desire of the man for everyone but the woman casting the spell. The candle becomes emblematic of the man's nafs.

Pots, Dirt, Dogs, and Hyenas:
The Use of Emblems in Magical Discourse

The importance of household objects such as candles is particularly salient in discourse about magic. In the first narrative the woman uses honey, dates, and eggshells in her preparation. In the next narrative an unusual juxtaposition of household items is employed:

"They say (gal-lək): the milk, you take half a liter of milk and you put the cloth [with the semen] on it. And you put it in the pressure cooker. You close the cooker and it keeps boiling, boiling, boiling, until it dries and you open it. That's it. The husband is good [if it's dry; if it's still wet, he's bad].

"Or you take the cloth and throw it in a bottle of acid. And it starts disintegrating there. It's like that magic with the dirt, they say, you take from him the dirt from under his feet."

"The right one?"

"The right one. The right foot. And put it in wild honey and put it in a little cloth and hide it and it stays [there]."

"Or you put it in a tree," said Aisha. "As the tree moves, so he will move, too. Understand?"

Fatna nodded. "Now he's either... either his footprints or his shoes. And you take his right shoe and you take off that dirt and mix it with wild honey. And hang it on a tree. As she told you, 'as that tree moves, so he too, will move.' You find him always standing for you next to the house. That's if he's a boyfriend, not your husband."

Here a pressure cooker, a popular commodity, is used as a tool of divination. Certainly this method did not exist when Westermarck documented magical practices in 1926. Hybridization has played a role even in the tools and symbols of magic by mixing customary practices with a modern accoutrement of convenience.

The role of hot and cold in native conceptions of the body and its temperaments is pertinent here.[30] Cold is associated with malady and weakness, while hot connotes anger and passion, but also growth. People with a cold constitution tend to be moist, while heat is accompanied by dryness (see Khan 1986). If the cloth remains wet when heated (contradicting the "natural" tendencies of the body), this is a bad omen (the man is "bad").

In the following narrative the sorceress heats dirt the intended victim has touched, thereby controlling his "temperature" in regard to her. She throws the dirt under the feet of a dog, rendering the man "doglike."

"And if you want to make him crazy [about you]?" asked Zohra.

"If you want to make him crazy? Take the dirt from his foot and take it home and fry it in the frying pan. It gives off heat."

"Be quiet! Be quiet!" Aisha said.

Fatna continued uninhibited. "Look. Find a dog that barks and throw it on him."

"For him to eat?" asked Zohra.

"No. Just throw it under his feet [so he] walks on it. Then [the man] he'll just come and go."

"Like a dog," Aisha said.

"Like a dog."

In this narrative the bewitched man is made to return to his woman like a dog following its master, its tail between its legs. The equation of men with dogs is a shameful one in Morocco, as is their association with domestication.[31] The sorceress inverts categories of gender by making the man follow the woman faithfully. The fact that the man is humiliated (rendered dog-like) by the employment of dirt is also significant, for the dog, who always lives outside in Morocco, is not considered a clean pet. The dirt from the man's shoe (or dirt that he has stepped on) is virtually cooked, fried in a frying pan like food. Unlike food, however, it is thrown under the paws of a dog. Categories here are mixed up (*mkhallət*): dirt is like food, men are like dogs, and women are in control. The sensitive nature of such transgressions is registered in the discourse when Aisha, anticipating Fatna's words, tries to censor her impending explanation.

Rendered dog-like with ṣḥur, the man is put into a category of tabooed animality (cf. Leach 1973), exercising no self-determination. This is an essential theme of magic in Morocco: attempts are made to confound another in order to subsequently gain control. As in the lyrical discourse of the shikhat examined earlier, the terminology often used in ṣḥur is that of "making crazy," of inducing the loss of control.

"And if you want to make him crazy," continued Fatna.

"Where do you put it?" Zohra asked, "In your breasts?"

"And the cloth," added Aisha, "did you tell her about it? Just tell her."

"And the cloth," said Fatna, "burn it. His cloth, burn it for him. Boil it in a pot of earth. And it keeps boiling, boiling, boiling, boiling. And if you want to make him crazy and mad and wild so he becomes... so he begins to want [only] you, take the eye of the hoopoe bird, and the feathers of the hoopoe..."

"And the eye of the swallow," added Aisha.

"And the eye of the swallow," Fatna confirmed.

"And the feathers of the swallow."

"And the feathers of the swallow."

"And what do you do with them?" asked Zohra. "That's it?"

"Those, you just take them with you in a little cloth and put it in your bag. And if you want to make someone crazy [about you] and to make... you seem beautiful to him—whatever you want, he'll take care of things and everything—carry with you the brain of the hyena. Whoever sees you will redden like a hyena. And the skin of a tiger, a little bit of that, too!

The women laughed.

"Really?" asked Zohra, a bit incredulous.

"Yeah, yeah. Take the charm to the fqih and say... Have a *jədwəl* [an amulet, inscribed with a geometrical design] made at the fqih's. And go sit with him [the man you want] and begin to laugh with him and hit him with it [the jədwəl] between his shoulders. And he'll begin to die for you!"

"There are also those who prepare jədwəl," said Aisha, "and they put it on the leg of a dove and she flies."

"The dove flies?"

"Yeah. The dove flies, by the truth of God! One guy, they did it to him, on the dove. He just started staying around next to the door, just going and coming [home]. Strange! Some... this one woman, her daughter was married; they put that wonder on the dove for him [and] he became as if he were crazy. Well, dear woman, you go to the fqih and sometimes you give him two thousand [riyals] or sometimes three thousand.[32] He keeps ringing you, by God!"[33]

The women laughed at Fatna's portrayal of the fqih as a charlatan who takes your money.

"Well, he writes three or four for you. This one, put it in a tree; he writes you [something about] the wind: you hang it on a tree. And he writes you one about fire: you burn it. You can use those amulets. Sometimes you do it at one o'clock, or at twelve. He gives you, like that, about three for you to use each day. Well, for three days you burn those 'books.'"

Fatna suggests the "brain of the hyena" to make a man "redden like a hyena." This phrase has a parallel structure to the 'attar's formulae (*l-ḥarmal bəsh y-ji kay-tḥarəm*), evidencing that the canon of magic is constructed discursively and poetically. The figure of the hyena is often present in talk about magic.[34] Someone who is bewitched is said to be "hyena-ed." In folk belief, hyenas are thought to urinate on their victims in order to stun and stupefy them. A person who is "hyena-ed" is able to be completely manipulated. The actual brain of the hyena is used to render the victim stupid—brain-less. In this case, the spell acts like urine to incapacitate the victim.

Also noteworthy in this segment are the terms in which the fqih is discussed. He is paid an impressive sum of money and keeps the client coming back. His charms (here called "books") refer to a time when the fqih's literacy had magical properties in itself. These books are "burned" in the course of the spell, destroying the evidence of the fqih's meditation.[35]

The Replacement of the Fqih

The fqih is a man of considerable standing, largely due to his literacy and religious training in the Qur'an (see Spratt and Wagner 1986). His engagement with marketplace practices, however, seems to undermine his stature in Fatna's eyes. In the following narrative, she delineates the fqih as someone of low status, who takes advantage of a woman who comes to him for professional services. The woman in this scenario is portrayed as "hot" and in desperate need of cooling down, to the extent that she is ready to pay any price for it. The fqih, much like the maids examined earlier, is constructed as an agent of disorder, without morals, low and self-interested. This represents a complete inversion of his traditional role as a representative of religious morality in the community.

"Anyway (*l-muhim*), her husband left her and all that. And she began to give herself to magic. All of a sudden she went to a fqih and… and she's pretty, she's very pretty. Anyway, he began wanting her (it was the fqih who wanted her) and she started, the poor thing, to pay the price [for her mistakes]; that is, to pay the price with her morals.

"She began to go to his place and he imposed some things on her. Like now, he wants to sleep with her and all that. No one…"

"Turn off, turn off that recorder, my sister!" said Aisha.

Fatna ignored the request and continued. "Anyway, the woman began to please the fqih. And he said to her, 'If you want me to (*za'ma*) help you out and be at your side and all that, well, I want you, too.'

"Anyway, she began, the poor thing, to see what she should or should not do. She said, 'That's it. I'm going… anyway, I just need to attain my goal.' Because concerning questions of magic, she just had to arrive… at, at… something that would cool her off. And that's it.

"Anyway, she started, the poor thing, to pay with her morals. Like that. She used to meet him… He was just fooling around with her and up until now, I've never seen a fqih, that is (*za'ma*), who took care of things in this way. That is, the truth is, magic is plentiful and is mentioned in the

Qur'an. But I never could, that is, I couldn't imagine, except when I saw people, women, that is, in their homes; that is, they've started to do that in their homes.

"I say [that] it gives results. But the fqih I don't think he can do anything."

The form of this discourse is noteworthy for its style. Fatna repeats two phrases frequently: "anyway" (*l-muhim*, literally "the important thing is…") and "that is" (*za'ma*, from the classical Arabic verb *za'ama*, meaning "allegation," or "claim"). These phrases are "contextualization cues" (Gumperz 1982:131). They add little to the literal meaning of the narrative, but function rhetorically as emphatics, calling attention to what Fatna considers her main points. These phrases, very common in colloquial speech, also act as hedges, said in moments of hesitation or in thinking of the next thing to say (much like "ummm" or "ah" in English). The increased frequency with which Fatna repeats these phrases alerts us to her return from a more self-conscious and "educated" register of Arabic to a more everyday parlance. They also cue the listener to important junctures of hesitation — occurring notably when Fatna talks about acts that are particularly transgressive. Her sister registers the licentiousness of Fatna's speech when she directs her to turn the tape-recorder off. But Fatna seems to delight in this small scandal.

Fatna again portrays the fqih here as ineffective and always "eating" the money of others, without giving them any results:

"Anyway, a woman, my friend, her husband is married to a second wife and they have children. She said to you, anyway, one day we talked about the question of magic. And I found her always practicing magic, *surtout* on religious holidays. Well, I would always ask her, she said to you, 'No, now I have problems with the second wife and I need a condition (*hal*) that will always bring my husband to me.' And suddenly, whenever I went to her house, I would find her using different methods, to the extent that the man… that magic gave a result. The man began always to be on her side. Or, that is, he would come to her place, he would come to her [often] to the extent that he forgot his children. I didn't used to believe in this, but when I saw, I went back, went back and was sure.

"For example, one day I went in and found her doing three things; each having a different effect. I found her using the brazier. And the brazier, what was in it? They call it, they call it "the incubation" (*l-ḥadana*).[36] Now she had ḥadana in the brazier. And this ḥadana is known, that is, it's known in Morocco by this name. The brazier is incubating. It is incubating all those things that I'm going to tell you about.

"Anyway, I found the piece of cloth; it's the most important element with which they do this magic. If there's no cloth [with semen on it] there's not going to be anything. The cloth is the most important, the most important thing to put the herbs in. The herbs are known. Whatever herbalist you go to, you tell him what herbs [you want] and he gives them to you.

"Anyway, the herbs, she's holding them on the cloth. She cut it in pieces and every piece she put into something. Like, for example, she put [a piece] in an orange, she put it in a lemon and in a bottle and in a light bulb that's been emptied. And she put in that cloth with the herbs. And she put it in dates, in a candle, she put it in an apple. Anyway, she takes that ḥadana and a sea onion. And you empty the sea onion in the middle and you pound those things in it with a spoon. Anyway, she takes that ḥadana, [and] she puts charcoal on the top of it. That's it. And it cooks by itself.

"And then she took a teapot and she put in those herbs and the cloth and she put tea and sugar and she put a little of, ah… oil and a little ḥarmal. And she put in boiling water. It boils on top of that brazier that we spoke about.

"For the third method, she took seven candles. Those, they're called the wicks. Anyway, she rolled them up and put them in a… like a clay cooking pot (ṭajin) and she lit them. And she began to read a little, those words of… those [words] of… something spiritual (ruḥaniyin). She sent him one like this:

'I took a swing at you with maru,
it returns the unhappy one to his house.'

(shiyrt 'l-ik bl-l-maru
tay-rad l-ghədban l-dar-u)

"Like that. Something that she notifies the spiritual beings with. And, anyway, she lit those wicks, all seven and she lit the ḥadana and that teapot I told you about. Everything is boiling, and she created a climate, that is, you could be afraid of it, frightened of it.

"And meanwhile, she did this for about twenty-four hours, until her husband came to her with exactly the characteristics that she predicted. She told me that he might get some small pimples; he could get a headache, he could… anyway, those things, I returned to see them and then was assured that there's such a thing as magic. But as far as the fqih is concerned, the fqih is always eating you, he's always eating you. He keeps eating your money. He only has handwriting. He's no longer important. There are some people, some fqihs like those Souassa.[37] It's *given* to them, those Souassa, because they are astrologers and they study this science. But here in Beni Mellal, I think the woman is the one who is capable of doing that by herself. The cloth is everything. The cloth, that is, is easy, it's easy."

The fqih in Beni Mellal "only has handwriting." Since this is no longer a coveted commodity, he is "no longer important." Literacy is now common-place, thus its value as an item of social exchange has diminished as has its ritual value and symbolic power.

Despite the lessening importance of the fqih, magical practices flour-ish, largely because the woman, as Fatna asserts, has become "capable of doing that by herself"; she has appropriated the knowledge of the fqih and become a specialist. In the absence of the fqih, women practitioners forge their own bridges between religion and magic; the expert in shur portrayed here practices her most "frightful" magic on religious holidays. As a semi-professional, the woman who specializes in magic does not "eat" all her clients' money, as the fqih does:

"If the sorceress has everything, she doesn't ask for much money. Like one time, she took a big candle — according to the color of the husband. If he's brown, you get a red candle for him. If he's white, you get a white candle for him. And when you take that cloth and spread it out and put a little pure honey in it, you take... ah... tobacco, the tobacco that men smoke. It's known in any tobacco store. You tell them, 'give me tobacco,' and they give it to you. You take it and put it on top of that cloth. You add some honey to it. You put a box of matches [there], you spread it on top and you roll it up. You take a white cloth and you tie it so the cloth doesn't open with the candle. And you always leave two matches so you can light it.

"Anyway, in the afternoon you take and you strike the match. And you light it and it becomes like... it goes out in such a manner, quickly! With tobacco and matches and what's-it-called, right away it takes fire."

"It melts?" asked Zohra.

"Yeah. Anyway, she had a little notebook and I used to read it to her."

The literacy skills of the fqih are now in the hands of women, who keep notebooks of incantations and spells, incorporating their own writing power. If they are not literate, they use women who are. And provided they are not needy, sorceresses don't charge a lot of money. Their currency, or medium of exchange, is of a different order. Complicity between women plays a role here, as they are weaned from reliance on the fqih.

The sorceress works some of her more powerful magic by mixing ingredients that are incompatible by social norms: for example, semen and acid or bleach and the blood of a leech. She ignites alcohol and semen, or she bottles up caustics that bubble and eat away at the cloth:

"She used to take the cloth and put some wild honey in it. And she put matches in it, the same way. Anyway, she would buy a bottle of alcohol and pour it on top of the candles — but she has to keep her face away. Now alcohol with matches, right away it ignites. You strike a match and you light it. That's it. It becomes like a bonfire.

"There are candles that the fqih writes on. He writes on it and she brings it home and she lights it. But the cloth, the cloth is the most important element of all those things. The cloth is everything.

"And kerosene. Ah! Then again, there's the cloth, kerosene, bleach. You take it and soak it for seven days. You take the cloth like this, for example, and you put it in a mug, a mug made of iron. You take the kerosene and keep pouring it on for seven days. You take a little kerosene and pour on a little bleach. You take a little kerosene and pour on a little bleach. Seven days and it boils by itself."

"There's another way. That's with acid. You take the cloth, you take some soft lime. You go to the seller of lime and he gives it to you. You say, 'Give me the lime that melts right away.' Anyway, you take that lime and pound it a little and put it in a glass bottle. It has to be well washed! You take the cloth. You take a live leech and you crack it until its blood comes out and you add the leech to it, the leech and *maru* and a little *ḥarmal* and also some *shdəq j-jmal*. All of that, you take it and put it in that cloth and throw it in that bottle on top of the lime. You're going to pour a bottle of acid. You're going to close it so tight that you'd say it was going to explode. With the lime and the acid, you're going to say, it's going to explode.

"You close it tightly and it begins to bubble all by itself. Anyway, I never did it, but I lived it and saw it {to the extent that [CA]} I began to believe it. I didn't use to trust it. I've begun to believe in a lot of things… He comes home at one o'clock at night, he starts calling, he's troubled. [But] it doesn't last. You have to always do it anew, so his attention is always on that woman. And that's it."

"Forty days, right?"

"I, myself, heard one say fourteen days. She said to you, every fourteen days."

The semantic "collision" of these ingredients evokes a certain shock value among Moroccan women; the mixing of semen and acid being somehow blasphemous, almost murderous—a murder of categories and what belongs in them. Such descriptions elicit awe even from the speaker: "I never did it, but I lived it and saw it... I've begun to believe in a lot of things." The women here speak of these things in hushed tones, as if passing clandestine information. The more subversive the procedure, the more the other women present fall silent before the speaker:

"And there's that one... That's to say, this subject has many branches, because everyone has her special way. There are those that do it with names. There are those that tell you, for example, Mohamed has Wednesday and Saturday. Or Mustapha is on Monday and Thursday. Every name, that is, goes with a day on which it has to work.

"Like, ah... what's it called... another way... You put milk on it. You take a half a liter of milk and you put it in a small pot and it starts to boil. And you put the cloth [in] and you add ginger and *ḥarmal* and cloves. And you keep stirring and stirring until the milk overflows. Afterwards, after the milk overflows, that's it. You dry the cotton. You dry it.

"Anyway, you're going to take it and cook it the way you want to barbecue meat. Don't burn it. It needs just to broil like that. Broil. That's it. And you take it, that morsel of it and you're going to put it in a piece of meat and he's going to eat it. You give it to a dog to eat. That's a way that they say is good. But to be honest, I never used it.

"But, there *is* this stuff. Because this—{to the extent that [CA]} you see a man, he's "hyena-ed." You find him afraid and his heart shivers. You find that his head hurts. {To the extent that [CA]}, I don't know, that is, the motivation. I don't know the most important reason in all this.

"The cloth with magic, like that and the man gets in that state. That stuff, you can't imagine. But people they live these problems. They feel that these things are real."

As the magic Fatna describes becomes more sinister, she is careful to assert her inexperience with it: she reports rather than testifies. Her construction of distance from the subject matter is both thematic ("sincerely, I never used it") and formal, evidenced in her use of code-switching. The repetition of a gramatical phrase in classical Arabic — "to the extent that" — (*li daraja 'anna*) [38] — breaks the colloquial flow of her narrative. Its use testifies to her education (she went through high school, though did not pass her final baccalaureate exams). As mentioned earlier, many educated women an men reject the practice of magic, associating it with backwardness and superstition (see Webber 1991). Fatna's code-switching signals her knowledge of these alternative perceptions and situates her somewhat uncomfortably between them.

Similarly, the substances she enumerates are also between categories. In her narrative, semen is mixed with milk and broiled like meat. It is then given to a dog to eat. This renders the man "hyena-ed" — stupefied and malleable. Semen, a "raw" bodily substance, is cooked — "enculturated," according to Lévi-Strauss (1969b). But the "food" is not for human consumption. Feeding food that has been culturally manipulated or controlled to a dog, a symbol of dirt and lack of self-control, is a transgression of categories. Likewise, a woman asserts control by reversing relations of hierarchy:

"Ah. Ah! There's another state — this [one] without the cloth. They say to you, 'Now your husband will be quiet.' That's it. He'll always stay quiet for her. She said (to you), you go to the herbalist and you say, 'Give me *s-sakta* and *l-məskuta* and *l-gəri* seeds and *l-ghaləb*.' Those four herbs. And you pound them well and take a small piece of cloth and you're going to put that stuff in it. And you have to be ritually pure.

"Anyway, the herbs spend the night at your place and in the morning you start giving him [some], for example, in his coffee or in his harira [39] or in his vegetable soup or in something. Anyway, she said to you, he doesn't speak any longer. He doesn't talk anymore."

"He shuts up?"

"He shuts up. He always stays quiet. The woman becomes... it's in her hands. She holds the reins of power. She's the one that begins to rule. She's the winner."

S-sakta l-məskuta, as it is popularly known, is a potion that affects the vocal chords. Whoever eats or drinks it can no longer speak for twenty-four to forty-eight hours. This temporary silencing of the man makes the woman a "winner," for a man who cannot speak cannot possess "the word"; he cannot exercise his authority. Here, his un-voicing precedes the appropriation and transformation of her voice.

A similarly clandestine tactic is found in the magic of *tqaf* (see Rosander 1991). Literally "the closing," this magic works to render a man impotent and thus threatens his nafs as well as his soul (ruḥ).

Tqaf: Money, Food, and Knots

The business of "closing" is taken very seriously in Morocco. All sorts of charms are used to prevent tqaf on a wedding night, for example.[40] Both women and men are liable to be "closed" by tqaf. In the woman's case, it is often a resistant hymen that brings on accusations of tqaf. In the man's case, the "closing" is more figurative than literal. It is expressed in terms of a "knot" that has been tied and that renders him impotent until untied. Tqaf prevents adultery by rendering a man selectively impotent; he loses the capacity to "exercise" with anyone but his wife. Of course, some men are "closed" for everyone. This decision is in the hands of the sorceress:

"There are some things, a lot [of things]... the man has to... He shouldn't look at women. He shouldn't. Like the business of tqaf. They..."

"That tqaf. I had forgotten..." said Aisha.

"Yeah. They make him impotent. So he can no longer, he can no longer function with just anyone, that is. He can't exercise... ah, ah..."

"Sex!" Zohra said.

"Sex," Fatna repeated, "with anyone except his own wife. Now, they take a match, for example. They open [the matchbox], they spread them out. They leave some here and some there. He crosses [over] them. They gather the matches. They hide them. Like that *gǝrsh*,[41] that gǝrsh that we call... that money. Those old coins that we used to use.

"You take them and divide them. You put one on this side and one on that side. He crosses over them. Anyway, he crosses over them and there's one word that they say: 'I closed you.'

"Like now if he's leaving her place... he's leaving and she gets up and gets those *grush* (pl.). She puts them together and she says to him, '*tǝqqaft-ǝk*':

'*Tǝqqaft-ǝk* with a hundred [piece *gǝrsh*] and a hundred,
    just me and my freedom.'

That's to say, I make you impotent for all women. And, indeed, this happens.

"How many times — there are some people whose wives have died and the men remain impotent to this day. They still don't exercise, they don't exercise their sex. They stay that way. That repression of theirs, it stays like that, that knot.

"Or he stays in a world of forgetfulness. No one knows him anymore. He's the only one who knows that he doesn't get excited. He doesn't, that's to say…"

"He doesn't exercise," said Aisha.

"Ah, then again, they do some things; for example, they do it in some forgotten graveyard. He doesn't… that is, the man becomes a tramp; he neglects all that could attract [his attention], all that a woman could attract him with. This subject is a big ocean. One can't talk about it all. There's a lot to say. That is, how is this man able… he can no longer, he can no longer practice with any women except his wife. Then even this gərsh, even this step has importance. It can open the knot of women."

Tqaf is enacted by separating two or more things of a set: matches from a matchbox, two of the same coins, or a kohl bottle and its applicator. The man crosses over the separated materials and the woman intones *təqqaft-ək*, "I closed you." They are then rejoined by the sorceress, rendering the man impotent. The gərsh coins used in this process are obsolete currency found in abundance at the suq and used as amulets and charms. There is an explicit correlation between the symbol of money and freedom, here expressed in rhyme:

təqqaft-ək 'la miya u miya
ghir ana u l-ḥurriya

I closed you with a hundred [piece coin] and a hundred
just me and my freedom.

Money — the true symbol of the marketplace — buys freedom here, having a direct bearing upon the state (ḥal) of the sorceress and the desire-life (nafs) of her subject. Freedom is bought by symbolically imprisoning another, using currency that is only valued by some women. Freedom is thus obtained by challenging the prevailing system of patriarchal value with an alternate "capital." This symbolic capital cannot be banked in the male-dominated marketplace; it defies that system and subverts it.

Magic is a separatist politics. And just as adults may have trouble rid-

ding themselves of the belief in *jnun* (genies or spirits) that is inculcated in
early childhood, so do adult males carry with them the fear of witchcraft.
Because everyone knows that the system exists, it always looms as a threat
in the psyches of men who are socialized not to trust women (other than
their mothers), as women are also socialized not to trust men. Even the
most common household objects and actions may instill fear: [42]

"Like now, you take this little coin. It's really old. The coin and milk
and a little sugar. You spend the night with them for three days under the
stars. And you take a needle and thread and a little, ah... you take a shirt
that he wears or a sweater. You take it and you sew it with... the string has
to be *n-nira* string. *N-nira* string is what women weave with. And you
sew that shirt with it like you're darning. And you leave it for three days.
Anyway, those three days pass and you take a plastic bag and you're going
to put in it all that I told you: milk and what's it called and you're going to
add some Bouzkri dates to it.

"That string, you're going to put that also in the plastic bag and half
of it you're going to tie the plastic bag with. And you're going to take it and
you're going to shroud it and put it in a forgotten graveyard. That's what
they say and it has its effect."

Money, ritual food (milk and dates), and clothing here are combined, put
in a plastic bag, shrouded, and buried. The plastic bag, which became common in the seventies, is a symbol of modernity. Like the pressure cooker
mentioned earlier, it provides enclosure for the various ingredients of
magic. Women's magic involves enclosed spaces and enclosing procedures.
The ingredients are then buried in "a forgotten graveyard," signifying the
death of the man's nafs:

"There's another way. For example, you put the cloth... They call this
'boiling,' that is, it keeps boiling. You take and put a little ḥarmal and some
cloves and herbs. Then you simmer a pot of tea, a pot of tea as if we want
to set it down for a guest. With sugar, with mint, everything. And that's it.

"You pour that tea and it stays boiling for seven days. Usually, what's
left of it shouldn't be thrown out, for example, in the toilet or... You should
take something to dig with if you have a garden, or else a dog might get it.
Throw it in a place far away. Don't throw it in the toilet or it [the plumbing]
will get ruined.

"That's what I know. And this door leads far. Because anyone you talk to, she tells you something else, another kind [of spell]. This area is wide and that's it."

The confluence of food and drink with substances so abrasive that they ruin plumbing and must even be kept away from dogs contributes to the power of magic. In the previous spell, dates and milk — foods that are fed to the bride by her groom and offered to honored guests as symbols of abundance and welcome — are buried, to decompose like a corpse. In the above narrative, harmful substances are assembled and mixed in a teapot ceremoniously, as if for a guest. Not only are non-compatible categories mixed, but appearances disguise improbable contents: a grave harbors wedding food and a teapot holds poison. Disguise in magic lends it an element of trickery and makes the sorceress a sort of trickster, as acknowledged by Fatna:

"You always stay in the frame of this trickery and this magic. And there's a thing that they call *tnakir*.[43] With tnakir, the woman tries to make someone separate [from someone else]. For example, a woman from her husband or her boyfriend. Like that. Some boyfriend that she has an understanding with. This is the ugliest one of all, because she takes recourse in these things so that they'll part from each other.

"Like now she'll take that ḥadja and asphalt and all the ugly things that the ʿaṭṭar sells. She goes to him and she tells him, 'tnakir,' like that. And he gives her from what he has. He knows. And she takes those things. When she throws them a noise[44] occurs and a confusion. And it happens; each one and the way that they're pushing."[45]

"And tnakir, that is, it shows. That's what's rough. This and tqaf. The tqaf is the most dangerous, the most dangerous of all these magics. And tnakir also. They have consequences that are rough, from the doings of the woman. That's it. When she does this, the woman is jealous and her eyes are closed. She takes recourse in those things to the extent that the son parts with his family or from his brothers or from his mother or from... He doesn't see anymore. That's it.

"A big clamor happens and confusion. So much that he separates, he runs away with his wife. His wife becomes... she's his sister, she's his mother, she's his brother and sister and she's his everything. That is, tqaf is really hard. It has some very ugly results."

Like the merchant, the sorceress is both trickster and anti-trickster; her deception involves the disguise of appearances, but her methods of deception are taken quite seriously by herself, her clientele and her community. As Fatna acknowledges, the sorceress always stays "in the frame of this trickery" and those who would engage with her, in common pursuits or in contest, must also situate themselves within this frame. Although she can be trivialized as representing a marginal and illegitimate sector of society, the effects of her marginal behavior are perceived as a real threat by many; this is confirmed by the large numbers of men and women who gather on suq days around the herbalists and orators in the ḥalqa who hold forth on the effects of magic and how to counter them.

The chaos that the sorceress can create has consequences for many. Like the shikha, she is seen as an agent of family disorder, whose motives are selfish rather than community-minded. Fatna condemns the breaking up of the extended family by the use of tnakir, despite the fact that the woman becomes the man's "everything" as a result. When a woman replaces a man's mother, sister, and brother via magic, managing to place herself over all other social relations, what else can she be but a witch?

Power to Close and Power to Open

If a woman can control the nafs of the man through tqaf, or control his destiny through tnakir, she can also return him to himself by admitting her actions and voluntarily reversing them. Her verbal confession serves to reveal her true powers to her husband, to let him know that it is she indeed who "holds the reins of power." But if she neither confesses nor reverses her work, there may be lasting and devastating consequences for the man, especially in the case of divorce. If the spell-maker does not want to disclose the hiding place of a knife used in her spell, for example, the man may remain permanently impotent, his "normalcy" left in her hands:

"And the one about the knife?" prompted Zohra.
"Ah! The knife and tqaf."
"Ahuh."
"Ahu:h, about that I heard that the knife, they pass it [over]. She measures it and passes it over him at the time that he's "exercising" with her. And the knife [magic], that, too, is very rough. And they bury it and no one knows where it is. But the woman commits a big wrong. Especially if she dies or if she divorces him and doesn't want to give it to him. That is, she doesn't want to give it to him so he [can] disengage from that tqaf of

his. It's really rough. Like now they'll take those kohl applicators — those [things] for the eyes, the kohl stick and the bottle. They take them and they divide them. They put the bottle on the right and — what's it called — on the left. And when he's out [of the house], she takes the kohl stick and puts it back in its bottle. And that's it. She closes it.

"The man can't know what made him impotent except from the woman. The woman can tell him. And if she wants to break his tqaf she puts the kohl bottle back in its place and the kohl stick back in its place and he has to enter [the house] before she separates them. Then she separates them and that's it; it's like she's severed him from his impotence. And that's it. He becomes a natural person, a normal person."

Conclusion: Magic as a Counter-Hegemonic Discourse

Unlike the majduba, the sorceress does not appropriate and revoice male speech genres in order to establish her authority, nor does she invoke religious scripture like the 'ashshaba. Her words, like those of the shikha, are enclosed in a feminine discourse that does not seek male validation. The incantation that Fatna recited above, for example, is reminiscent of shikha lyrics in its expression of loss of family and the equation of such loss with the marketplace:

> I twisted you around my right thigh
> to sleep with it
> to wake up with it
> with it to forget your full brother
> with it to forget the prostitutes that are lost in the marketplaces.

What is revoiced, then, is a feminine discourse; but whereas the shikha mourns the loss of family, the sorceress creates it, transforming the voice of lament into the voice of contestation. The sorceress embodies the quality of disorder that male society projects on women in general. The sorceress does not refute the stereotype; rather, she incorporates and exaggerates it, like the woman who says, "now you know what a woman's war is!"

Although the role of the sorceress is forbidden according to the Qur'an, practitioners of magic do not denounce religion. To the contrary; the fqih who writes charms has already provided the model for the compatibility of the two systems. Yet the prescribed role of the sorceress, again like that of the shikha, is socially pre-scripted outside the bounds of the dominant moral ethic. She is the female "criminal," someone who does not play within the rules laid down by the institutions of family, scripturalist religion, and community.

But if male practices are not being appropriated (as they are in the marketplace), the territory of male authority figures is being usurped and replaced. The sorceress is fast taking over the function of the fqih in the knowledge and practice of shur, appropriating his ritual authority and re-making it in feminine guise. The fqih's change of status in matters of magic radicalizes the system of shur, which no longer depends on male mediation and a presiding religiosity. Women are elaborating on the magical canon, weaving the sacredness of religious holidays into their practice of magic, and keeping their own "notebooks."

Though the successful businesses of traditional druggists attest to the link between magic and the marketplace, there is very little bargaining activity that takes place over the ingredients for magic. Not only are women counseled *not* to bargain for certain materials, but the druggists know that women with belief in matters of magic will pay as much as they can afford. The relatively high prices that the traditional druggist charges for special potions (often between one hundred and one hundred-fifty dirhams, or fifteen to twenty dollars) is seen to reflect their value in efficacy. Women's passive interaction with the market in acquiring the "goods" of magic changes considerably once the goods are in their hands. More and more, women frequent the 'attar only to buy herbs and not for advice in shur. Like the modern marketplace, magic challenges the moral economy of honor and reciprocity, yet it differs from the system of commodification in important ways: its voice is subaltern and its power demeaned by all official discourses.

Magic is in many senses a reaction to the hegemonic practices of patriarchy. It seeks to counter them and to undo them subversively. It is no secret that the system of magic is most appealing to women who are most socially impotent. Only those with little to lose risk involvement in activities that are classified as reprehensible by both religious authorities and a majority of the population.

The power of magic is partly due to its ability to confound, to transgress the circumscription of taboo and to mix sacred materials or words from the Qur'an with symbols of modern secularity like money and pressure-cookers. Yet the hybridizing force of magic extends primarily to the symbolism of its material economy, not to the larger economy of gender.

Magic, as it is recreated in female discourse, constitutes the very gender polarities that necessitate its existence to begin with: within the realm of magic, women and men are constructed as antagonistic "others," an antagonism whose effects can only be countered coercively. Given these processes of objectification, we have to ask whether feminine discourse on magic can ever compete with that of the male-informed marketplace. Are women destined to infiltrate, appropriate, and revoice male discourse in order to gain social acceptance of their authority?

Notes

1. Fatna uses the word "woman" as a synonym for sorceress throughout her discourse.

2. The "fixing" isn't always efficacious.

3. *Ḥayati* is a white, semi-transparent, cotton-blend cloth. *Ḥayati*, in Arabic, means "my life."

4. Astrology symbolizes "the indissoluble marriage between heaven and earth and the derivation of all things from their celestial counterparts" (Nasr 1964:152).

5. See Doutté (1984 [1908]) for a discussion of the history of magic in North Africa. Doutté notes that since a woman is "exclue par la religion du commerce des choses sacrées ou interdites, elle y revient sous le couvert de la magie, qui devient pour elle une sorte de religion d'ordre inférieur" (1984:33). Since a woman is "excluded by religion from participating in sacred affairs, she comes back under the cover of magic, which becomes for her a sort of religion of an inferior order."

6. Westermarck first went to Morocco in 1898 and made twenty-one voyages there before his last in 1926. He is the most thorough documenter of Moroccan "ritual and belief," but is also known as a theorist of ethical relativism, a school of thought that situates moral principles in social institutions (see *Ethical Relativity* 1932). Connected with Westermarck's theoretical concerns was his interest in marriage as it intersected with issues of morality and social life. On that subject, his best-known works are *The History of Human Marriage* (1891) and *Marriage Ceremonies in Morocco* (1914).

The history of scholarship on Morocco and the history of folklore scholarship collide in Westermarck. As a Finn, he shared the heritage of the Krohns, whose role in the development of Finnish Folklore and the historical-geographical method of folklore analysis made Finland a forerunner in folklore scholarship. He was also heavily influenced by James George Frazer. In fact, Westermarck's detailed investigation of almost every aspect of folklife and lore (except folktales) may be seen, in Frazerian terms, as a search for the memory of the "savage forefathers" that Frazer saw exemplifying the "first stage of human thought" (Cocchiarra 1980:413). Magical beliefs and superstitions thus held a fascination for Westermarck (see particularly *The Belief in Spirits in Morocco* 1920 and *Pagan Survivals in Muhammedan Civiliza-*

tion 1933). Westermarck's work on the history of marriage also exemplifies his pre-occupation with finding the "survivals" of an ancient past in popular tradition.

Westermarck wrote the definitive work on Moroccan proverbs in 1930 (*Wit and Wisdom in Morocco: A Study of Native Proverbs*), grouping them somewhat novelly "according to subjects or situations on which they have a bearing" (ibid.). In his long introduction to the book, dedicated to Sir James G. Frazer, Westermarck not only analyzes the several forms of Moroccan proverb, but emphasizes the necessity of contextualization in their interpretation.

Morocco is portrayed as an archaic civilization by Westermarck and other writers of the period. Here again we find the influence of Frazer, but Durkheim cannot be ignored as an important influence in the early part of the twentieth century. His notions of solidarity and the undifferentiated social state are implicit in Westermarck's writing.

7. Lévi-Strauss notes that

the first difference between magic and science is therefore that magic postulates a complete and all-embracing determinism. Science, on the other hand, is based on a distinction between levels: only some of these admit forms of determinism; on others the same forms of determinism are held not to apply. One can go further and think of the rigorous precision of magical thought and ritual practices as an expression of the unconscious apprehension of the truth of determinism, the mode in which scientific phenomena exist. In this view, the operations of determinism are divined and made use of in an all-embracing fashion before being known and properly applied, and magical rites and beliefs appear as so many expressions of an act of faith in a science yet to be born. (1966:11)

8. See Hart (1976:149–74) for parallel practices among the Ait Waryaghar of Northern Morocco.

9. Fqihs commonly write a verse of the Qur'an on a piece of paper with particular geometrical designs. Incantation of Qur'anic verse is often simultaneous. The charm, which is called a *jədwəl*, may be solicited to make a man love a woman.

10. The root of the word ʿaṭṭar comes from the verb "to perfume" or "to scent"; the ʿaṭṭar sells aromatics such as rose and orange blossom water as well as cooking spices (*l-ʿaṭriya*). Although also an herbalist, the ʿaṭṭar is different than the ʿashshaba discussed earlier in that he sells a much larger variety of goods—including traditional medicines, but extending also to daily-need items such as washcloths, soap, and ḥənna. In order to avoid confusion between the two, I have translated ʿaṭṭar as "traditional druggist."

11. See Rosander (1991:247–54) for a discussion of some Moroccan responses to perceived magical intervention.

12. *D-din b-n-niya u shur b-n-niya, Kulshi b-n-niya.*

13. Descendants of the Prophet are called *shrif* (masc.) and *shrifa* (fem.). The ʿaṭṭar uses the title here as a somewhat exaggerated term of honor.

14. She's buying this for another.

15. Moulay Bouazza is a saint's tomb and pilgrimage center; see chap. 3 on the saint's tomb, Moulay Ibrahim.

16. This saying in classical Arabic is from the ḥadith, the reported sayings of the Prophet. Niya, in this context, is best translated as "good intention."

17. See Kirshenblatt-Gimblett and Sherzer (1976) on play and verbal art.

18. Ḥarmal is *peganum harmala*; it contains harmaline, "a hallucinogenic alkaloid . . . found in several plants . . . and used as in medicine as a stimulant of the central nervous system" (*Webster's Ninth New Collegiate Dictionary*). Although it is being prepared as incense here, it is also ingested.

The word *ḥaram* includes notions of both the sacred and the forbidden. In classical Arabic it is a sacred possession, used as a synonym for a wife, and related to the adopted English word "harim," which includes all the female members of a family. In Moroccan Arabic it usually means what is disallowed by religion. A man who *kay tḥarəm* as a result of magic seeks the shelter of women's refuge; he is someone who is vulnerable and somewhat cowed.

19. *ashan* is lichen moss.

20. Ḥalḥal is a plant in the *Lavendula Vera* family, while *shdəq j-jmal* is in the *Solanacae* family (Linnaeus classifies it as *batura stramonium*) (Abdelhai Diouri, personal communication).

21. When the genie comes out of the magic lamp in colloquial renderings of the tales of Aladdin, the genie says, *shubb-ik lubb-ik, ana 'abd bin id-ik*, "I'm ensnared and obedient, I'm a slave between your hands."

22. Karim code-switches, using the French *normale* here.

23. From the verb *'akala*, "to eat."

24. Muslim fqihs are part of the legal and juridical system in Morocco and still enjoy much respect and importance. Not all fqihs write charms. In these narratives, however, the fqih is equated with these activities, taking on the role of the somewhat corrupt country priest.

25. Webber notes a marginalization of all practitioners of magic in Tunisia:

> There are other kinds of folk knowledge now banished to the countryside as dangerous, irreligious, obsolete or useless . . . practitioners of magic, writers of charms or spells or amulets or potions . . . have gradually been literally as well as figuratively pushed to the edges of town. Now if a young wife, for example, seeks a magician to help her control her husband or a husband his wife or in-laws, she or he must seek this magic in the countryside. This behavior, if it becomes known, is now a source of embarrassment, amusement, or alarm to other community members. (1991:173)

26. Literally "water," *l-ma* [MA].

27. Ten years ago, when there was an open market for women educators and federal employees, the "control over others" was less important than control over one's own destiny. Now, however, there is high unemployment and inflation, and even the women who have managed to get jobs with the state have realized that their personal power is very limited in the larger economy. Their power in the home has also been diminished — even in regards to their children, who are influenced by education and the media to a much greater extent that they or their parents were.

28. This was exemplified in the realm of domestic employment examined in Chapter 7.

29. Bargaining with the ʿaṭṭar for anything except trivial items such as ḥənna and washcloths is extremely rare. The ʿaṭṭar gets the prices he asks for, usually without any question.

30. The traditional Arabic medical system is based on balancing "humors," considered hot and cold, moist and dry (Hamarneh 1984; Nasr 1964). This system is not unique to Arabic medicine, but exists also in European ideologies of the Middle Ages, Ancient Greek medicine, and contemporary Asian medical traditions.

31. As for donkeys, mention of dogs is usually followed by the phrase ḥashak, which is the equivalent of, "forgive me for mentioning it" (Bourdieu 1966:224 translates ḥashak as "saving your presence"). Ḥashak is also said after all words that connote dirt and contagion (donkeys or prostitutes, for example). Such categories inhabit a field of ambiguity in the Moroccan imagination; they are domesticated, yet still somewhat embarrassing in their public display of sexual behavior and their resistance to social control (packs of wild dogs are still a common sight in Beni Mellal).

32. Two thousand riyals is the equivalent of one hundred dirhams, about fourteen dollars; three thousand riyals equals one hundred fifty dirhams, or about twenty dollars. This represents quite a bit of money for the narrator.

33. In other words, he keeps you coming back; he keeps taking your money.

34. The Ait Waryaghar employ the word "hyena" as a synonym for a feminine jinn, or spirit (Hart 1976:156).

35. "Writing" charms that consist of Qur'anic verses serves to materialize the jnun that are causing trouble. The jnun are then made to disappear by the burning of the paper on which the verses were written; see Hart (1976:156).

36. This also means "the hatching (of an egg)."

37. Berbers from the region of the Souss, the southwest region of Morocco.

38. In classical Arabic the phrase is li darajati 'anna. Fatna dropped the ending vocalization.

39. L-ḥarira is a tomato-based soup made with lentils, beef, and chick peas. Any other kind of soup is just called ṣ-ṣuba.

40. For example, the placing of a needle in the slipper of the groom.

41. Gərsh is an old Moroccan coin that is no longer in circulation. They are still plentiful and are sold at the suq or at an ʿaṭṭar's shop.

42. Women are perhaps even more sensitive to the magical import of daily actions and household objects. I was present when one woman found a sewing needle on the threshold of her door. She was absolutely convinced that someone was trying to work a spell on her husband to make him part with her.

43. From the noun nakir, which means "denial" or "rejection." Nakir is also the name of one of two Angels of Death (the other is Munkir), who "examine the dead in their graves as to their faith" (Wehr 1971).

44. "Noise" in this context means a social or psychological upheaval.

45. In other words, "each one pushes in a different direction."

10. Conclusion: Hybridization and the Marketplace

The significance of this study is not in recognizing that daily life is comprised of small-scale displacements, replacements, and hybridizations of cultural forms (as opposed to the dramatic paradigm shifts that Kuhn describes 1962); nor is the attribution of responsibility for such processes to the market new (Appadurai 1990; Hannerz 1987). Rather, the study illuminates how incremental changes leading to larger paradigm shifts take place discursively and in relation to the marketplace, indicated by subtle transformations of both speech genres and larger conceptual categories.

It is evident that new notions of community are asserted in the genre of bargaining. For example, the woman merchant cleverly maneuvers her male client to admit that women merchants are Muslims like everyone else, and that their place in the market is therefore not shameful. The client's laughter at this tactic acknowledges the vendor's strategy and the discomfort caused by her attempts at persuasion, yet the effect is not diminished. The bargaining discourse demonstrates the agonistic aspect of marketplace exchange, as well as establishing women's solid place in the game. They are even found to be expert players, capitalizing on their adhesive role in the family to essentially shame clients into "eating" profit with them. Hybridization, in this case, relates to the actualization of intersexual negotiation, to women sellers participating in a genre of speech that has customarily been male. Were the phrase, "Aren't we all Muslims?" not a common one in the male repertoire, it would not carry the weight that it does in this discourse.

The speech of the majduba exemplifies a different kind of collision of forms. Although she, too, revoices speech that has formerly been in the mouths of others (using religious genres of supplication, cursing, proverbs, and traditional sayings), her discourse changes the rules for what kind of expressive behavior is permissible in the public domain. She thus hybridizes what were previously separate gender spheres and codes of comportment. The majduba's clients are actually counseled by her — not behind the flaps

Figure 21. Research assistants Abdelmajid Hafidi (left) and Si Mohamed Zidouh.

of a tent or behind closed doors, as has been customary in Beni Mellal, but in the open air of the suq. The client, in expressing her story to the surrounding crowd, is in a position of *performing* her personal vulnerability. Both the majduba and the ʿashshaba are aware of the fragility of such social openings and are careful to stress the continuity of the client/merchant-counselor relationship by telling the audience their suq itinerary and promising to return. These women embody the authority to direct the words and actions of others, whether in the divination and prescription employed by the majduba, or in the call-and-response techniques used by the herbalist.

The performance of public emotion is not unique among women, the appointed wailers in times of grief, but it is unique in the heterosexual marketplace. The majduba's audience was comprised primarily of other women, though the fact that men join the circle at will makes this performance exemplary, attesting to new definitions of the permissible in mixed-gender contexts. Not only are notions of what is appropriate here put into question, but display of this kind of emotion in the marketplace signifies the forging of a new level of public relationship. The rearrangement of the material economy, and its laws or rules for the physical and social body, has influenced the transformation of the moral code. What was formerly considered private and feminine behavior is now public behavior in the heteroglossic marketplace.

With boundaries being overstepped, limits refuted, and notions of personhood and category challenged, transgression plays a major role in the hybridization process. This is nowhere more evident than in the speech of the 'ashshaba, whose words clearly put all notions of propriety into question. Her preoccupation with paying respect to the elders, her pronounced use of religious quotation in the high register of classical Arabic and her verbal denial of the very market conditions in which she is working in favor of an ethic of kinship and reciprocity, formally link her to the values of the early days (*bəkri*). Yet the herbalist breaks with marketplace customs of the past in important ways, most notably in her feminine revoicing of male-informed oratory. The 'ashshaba embodies an authoritative voice that women have rarely exercised in the public realm, setting herself up as a counselor of body and soul, capable of medical and religious discourse, a specialist. Within her oratory, two world views collide: the official and orthodox view of patriarchal and religious doctrine, and an unofficial and heterodox view that very subtly subverts the former by infiltrating its expressive forms with themes and meanings incongruous to it.

The 'ashshaba elaborates on topics that are considered taboo, yet there is an important difference between her transgression and that of the shikha, for example. The shikha is, in effect, less transgressive than the woman orator in that her role as an outsider is pre-scripted into the social hierarchy and carries the weight of historical precedence. The shikha is a category of woman whose low and peripheral stature has always helped define the high and socially central by providing its contrast. Yet today the social role of the shikha is undergoing important change. Her ability to earn substantial amounts of money, owning property and gold, gives her access to status mobility. A shikha may buy a house in a very posh section of town and begin to call herself a *mughanniya*, a singer. Her material success also gives her access to public renown, for it is becoming the rule for groups of shikhat to go to Casablanca in order to produce tape recordings and videos. This kind of exposure is personally gratifying, making the contemporary role of the shikha/mughanniyya less compromising, or even attractive, for many youth. The commercial success of shikhat music is also significant in that the more people listen to the lyrics of shikhat music, the more its subaltern ethic becomes commonplace. Witchcraft, extra-marital love, parental defiance, and other descriptions of "dishonorable" behavior are given considerable exposure, with Moroccan youth easily identifying with these themes.

If the shikha has long been the social representative of the low and the unclean in Moroccan history, the discursive construction of the maid in similar terms is now taking place. This phenomenon is contemporary with the emergence of the middle class and its emblematic desire for material acquisition. The maid becomes, in effect, an object of desire, a commodity which is necessary and status-endowing. But the inability of the woman of the house to fully control the maid gives rise to a discourse of contamination and danger. The maid becomes the enemy of the insular and clean domain of the nuclear family, "a daughter of sin," an agent of social disorder. This discursive construction of the maid effectively disempowers her, rendering her controllable—if not on a person-to-person level, then on a class basis. Selling one's labor into the private home often means selling oneself into tyranny.

The discourse on magic (shur) provides one example of how women have empowered themselves in the face of similar tyranny and stigmatization based on gender. The ability of women to symbolically take control of their lives and the lives of their men is not without consequence in general society. Apart from the effects of magic, the effects of the *discourse* about magic are also to be reckoned with. Shur is considered "forbidden" (*haram*) precisely because it poses a threat to the male-dominant power hierarchy. Engaging in talk about magical practices is thus an exploration of empowerment by those who are denied power, though it does not necessarily lead to an incorporation of that power. Talk about magic is hidden and subversive, infiltrating silently, attempting to rob its object of the most precious things it owns: desire, volition, and honorable personhood.

Concepts of personhood are clearly in flux in contemporary Morocco and the multi-costumed bride provides the most pertinent metaphor for the transitions that are taking place. Embodying several national and international identities, and able to be more physically and psychologically mobile than she has been in the past, the bride is still symbolically "held in hock" until someone pays for her "release." As in the marketplace, freedom must be bought. But will the new wife's participation in the market eventually liberate her? Is it freedom that the marketplace promises, or just a new set of circumstances in which to move, to acquire, and to lose?

The marketplace is the forum for transition, for transgression, and for hybridization — often experienced as rupture — and its aftermath, a promise of change. But the market is also the domain of lies and deceit, a place that requires abandoning all notions of cherished authenticity in favor of a "buyer beware" cynicism. Things are not what they seem and values fluctuate before changes can be registered.

Concepts of gender are clearly on the market in contemporary Morocco. The separate spheres described by scholars[1] are now mixing, colliding, and producing new species of cultural forms and ideations. Many dialogues contribute to this process; among them, the dialogue of women vendors with men and other women, the dialogue of maids with employers, of shikhat with "respectable" society, of the (inter)national media with the *sha'b*, or of sorceresses with foreign ethnographers via the mediation of a tape recording. Whether we can expect Moroccan women's presence in the marketplace to become as characteristic as the ḥalqa or as codified as the genre of bargaining, or by contrast, whether the values currently on the market will be undermined as quickly as they have appeared, remains an open question. In a climate where negotiation is diminishing in favor of fixed prices, there is reason for skepticism. Yet if there is one thing that we can depend upon, it is that marketplace interactions are always open-ended and precarious. The amplification of women's voices in the suq and their revoicing of tradition and authority in society at large, affirms an agency too long denied. In the words of Canto (1985 : 339):

> Everything depends . . . on presence. Feminist politics is real only if women, together with their bodies, their works, their labor, and their voice, are present in a place where everyone can see them — let us say, in the marketplace.

Note

1. See Bourdieu 1966; Crapanzano 1980 : 31; Geertz 1979 : 240.

Appendix 1:
Discourse of the Majduba

ṣalli ʿla rasul aḷḷah.
fin jdud-na?
fin walidi-na u fin n-nabi, ṣalla aḷḷah ʿl-ih wa səlləm.
ʿad ḥnaya bghina n-wərtu-ha wa bghina n-diu-ha?
wayli, wayli.   5
saghiru turab daratu l-muʿid.
al-yum lli ma y-nafʿ-ək wald-ək l-kbir.
zidi alalla, aḷḷah y-rḥəm l-walidin.
lli bgha shi baruk, marḥba,
u lli ma bghash, marḥba gaʿ b-juj.   10
Client: ayyəh.
Majduba: ḥna ghir dəllalin l-khir.
ana ghir majduba bənt mulay ibrahim.
hada ḥal-i wa ana mulat-u.
ila kant ʿaziba, t-ʿaml ḥajrət l-fək wa l-fasukh.   15

ila kant mra ma bin-ha u bin wlidat-ha, nhar j-jəmʿa.
ila kanu l-wlidat ʿla qraia, nhar l-tnin.
ila kanu bhaymat, nhar l-tnin.
bhaymat ma sakhru,
wlidat ma qraw —   20
l-məjmaʿ ḥar.
Ha l-mqab,
ganfud l-bḥar,
umm n-nas,
u n-nila,   25
u l-mərjan,
u n-nil l-watqa,
l-ʿarʿar, u d-dərdar.
kul mən ḥaja mən-ha naṣib dyal-ha,
kif ila ṣalli-ti ʿla rasual aḷḷah.   30
shkun lli y-tuwakkəl mʿaya ʿla aḷḷah?
wa lli gal s-shur ma kaynsh,
y-ṭlaʿ l-jəddi mulay ibrahim,
u buya ḥamid,
u y-ṭlaʿ l-buya ʿomar,   35

*The Soussi Berbers are known for their expertise in magic.

Pray on behalf of the Prophet.
Where are our grandparents?
Where are our parents and where is the Prophet? (God bless him and
    grant him peace)
We want to inherit worldly goods and we want to take them with us?
Wayli, wayli!   5
The smallest on earth has a meeting [on Judgment Day].
That day when your oldest son won't avail you.
Come closer, woman, May God have mercy on your parents.
Whoever wants some blessings [=incense], welcome.
And whoever doesn't want any, welcome you, too.   10
Client: Yeah.
Majduba: We're just the guides to goodness.
I'm just a majduba, daughter of Moulay Ibrahim.
That's my state and I'm the owner of it.
If she's a little virgin, use the "rock of severing" and "the abolisher."   15
If she's a woman and there's something between her and her children,
    [use them] on Friday.
If it's something to do with children and their studies, on Monday.
If it's [herd] animals, on Monday.
If the animals aren't subjugated,
the children aren't studying,   20
the [family] gathering is bitter.
Here's *maqab*
sea urchin
"mother of people"
and indigo   25
and coral
and *nil l-watqa*
'ar'ar or *dərdar*.
Every one of these [packets] has a piece of each one of these [herbs],
as if you prayed to the Prophet.   30
Who will trust in God with me?
And whoever says there's no such thing as magic,
go up to the tomb of my grandfather Moulay Ibrahim,
and my father Hamid.
And go up to [the tomb of] my father Omarr.   35

u y-shuf shḥal mən shab u shḥal mən shabba mkətfin b-snasəl b-shghul
    iblis.
shḥal mən ʿarusa, alalla, tay-khlliu-ha ḍala,
mkətfa məskina,
u t-gul,
"ana fi ʿar-ək a ʿomar."   40
Majduba: ah alalla.
Majduba: "ḥarqu-ni b-n-nar ʾa ʿomar."
Majduba: aji alalla, n-gul-lək.
Majduba: "ana fi ʿar-ək ʾa mulay ibrahim."
Majduba: ana bghit n-ʿawəd-lək ʿla waḥəd l-bənt.   45
Majduba: ṣalli ʿla rasul alḷah.
Majduba: hiya makhṭuba u kətbət ʿli-ha…
Majduba: ayyəh, ayyəh.
Majduba: u z-zawj dayr wəḥda ukhra laṣqat fi-h.
Majduba: aywa, ʿlash?   50

Majduba: hadik umm-ha ḥadga u nti naʿsa məskina.
ṣalli ʿla rasul alḷah.
Client: ḥətta gaʿ taḥ lʿaqd u kulshi u dda wəḥda ukhra.
Majduba: səmʿini alalla, ṣalli ʿla rasul alḷah.
ayyəh, swasa l-ḥrar!   55
Client: hiya ma tlatsh bghat-u.
Majduba: alḷah, alḷah ʿl-ik ʾa jədd-na mulay ibrahim.
la, la, sm'ini,
bəssif ma tlatsh t-bghih,
li'annahu, alalla, daru bi-h.   60
ḥna l-ʿyalat ṣʿab.
ila ḥabbu-k y-wakklu-k
wa ila karhu-k, y-saḥru-k.
Client: hiya luwla li-h.
Majduba: ya d-dakhel suq n-nsa rəd bal-ək,   65
y-biynu-lək mən r-rbəḥ qanṭar
wa y-khəsru-k f-ras mal-ək.
    kid n-nsa, kid-hum,
    mən kid-hum jit harəb.
    ya l-mḥazmat b-l-ḥnash   70
    wa l-mʿawdat b-l-ʿgarəb.
ṣalli ʿla rasul alḷah.
ayyəh, l-ʿyalat lli hiya mra, ʿmmər-ha ma t-dir ḥbibt-ha mra.
diri, alalla, ḥajrət l-fək
ila ṭṭarṭqat li-ha, alalla,   75
jibi-li triyba mən taḥt rjəl-ha limna.
u ḥsəb-ha nti mashi umm-ha
ana hiya lli umm-ha.
u ghadi n-khdəm li-ha sh-shghul
u binat-na alḷah u jəddi mulay ibrahim.   80

And see how many women and men are shackled by chains by the work
    of Satan!
And how many brides, dear woman (*alalla*), they leave them abandoned.
She's shackled, poor thing,
and she says,
"I'm begging your protection, Oh Omarr.'"   40
Client: Ahh, my dear woman!.
Majduba: "They burned me with fire, oh Omarr!"
Client: Come here, woman, let me tell you.
Majduba: "I'm begging your protection, oh Moulay Ibrahim!"
Client: I want to tell you about one girl.   45
Majduba: Pray to the Prophet.
Client: She's engaged and she has her marriage certificate.
Majduba: Yeah, my woman.
Client: And [her] husband took someone else who's stuck to him.
Majduba: Well, why?   50
That mother of the other one is awake and you, her mother, are asleep,
    poor thing!
Pray to the Prophet.
Client: Until the act fell and everything and he took someone else!
Majduba: Listen to me, *alalla*, pray on behalf of the Prophet.
Yeah! Pure Soussis!" *   55
Client: She doesn't want him anymore.
Majduba: God, God be with you, [and] our grandfather Moulay Ibrahim.
No, No, listen to me.
Of course, she doesn't want him anymore,
because, alalla, they've turned around him [with magic].   60
We women are hard!:
If they love you, they'll feed you
and if they hate you, they'll bewitch you.
Client: She's the first.
Majduba: *He who enters the women's suq, beware!*   65
They'll show you a ton of profit
and make you lose your salary!
    The ruses of women are their own.
    From their ruses I came running!
    Oh the women belted with snakes   70
    and those wrapped with scorpions!
Pray on behalf of the Prophet.
Yeah, oh woman, whoever is a woman never hold a[nother] woman dear.
Use, *lalla*, the "rock of redemption."
If it explodes for her lalla,   75
bring me a little dirt from under her right foot.
And consider that you're not her mother.
I'm her mother.
And I'm going to take care of her business.
And between us is God and our grandfather Moulay Ibrahim.   80

Client: ana druk bghit…
Majduba: hadi alalla duggi-ha u bakhri bi-ha səbʿ ʾayyam.
ila kan s-sḥur u ṭṭarṭqat li-ha
kan gul-lək
jib-li triyba mən taḥt rəjli-ha   85
bəsh n-ʿṭi-ha l-ma dyal səbʿat l-mwaj
u l-ma dyal səbʿat l-ḥaddada,
u l-ma dyal səbʿat l-byar
u l-ma dyal r-rḥa dyal jəddi mulay ibrahim
t-ʿum bi-hum.   90
Client: ana bghit…
Majduba: səmʿini
khalli-na ʿl-ik mən l-hadra dyal-lək.
daba daqqiti ʿl-iya, khalli-ni n-wajb-ək.
Client: ayyəh.   95
Majduba: bghiti marḥba
ma bghitish siri
allah y-ʿarḍ-ək l-khir.
{mrzighfar}
{agharas, agharas}   100
ma fiya la tu tu tu, u la t-khabbi ʿl-iya.
səmʿini n-gul-lək.
duggi hada f-l-məhraz dyal l-ʿud.
u bakhri bi-h səbʿ ʾayyam.
u hada diri-h li-ha f-l-məjmar buḥdu.   105
ila ṭṭarṭqat l-ḥajra
aji u jib-li t-triyba lli gult-lək
wakhkha s-sḥur y-kunu dayrin-u ma n-ʿraf fin
b-jəhd allah u jəddi mulay ibrahim…
ash mən suq dyal-kum?   110
ash mən suq ʿand-kum?
dima tat-jiu l-hna?
mnin s-suq dyal-kum?
{mani?}
Client: {mani?}   115
Majduba: ayyəh.
Client: l-khmis dyal ulad ʿayyad.
Majduba: aywa. rah ana tan-kun f-ulad ʿayyad f-l-khmis.
rah, tan-kun f-r-raḥba dyal d-djaj.
ṣalli ʿla rasul allah.   120
ila t-kuni f-s-sabt, ana rah tan-kun f-s-sabt.
t-kuni f-ḥad l-bradiya ana f-ḥad l-bradiya.
ma tan-khalli, alalla, ḥətta suq.
bi smi llah bi smi llah.
ana n-kun s-sabab u l-kaməl dyal rabbi   125
Client: {incomprehensible [B]}

Client: I, now... I want...
Majduba: This, lalla, pound it and light this incense for her for seven days.
If it was magic and it explodes for her,
I'll tell you,
bring me a little dirt from under her foot   85
in order that I give her the water of seven waves,
and the water of seven ironsmiths,
and the water of seven wells,
and the water of the mill of Moulay Ibrahim,
so she can bathe with them.   90
Client: I want...
Majduba: Listen to me!
Spare me your words.
Now, you knocked, let me answer you.
Client: Yeah.   95
Majduba: You want it, welcome,
you don't want it, go,
may God make you meet the good thing.
{incomprehensible [B]}
{What's straight is straight [B]}   100
I don't tu, tu, tu [=whisper] and don't you hide it from me.
Listen to what I'm going to tell you!
Pound this in a mortar and pestle of wood.
And light it as incense for seven days.
And this, put it in the brazier by itself.   105
If the rock explodes,
come and bring me that little bit of dirt that I told you about.
Even if they've put the magic I don't know where,
with the strength of God and Moulay Ibrahim...
Which suq is yours?   110
What suq is near you?
Do you always come here?
Where is your suq?
{Where? [B]}
Client: {Where? [B]}   115
Majduba: Yeah.
Client: Thursday's suq [at] Ouled Ayyad.
Majduba: Well, I'm also at Ouled Ayyad on Thursdays.
You see, I'm at the place where they sell chickens.
Pray on behalf of the Prophet.   120
If you're in Sebt, I'm also in Sebt.
If you're in Hed el-Bradiya, I'm also at Hed el-Bradiya.
I don't leave, lalla, a single suq untouched.
In the name of God, In the name of God.
I'll be the reason [for the cure] and completion is God's.   125
Client: {incomprehensible [B]}.

Majduba: ayyəh alalla. {incomprehensible [B]}
dayra n-nabbata f-l-khalwa dyal mulay ibrahim.
hadi alalla, duggi-ha u t-bakhri bi-ha səb' 'ayyam.
Client: u səb'atu rijal?   130
Majduba: ayyəh alalla. AYYƏ:H, AYYƏ:H
{lā ḥawla wa lā qūwwata illā bi-llāh al-'alī al-'aẓīm.
la ilāha illa allāh, sayyidunā muḥammad rasūlu allāh [CA]}
ha l-ḥbiba.
rah, tay-fərqu l-khu 'la kha-h   135
rah, tay-fərqu l-wald 'la bba-h.
rah, tay-fərqu sh-shab 'la l-mwima.
rah, ta-y-fərq-u l-bəgra 'la l-lban u s-sman.
rah, ta-y-fərq-u d-djaja 'la…
ta-yəbsu li-ha l-biḍ dyal-ha.   140
ga'da 'li-h d-djaja
wəllat kərmat fuq l-biḍ,
hiya u l-biḍ.
ayyəh. ṣalli 'la rasul aḷḷah.
aḷḷah y-shəttət 'ash-hum.   145
allah y-shəttət shməl-hum kama rabu d-dyur f-l-'ashiya.
sir ya l-mra s-saḥara.
sir ya l-mra l-khadda'a.
sir ya l-mra l-ghadra rdi't-ha u jart-ha
l-ghadra l-'azba u l-ghadra sh-shab.   150
Client: da'au m'aya.
Majduba: allah y-khli 'ash-ha kama khla s-suq f-l-'ashiya.
bi smi ḷḷah.
ṣalli 'la rasul aḷḷah.
Client: yak, hadi kif kif?   155
Majduba: bḥal bḥal alalla.
lli 'ajbu y-ddi-h.
HA.
hadu mashi huma.
hadu huma.   160
un nti mdarba ghir m'a izar-ək,
wa t-guli-li,
jab 'li-ha wəḥda ukhra.
rah y-jib ḥətta rub'a ila kant umm-ha bḥal hakka.
ghir sir-i f-ḥal-ək.   165
Client: alalla ḥna ma kan-fahmush
Majduba: ha hiya, ha hiya, ha.
t-kuni bant lalla u sidi.
{Berber: God help you}
Client: amin.   170
Majduba: {Put your [B] faith in God. [MA]}
Client: amin

Majduba: Yeah, lalla {incomprehensible [Berber]}
They put its seeds in the woods of my grandfather Moulay Ibrahim
This, lalla, pound it and burn it as incense for seven days.
Client: And the 'seven men'?   130
Majduba: Yeah, lalla, YEA:H, YEA:H.
{There's no might or power except with God, the High, the Great.
There's no God but God and Mohamed is his Prophet [CA].}
Here, my dear.
They part brother from his brother.   135
They part the son from his father.
You see, they part the youth from his little mother.
They part the cow from buttermilk and aged butter.
They part the chicken…
Her eggs dry up on her.   140
She's sitting on them
and she becomes stiff on top of the eggs,
both she and the eggs.
YEAH. Pray on behalf of the Prophet.
May God scatter their nest [those who bewitch].   145
God scatter them, may their house be devastated in the afternoon.
Go, oh woman witch!
Go, oh woman cheat!
Go, oh woman, who deceives the one who suckled her and her neighbor!
She deceives the virgin and she deceives the youth!   150
Client: Plead to God with me.
Majduba: God leave her nest like the suq in the afternoon!
In the name of God,
Pray on behalf of the Prophet.
Client: That's the same stuff, right?   155
Majduba: Yeah, lalla. It's the same.
Whoever wants it, take it.
Here.
Those, those aren't like the others.
HERE they are.   160
And you, you're just fighting with your sheet all the time
and you say to me,
'He brought someone else to her.'
You see, he can bring as many as four, if her mother is like that [you].
Just go on your way.   165
Client: *Lalla*, we don't understand.
Majduba: Here it is, here it is, here.
Be the daughter of a lady and a sir…
{God help you [B]}
Client: Amen.   170
Majduba: {Put your [B] faith in God [MA]}
Client: Amen.

Majduba: {Peace [MA] incomprehsible [B]}
Client: amin.
Majduba: l-kamal mən 'and llah subḥana-h.   175
Client: amin.
Majduba: ya rabbi
l-'abd 'abd-ək
u l-khliqa khliqt-ək
u l-kamal mən 'and-ək.   180
ṣalli 'la rasul allah.
shkun lli y-tuwakkəl m'aya 'la allah?
ana ghadi n-ji-k l-ulad 'ayyad f-l-khmis in sha' llah.
{ighan [B]} t-mut y-rḥəm rabbi.
ṣalli 'la rasul allah.   185
shkun lli y-tuwakkəl m'aya 'la allah?
shkun lli gal bi smi llah?
ayyəh.
sh-shuf ma y-bərrəd aj-juf.
u n-naga ma t-raḍə' l-khruf.   190
u lli bgha y-rkəb, y-rkəb 'la 'awd ma'luf.

Majduba: {Peace [MA] incomprehensible [B]}
Client: Amen.
Majduba: Completion is from God sublime...   175
Client: Amen.
Majduba: My God
a slave [is] your slave.
The created [is] your creation.
And completion is from you.   180
Pray on behalf of the Prophet.
Who will trust in God with me?
I'm going to come to you in Ouled Ayyad on Thursday insha'allah.
{But if [B]} you die, May God have mercy.
Pray on behalf of the Prophet.   185
Who will trust in God with me by God?
Who will say, In the name of God?
Yeah.
Looking won't chill the belly.
And the camel doesn't nurse the lamb.   190
And whoever wants to ride, he rides the fattened horse.

Appendix 2:
Discourse of the 'Ashshaba

nta 'aṭa-k rabbi khamsa itru dyal d-dam.
ḥna 'aṭa-na rabbi səb'a itru dyal d-dam —
dam l-ḥida wa dam n-nifas.
'lash r-rijal ntuma zinin b-tlata u ḥna zinat b-rb'a?
ntuma 'aṭa-kum rabbi shahiyya wəḥda, ḥna 'aṭi-na ts'ud u ts'in.
ara 'and-kum ghir shahiyya wəḥda.
ila khṭat-ək,
rah sh-sharaf ma y-bqash 'and-ək f-d-dar.
t-wəlli l-mra t-ban qədam-ha ki-l-ḥmar.
rah ma kaynsh lli mqaddr-ək u msharrf-ək illa n-nafs.
ila mshat ḥətta khṭat-ək, hsəb ruḥ-ək l-qima ma t-bqash 'and-ək.
rah ḥətta d-din w ḍ-ḍərr ma fihsh l-ḥya.
ḥna 'aṭi-na rabbi ts'ud u ts'in shahiyya.
'lash r-rajəl zin b-tlata w l-mra zina b-rb'a?
shnu z-zin dyal-na, ḥna l-'yalat?
shnu z-zin dyal-kum ar-rjal?
u llah, r-rajəl y-thalla f-l-kəlma.
z-zin dyal-kum u sharaf-kum u mal-kum u naẓar-kum, hiya l-kəlma.
lli kay tba'u u y-tshrau b-tlatin məlyun u rb'yn məlyun ghir b-l-kəlma.
ila shafti r-rajəl l-'aṣṣaba hiya hadik,
wa l-waqfa hiya hadik,
wa j-jəllaba hiya hadik,
w ila ji-ti ṭala'-ti 'l-ih
kat-lqa-h kəlmət l-mra hsən mənn-u huwa.
ila bgha y-mshi 'and mul l-ḥanut,
ma y-ṭlq-u ḥətta b-rubṭa dyal n-na'na'.
lli ma 'and-u kəlma wa lli ma 'and-u kəlma,
ma y-tsahlsh y-kun rajəl.
'lash r-rajəl zin b-tlata u l-mra zina b-rb'a?
{u la t-talta, t-taniya}
allah y-'ṭi l-sidi l-khir.
thalla f-n-nafs, t-bqa ḥayya.
'andak t-ghərr-ək l-mra u t-gul-lək,
"rak rajli u 'ziz 'l-iya u ila mətti, rani n-mshi n-ḥzən 'l-ik."
la t-tiqush.
wa-llah ila kan-nafqu-kum fi-ha.

ḥit huma rbʿa kay-aklu ma kay-shəbʿush.
ḥsəb mʿa-ya, asidi, llah y-ʿṭi-k l-khir.
luwla, l-ʿayn kat-akul, ma kat-qnaʿsh mən n-naẓar.
t-taniya, l-udən kat-akul, ma kat-qnaʿsh mən s-səmʿ u l-khabar.
t-talta, l-ʾarḍ kat-akul, ma kat-qnaʿsh mən l-maʾ u l-maṭar.
u r-rabʿa, lli fahəm y-kəmməl mən ʿaql-u,
sharrafa llah qadr syadi r-rjal.
u llah t-khṭa-k sh-shahiyya ḥətta t-bat-lək l-mra ʿand s-sərah dyal
    l-ghaba.
Fiyq mən l-gəlba u kun rajəl.
ntuma r-rjal ʿlash kat-bghiu-na?
ashnu z-zin dyal-na lli kat-bghiu-na ʿli-h?
ʿlash ḥna qrabat l-jənna u qrabat l-jahannam u qrabat l-sh-shayṭan?
qala rasulu llahi (ṣalla llahu ʿalay-hi wa salləm)
"l-mra ila ṭaʿat zawja-ha…"
kayn daba lli fi-kum wakhəd ghir mra zaniya.
ma kaynsh lli kay-ṭayyəḥ qimt-kum ar-rjal, ghir n-nsa.
la ma ṭayḥət-lək qimt-ək mart-ək, ṭṭayḥa-lək bant-ək —
t-ji ḥamla u lla t-khrəj bant-ək shikha.
ʾila ma ṭayḥət-ha l-ik mart-ək u la bant-ək, ṭṭayḥa-lək kht-ək u la
    umm-ək.
rah, klam-i mʿa haduk lli lli f-ʿqul-hum f-qlub-hum,
mashi klam-i mʿa hadak lli y-akul u y-zənnəd-ha w y-təkka ḥda-k kif
    l-khənsha dyal s-sima,
wa y-bul n-nuṣ f-l-ʾarḍ u l-baqi ʿla fkhad-u.
allah y-ʿṭi l-sidi l-khir.
ila ma fiyq mən l-gəlba.
ḥətta r-rajəl lli y-ẓal khaddam u l-mra ẓal t-zni —
u t-ʿqal ʿla waqt-u, ʿarfa waqt-u imta kay-dkhəl.
ghir huwa y-dkhəl u hiya t-sabq-u t-jib ḥamda t-qsəm-ha ʿla juj,
u ddir wəḥda hna, u wəḥda hna,
t-ʿgud ras-ha b-kharqa u t-rgud tay-ji r-rajəl ʿla niyt-u:
"mal-ək, aflana?"
tat-gul li-h, "məlli mshiti ṣ-ṣbaḥ u ana ḥatta ras-i ʿla l-əmkhadda."
siri, llah y-nəzzal ʿl-ik n-naʿla kama nəzlat sh-shta ʿla l-ʾarḍ.
l-mra ila ṭaʿat zawj-ha
u ṣallat waqt-ha
u ṣamət shhar-ha
u ḥasnat farj-ha
fa ʾila l-jənna maʾwa-ha.
r-rjal fi-kum lli bhga t-bqa shəmʿt-u shaʿla,
u t-bqa nawart-ək gadiya.
u-zin-ək ma y-dbal u shməʿt-ək ma t-ṭfa,
dakhalt ʿli-kum b-llah ila ma waqru waḥəd r-rubʿa
la baqish t-diru-hum ar-rjal l-l-ʿyalat:
n-wərri-hum li-kum.

ma sma'tsh lli gal ḷḷah y-rḥəm l-walidin.

ḷḷah y-rhəm l-walidin

shəfti lli waqr fi-kum had r-rub'a wa-ḷḷah 'ila rajəl.

shəfti lli dar hadu rb'a u ḷḷah 'ila l-ḥmar ḥsən mənn-u.

lli bgha nawart-u t-bqa dawiya

u shmə't-u t-bqa sha'la

y-waqər hadu rb'a la baqish y-dir-hum:

luwla mən-hum ila ṣalli-na 'la rasul-aḷḷah

ṣalla ḷḷah 'l-ih wa səlləm

hani ghadiya n-haz l-mizan hada, ha huwa.

{incomprehensible}

n-'məl-lək l-mizan bḥal-i ana hakda.

l-marḍ lli fi-k ana n-wərri-h l-ik.

la t-shkish 'l-iya, shki 'la ḷḷah.

'ṭi-ni ghir idd-ək u skut.

kullu huwa l-marḍ lli fi-k ghadi n-gulu-lək,

walakin 'ila khdəm-lik l-mizan f-idd-ək.

'ila ma khdəmsh l-mizan f-idd-ək,

u ḷḷah wakha t-shəd-ha sa'tayn f-idd-ək, u ḷḷah, mən blaṣt-ha la t-ḥarkat.

'ila t-khalləṣ-ni fi-ha, u la t-'ṭi-ni fi-ha shi ḥaja,

ḷḷah y-ḥarg-ək bi-hum.

u la n-dir idd-i ḥətta 'anaya u n-tkhalləṣ mənn-ək fi-hum,

ḷḷah y-ḥrag-ni bi-hum.

l-khlaṣ lli baghiya n-sma' ma sma'tush:

gulu ḷḷah y-rḥəm l-walidin.

aḷḷah y-rhəm l-walidin.

rb'a waqru-hum ḷḷah y-'ṭi l-syadi l-khir.

luwla mən-hum 'ila ṣalli-na 'la rasul aḷḷah.

ṣalla aḷḷah 'li-h wa səlləm.

luwla n-bghi t-waqər rfaqət mən wala.

'ila bghiti t-rafəg rafəg ḥsən mənn-ək mashi kraf mənn-ək.

t-taniya, ḷḷah y-'ṭi l-sidi l-khir,

bghit-ək t-waqər l-fruj.

ga' lli kay-tba' ta' z-zənqa hadak ḥsəb ma y-bqash rajəl.

li'anna l-mra ash kat-tsəmma?

u ḷḷah, ma n-ḥshəm mənn-ək.

l-mra ash kat-tsəmma?

bir, u r-rajəl kay-tsəmma dlu.

l-mra kat-tsəmma dwaya, u r-rajəl kay-tsəmma qləm.

l-mra kat-tsəmma ḥawḍ u r-rajəl kay-tsəmma saqiya.

l-mra kat-tsəmma frash u r-rajəl ghṭa.

kayn r-rajəl lli kay-laqqəṭ l-khnəz ghir mən l-'yalat.

t-talta, ḷḷah y-'ṭi l-sidi l-khir,

ma t-shrəbsh l-ma f-l-ḥammam,

rah, kif j-jamra li kant sha'la 'ila ṭfat.

ma t-shrəbsh qar'at l-munada f-l-ḥal skhun u nta 'argan.

rah, 'mər n-nafs la ḥyat,
la t-shrəbsh l-ma dyal l-frijidir,
rah, 'mər n-nafs la drakti-ha.
la t-fṭarsh b-l-qahwa kaḥla,
rah kat-qtəl n-nafs.
ḥna l-'yalat wakha n-aklu l-ḥjar, y-khrəj
'la ḥaqq-ash 'and-na l-ḥkak dyal-na 'raḍ.
r-rjal 'and-hum l-klawi kif z-zif dyal ḥayati.
la t-kunsh 'argan u t-təkka 'la l-ḥayṭ,
rah hadak huwa l-marḍ dyal l-'amud l-fiqari.
la t-kun-sh 'argan u t-hawwəd mən ṭ-ṭumubil u nta 'argan,
rah hadak huwa l-mani tay-krəm f-l-klawi.
u rabbi qal f-l-qur'an,
la qawli-hi ta'ala,
ba'd *a'ūdu bi llāhi mina ash-shayṭāni ar-rajīm,*
fal ya-nẓuri al-'insānu mimma khuliqa.
wəsh had l-'aya qal-ha rabbi u la mzawra?
fal ya-nẓuri al-'insānu mimma khuliqa
khuliqa min mā'in dāfiqin ya-khruju min bayni aṣ-sulbi wa at-tarā'ib.
dik n-nuṭfa dyalt l-ma lli kat-khrəj lək mən s-səlsul dyal z̧-z̧har,
fin kat-farrəgh-lək?
n-nuṣ dyal-ha kay-mshi l-had l-kəlwa u n-nuṣ l-had l-kəlwa.
ash kat-luḥ fi-ha, d-dam 'au l-qiḥ?
lli kay-kun 'argan u kay-hbat mən ṭ-ṭumubil,
l-mani kay-krəm f-s-səlsul dyal z̧-z̧har.
r-rab'a, waqru-ha, llah y-'ṭi-kum l-khir,
la təjtamə' b-l-mra u 'li-ha l-ḥiḍa.
rabbi waṣṣa-k 'la l-maḥiḍ.
qala rasulu llah, ṣalla llahu 'alay-hi wa salləm,
man naẓar mra b-dam-ha,
bḥal ila kal l-f'a b-sam-ha.
bghit-i t-bqa rajəl zin u nqi, ḥaja wəḥda ghadi n-wərri-ha li-kum.
ma sma't-sh lli gal llah y-rḥəm l-walidin.
allah y-rḥəm l-walidin.
aji a s-si khalid.
lli jma' m'aya idd-u, bghit 'mər sh-shuka ma dduggu f-l-'ḍam.
lli t-kabbər 'l-iya y-ddi-ha ragda 'la jənbu.
'ara idd-i-kum m'aya huk.
diru m'aya idd-i-kum u jm'u m'aya idd-i-kum,
wa-llah y-'ṭi l-sidi l-khir.
u rani l-yum m'a-kum, shhar m'a-kum, w ana hna.
ana ghadiya n-farrəq l-adrisa dyal dar-i 'li-kum kamlin.
s-sukna f-d-dar l-biḍa u s-sukna f-mərraksh.
s-sukna f-dukkala.
u kəddab 'li-kum, y-'ma mən 'ayn-ih b-juj.
'and-i l-ḥanut dyal-i f-l-qri'a f-d-dar l-biḍa.

kan-biʿ u n-shri f-l-ʾadwiya, f-l-ʿshub.
kayn ʿand-i l-ʿashba lli kat-swa ʿand-i khams myat alf frank l-kilu,
b-ṭurizasyun, b-kwaghṭ-i
u ra-ni bant l-ʿruq mashi bant l-khruq.
t-shab-lək had l-mihna tabʿa fi-ha?
ra-ni tabʿa jdud jdud-i.
uqaf ghir qəddam-i.
ma-t-gul-i, "ha lli ḍarr-ni."
l-marḍ lli fi-k, n-gulu-lək ghir b-ʿayn-i,
b-la ma n-ʿməl lək had l-mizan f-idd-ək.
khmsat l-ḥajjat ʿand-i f-rasul ḷḷah.
sbʿa-t l-ʿumrat mduza-hum f-qbar n-nbi.
hani labsa ḥaq ḷḷah.
shhar u khamsṭ-ashr yum bash ḍaʿ liya z-zawj.
ma mraḍ la nhar la yumayn, la saʿa la saʿtayn.
rgəd, mul l-ʾamana dda ʾamant-u.
binu-u-bin l-walid dyal-i shahrayn.
fin t-fakkər-na rabbi f-ḥukmu.
qal-lək, ʾida ʾarada shayʾun
ya-qulu la-hu "kun fa ya-kun."
daba rah miyt druk u waqəf mʿaya.
ma ʿraf-kum ntuma u la ʾanaya.
wa lli labsa had l-kswa khaṣṣ-ha ma-t-hdarsh l-klam dyal s-sufh.
ma-t-hdarsh l-tnəmnim.
liʾannahu rak dakhla f-ḥaq ḷḷah.
ʿashrat l-ulad ʿand-i.
n-ḥməd rabbi u n-shəkru.
u ʿand-i r-rjal sbuʿa.
ma n-qdarsh n-wərri-hum-lək fin kaynin
ḥətta ʾila bghiti n-wərri-hum-lək, n-wərri-hum-lək.
u rah kay gulu l-ʿaqlin,
l-ʿud lli y-dḥak-lək,
huwa lli y-ʿmi-lək ʿayn-ək.
n-ḥməd rabbi u n-shəkru.
ʿmər ṭ-ṭbib ma tkashəf-liya ʿla ṣaḥt-i.
u ʿmər ṭ-ṭbib ma dkhəl ʿliya.
u ʿmr l-bra ma jat-liya f-l-aḥm-i.
ḷḷah y-jʿal ṣaḥt-i t-kun ṣaḥət-kum ntuma.
ṭarf dyal d-dhab lli ka-n ʿməl l-ruḥ-i.
ghadiya n-shri l-maʿrifa dyal-ti mʿa waḥəd r-rajəl u ulla mra.
bghit nhar t-tlat y-suwəl ʿliya hna.
ghadi n-rḥəm-kum bi-h,
naṣib,
naṣib,
naṣib,
naṣib.

ma sma'tsh lli gal ḷḷah y-rḥəm l-walidin.
ḷḷah y-rḥəm l-walid-in.
had shwiya lli ghadi n-'ṭi-k lash y-liq?
wa-ḷḷahi ma-n-gul li-kum lash y-liq ḥətta t-gul-u ntuma "lash."
lash y-liq alalla?
u ḷḷahi ma sma't-kum!
lash y-liq?
sma' 'ash ghadiya n-gul u 'qal 'la klam-i.
'ila ma dkhal-ti mən hna t-khrəj mən hna.
l-luwla 'ṭi-ni dak lli y-təm ghadi
u y-kali b-had l-id dyal-u l-klawi.
y-t-shəkka b-l-'amud l-fiqari.
hadu y-ghawwət bi-hum.
n-nuṣ hada mat li-h.
hadu zḥaf bi-hum.
n-nafs matət.
ma bqitish rajəl.
'qal ash kan-gul, rani kan-tkalləm m'a-k.
t-nud rub'a, khamsat l-marrat f-l-lilla.
l-bul ma t-shəddi-h.
sir suwəl 'liya f-l-ḥad dyal l-qṣiba,
rah s-sərbis hna u hna.
t-bat, dakhəl kharəj.
mra khanza li-ha l-walda.
ma bqitish rajəl
l-qaḥba malka-k, s-sifa mərgat.
'ila n-khalli shi ṭ-ṭbib baqi y-kshəf 'la dhat-ək,
bin-i u bin-ək, lli mshark-na kamlin, huwa rasul ḷḷah.
ṣalla ḷḷah 'l-ih wa sələm.
shahadat-ḷḷah.
shahadat-ḷḷah.
shahadat-ḷḷah.
shahadat-ḷḷah.
shahadat-ḷḷah.

Glossary

ajər: recompense
aṣl: origin
'aql: reason
'ashshaba: female herbalist
'aṭṭar: traditional druggist, herbalist
baraka: blessing, grace
bəkri: early; in earlier times; in the olden days
da'wa (pl. *da'wat*): a supplication to God, or a curse
fatḥa: a religious invocation
fitna: chaos, disorder
fqih: a Muslim cleric, a person learned in the Qur'an
gal-lək: he said to you
ḥadith: "report" or "narrative," the oral record (now transcribed) of the utterances
    and deeds in the Prophet
ḥal: a state (as of being)
ḥalal: permitted, lawful
ḥalqa: the section of the suq reserved for performance
ḥaq: a right, a share, truth
ḥaram: forbidden
ḥashak: "sparing your presence," "forgive me for mentioning it"
ḥshuma: something shameful
ḥashshumi (masc.)/*ḥashshumiya* (fem.): shy, modest, reserved
ḥammam: public bath
ḥikam: aphorisms
ḥlayqi: a performer or hawker in the ḥalqa
ḥəfla: party
ḥənna: a plant that dyes the skin and that is used for ornate body decoration
hadra: talk, gossip, speech
insha'llah: God willing
jnun: spirits
kəlma: word, authority
khəddama (fem.): maid
lalla: form of address: "my lady," "lady." [sometimes pronounced *alalla*]
majduba (fem.): a possessed or "attracted" one, a renouncer, a doomsayer
ma'rifa: knowledge, having connections
maṭluq: loose, open, relaxed
mkhalləṭ: mixed, hybrid
mra dyal d-dar: housewife

mul d-dar: the "owner" or "master" of the house
mulat d-dar: the "mistress" of the house
nafs: carnal spirit or desire nature, self
nas sha'biyin: the populace, the folk
niya: good intention, belief, naiveté
nəggafa: professional adorner, caretaker of the bride
nəqqasha: a henna artist, a professional body-painter
prix fixe: "fixed price," no bargaining
qa'ida: custom, the ways things are done
qaṣəḥ: hard
ruḥ: soul
sahhara: a woman adept at magic, a witch
ṣbər: patience
shur: magic
suq: marketplace
shahada-llah: a witness before God
sha'b: the folk
shikha: a female performer
shṭara: bargaining
taqalid: tradition
təfliya: a conversational genre of speech which involves joking and teasing in a
        performative mode
tqaf: "closing"; in magic, rendering someone impotent, unable to have sexual
        intercourse
tukal: a magic potion which is ingested and which has harmful results
wajib: obligation, including filial piety
wayli or *wili-wili*: "oh my hell!", damnation
za'ma: that is [to claim]

Bibliography

Abbassi, Abdelaziz. 1977. A sociolinguistic analysis of multilingualism in Morocco. Ph.D. dissertation, University of Texas at Austin.

———. 1994. personal communication.

Abdel-Massih, Ernest T. 1974. *Advanced Moroccan Arabic*. Ann Arbor, MI: University of Michigan Press.

Abrahams, Roger D. 1969. The complex relation of simple forms. *Genre* 2 (2): 124–28.

———. 1970. A performance-centered approach to gossip. *Man* 5: 290–301.

———. 1977. Towards an enactment-centered theory of folklore. *Frontiers of folklore*. Boulder, CO: Westview Press. 79–120.

———. 1983. *The man-of-words in the West Indies: performance and the emergence of creole culture*. Baltimore and London: Johns Hopkins University Press.

———. 1985. A note on neck-riddles in the West Indies as they comment on emergent genre theory. *Journal of American Folklore* 98 (387): 85–94.

———. 1986. Ordinary and extraordinary experience. *The anthropology of experience*. Urbana and Chicago: University of Illinois Press.

———. 1987. An American vocabulary of celebration. *Time out of time*. Albuquerque: University of New Mexico Press.

———. 1993. Phantoms of romantic nationalism in folkloristics. *Journal of American Folklore* 106 (Winter): 3–37.

———. n.d. Folklore at the marketplace.

Abrahams, Roger D. and Richard Bauman. 1978. Ranges of festival behavior. *The reversible world: symbolic inversion in art and society*. Ithaca, NY: Cornell University Press. 193–208.

Abu-Lughod, Janet L. 1980. *Rabat: urban apartheid in Morocco*. Princeton, NJ: Princeton University Press.

Abu-Lughod, Lila. 1986. *Veiled sentiments: honor and poetry in a Bedouin society*. Los Angeles and London: University of California Press.

———. 1989. Zones of anthropology in the Arab world. *Annual Review of Anthropology* 18: 276–306.

———. 1990a. The romance of resistance: tracing transformations of power through Bedouin women. *American Ethnologist* 17: 14–55.

———. 1990b. Shifting politics in Bedouin love poetry. *Language and the politics of emotion*. New York: Cambridge University Press. 24–45.

———. 1991. Writing against culture. *Recapturing anthropology*. Sante Fe, NM: School of American Research Press. 137–62.

———. 1993. *Writing women's worlds: Bedouin stories*. Berkeley: University of California Press.

Accad, Evelyne. 1978. The themes of sexual oppression in the North African novel. *Women in the Muslim world*. Cambridge, MA and London: Harvard University Press. 617–628.

Adonis. 1990. *An introduction to Arab poetics*. Austin: University of Texas Press.

Africanus, J.-L. (Leo L'Africain). 1980. *Description de l'Afrique*. Paris: Maisonneuve.

Agnew, Jean-Christophe. 1986. *Worlds apart: the market and the theater in Anglo-American thought, 1550–1750*. Cambridge and New York: Cambridge University Press.

Ahmed, Akbar S. 1986. *Toward Islamic anthropology: definition, dogma, and directions*. Herndon, VA: International Institute of Islamic Thought.

Akhmisse, M. 1985. *Médecine, magie et sorcellerie au Maroc: ou l'art traditionnel de guérir*. Casablanca: Imprimerie Eddar El Beida.

al-Hibri, Azizah, Ed. 1982. *Women and Islam*. New York: Pergamon Press.

al-Majdub, 'Abd al-Rahman. 1966. *Les Quatrains de Mejdoub le Sarcastique: poète Maghrebin du XVIième siècle*. Published Arab texts with notes and comments by Jeanne Scelles-Millie with the collaboration of Boukhair Khelifa. Paris: Maisonneuve.

Anderson, Benedict R. O. 1983. *Imagined communities: reflections on the origin and spread of nationalism*. London: Verso.

Anderson, Jon W. 1982. Social structure and the veil: comportment and the composition of interaction in Afghanistan. *Anthropos* 77: 397–420.

———. 1985. Sentimental ambivalence and the exegesis of "self" in Afghanistan. *Self and society in the Middle East*. Special issue of *Anthropological Quarterly*. Washington, DC: Catholic University of America.

Antoun, Richard T. 1976. The state of the art in Middle East studies. *The study of the Middle East research and scholarship in the humanities and the social sciences*. New York: Wiley.

———. 1989. *Muslim preacher in the modern world: a Jordanian case study in comparative perspective*. Princeton, NJ: Princeton University Press.

Appadurai, Arjun. 1986a. Introduction: commodities and the politics of value. *The social life of things: commodities in cultural perspective*. Cambridge and New York: Cambridge University Press. 3–63.

Appadurai, Arjun, ed. 1986b. *The social life of things: commodities in cultural perspective*. Cambridge and New York: Cambridge University Press.

———. 1990. Disjuncture and difference in the global cultural economy. *Public Culture* 2 (2).

Appadurai, Arjun, Frank J. Korom, and Margaret Mills, eds. 1991. *Gender, genre, and power in South Asian expressive traditions*. Philadelphia: University of Pennsylvania Press.

Austin, J. L. 1962. *How to do things with words*. Cambridge, MA: Harvard University Press.

Babcock, Barbara. 1980. Reflexivity: definitions and discriminations. *Semiotica* 30 (1/2): 1–14.

———, ed. 1978. *The reversible world: symbolic inversions in art and society*. Ithaca, NY: Cornell University Press.

Bakhtin, Mikhail M. 1981. *The dialogic imagination*. Austin: University of Texas Press.
———. 1984a. *Problems of Dostoevsky's poetics*. Minneapolis: University of Minnesota Press.
———. 1984b. *Rabelais and his world*. Bloomington: Indiana University Press.
———. 1986. *Speech genres and other late essays*, trans. Vern W. McGee, ed. Caryl Emerson and Michael Holquist. Austin: University of Texas Press.
Banfield, Ann. 1982. *Unspeakable sentences: narration and representation in the language of fiction*. Boston: Routledge and Kegan Paul.
Barthes, Roland. 1967. *Elements of Semiology*. New York: Hill and Wang.
———. 1972. *Mythologies*. New York: Hill and Wang.
———. 1975. *The pleasure of the text*. New York: Hill and Wang.
———. 1977. *Image, music, text*. New York: Hill and Wang.
———. 1978. *A lovers' discourse: fragments*. New York: Hill and Wang.
Basset, René. 1987. Recherches sur Si Djoh'a et les anecdotes que lui sont attribuées. *Les fourberies de Si Djeh'a*. Paris: La Boite à Documents.
Basso, Ellen B. 1987. *In favor of deceit: a study of tricksters in an Amazonian society*. Tucson: University of Arizona Press.
Basso, Keith H. 1976. "Wise words" of the western Apache: metaphor and semantic theory. *Meaning in anthropology*. Albuquerque: University of New Mexico Press. 93–122.
———. 1988. Speaking with names: language and landscape among the Western Apache. Cultural Anthropology 3 (2): 99–130.
Basso, Keith H. and Henry A. Selby, eds. 1976. *Meaning in anthropology*. School of American Research Advanced Seminar Series. Albuquerque: University of New Mexico Press.
Bateson, Gregory. 1972. *Steps to an ecology of mind*. New York: Balantine Books.
Baudrillard, Jean. 1990. *Seduction*. New York: St. Martin's Press.
Bauman, Richard. 1977. *Verbal art as performance*. Prospect Heights, IL: Waveland Press.
———. 1986. *Story, performance, and event: contextual studies of oral narrative*. New York: Cambridge University Press.
———. 1989. American folklore studies and social transformation: a performance-centered perspective. *Text and Performance Quarterly* 9 (3): 175–184.
———. 1992. Contextualization, tradition and the dialogue of genres: Icelandic legends of the kraftaskald. *Rethinking context*. Cambridge: Cambridge University Press.
Bauman, Richard and Charles L. Briggs. 1990. Poetics and performance as critical perspectives on language and social life. *Annual Review of Anthropology* 19 : 59–88.
Bauman, Richard and Joel Sherzer, eds. 1974. *Explorations in the ethnography of speaking*. London and New York: Cambridge University Press.
Beck, Lois and Nikki Keddie, eds. 1978. *Women in the Muslim world*. Cambridge, MA: Harvard University Press.
Beeman, William O. 1986. *Language, status, and power in Iran*. Bloomington: Indiana University Press.

Behar, Ruth. 1990. Rage and redemption: reading the life story of a Mexican marketing woman. *Feminist Studies* 16 : 223–58.

Belarbi, Aicha. 1988. Salariat feminin et division sexuelle du travail dans la famille: cas de la femme fonctionnaire. *Femmes partagées: famille-travail.* Casablanca: Le Fennec, 79–98.

Belshaw, Cyril S. 1965. *Traditional exchange and modern markets.* Englewood Cliffs, NJ: Prentice-Hall.

Ben Jelloun, Tahar. 1989. *The sacred night.* London: Quartet Books Limited.

———. 1991. *Silent day in Tangier.* London: Quartet Books.

Ben-Amos, Dan. 1972. Toward a definition of folklore in context. *Towards new perspectives in folklore.* Austin: University of Texas Press.

———. 1976. Analytical categories and ethnic genres. *Folklore genres.* Austin: University of Texas Press. 215–42.

Bensman, Joseph and Robert Lilienfeld. 1979. *Between public and private: the lost boundaries of the self.* New York: Free Press.

Benstock, Seymour L. 1991. *Textualizing the feminine: on the limits of genre.* Norman: University of Oklahoma Press.

Berrechid, Abelkrim. 1977. Alif ba: al-wāqiʻiya al-iḥtifāliya. *At-taqafa al-Jadida* 7 (Spring) 156.

———. 1993. *Al-iḥtifāliya: mawāqif wa mawāqif muḍadda.* Marrakech: Tansift.

Besnier, Niko. 1989. Information withholding as a manipulative and collusive strategy in Nukulaelae gossip. *Language in Society* 18 : 315–41.

———. 1989. Literacy and feelings: the encoding of affect in Nukulaelae letters. *Text* 9 : 69–91.

———. 1990a. Conflict management, gossip and affective meanings on Nukulaelae. *Disentangling: Conflict discourse in Pacific societies*, ed. Karen Ann Watson-Gegeo and Geoffrey M. White. Stanford, CA: Stanford University Press. 290–334.

———. 1990b. Language and affect. *Annual Review of Anthropology* 19 : 419–51.

Betteridge, Ann. 1985. Gift exchange in Iran: the locus of self-identity in interaction. *Anthropological Quarterly* 58 (4): 182–202.

Bloch, Maurice, ed. 1975. *Political language and oratory in traditional society.* London: Academic Press.

Boddy, Janice P. 1989. *Wombs and alien spirits: women, men, and the zar cult in Northern Sudan.* Madison: The University of Wisconsin Press.

———. 1988. Spirits and selves in Northern Sudan: the cultural therapeutics of possession and trance. *American Ethnologist* 15 (February): 4–27.

Bohannan, Paul and George Dalton. 1962. *Markets in Africa.* Northwestern University Press.

———, eds. 1965. *Markets in Africa: eight subsistance economies in transition.* Garden City, New York: Doubleday.

Booth, Wayne C. 1984. Introduction. Mikhail M. Bakhtin, *Problems of Dostoevsky's poetics.* Minneapolis: University of Minnesota Press.

Boughali, Mohamed. 1974. *La représentation de l'espace chez le Marocain illettré: mythes et tradition orale.* Paris: Editions Anthropos.

Bouhmid, Mohamed. 1995. ʼInnahum yurīdūna al-ʻaita ka ḍajījin li jamʻi al-ḥushūdi?

as-sulṭa fi al-maghribi lam tafham 'anna iḥtirāma al-ʿaiṭa fi-hi jānibun min ja-wānibi al-ḥifḍi ʿalā shakhsiyatinā. *al-Ittiḥad al-Ishtiraqi* April 15 : 6.

Bourdieu, Pierre. 1966. The sentiment of honour in Kabyle society. *Honour and shame: the values of Mediterranean society.* London: Weidenfeld and Nicolson.

———. 1977a. The economics of linguistic exchange. *Social Science Information* 16 (6): 645–668.

———. 1977b. *Outline of a theory of practice.* New York: Cambridge University Press.

———. 1984. *Distinction: A social critique of the judgement of taste.* Cambridge, MA: Harvard University Press.

Bourdieu, Pierre and Jean-Claude Passeron. 1977. *Reproduction: in education, society and culture.* Beverly Hills, CA: Sage.

Bourquia, Hassan. 1995. al-Jasad wa al-ḥanīn al-muʾriq: taʾamulāt fi ʿaita maḥaliyya: "ghufal." *al-Ittiḥad al-Ishtiraqi* April 22 : 7.

Bowen, John R. 1993. A modernist Muslim poetic: print, politics, and religious ideology. *Journal of Asian Studies* 52 (3): 629–46.

Bowles, Paul. 1982. *The spider's house.* Santa Barbara, CA: Black Sparrow Press.

Brandes, Stanley. 1980. *Metaphors of masculinity: sex and status in Adalucian folklore.* Philadelphia: University of Pennsylvania Press.

Braudel, Fernand. 1975. *Capitalism and material life, 1400–1800.* New York: Harper Colophon.

———. 1982–84. *Civilisation and capitalism: 15th–18th century.* New York: Harper and Row.

Brenneis, Don L. 1984a. Grog and gossip in Bhatgaon: style and substance in Fiji Indian conversation. *American Ethnologist* 11 : 487–506.

———. 1984b. Straight talk and sweet talk: political discourse in an occasionally egalitarian community. *Dangerous words: language and politics in the Pacific.* New York: New York University Press. 69–84.

———. 1986. Shared territory: audience, indirection and meaning. *Text* 6 (3): 339–47.

———. 1987. Performing passions: aesthetics and politics in an occasionally egalitarian community. *American Ethnologist* 14 : 236–50.

———. 1990. Shared and solitary sentiments: the discourse of friendship, play and anger in Bhatgaon. *Language and the politics of emotion.* Cambridge: Cambridge University Press. 113–125.

Brenneis, Don L. and Fred R. Myers, eds. 1984. *Dangerous words: language and politics in the Pacific.* New York: New York University Press.

Briggs, Charles L. 1988. *Competence in performance: the creativity of tradition in Mexicano verbal art.* Philadelphia: University of Pennsylvania Press.

———. 1992. "Since I am a woman, I will chastise my relatives": gender, reported speech and the reproduction of social relations in Warao ritual wailing. *American Ethnologist* 19 (2): 337–361.

———. 1993. Textual practices and scholarly authority in folkloristics. *Western Folklore.*

Briggs, Charles L. and Richard Bauman. 1992. Genre, intertextuality, and social power. *Journal of Linguistic Anthropology* 2 (2): 131–72.

Brown, Kenneth. 1977. Changing forms of patronage in a Moroccan city. *Patrons and clients in Mediterranean societies*. London: Duckworth.

———. 1982. The "curse" of Westermarck. *Ethnos* 3/4 : 197–231.

Brown, Penelope and Stephen Levinson. 1978. Universals in language usage: politeness phenomena. *Questions and politeness: strategies in social interaction*, ed. Esther Goody. Cambridge and New York: Cambridge University Press.

Brown, Roger and Albert Gilman. 1960. The pronouns of power and solidarity. *Style in language*. Cambridge, MA: MIT Press.

Brunvand, Jan H. 1986. *The study of American folklore*. New York: Norton.

Buitelaar, Marjo. 1993. *Fasting and feasting in Morocco: women's participation in Ramadan*. Oxford and Providence, RI: Berg.

Bynum, Caroline Walker. 1984. Women's stories, women's symbols: A critique of Victor Turner's theory of liminality. *Anthropology and the study of religion*. Chicago: Center for the Scientific Study of Religion. 105–25.

Caillois, Roger. 1961. *Man, play, and games*. New York: Free Press.

Campbell, Donald. 1926. *Arabian medicine and its influence on the Middle Ages*. London: Kegan Paul, Trench, Trubner.

Canclini, Nestor García. 1990. *Culturas hibridas: estrategias para entrar y salir de la modernidad*. México: Grijalbo.

———. 1993. Too much determinism or too much hybridization? *Travesia* 3 : 161–70.

Canto, Monique. 1985. The politics of women's bodies: reflections on Plato. *The female body in Western culture: contemporary perspectives*. Cambridge, MA; and London: Harvard University Press. 339–353.

Caraveli, Anna. 1986. The bitter wounding: the lament as social protest in rural Greece. *Gender and power in rural Greece*. Princeton, NJ: Princeton University Press. 169–194.

Caton, Steven Charles. 1990. *"Peaks of Yemen I summon": poetry as cultural practice in a North Yemeni tribe*. Berkeley: University of California Press.

Chafik, Mohamed. 1988–89. *Recherches sur l'identité du théâtre Marocain*. Thèse de Doctorat. Paris VIII.

Chebel, Malek. 1984. *Le corps dans la tradition du Maghreb*. Paris: Presses Universitaires de France.

Cixous, Hélène. 1980. The laugh of the medusa. *New french feminisms*. New York: Schocken Books.

Cixous, Hélène and Cathérine Clement. 1975. *La jeune née*. Paris: UGE.

———. 1986. *The newly born woman*. Minneapolis: University of Minnesota Press.

Cixous, Hélène, Madeleine Gagnon, et al. 1977. *La venue à l'écriture*. Paris: UGE.

Clark, Katerina and Michael Holquist. 1984. *Mikhail Bakhtin*. Cambridge, MA and London: Harvard University Press.

Coates, Jennifer. 1989. Gossip revisited: Language in all-female groups. *Women in their speech communities: new perspectives on language and sex*. New York and London: Longman.

Cocchiara, Giuseppe. 1980. *The history of folklore studies in Europe*. Philadelphia: Institute for the Study of Human Issues.

Combs-Schilling, M. E. 1989. *Sacred performances: Islam, sexuality and sacrifice*. New York: Columbia University Press.

Crapanzano, Vincent. 1973. *The Ḥamadsha: study in Moroccan ethnopsychiatry.* Berkeley: University of California Press.

———. 1980. *Tuhami: portrait of a Moroccan.* Chicago: University of Chicago Press.

———. 1992. *Hermes' dilemma and Hamlet's desire: on the epistemology of interpretation.* Cambridge, MA: Harvard University Press.

Csordas, Thomas J. 1993. Somatic modes of attention. *Cultural Anthropology* 8 (2): 135–156.

Dargan, Amanda and Steven Zeitlin. 1983. American talkers: expressive styles and occupational choice. *Journal of American Folklore* 96 : 3–33.

Davis, Natalie Zemon. 1978. Women on the top: Symbolic sexual inversion and political disorder in early modern Europe. *The reversible world: symbolic inversion in art and society.* Ithaca, NY: Cornell University Press. 147–90.

Davis, Susan Schaeffer. 1978. Working women in a Moroccan village. *Women in the Muslim world.* Cambridge, MA and London: Harvard University Press. 416–433.

———. 1983. *Patience and power: women's lives in a Moroccan village.* Cambridge, MA: Schenkman.

Davis, Susan Schaeffer and Douglas A. Davis. 1989. *Adolescence in a Moroccan town: making social sense.* New Brunswick, NJ and London: Rutgers University Press.

Delaney, Carol L. 1991. *The seed and the soil: gender and cosmology in Turkish village society.* Berkeley: University of California Press.

Derrida, Jacques. 1978. *Writing and difference.* Chicago: University of Chicago Press.

———. 1980. The law of genre. *Glyph.* Baltimore: Johns Hopkins University Press. 202–32.

Desjarlais, Robert. 1992. *Body and emotion: the aesthetics of illness and healing in the Nepal Himalayas.* Philadelphia: University of Pennsylvania Press.

Diouri, Abdelhai. 1984. La résistance du nom. *Bulletin Économique et Social du Maroc* 153–53 : 25–31.

Donaldson, Dwight M. 1943. Truth and falsehood in Islam. *Moslem Word* 33 : 276–85.

Dorson, Richard M., ed. 1983. *Handbook of American folklore.* Bloomington: Indiana University Press.

Dorst, John. 1983. Neck riddle as a dialogue of genres. *Journal of American Folklore* 96 : 313–433.

———. 1990. Tags and burners, cycles and networks: folklore in the telectronic age. *Journal of Folklore Research* 27 (3): 179–90.

Douglas, Mary. 1982/1970. *Natural symbols: explorations in cosmology.* New York: Pantheon.

———. 1988/1966. *Purity and danger: an analysis of the concepts of pollution and taboo.* London and New York: Ark Paperbacks.

Doutté, Edmond. 1984. *Magie et religion dans L'Afrique du Nord.* Paris: J. Maisonneuve, P. Geuthner S.A.

Dundes, Alan and Alessandro Falassi. 1975. *La terra in piazza: an interpretation of the Palio of Siena.* Berkeley: University of California Press.

Duranti, Alessandro. 1986. The audience as co-author: an introduction. *Text* 6: 239–247.

———. 1993. Truth and intentionality: an ethnographic critique. *Cultural Anthropology* 8 (2): 214–45.

Duranti, Alessandro and Charles Goodwin, eds. 1992. *Rethinking context: language as an interactive phenomenon.* Studies in the Social and Cultural Foundations of Language. Cambridge: Cambridge University Press.

Dwyer, Daisy Hilse. 1978a. *Images and self-images: male and female in Morocco.* New York: Columbia University Press.

———. 1978b. Women, sufism and decision-making in Moroccan Islam. *Women in the Muslim world.* Cambridge, MA and London: Harvard University Press. 585–598.

Dwyer, Kevin. 1982. *Moroccan dialogues: anthropology in question.* Baltimore: Johns Hopkins University Press.

Eickelman, Dale F. 1976. *Moroccan Islam: tradition and society in a pilgrimage center.* Austin: University of Texas Press.

———. 1977. Time in a complex society: a Moroccan example. *Ethnology* 16 (1): 39–55.

———. 1978. The art of memory: Islamic education and its social reproduction. *Comparative Studies in Society and History* 20: 485–516.

———. 1981. *The Middle East: an anthropological approach.* Englewood Cliffs, NJ: Prentice Hall.

———. 1983. Religion and trade in western Morocco. *Research in Economic Anthropology* 5: 335–48.

———. 1985. *Knowledge and power in Morocco: the education of a twentieth century notable.* Princeton, NJ: Princeton University Press.

———. 1992. Mass higher education and the religious imagination in contemporary Arab societies. *American Ethnologist* 19 (4): 643–55.

Eickelman, Dale F. and James Piscatori. 1990. Social theory in the study of Muslim societies. *Muslim travellers: pilgrimage, migration, and the religious imagination.* Berkeley: University of California Press. 3–25.

Ejxenbaum, Boris M. 1971. The theory of the formal method. *Readings in Russian poetics: formalist and structuralist views.* Cambridge, MA: MIT Press. 3–37.

El-Shamy, Hassan M. 1980. *Folktales of Egypt.* Chicago: University of Chicago Press.

Elias, Norbert. 1978. *The civilizing process: The history of manners.* New York: Pantheon.

Elkhadem, H. 1990. *Le taqwīm al-sihha tacuini sanitanis, d'Ibn Butlan: un traité médical du XIe siècle.* Lovanii: Aedibus Peeters.

Ennaji, Mohammed. 1994. *Soldats, domestiques et concubines: l'esclavage au Maroc au XIX ième siècle.* Casablanca: Éditions Eddif.

Ervin-Tripp, Susan. 1976. Speech acts and social learning. *Meaning in anthropology.* Albuquerque: University of New Mexico Press. 123–54.

Esposito, John L. 1982. *Women in Muslim family law.* Syracuse, NY: Syracuse University Press.

Fabian, Johannes. 1983. *Time and the other: how anthropology makes its object.* New York: Columbia University Press.

————. 1990. *Power and performance: ethnographic explorations through proverbial wisdom and theater in Shaba, Zaire*. Madison and London: University of Wisconsin Press.

Falassi, Alessandro. 1987. Festival: definition and morphology. *Time out of time: essays on the festival*. Albuquerque: University of New Mexico Press.

Favret-Saada, Jeanne. 1977. *Deadly words: witchcraft in the Bocage*. New York London: Cambridge University Press.

Feld, Steven. 1982. *Sound and sentiment: birds, weeping, poetics, and son in Kaluli expression*. Philadelphia: University of Pennsylvania Press.

————. 1990. Wept thoughts: the voicing of Kaluli memories. *Oral Tradition* 5 (2/3): 241–66.

————. 1995. From schizophonia to schismogenesis. *Music grooves*. Chicago: University of Chicago Press.

Fernandez, James W. 1986. *Persuasions and performances: the play of tropes in culture*. Bloomington: Indiana University Press.

Fernea, Elizabeth Warnock, producer/director. 1978. *Saints and spirits*. Video. University of Texas at Austin.

————. 1980. *A street in Marrakech*. Garden City, NY: Anchor Books, Doubleday.

Fernea, Robert and James H. Malarkey. 1975. Anthropology of the Middle East and North Africa: a critical assessment. *Annual Review of Anthropology* 4 : 183–206.

Fine, Elizabeth C. 1984. *The folklore text: from performance to print*. Bloomington: Indiana University Press.

Flood, B. P. J. 1968. *Macer Floridus: A Medieval herbalism*. PhD dissertation, University of Colorado.

Foster, Hal, ed. 1983. *The anti-aesthetic: essays on postmodern culture*. Port Townsend, WA: Bay Press.

Foucauld, Charles de. 1888. *Reconnaissance au Maroc*. Paris: Challamel, Librairie Coloniale.

Foucault, Michel. 1981. The order of discourse. *Untying the text: a post-structuralist reader*. Boston: Routledge and Kegan Paul. 48–78.

Fox, James J., ed. 1988. *To speak in pairs: essay on the ritual languages of eastern Indonesia*. Cambridge Studies in Oral and Literate Culture. Cambridge: Cambridge University Press.

Fox, T. and Mohamed Abu-Talib. 1966. *A Dictionary of Moroccan Arabic: Arabic-English*. Washington, DC: Georgetown University Press.

Franco, J. 1993. Border patrol. *Travesia* 3 : 134–42.

Fraser, Nancy. 1992. Rethinking the public sphere: a contribution to the critique of actually existing democracy. *Habermas and the public sphere*. Cambridge, MA and London: MIT Press. 109–42.

Frazer, George H. 1911. *The magic art and the evolution of kings*. London: Macmillan.

Friedrich, Paul. 1966. Structural implications of Russian pronominal usage. *Sociolinguistics*. The Hague: Mouton. 214–59.

Gal, Susan. 1989. Language and political economy. *Annual Review of Anthropology* 18 : 345–67.

————. 1990. Between speech and silence: The problematics of research on language and gender. In *Toward a new anthropology of gender*, ed. Micaela Di Leonardo. Berkeley: University of California Press.

Geertz, Clifford. 1968. *Islam observed: religious development in Morocco and Indonesia*. Chicago: University of Chicago Press.

———. 1976. From the native's point of view: on the nature of anthropological understanding. *Meaning in anthropology*. Albuquerque: University of New Mexico Press. 221–238.

———. 1979. Suq: the bazaar economy in Sefrou. *Meaning and order in Moroccan society: three essays in cultural analysis*, ed. Clifford Geertz, Hildred Geertz, and Lawrence Rosen. Cambridge: Cambridge University Press.

———. 1983. Blurred genres: the refiguration of social thought. *Local knowledge*. New York: Basic Books.

Geertz, Hildred. 1979. The meaning of family ties. *Meaning and order in Moroccan society*. Cambridge: Cambridge University Press.

Gellner, Ernest. 1969. *Saints of the Atlas*. Chicago: University of Chicago Press.

Gennep, Arnold van. 1960. *The rites of passage*. Chicago: University of Chicago Press.

Gerhardt, Mia. 1963. *The art of storytelling: a literary study of the Thousand and One Nights*. Leiden: E. J. Brill.

Gilligan, Carol. 1982. *In a different voice: psychological theory and women's development*. Cambridge, MA: Harvard University Press.

Gilsenan, M. 1976. Lying, honor and contradiction. *Transaction and meaning: directions in the anthropology of exchange and symbolic behavior*. Philadelphia: Institute for the Study of Human Issues. 191–219.

Gluckman, Max., ed. 1962. *Essays on the ritual of social relations*. Manchester: Manchester University Press.

———. 1963. Gossip and scandal. *Current Anthropology* 4:307–16.

———. 1968. Psychological, sociological, and anthropological explanations of witchcraft and gossip. *Man* 3:20–34.

Goffman, Erving. 1974. *Frame analysis*. New York: Harper and Row.

———. 1981. *Forms of talk*. Philadelphia: University of Pennsylvania Press.

Goodman, Lenn Evan. 1992. *Avicenna*. London: Routledge.

Goodwin, Charles and Alessandro Duranti. 1992. Rethinking context: an introduction. *Rethinking context*. New York: Cambridge University Press. 1–42.

Goodwin, Marjorie H. 1990. *He-said-she-said*. Bloomington and Indianapolis: Indiana University Press.

Goody, Esther N. 1978. Towards a theory of questions. *Questions and politeness: strategies in social interaction*. Cambridge and New York: Cambridge University Press.

Goux, Jean-Joseph. 1990. *Symbolic economies: after Marx and Freud*. Ithaca, NY: Cornell University Press.

Graham-Brown, Sarah. 1988. *Images of women: the portrayal of women in the photography of the Middle East 1860–1950*. New York: Columbia University Press.

Gramsci, Antonio. 1971. *Selections from the prison notebooks*. New York: International Publishers.

Grice, Paul. 1975. Logic and conversation. *Syntax and semantics*. New York: Academic Press.

Grima, Benedict. 1992. *The performance of emotion among Paxtun women: "The misfortunes which have befallen me."* Austin: University of Texas Press.

Gross, Elizabeth. 1986. Philosophy, subjectivity and the body: Kristeva and Irigaray. *Feminist challenges: social and political theory.* Boston: Northeastern University Press.

Gross, Joan, David McMurry and Ted Swedenburg. 1994. Arab noise and ramadan nights: rai, rap and Franco-Maghrebi identities. *Diaspora.*

Gumperz, John Joseph. 1982. *Discourse situations.* London: Cambridge University Press.

Habermas, Jurgen. 1991. *The structural transformation of the public sphere: an enquiry into a category of bourgeois society.* Cambridge, MA: MIT Press.

———. 1992. Further reflections on the public sphere. *Habermas and the public sphere.* Cambridge, MA and London: MIT Press. 421–61.

Hajjarabi, Fatima. 1987. *Les souks feminins du Rif Central: anthropologie de l'échange féminin.* Thèse de Doctorat: Paris VII.

———. 1988. Les souks féminins du Rif Central: rareté des biens et profusions sociale. *Femmes partagées: famille-travail.* Casablanca: Le Fennec.

Hamarneh, Sami Khalif. 1983. *Health sciences in early Islam.* Blanco, TX: Zahra Publications.

Hammoudi, Abdellah. 1988. *La victime et ses masques: essai sur le sacrifice et la mascarade au Maghreb.* Paris: Seuil.

Hanks, William F. 1987. Discourse genres in a theory of practice. *American Ethnologist* 14 (4): 668–92.

———. 1989. Word and image in a semiotic perspective. *Word and image in Maya culture: explorations in language, writing, and representation.* Salt Lake City: University of Utah Press. 8–21.

———. 1990. *Referential practice: language and lived space among the Maya.* Chicago: University of Chicago Press.

Hannerz, Ulf. 1987. The world in creolization. *Africa* 57 (4): 546–59.

Haring, Lee. 1992a. *Verbal arts in Madagascar: performance in historical perspective.* Philadelphia: University of Pennsylvania Press.

———. 1992b. Parody and imitation in West Indian Ocean oral literature. *Journal of Folklore Research* 29 (3): 199–224.

Harrell, Richard S. 1962. *A short reference grammar of Moroccan Arabic.* Washington, DC: Georgetown University Press.

Harrison-Pepper, Sally. 1990. *Drawing a circle in the square: street performing in New York's Washington Square Park.* Jackson: University Press of Mississippi.

Hart, David M. 1976. *The Aith Waryaghar of the Moroccan Rif: an ethnography and history.* Tucson: University of Arizona Press.

Harway, Michele and Marsha B. Liss. 1988. Arab mothers in Morocco: responsibilities without rights. *The different faces of motherhood.* New York: Plenum Books.

Haviland, John B. 1977. *Gossip and knowledge in Zinacantan.* Chicago: University of Chicago Press.

———. 1986. "Con buenos chiles": talk, targets and teasing in Zinacantan. *Text* 6 (3): 249–282.

———. 1989. 'Sure, sure': Evidence and affect. *Text* 9 (1): 27–68.

Heath, Jeffrey. 1987. *Ablaut and ambiguity: phonology of a Moroccan Arabic dialect*. Albany: State University of New York Press.

Herzfeld, Michael. 1985. *The Poetics of manhood*. Princeton, NJ: Princeton University Press.

———. 1990. Silence, submission, and subversion: Towards a poetics of womanhood. *Contested identities: gender and kinship in modern Greece*. Princeton, NJ: Princeton University Press.

Hobsbawm, Eric. 1983. Introduction: inventing traditions. *The invention of tradition*. Cambridge and New York: Cambridge University Press. 1–14.

Hochschild, Arlie. 1990. *The second shift*. New York: Avon Books.

Holquist, Michael. 1986. Introduction, Mikhail M. Bakhtin, *Speech genes and other late essays*. Austin: University of Texas Press.

Hopper, Paul J. and Sandra A. Thompson, eds. 1982. *Syntax and semantics: studies in transitivity*. Syntax and Semantics 5. New York: Academic Press.

Hubert, R. and Marcel Mauss. 1950. Esquisse d'une théorie générale de la magie. *Sociologie et anthropologie*. Paris: Presses Universitaires de France.

Huizinga, Johan. 1967/50. *Homo ludens: a study of the play element in culture*. Boston: Beacon Press.

Humphreys, R. Stephen. 1991. *Islamic history: a framework for inquiry*. Princeton, NJ: Princeton University Press.

Hymes, Dell. 1964. Introduction: toward ethnographies of communication. *The ethnography of communication*, ed. John Joseph Gumperz and Dell Hymes. Special publication of *American Anthropologist*.

———. 1971. Introduction. *Pidginization and creolization of languages*, ed. Dell Hymes. Cambridge: Cambridge University Press. 65–90.

———. 1974. *Foundations in sociolinguistics: an ethnographic approach*. Philadelphia: University of Pennsylvania Press.

———. 1975. Breakthrough into performance. *Folklore: performance and communication*. The Hague: Mouton. 11–74.

Irigaray, Luce. 1991. *The Irigaray reader*. Cambridge, MA: Basil Blackwell.

Irvine, Judith T. 1979. Formality and informality in communicative events. *American Anthropologist* 81:773–790.

———. 1989. When talk isn't cheap: language and the political economy. *American Ethnologist* 16 (2): 246–267.

Jackson, Michael. 1989. *Paths toward a clearing: radical empiricism and ethnographic inquiry*. Bloomington: Indiana University Press.

Jakobson, Roman. 1960. Concluding statement: linguistics and poetics. *Style in language*. Cambridge, MA: MIT Press.

———. 1966. Grammatical parallelism and its Russian facet. *Language* 42:399–429.

———. 1968. Poetry of grammar and grammar of poetry. *Lingua* 21:597–609.

———. 1971. The Dominant. *Readings in Russian poetics: formalist and structuralist views*. Cambridge, MA: MIT Press.

———. 1981. *Selected writings: poetry of grammar and grammar of poetry*. The Hague: Mouton.

Jameson, Fredric. 1981. *The political unconscious: narrative as a socially symbolic act*. Ithaca, NY: Cornell University Press.

———. 1981. *The political unconscious: narrative as a socially symbolic act*. Ithaca, NY: Cornell University Press.

———. 1983. Postmodernism and consumer society. *The anti-aesthetic: essays on postmodern culture*, ed. Hal Foster. Port Townsend, WA: Bay Press. 11–125.

Johnson, Mark. 1987. *The Body in the mind*. Chicago: University of Chicago Press.

Johnstone, Barbara. 1987. Perspectives of repetition: an introduction. *Text* 7 (3): 205–214.

Jones, Ann Rosalind. 1986. Surprising fame: renaissance gender ideologies and women's lyric. *The poetics of gender*. New York: Columbia University Press. 74–95.

Joseph, Roger. 1983. The semiotics of reciprocity: A Moroccan interpretation. *Semiotica* 46 : 211–31.

Joseph, Terri Brint. 1980. Poetry as strategy of power: The case of the Riffian Berber women. *Signs* 5 (3): 418–34.

Juwiti, Abdelkrim. 1995. Al-ʿaiṭa al-mallaliya: al-bihishiya fī muwājahāt al-qubṭān biruni. *al-Ittiḥād al-Ishtiraki* April 22.

Juynboll, G. H. A. 1983. *Muslim tradition: studies in chronology, provenance and authorship of early ḥadith*. Cambridge: Cambridge University Press.

Kamal, Hassan. 1975. *Encyclopedia of Islamic medicine*. Cairo: General Egyptian Book Organization.

Kanafani, Aida Sami. 1983. *Aesthetics and ritual in the United Arab Emirates: the anthropology of food and personal adornment among Arab women*. Beirut: American University of Beirut.

Kandiyoti, Deniz, ed. 1991. *Women, Islam and the state: women in the political economy*. Philadelphia: Temple University Press.

Kapchan, Deborah A. 1993. Moroccan women's body signs. *Bodylore*, ed. Katharine Young. Knoxville: University of Tennessee Press.

———. 1993a. Hybridization and the marketplace: emerging paradigms in folkloristics. *Western Folklore* 52 : 303–326.

Keenan, Elinor. 1975. A sliding sense of obligatoriness: the polystructure of Malagasy oratory. *Political language and oratory in traditional society*. London: Academic Press. 93–112.

Kertzer, David I. 1988. *Ritual, politics and power*. New Haven, CT and London: Yale University Press.

Khan, Muhammad Salim. 1986. *Islamic medicine*. London: Routledge and Kegan Paul.

Kharaz, Mohamed. al-Kharraz. 1995. Al-buʿd as-siyyāsi fi l-ʿaiṭa ash-shaʿbiya. *Al-Saḥara al-Maghribiya*. April 29.

Khatibi, Abdelkebir. 1983. *Maghreb pluriel*. Paris: Denoel.

Khuri, Fuad Ishat. 1967. The etiquette of bargaining in the Middle East. *American Anthropologist* 70 : 698–706.

Kilito, Abdelfattah. 1992. *L'oeil et l'aiguille: essai sur "les mille et une nuits"*. Paris: Éditions la Découverte.

Kirshenblatt-Gimblett, Barbara, ed. 1976. *Speech play*. University of Pennsylvania Publications in Conduct and Communication. Philadelphia: University of Pennsylvania Press.

———. 1989. Authoring lives. *Journal of Folklore Research* 26 (2): 123–150.

———. 1992. Presidential Address. American Folklore Society Annual Meetings.

Kirshenblatt-Gimblett, Barbara and Joel Sherzer. 1976. Introduction. In *Speech play*, ed. Barbara Kirshenblatt-Gimblett. University of Pennsylvania Publications in Conduct and Communication. Philadelphia: University of Pennsylvania Press.

Kopytoff, Igor. 1986. The cultural biography of things: commoditization as process. *The social life of things: commodities in cultural perspective*. New York: Cambridge University Press.

Kuhn, Thomas S. 1962. *The structure of scientific revolutions*. Chicago: Chicago University Press.

Kuipers, Joel C. 1990. *Power in performance: the creation of textual authority in Weyewa ritual speech*. Philadelphia: University of Pennsylvania Press.

Lacoste-Dujardin, Camille. 1985. *Des mères contre des femmes: maternité et patriarcat au Maghreb*. Paris: La Découvert.

Laquer, Thomas W. 1986. Orgasm, generation, and the politics of reproductive biology. *Representations* 14: 1–35.

Laroui, Abdellah (al-ʿArawi). 1982. *L'histoire du Maroc: un essai de synthèse*. Paris: François Maspero.

Lauer, Mirko. 1993. Modernity, a foreign body: Nestor García Canclini's "Culturas Hibridas." *Travesia* 3: 125–33.

Lavie, Smadar, Kirin Narayan, and Renato Rosaldo. 1993. *Creativity/anthropology*. Anthropology of Contemporary Issues. Ithaca, NY: Cornell University Press.

Leach, Edward. 1964. Anthropological aspects of language: animal categories and verbal abuse. *New directions in the study of language*, Cambridge, MA: MIT Press. 23–63.

Lee, Benjamin. 1991. Textuality, mediation, and public discourse. *Habermas and the public sphere*. Cambridge, MA and London: MIT Press. 402–418.

———. 1993. Going public. *Public Culture* 5 (2): 165–178.

Lévi-Strauss, Claude. 1949. The principle of reciprocity. *Sociological theory*. New York: Macmillan.

———. 1963. *Structural anthropology*. New York: Basic Books.

———. 1969. *The elementary structures of kinship*. London: Eyre and Spottiswoode.

———. 1969. *The raw and the cooked*. New York: Harper and Row.

———. 1974. *Tristes tropiques*. New York: Atheneum.

———. 1978. *The origin of table manners: mythologies*. New York: Harper and Row.

Levinson, Steven. 1983. *Pragmatics*. Cambridge: Cambridge University Press.

Limón, José Eduardo. 1989. Carne, carnales, and the carnivalesque: Bakhtinian bathos, disorder, and narrative discourse. *American Ethnologist* 16: 471–86.

Lindstrom, Lamont. 1992. Context contests: debatable truth standards on Tannu Vanvatu. *Rethinking context: language as an interactive phenomenon*. Cambridge: Cambridge University Press.

Lortat-Jacob, Bernard. 1980. *Musique et fêtes du Haut-Atlas*. Paris and New York: Mouton.

Lucy, John Arthur. 1993. Metapragmatic presentationals: reporting speech with quotatives in Yucatec Maya. In *Reflexive language: reported speech and metapragmatics*, ed. John Arthur Lucy. Cambridge: Cambridge University Press.

————, ed. 1993. *Reflexive language: reported speech and metapragmatics*. Cambridge, New York: Cambridge University Press.

Lutz, Catherine A. 1990. Engendered emotion: gender, power, and the rhetoric of emotional control in American discourse. In *Language and the politics of emotion*, ed. Catharine Lutz and Lila Abu-Lughod. New York: Cambridge University Press. 69–91.

MacLeod, Arlene E. 1991. *Accommodating protest: working women, the new veiling, and change in Cairo*. New York: Columbia University Press.

Maher, Vanessa. 1974. *Women and property in Morocco*. Cambridge: Cambridge University Press.

————. 1978. Women and social change in Morocco. *Women in the Muslim world*. Cambridge, MA and London: Harvard University Press. 120–23.

Malti-Douglas, Fedwa. 1991. *Woman's body, woman's word*. Princeton, NJ: Princeton University Press.

Mauss, Marcel, ed. 1950. *Sociologie et anthropologie*. Paris: Presses Universitaires de France.

————. 1967. *The gift: forms and functions of exchange in archaic societies*. New York: W. W. Norton.

————. 1973. Techniques of the body. *Economy and Society* 2:70–88.

McDowell, John H. 1985. The poetic rites of conversation. *Journal of Folklore Research* 22:113–32.

Meakin, Budgett. 1905. *Life in Morocco*. London: Chatto & Windus.

Medvedev, P. N. and Mikhail M. Bakhtin. 1985/1928. *The formal method in literary scholarship*. Cambridge, MA: Harvard University Press.

Meeker, Michael E. 1979. *Literature and violence in North Arabia*. Cambridge: Cambridge University Press.

Mernissi, Fatima. 1982a. Virginity and patriarchy. *Women and Islam*. New York: Pergamon Press. 183–92.

————. 1982b. Zhor's world: A Moroccan domestic worker speaks out. *Feminist Issues* 2 (1): 3–32.

————. 1987. *Beyond the veil: male-female dynamics in modern Muslim society*. Bloomington: Indiana University Press.

————. 1988. Comment priver une ouvrière de son salaire minimum. *Femmes partagées: famille-travail*. Casablanca: Le Fennec. 59–78.

————. 1989. *Doing daily battle: interviews with Moroccan women*. New Brunswick, NJ: Rutgers University Press.

————, ed. 1990. *Femmes et pouvoirs*. Casablanca: Le Fennec.

Messick, Brinkley M. 1989. Subordinate discourse: women, weaving, and gender relations in North Africa. *American Ethnologist*.

Metcalf, Barbara Daly. 1993. Living hadith in the Tablighi Jama'at. *Journal of Asian Studies* 52 (3): 584–608.

Meyerhof, Max. 1940. *Sarh asma al-'uqqar, l'explication des noms de drogues: un glossaire de matière médicale composé par Maimonide*. Cairo: Imprimerie de l'Institut Français D'Archéologie Orientale.

Mills, Margaret. 1991. *Rhetorics and politics in Afghan traditional storytelling*. Philadelphia: University of Pennsylvania Press.

Mitchell, T. S. 1957. The language of buying and selling in Cyrenaica. *Hesperis* 44.

Mniai, Hassan. 1990. *Hunā al-masrah al-ʿarabī, hunā baʿdu tajalliyātih.* Meknes: As-Safir

Moi, Toril. 1988. *Sexual/textual politics: feminist literary theory.* London and New York: Routledge.

Moulieras, Auguste Jean. 1987. *Les fourberies de Si Djehʾa.* Paris: La Boite à Documents.

Munn, Nancy D. 1986. *The fame of gawa: a symbolic study of value transformation in a Massim Papua New Guinea society.* Cambridge: Cambridge University Press.

Munro, Pamela. 1982. On the transitivity of "say" verbs. *Syntax and semantics.* New York: Academic. 310–318.

Naamane-Guessous, Soumaya. 1990. *Au-dela de toute pudeur: la sexualité féminine au Maroc.* Casablanca: Éditions Eddif.

Naamouni, Khadija. 1993. *La culte de Bouya Omar.* Casablanca: Editions Eddif.

Naficy, H. 1993. *The making of exile culture: Iranian television in Los Angeles.* Minneapolis: University of Minnesota Press.

Nasr, Sayyed Hossein. 1964. *An introduction to Islamic cosmological doctrines.* Cambridge, MA: Harvard University Press.

Ngole, J.-P. 1988. *Bargaining strategies as performance: an ethnographic and sociolinguistic study of Congolese women fishsellers.* PhD dissertation, Indiana University.

Noyes, Dorothy. 1992. *The mule and the giants: struggling for the body social in a Catalan Corpus Christi festival.* PhD dissertation, University of Pennsylvania.

Ochs, Elinor. 1986. From feelings to grammar. *Language socialization across cultures.* Cambridge: Cambridge University Press.

Ochs, Elinor and Bambi Schieffelin. 1989. Language has a heart. *Text* 9 (1): 7–27.

O'Neill, John. 1985. *Five bodies: The human shape of modern society.* Ithaca, NY and London: Cornell University Press.

Ossman, Susan. 1994. *Picturing Casablanca: portraits of power in a modern city.* Berkeley and Los Angeles: University of California Press.

Pandolfo, Stefania. 1989. Detours of life: space and bodies in a Moroccan village. *American Ethnologist* 16 (1): 3–23.

Pateman, Carole. 1988. *The sexual contract.* Stanford, CA: Stanford University Press.

———. 1989. *The disorder of women: democracy, feminism, and political theory.* Cambridge: Polity Press.

Pelton, Robert D. 1980. Interpreting the trickster. *The trickster in West Africa: A study in mythic irony and sacred delight.* Berkeley: University of California Press.

Peristiany, Jean G., ed. 1966. *Honour and shame: the values of Mediterranean society.* London: Weidenfeld and Nicolson.

Perloff, Marjorie. 1992. *Postmodern genres.* Norman: University of Oklahoma Press.

Philips, Susan U. 1980. Sex differences and language. *Annual Review of Anthropology* 9:523–44.

Radner, Joan N. and Susan S. Lanser. 1987. The feminine voice: strategies of coding in folklore and literature. *Journal of American Folklore* 100 (398): 412–425.

Rahmouni, H. 1988. Les mutations des fonctions contributives de la femme marocain au développement par l'apparentissage de métiers non traditionnels. *Femmes partagées: famille-travail.* Casablanca: Le Fennec. 99–109.

Ricoeur, Paul. 1971. What is a text? Explanation and interpretation. *Mythico-symbolic language and philosophical anthropology: A constructive interpretation of the thought of Paul Ricoeur*, ed. David M. Rasmussen. The Hague: Martinus Nijhoff. 135–50.

———. 1976. *Interpretation theory: discourse and the surplus of meaning*. Fort Worth: Texas Christian University Press.

———. 1979. The model of the text: meaningful action considered as text. *Interpretive social science: a reader*. Berkeley: University of California Press. 73–101.

Roberts, John W. 1989. *From trickster to badman: the black folk hero in slavery and freedom*. Philadelphia: University of Pennsylvania Press.

Robertson, Claire C. 1984. *Sharing the same bowl: a socioeconomic history of women and class in Accra, Ghana*. Bloomington: Indiana University Press.

———. 1993. personal communication.

Rosaldo, Michele Zimbalist and Louise Lamphere, eds. 1974. *Women, culture, and society: a theoretical overview*. Stanford, CA: Stanford University Press.

Rosander, Eva Evers. 1991. *Women in a borderland: managing Muslim identity where Morocco meets Spain*. Stockholm: Stockholm Studies in Social Anthropology.

Rose, Dan. 1991. Wordly discourses: reflections on pragmatic utterances and on the culture of capital. *Public Culture* 4 (1): 109–27.

Rosen, Lawrence. 1978. The negotiation of reality: male-female relations in Sefrou, Morocco. *Women in the Muslim world*. Cambridge, MA: Harvard University Press.

———. 1984. *Bargaining for reality: the construction of social relations in a Muslim community*. Chicago and London: University of Chicago Press.

Rosner, Fred, ed. 1979. *Moses Maimonides: glossary of drug names*. Memoirs of the American Philosophical Society. Philadelphia: American Philosophical Society.

Rossi-Landi, Ferrucio. 1983. *Language as work and trade: a semiotic homology for linguistics and economics*. South Hadley, MA: Bergin and Garvey.

Rothenberg, Jerome and Diane Rothenberg, eds. 1983. *Symposium of the whole: a range of discourse toward an ethnopoetics*. Berkeley: University of California Press.

Rubin, Gayle. 1975. The traffic in women: notes on the "political economy" of sex. *Toward an anthropology of women*. New York: Monthly Review Press. 157–210.

Saddiki, Tayeb. 1991. *Les sept grains de beauté: contes et légendes en dix-huit voyages*. Casablanca: Éditions Eddif.

Sahlins, Marshall D. 1972. *Stone age economics*. Chicago: Aldine-Atherton.

Sapir, Edward. 1921. *Language: an introduction to the study of speech*. New York: Harcourt, Brace and World.

———. 1933. Language. *Encyclopedia of the social sciences*. New York: Macmillan.

———. 1963. *Selected writings of Edward Sapir*. Berkeley: University of California Press.

Scelles-Millie, Jeanne with Boukhari Khelifa, eds. 1966. *Les Quatrains de Mejdoub le Sarcastique: poète Maghrébin du XVIième siècle*. Paris: Maisonneuve.

Schechner, Richard. 1977. *Essays on performance theory*. New York: Drama Books Specialists.

Schegloff, Emanuel and Harvey Sacks. 1973. Opening up closings. *Semiotica* 8: 289–327.

Schiffren, Deborah. 1987. *Discourse markers*. Studies in Interactional Sociolinguistics, ed. John J. Gumperz.

Schimmel, Annemarie. 1975. *Mystical dimensions of Islam*. Chapel Hill: University of North Carolina Press.

Scott, James C. 1985. *Weapons of the weak: everyday forms of resistance*. New Haven, CT: Yale University Press.

———. 1990. *Domination and the arts of resistance: hidden transcripts*. New Haven, CT: Yale University Press.

Searle, John R. 1975. Indirect speech acts. *Speech acts*. Syntax and Semantics 4. New York: Academic Press. 59–82.

Sebeok, Thomas A., ed. 1958. *Style in language*. Cambridge, MA: MIT Press.

Seddon, David. 1981. *Moroccan peasants: a century of change in the eastern Rif*. Folkestone, Kent: Wm Dawson and Sons.

Seligmann, Linda J. 1993. Between worlds of exchange: ethnicity among Peruvian market women. *Cultural Anthropology* 8 (2): 187–213.

Seremetakis, C. Nadia. 1991. *The last word: women, death, and divination in Inner Mani*. Chicago: University of Chicago Press.

Sherzer, Joel. 1976. Play languages: implications for socio-linguistics. *Speech play: research and resources for studying linguistic creativity*. Philadelphia: University of Pennsylvania Press. 19–36.

———. 1981. Tellings, retellings, and tellings within tellings: the structuring and organization of narrative in Kuna Indian discourse. *Working Papers in Sociolinguistics*. Austin, TX: Southwest Educational Development Laboratory.

———. 1983. *Kuna ways of speaking: an ethnographic perspective*. Austin: University of Texas Press.

———. 1987. A diversity of voices: men's and women's speech in ethnographic perspective. *Language, gender, and sex in comparative perspective*, ed. Susan U. Philips, S. Steele and C. Tanz. Cambridge and New York: Cambridge University Press. 95–120.

———. 1990. *Verbal art in San Blas: Kuna culture through its discourse*. Cambridge: Cambridge University Press.

———. 1993. On puns, comebacks, verbal dueling, and play languages: speech play in Balinese verbal life. *Language in Society* 22: 217–233.

Sherzer, Joel and Greg Urban, eds. 1986. *Native South American discourse*. Berlin and New York: Mouton de Gruyter.

Shweder, Richard A. and Robert A. Levine, eds. 1984. *Culture theory: essays on mind, self, and emotion*. Social Science Research Council Committee on Social and Affective Development During Childhood. Cambridge: Cambridge University Press.

Silverstein, Murray. 1976. Shifters, linguistic categories, and cultural description. *Meaning in anthropology*, ed. Keith H. Basso and Henry A. Selby. Albuquerque: University of New Mexico Press. 11–56.

Singer, Murray. 1989. Pronouns, persons and the semiotics of self. *Semiotics, self, and society*. Berlin and New York: Mouton de Gruyter.

Slyomovics, Susan. 1987. *The merchant of art: an Egyptian Hilali oral epic poet in performance*. Berkeley: University of California Press.

Slyomovics, Susan and Amanda Dargan, directors/producers. 1990. *Wedding song: henna art among Pakistani women in New York City*. 40 minutes. 3/4" or 1/2" format video.

Smith, Robert Jerome. 1972a. The structure of esthetic response. *Towards new perspectives in folklore*, ed. Richard Bauman and Americo Paredes. Austin: University of Texas Press.

———. 1972b. Festivals and celebrations. *Folklore and folklife*. Chicago: University of Chicago Press.

———. 1975. *The art of the festival*. Lawrence: University of Kansas Press.

Sobleman, Harvey and Richard S. Harrell, eds. 1963. *A dictionary of Moroccan Arabic: English-Moroccan*. Arabic Series: Institute of Languages and Linguistics, Georgetown University. Washington, DC: Georgetown University Press.

Spacks, Patricia Meyer. 1985. *Gossip*. New York: Alfred A. Knopf.

Spellberg, D. A. 1994. Introduction: approaches to the study of a legacy. *Politics, gender, and the Islamic path: the legacy of 'A'isha Bint Abi Bakr*. New York: Columbia University Press.

Spivak, Gayatri Chakravorty. 1993. *Outside in the teaching machine*. New York: Routledge.

Spratt, Jennifer E. 1992. Women and literacy in Morocco. *Annals of the American Academy of Political and Social Science* 520 (March): 54–65.

Spratt, Jennifer E. and Dan A. Wagner. 1986. The making of a fqih: the transformation of traditional Islamic teachers in modern times. *The cultural transition: human experience and social transformation in the Third World and Japan*, ed. Merri I. White and Susan Pollak. New York: Routledge and Kegan Paul.

Stahl, Sandra. 1983. Personal experience stories. *Handbook of American Folklore*, ed. Richard M. Dorson. Bloomington: Indiana University Press. 268–276.

Stallybrass, Peter and Allon White. 1986. *The politics and poetics of transgression*. Ithaca, NY: Cornell University Press.

Stewart, Kathleen. 1991. On the politics of cultural theory: A case for "contaminated" cultural critique. *Social Research* 58 (2): 395–412.

Stewart, Susan. 1978. *Nonsense: aspects of intertextuality in folkore and literature*. Baltimore: Johns Hopkins University Press.

———. 1984. *On longing*. Baltimore: Johns Hopkins University Press.

———. *Crimes of writing*. New York: Oxford University Press.

Stillman, Yedida. 1995. personal communication.

Stoeltje, Beverly. 1981. Cowboys and clowns: rodeo specialists and the ideology of work and play. *"And other neighborly names": social process and cultural image in Texas folklore*, ed. Richard Bauman and Roger D. Abrahams. Austin: University of Texas Press. 123–151.

———. 1983. Festival in America. *Handbook of American folklore*. Bloomington: Indiana University Press. 239–46.

———. 1987. Riding, roping, and reunion: cowboy festival. *Time out of time*, ed. A. Falassi. Albuquerque: University of New Mexico Press. 137–51.

———. 1988a. Introduction: feminist revisions. *Journal of American Folklore* 25 (3): 141–53.

———. 1988b. Gender representations in performance: the cowgirl and the hostess. *Journal of Folklore Research* 25 (3): 219–41.

———. 1988c. Festival. *Encyclopedia of communications*. Oxford: Oxford University Press.

Stoller, Paul. 1989a. *Fusion of the worlds: an ethnography of possession among the Songhay of Niger*. Chicago: University of Chicago Press.

———. 1989b. *The taste of ethnographic things: the senses in anthropology*. Philadelphia: University of Pennsylvania Press.

Stoller, Paul and Cheryl Olkes. 1987. *In sorcery's shadow: a memoir of apprenticeship among the Songhay of Niger*. Chicago: University of Chicago Press.

Strathern, Marilyn. 1988. *The gender of the gift: problems with women and problems with society in Melanesia*. Berkeley: University of California Press.

Street, Brian V. 1984. *Literacy in theory and practice*. Cambridge and New York: Cambridge University Press.

———, ed. 1993. *Cross-Cultural approaches to literacy*. Cambridge Studies in Oral and Literate Culture. Cambridge: Cambridge University Press.

Suleiman, Susan R., ed. 1985. *The female body in western culture: contemporary perspectives*. Cambridge, MA: Harvard University Press.

Sutton-Smith, Brian. 1972. *Games of order and disorder*. Paper given in panel, Forms of Symbolic Inversion, American Anthropological Association Annual Meetings.

Tadros, Helmi R., Mohamed Feteeha, and Allen Hibbard. 1990. *Squatter markets in Cairo*. Cairo: American University in Cairo Press.

Tannen, Deborah. 1980. The oral/literate continuum in discourse. *Spoken and written language*. Norwood, NJ: Ablex.

———. 1987. Repetition in conversation as spontaneous formulaicity. *Text* 7 (3): 215–243.

———. 1989. *Talking voices: repetition, dialogue, and imagery in conversational discourse*. Cambridge and New York: Cambridge University Press.

Tapper, Nancy. 1990. Ziyaret: gender, movement, and exchange in a Turkish community. *Muslim travellers: pilgrimage, migration, and the religious imagination*, ed. Dale Eickelman and James Piscatori. Berkeley: University of California Press. 236–255.

———. 1991. *Bartered brides: politics, gender and marriage in an Afghan tribal society*. Cambridge: Cambridge University Press.

Tapper, Nancy and Richard Tapper. 1987. The birth of the Prophet: ritual and gender in Turkish Islam. *Man* 22 (March): 69–92.

Taussig, Michael T. 1980. *The devil and commodity fetishism in South America*. Chapel Hill: University of North Carolina Press.

Tedlock, Dennis. 1983. *The spoken word and the work of interpretation*. Philadelphia: University of Pennsylvania Press.

Thompson, E. P. 1991. The moral economy of the English crowd in the eighteenth century. *Customs in common*. London: Merlin Press. 185–258.

Thompson, Stith. 1955–58. *Motif-index of folk-literature*. Bloomington: Indiana University Press.

Todorov, Tzvetan. 1982. *Symbolism of interpretation*. Ithaca, NY: Cornell University Press.

———. 1990. *Genres in discourse*. Cambridge and New York: Cambridge University Press.

Troin, Jean-François. 1975. *Les souks Marocains: marchés ruraux et organisation de l'espace dans la moitié nord du Maroc*. Aix-en-Provence: EDISUD.

Tsing, Anna Lowenhaupt. 1993. *In the realm of the diamond queen: marginality in an out-of-the-way place*. Princeton, NJ: Princeton University Press.

Turner, Victor. 1974. Liminal to liminoid, in play, flow and ritual: An essay in comparative symbology. *The anthropological study of human play*, ed. Edward Norbeck. Rice University Studies. Houston, TX: Rice University Press.

———. 1977/69. *The ritual process: structure and anti-structure*. Ithaca, NY: Cornell University Press.

———. 1982. *From ritual to theater*. New York: PAJ Publications.

———. 1986. *The anthropology of performance*. New York: PAJ Publications.

———. 1987. Carnival, ritual and play in Rio de Janeiro. *Time out of time: essays on the festival*, ed. Alessandro Falassi. Albuquerque: University of New Mexico Press. 76–89.

———. 1990. Are there universals of performance in myth, ritual, and drama? *By means of performance: intercultural studies of theatre and ritual*. Cambridge and New York: Cambridge University Press. 8–18.

Urban, Greg. 1984a. The semiotics of two speech styles in Shokleng. *Semiotic mediation: sociocultural and psychological perspectives*, ed. Elizabeth Mertz and Richard J. Parmentier. Orlando, FL: Academic Press. 311–329.

———. 1984b. Speech about speech in speech about action. *Journal of American Folklore* 97 (385): 310–28.

———. 1989. The "I" of discourse. In *Semiotics, self and society*, ed. Benjamin Lee and Greg Urban. Berlin and New York: Mouton de Gruyter. 27–52.

———. *A discourse-centered approach to culture: native South American myths and rituals*. Austin: University of Texas Press.

Vaughan, Genevieve. 1980. Communication and exchange. *Semiotica* 29 (1/2): 113–143.

Volosinov, V. N. 1973. *Marxism and the philosophy of language*. Cambridge, MA: Harvard University Press.

Wagner, Daniel A. 1993. *Literacy, culture and development: becoming literate in Morocco*. Cambridge and New York: Cambridge University Press.

Wagner, Daniel A., Brinkley M. Messick, et al. 1986. Studying literacy in Morocco. *The acquisition of literacy: ethnographic perspectives*, ed. Bambi Schieffelin and Perry Gilmore. Norwood, NJ: Ablex.

Waterbury, John. 1972. *North for the trade: the life and times of a Berber merchant*. Berkeley: University of California Press.

Webber, Sabra J. 1985. Women's folk narratives and social change. *Women and the family in the Middle East: new voices of change*. PhD dissertation, University of Texas at Austin.

———. 1991. *Romancing the real: folklore and ethnographic representation in North Africa*. Philadelphia: University of Pennsylvania Press.

Wehr, Hans. 1971. *A Dictionary of modern written Arabic*. Ithaca, NY: Spoken Language Services.

Weiner, Annette B. 1984. From words to objects to magic: "hard words" and the boundaries of social interaction. *Dangerous words: language and politics in the Pacific*, ed. Don Brenneis and Fred Myers. New York: New York University Press.

———. 1992. *Inalienable possessions: the paradox of keeping-while-giving*. Berkeley: University of California Press.

Weir, Shelagh. 1989. *Palestinian costume*. Austin: University of Texas Press.

West, Cornell. 1990. The new cultural politics of difference. *Out there: marginalization and contemporary cultures*, ed. Russell Ferguson, Martha Gever, T. Minhha Trinh and Cornell West. Cambridge, MA: MIT Press.

Westermarck, Edward A. 1891. *The history of human marriage*. London and New York: Macmillan.

———. 1914. *Marriage ceremonies in Morocco*. London: Macmillan.

———. 1926a. *Ritual and belief in Morocco*. London: Macmillan.

———. 1926b. *Short history of marriage*. New York: Macmillan.

———. 1980/1930. *Wit and wisdom in Morocco: a study of native proverbs*. London: Routledge.

Whinnom, Keith. 1971. Linguistic hybridization and the "special case" of pidgins and creoles. *Pidginization and creolization of languages*. Cambridge: Cambridge University Press. 91–115.

Williams, Raymond. 1977. Genres. *Marxism and literature*. Oxford: Oxford University Press. 180–185.

Willis, Susan. 1991. *A primer for daily life*. London and New York: Routledge.

Woolard, Kathryn A. 1985. Language variation and cultural hegemony: towards an integration of sociolinguistic and social theory. *American Ethnologist* 12 (November): 738–748.

World Bank. 1990. *World Development Report 1990*. New York: Oxford University Press.

Zartman, I. William. 1987. *The political economy of Morocco*. New York: Praeger.

Zeggaf, Abdelmjid. 1989. Ḥawla baʿḍa khaṣāʾiṣi al-naṣṣi al-ʾdabī ash-shaʿbī. *Littérature Populaire Marocaine*. Rabat: Éditions Okad.

———. 1990. Personal communication.

Zeitlin, Amanda Dargan. 1992. *American talkers: the art of the sideshow carnival pitchman and other itinerant showmen and vendors*, PhD dissertation, University of Pennsylvania.

Subject Index

Author Index